Positive Behavioral Support
in the Classroom

Positive Behavioral Support in the Classroom

Principles and Practices

by

Lewis Jackson, Ed.D.
University of Northern Colorado
Greeley, Colorado

and

Marion Veeneman Panyan, Ph.D.
Drake University
Des Moines, Iowa

with invited contributors

·P·A·U·L·H·
BROOKES
PUBLISHING Co

Baltimore • London • Toronto • Sydney

Paul H. Brookes Publishing Co.
Post Office Box 10624
Baltimore, Maryland 21285-0624

www.brookespublishing.com

Typeset by PRO-IMAGE Corporation, York, Pennsylvania.
Manufactured in the United States of America by Versa Press, Inc., East Peoria, Illinois.

Permission to reprint the following is gratefully acknowledged:

Excerpt on page 41 from THE COLLECTED POEMS OF WALLACE STEVENS by Wallace Stevens, copyright © 1954 by Wallace Stevens. Used by permission of Alfred A. Knopf, a division of Random House, Inc.

Excerpt on page 303 by Dylan Thomas, from THE POEMS OF DYLAN THOMAS, copyright © 1939 by New Directions Publishing Corp. Reprinted by permission of New Directions Publishing Corp.

The vignettes in this book are based on the authors' experiences. Some of the vignettes represent actual people and actual circumstances. The names and other identifying information of individuals have been changed to protect their identities. Some of the vignettes are composite accounts that do not represent the lives or experiences of specific individuals, and no implications should be inferred.

Purchasers of *Positive Behavioral Support in the Classroom: Principles and Practices* are granted permission to photocopy the blank forms appearing in the appendix, Intervention Planning Forms. Photocopying privileges are for educational purposes only; none of the forms may be reproduced to generate revenue for any program or individual. Photocopies must be made from an original book.

Library of Congress Cataloging-in-Publication Data

Jackson, Lewis (Lewis B.)
   Positive behavioral support in the classroom : principles and practices / by Lewis Jackson and Marion Veeneman Panyan.
      p.   cm.
   Includes bibliographical references and index.
   ISBN 1-55766-523-0
   1. Classroom management.   2. School discipline.   3. Problem children—Education.   4. Behavior modification.   I. Panyan, Marion V.   II. Title.

LB3013 .J33 2002
371.93—dc21

2001037440

British Library Cataloguing in Publication data are available from the British Library.

Contents

Section I   The Origins of Positive Behavioral Support

About the Authors

Lewis Jackson, Ed.D., Professor, Division of Special Education, College of Education, University of Northern Colorado, McKee Hall, Greeley, CO 80639

Dr. Jackson has been active as a university professor, researcher, teacher, and advocate for students with behavioral issues and other disabilities and their families for 30 years. He has worked in a variety of settings, including residential institutions, self-contained classrooms, correctional facilities, and inclusive schools. He has also developed graduate and undergraduate programs for teachers serving students with special needs at The Johns Hopkins University and at the University of Northern Colorado, and he has taught courses for both general and special educators who are preparing for the teaching profession. Dr. Jackson has published and presented nationally and internationally on the subjects of inclusive education, behavioral challenges, discipline concerns, positive behavioral support, and social skills and language development. His current research focuses on how the roles of special and general educators and other educational professionals change when students with special needs are served in general education classes and settings.

Marion Veeneman Panyan, Ph.D., Professor and Chair, Department of Teaching and Learning, School of Education, Drake University, 3206 University Avenue, Des Moines, IA 50311

Dr. Panyan has developed graduate programs at The Johns Hopkins University and at Drake University for teachers serving students with special needs; the most recent program prepares teachers to work in inclusive early childhood settings. She is leading efforts to recruit new teachers, promote literacy, and implement character development initiatives in public schools. She also serves as a mediator for the Iowa State Department of Education to successfully resolve differences between parents and schools. Dr. Panyan's publications and presentations have focused on applied behavior analysis, teacher training, technology integration, and multiple intelligences. She serves on grant review panels and editorial boards of journals in these areas. Her current research examines the infusion of positive behavioral support concepts and competencies in preservice programs.

Foreword

In this new millennium, the field of education is embroiled in major transitions. Many of those transitions influence services both for students with identified disabilities and without identified disabilities. Two particular trends are having profound effects on how we view special education services and their role within the general education context. The first of these trends is a shift away from the provision of separate educational services for students with and without disabilities to the provision of inclusive educational services that incorporate appropriate supports to meet all students' needs in the same educational contexts—that is, general education contexts. Increasingly, all students, regardless of their educational labels and levels of need for support, are receiving effective instruction in the same general education activities, in the same general education classes, across each school day.

The second trend is a theoretical and philosophical shift in how we perceive and address a student's behavioral issues. We are making a transition from perceiving situations in which a student exhibits challenging behaviors as a problem with the student to perceiving these situations as a problem with the context, from responding to these situations in a way that manages the student's behavior so that teachers can teach to responding in a way that identifies and modifies contextual variables to improve the student's quality of life through meaningful participation with peers in authentic activities.

Together, these two trends have resulted in students who had previously been removed from general education until their challenging behavior was "managed" increasingly receiving positive supports that allow them to be successful in authentic general education contexts. Their success frequently has little to do with "specialized instructional strategies" or "individualized behavior management plans." Rather, their success frequently is a result of merely engaging them in authentic general education activities, with authentic materials that are related to authentic general education curriculum content, with peers who do not have disabilities, and with contextual supports that allow the students to be valued as contributing members of their school society.

Positive Behavioral Support in the Classroom: Principles and Practices incorporates these two trends and urges education professionals to reconceptualize the role that contexts play in students' behavior and to focus on modifying general education contexts to prevent challenging behaviors. This can be accomplished by facilitating the provision of support at the school, classroom, and individual student levels that enables all students to be valued as contributing members across authentic activities with peers throughout their school community. The provision of such supports can prevent the occurrence of many challenging behaviors. Furthermore, these two trends are embedded within the five principles on which this book is grounded: 1) schooling is viewed as a largely irreducible cultural experience, rather than as a cumulative skill-acquisition process; 2) schools serve as institutions for both the transmission of knowledge and the development of a complex myriad of roles and relationships with fellow citizens; 3) most youth who experience trauma, have difficult family situations, are invested in marginalized subcultures, have been labeled as having behavioral disorders, or use behavior to effectively protect themselves and meet personal needs can succeed in schools without unduly endangering the rights of others; 4) the routine use of behavioral support processes with specific students in general education classes does not erode the educational experiences of the other students; and 5) the roles and responsibilities of professionals who work in more restrictive settings must be configured such that their efforts directly contribute to the successful reintegration of students back into their home schools whenever possible. Together, these principles represent a new way of viewing schools and educational professionals, as well as the roles that they play in either contributing to or preventing students' challenging behavior.

I believe that the teachers, administrators, parents, guidance counselors, and other student support personnel who read this book will leave it with a better understanding of their contribution to the presence or absence of students' challenging behavior, as well as a renewed sense of purpose related to improving the educational experiences for all students in authentic general education contexts with peers. I believe that this understanding and sense of purpose will result in a redefinition of roles and responsibilities such that the resources that are currently used to remove students with challenging behavior from general education contexts will instead be used to modify the general education contexts and provide support for all students. The authors should be applauded for contributing so significantly to the field's understanding of these concepts, and readers should be commended for questioning their current beliefs and stretching their minds to reconceptualize their professional roles.

Diane Lea Ryndak, Ph.D.
Associate Professor
Department of Special Education
University of Florida

Introduction

RATIONALE, SCOPE, AND INTENDED AUDIENCE

Positive behavioral support represents a perspective on learning and behavior—as well as a methodology—that can be used to underwrite the provision of educational services to students with challenging behaviors within school and community settings. We believe that positive behavioral support is grounded in five basic precepts, which distinguish it from other models that focus on behavioral issues and behavior change processes.

First, schooling is viewed as a largely irreducible cultural experience rather than as a cumulative skill-acquisition process. Based on this tenet, the practice of denying students access to all facets of this experience through long-term placement in separate classes or alternative schools on the basis of behavior can significantly curtail their educational opportunity.

Second, schools serve as institutions for both the transmission of knowledge and the development of a complex myriad of roles and relationships with fellow citizens. The implication of this precept is that "therapeutic" services that are linked to behavior problems (e.g., counseling, language and communication therapy, social skills training) must be framed within this social learning context rather than treated in isolation via long-term pull-out services.

Third, most youth who experience trauma, who have difficult family situations, who are invested in marginalized subcultures, who have been labeled as having behavioral disorders, or who use behavior to protect themselves and meet personal needs can succeed in schools without unduly endangering the rights of others. This is accomplished not by creating educational goals that mirror their behaviors but by backing up the provision of typical educational experiences with activity and outcome modifications, crisis prevention and management assurances, lifestyle planning experiences, and supplemental learning opportunities.

Fourth, the routine use of behavioral support processes with specific students in the general education classroom does not erode the educational experiences of the other students. To the contrary, teachers who use these practices discover that they help *all* students learn and grow. Moreover, the other students find themselves better prepared to enter a world in which human diversity and differences govern the most essential conduct and interactions.

The fifth precept is based on the following reality: The social justice goal of moving from a society in which behavior problems are largely addressed by removal and exclusion to a society in which behavior problems are primarily addressed by prevention and support must be viewed as a long-range goal, at best. This means that, in the foreseeable future, self-contained classrooms, alternative schools, day treatment centers, and residential facilities will continue to be used for many students who have behavioral issues. Given the prominent educational role of natural school and community settings in behavioral support, the fifth precept is that the roles and responsibilities of professionals who work in more restrictive settings must be configured such that their efforts directly contribute to the successful reintegration of students back into their home schools whenever possible. This implies that professionals in these settings must focus less on teaching isolated skills and reducing behavior and more on effecting long-term change in students and community systems.

Even a casual examination of the implications for practice of these five precepts in relation to actual school practices reveals that behavioral support represents a significant departure from mainstream educational thought about behavior and behavior change. Hence, a comprehensive book that summarizes in a practical way what the field has learned is needed for individuals who are preparing—especially at the graduate level—to enter the fields of general or special education teaching, behavioral disorders, school counseling and psychology, and school administration. Accordingly, *Positive Behavioral Support in the Classroom: Principles and Practices* provides the following regarding positive behavioral support: 1) its historical, theoretical, and ethical background; 2) a comprehensive overview of its essential elements and recommended components for behavior intervention plans; 3) a discussion of traditional and emerging techniques of assessment for designing plans and evaluating results; 4) practical ideas and suggestions for designing and implementing plans for individual students given different degrees of concern; and 5) extensions of the concept from the individual level to the levels of the classroom and the broader school community.

This book can serve as a single text for a course about behavior change and classroom management. An instructor can also use it as one of two texts when presenting comprehensive accounts of the behavior change field from (at least) two perspectives or offering a two-course sequence in which multiple perspectives are addressed in some depth.

OVERVIEW OF THIS BOOK

Positive Behavioral Support in the Classroom: Principles and Practices is organized into five sections. The first section, "The Origins of Positive Behavioral Support," 1) describes past and current perspectives on how challenging behaviors are conceptualized, 2) outlines the historical antecedents of behavioral support, 3) discusses how behavioral support emerged from earlier perspectives and how it differs from these perspectives, and 4) offers a theoretical rationale for rethinking how classrooms are managed for optimal learning and behavior given the natural diversity that exists among learners.

The second section, "Understanding and Characterizing the Support Process," begins by envisioning the basic principles of a support perspective, then discusses the parameters that define the possibilities and boundaries of positive behavioral support. This discussion is followed by an in-depth review of the essential methodologies of positive behavioral support, including person-centered planning, the role of relationships, hypothesis-based intervention, and crisis management. The section ends with an examination of systems change processes and suggests a framework—guided inquiry—that can be used to develop innovative support efforts at the student and building levels.

The third section, "Planning and Assessment for Positive Behavioral Support," provides a planning protocol that covers the entire support process from plan creation to plan revision. It addresses corresponding assessment practices as well. A framework is also offered for thinking of plan development from a degree of concern perspective so that time, professional, and technical resources are used most efficiently and advantageously.

The fourth section, "Positive Behavioral Support Practices and Their Applications," gives practical details for planning, designing, and implementing support processes for individual students at three different degrees of concern. These levels are as follows: 1) enhancing one's positive behavioral support practices to focus on improving and refining one's classroom skills as a support provider, 2) developing and implementing a solution-focused behavior intervention plan for persistent and difficult behaviors, and 3) developing and implementing a comprehensive behavior intervention plan for more extreme problems and concerns.

The fifth section, "Positive Behavioral Support at the School and Community Levels," extends and elaborates on behavioral support concepts by linking them to the broader practices of schools and communities. This section focuses largely on different methods and models for accomplishing the task of making schools more amendable to positive behavioral support practices. The section concludes by considering larger attitudinal and treatment issues that must be reframed if positive behavioral support principles are to become primary guides for conduct in public schools and other human service settings.

Displays

Additional information is interspersed throughout the book in the form of display boxes. Drawn either from our experiences or from the experiences that have been reported by colleagues, these displays briefly illustrate or give insight about points that are being made in respective chapters. The displays often include reflection questions for the reader.

Works Cited and Suggested Readings

Although behavioral support is a relatively new concept in the education and special education fields, it has emerged from a long history of advocacy activities by people within the disability community, research and applications by some researchers within applied behavior analysis, and changing practices in therapeutic and school counseling. As we discuss different issues throughout this book, we make a point of describing critical research publications and offering practical ideas that are derived from the works of leading authors. In this way, readers have a direct link between their emerging information needs and the relevant background literature. In addition, for the reader who wishes to go more in-depth, a Suggested Readings list appears at the end of the book, which contains materials that relate to each chapter's specific content.

Terminology

Many books about discipline and behavior liberally employ technical vocabularies that are specific to a profession or a group of like-minded professionals. Although precise, technical language can be helpful when a book's audience consists exclusively of individuals who are well versed in that language, greater understanding by a larger readership is made possible when a more broad-based vocabulary is consistently used.

Certainly, *Positive Behavioral Support in the Classroom: Principles and Practices* 1) discusses abstract ideas that sometimes require reference to a technical term, 2) introduces a technical term to communicate something within an historical context, and/or 3) uses a technical term because it is associated with a contemporary terminology that is pervasive in discussions of behavioral issues. Yet, we have avoided technical jargon whenever possible, using either vernacular expressions or actual descriptions.

We have also tried to adhere to the positive behavioral support principle of honoring the dignity of people who receive behavioral support. Although some terms are difficult to avoid because of their widespread usage (e.g., "behavioral concerns," "challenging behaviors"), others that tend to dehumanize and marginalize (e.g., "maladaptive behavior," "self-stimulatory behavior") have been deliberately avoided when at all feasible.

To extend this principle, when discussing either the research literature or our own work, we do not use specific disability labels (e.g., "autistic," "emotionally and behaviorally disordered") unless they contribute to understanding the principle or intervention technique that is described in a particular study. Of course, there may be a place for describing learning principles or intervention techniques specifically in relation to conventional disability categories. Nevertheless, we do not believe that place to be this book, which offers universally applicable principles and techniques that have been drawn from literature reviews and personal experiences with numerous diverse students. Moreover, we believe that the alternative course of action—frequently using disability labels—perpetuates a discourse in which these labels influence the thoughts and actions of the individuals who are directly responsible for making instructional decisions about students with behavioral concerns. We prefer not to contribute to the maintenance of this discourse, given that serious questions can be raised about the utility of disability labels in positive behavioral support research and practice.

A CHALLENGE

Our position that students with challenging behaviors should be educated in general education classrooms may be unsettling for many people for reasons that are often quite understandable. Nevertheless, we have seen in our own work that it can be done and that the education of all students can benefit when the resources used to take children and youth out of general education are used to support these students instead. We are not saying that the process is always easy or successful when it is undertaken, but we challenge people to consider the possibility that a great deal more could and should be done before a restrictive placement option is even considered for a student.

We believe that the positive behavioral support processes described in this book can help make the foregoing practice more of a reality. Of course, we do not discourage a healthy skepticism regarding this claim. However, we do ask the reader to approach this book not from the standpoint that such a claim is impossible but, rather, from the standpoint that such a claim takes hard work and courage to enact and that there will be setbacks and pitfalls along the way. In the end, we believe that it will be the successes of such efforts that will tip the scales toward broader acceptance of the ideal that students can and should learn together in today's schools.

Acknowledgments

We thank the many individuals who have contributed to this book. Marcia Broden and Carl Smith gave cogent reviews and recommendations. Marisa Ehrlich, Theresa Koch, Anne Murr, and Tessy Huang supplied library research and document preparation. Jamie Ferrare, Jim Romig, and Kay Ferrell provided administrative support. David Henzi, Theresa Larson, Amy Switzer, and Diane Raba reflectively applied these concepts. Andrew, Natalie, and Caroline Imhoff shared their perceptions of contemporary schools. The staff at Paul H. Brookes Publishing Co., especially Jessica Allan and Nicole Schmidl, provided valuable assistance.

Thanks also to the many university students, practicing teachers, parents, and students with and without disability labels who provided their insights, experiences, feedback, and criticism. Without them, this book would not have been possible. We give special thanks to friends and colleagues in Colorado Springs, Brighton, and Boulder for providing multiple opportunities to explore and learn about positive behavioral support in authentic settings.

To my family for their understanding,
to Harold Klemp for his guidance,
and to the many students with behavioral issues
who have been and continue to be excluded from
the educational experiences that most of us take for granted

(LJ)

To my husband, Steve, and son, Eric,
for their encouragement and inspiration;
in loving memory of my parents

(MVP)

Section I

The Origins of Positive Behavioral Support

Chapter 1

Understanding Public Education's Responses to Challenging Behavior

*"The significant problems we face
cannot be solved at the same level of
thinking we were at when we created them."*
—Albert Einstein

In the profound video, *A Credo for Support* (Kunc & Van der Klift, 1995a), Kunc challenged people to rethink how they perceive and treat citizens who are characterized as "disabled" or "deviant." Through music and narrative, the video sequentially considers a variety of familiar educational and rehabilitative treatment practices, such as "behaviour management." The video lays bare the very roots of the fields of rehabilitation, corrections, and special education by connecting the practices of these fields to the feelings that they may generate in the people who receive the "interventions." The video unsparingly portrays how these practices have excluded and devalued the very people they are supposed to benefit; it raises questions about the motivations, attitudes, and values that could in some cases underlie the use of these practices given their effects on recipients; and it reveals the potential for abuse of power that is possible when these practices are inappropriately used by one group of people to change the skills and behaviors of others in the minority.

A Credo for Support dramatically expresses the viewpoint that pervasive, dichotomous concepts such as *ability* and *disability, normal* and *abnormal,* and *social* and *antisocial* are perhaps well intentioned but have contributed to the plight of the people that they were designed to serve (see Display 1.1). Yet, what is perhaps the most important contribution of the video is that it presents a doorway into a very different kind of future for how we perceive human differences. The video offers hope for a future in which the concepts that drive practices associated with changing the behaviors and skills of others might be more thoughtfully constructed to align with basic values such as acknowledging and honoring individual freedom and autonomy, adhering to democratic principles in educational decision making, and respecting the substantial natural diversity that is expressed by members of the human community. This hope, so movingly portrayed in this video, is captured in the notion of *support.*

DISPLAY 1.1—PERCEPTIONS OF DISABILITY

A teacher was helping a kindergartner with multiple disabilities put on her coat while the girl sat in her wheelchair. An adult volunteer walked by and, without consideration for the feelings of the young girl, said, "Oh, *what* is wrong with *her*?" expecting to get information from the teacher about the child's disability. The teacher glanced at the girl and asked, "Anything wrong today?" to which the girl shook her head "no." The teacher then looked directly at the volunteer and said, "Nope, nothing wrong with her today!"

What kinds of experiences did the volunteer likely have over the years that made her react to a child in a wheelchair differently from how she might react to other children?

What kinds of experiences must occur in her life for her to perceive a child with a disability as "just another child"?

How does a child's educational placement in school affect the development of deep and abiding perspectives on disability and differences in general?

From a support perspective, when a student in an appropriate general education class expresses difficulties with class or curriculum access or exhibits learning or behaviors that are sufficiently different from others to raise concerns, the school community will generate and apply a variety of accommodations and modifications so that the student can remain in that setting. Such a perspective might seem to be commonsense. Indeed, good teachers and other practitioners employ the support concept every day with children and youth in our schools. Nonetheless, this practice is not widespread when one considers what happens to many children and youth who exhibit behavioral differences or difficulties that are especially troublesome to the educational community. As described in this chapter, removing the child from the learning situation—as a form of consequence (e.g., suspension, expulsion, incarceration) or for treatment in a more restrictive environment (e.g., special education resource or self-contained room, separate school or facility)—is the more likely result. In order for the support model to have greater influence on the treatment of children and youth with behavioral concerns, a number of changes in our perspectives on discipline, many of which are already beginning to emerge (see Chapter 2), must become increasingly visible within our schools.

Although these changing views about discipline are still emerging at the beginning of the 21st century, one need not wait to begin applying support concepts in daily practice. In fact, change begins with the actions of individual teachers, family members, behavioral specialists, related services professionals, and administrators. Hence, most of this book is a treatise on practical and effective support tools and strategies that can be used to resolve discipline and behavioral concerns and to set an example for others.

Nevertheless, given how pervasive removal is in today's schools, a teacher's or school team's implementation of the support perspective requires an understanding of the ways professionals in schools, universities, and society at large have historically perceived behavioral challenges among children and youth. This is because the removal process is maintained by a number of different beliefs and values, and understanding them is one step toward rejecting removal as a primary discipline strategy and endorsing an alternative support perspective.

This chapter examines perceptions of behavior and conflict that have dominated thinking about children and youth who have behavioral challenges, and it shows how these perceptions have contributed to the removal and treatment models that are pervasive in today's schools. Because what is viewed as challenging depends to some degree on the overall function of schools, this discussion is framed within the broader context of the purposes of public education. These issues are explored from a general education perspective, then reexamined from a special education perspective. The discussion shows that contemporary approaches to challenging behaviors in both professions are troubling because they are based on potentially misleading popular knowledge about how discipline practices affect behavior, and they place students with behavioral challenges at risk for reduced educational opportunities. The chapter reviews some trends in education that signal emerging changes in perspectives and concludes that positive behavioral support offers a way to address behaviors and more successfully realize the purposes of education for all students.

DEFINING AND RESPONDING TO CHALLENGING BEHAVIOR

The way behaviors that disturb and distress others are described has changed considerably over the course of the 1990s. Although expressions such as "deviant," "maladaptive," and "antisocial" were common in the 1980s and before, "puzzling," "risky," or "challenging" are more often used at the turn of the 21st century to describe behaviors that differ significantly from the expectations of others. These changes in language may sometimes seem arbitrary, simply mirroring trends in culture and fashion within a profession or discipline. Nonetheless, these shifts in language also reflect changes in 1) knowledge about the origins and causes of behavior and 2) the ethical standards that govern the treatment of those who appear different.

Over the course of history, changes in knowledge and ethics have not always yielded benefits. For example, the eugenics movement within the scientific community of the early 20th century propagated approaches to human differences that are now viewed as unsound and unethical. Influenced by Darwin's theory of evolution, Mendel's theory of genes and inherited traits, and Goddard's perceptions of the heritability of intellectual capacity (Mackintosh, 1998; O'Brien, 1999; Smith, 1999), eugenics viewed human differences within a dichotomy that allowed for only "fitness" and "unfitness." Moreover, it treated differences as cancers to the body politic that must be removed for the greater health of society (Mackintosh, 1998). Hence, people who were labeled "mentally ill," "disabled," "feebleminded," or "criminal" were at risk for extended isolation, sterilization, aversive techniques of management; or worse. The eugenics movement reached a pinnacle in Nazi Germany, where the view of the hereditability of unfitness was expanded to cover ethnic groups, religions, and classes of people, and extermination became a tool of the state.

Although eugenics appears to be something of the past that need not concern us today, it is more accurate to say that its influences are now more difficult to trace. As generations of German families must come to grips with how their Nazi past continues to influence the present (Massing, 1993), educational and human services within the United States and elsewhere must also come to grips with how contemporary values, attitudes, and traditions of practice are influenced by dubious and questionable beliefs from an often murky past (see Lovett, 1996). Viewing behavioral differences as inherited and immutable—and using long-term isolation as a primary response to behaviors that are perplexing—may seem to be archaic and unacceptable. As previously noted, however, expulsion, out-of-school placement, and confinement remain stalwart practices in schools and other institutions. Walker and colleagues (1996) referred to the increasing reliance on placing youth who commit crimes into prison as an "incarceration frenzy." Can we say with certainty that such practices are not partially based on forms of reasoning with roots in eugenics? Given the tremendous influence of eugenics on American society within the 1920s and 1930s, to believe so is to deny the influence of history on contemporary thinking within schools and other institutions.

Of course, as Mackintosh (1998) indicated, exclusion within public education has much too deep a history to say that a particular 20th-century ideology wields such power that it alone can be blamed for a particular injustice. Mackintosh presented the case of how intelligence testing has sometimes been solely blamed for the exclusion of students from particular educational opportunities. Certainly, no one would deny that the misuse of the IQ test has contributed to injustices in public education. Nevertheless, it may be more fair to say that the use of intelligence tests to screen and place students in radically different educational experiences has simply added to the injustice of previously existing historical trends, which summarily excluded those with less ability or status from the more valued forms of educational opportunity (Hanson, 1993).

The same holds true for public education's changing perceptions of behavioral issues. The roots of perceptions of and responses to problem behaviors are extremely complex, and they are influenced by widely differing theoretical, social, and attitudinal themes within U.S. history and culture. Within education, points of view on the overall purpose of education represent a good starting point for developing an understanding of how problem behaviors have been conceptualized and addressed by practitioners and how these concepts are changing. Concepts such as *appropriate* and *inappropriate, normal* and *deviant,* and *adaptive* and *maladaptive* are, to some extent, dependent on what educators in schools are trying to accomplish with children and youth. Because general and special education have divergent views about education, these issues must be examined separately for these two fields.

Purpose of Education, Perceptions of Behavior, and Impact on Practices: General Education

The purpose of public education is a source of considerable contention within academia (e.g., Buras, 1999). Nevertheless, Goodlad (1990) offered a perspective that incorporates two major points of view on this topic. In his discussion of teaching, Goodlad noted that a rationale for teaching as a profession must evolve out of an understanding of what schools are about. He suggested that the function of schooling encompasses "such things as responsibility for critical enculturation into a political democracy, the cultivation (with the family) of character and decency, and preparation for full participation in the human conversation" (p. 28). Goodlad identified two particular perceptions of schooling that seem to capture the essence of what constitutes a purpose for education.

First, schools are major providers of many of the enculturation experiences that can prepare young people for community life and responsible citizenship. From this perspective, public schools should serve as microcosms of the concerns and issues that face adults both within specific communities and within democratic society as a whole. Students should develop the following from their experiences:

- The ability to define personal lifestyles and life patterns that are within the latitudes deemed as acceptable by the broader culture
- An understanding and acceptance of the lifestyle choices of others, given the diversity that human and cultural differences entail
- A capacity for collaborative activity and problem solving for the realization of broader social ends
- An appreciation for the historical, artistic, and literacy accomplishments that help define the worth of the groups in which a citizen has membership
- Skills to make a contribution to society through community membership and participation, child rearing, and career/vocational pursuits

Within this perspective on the purpose of education, some level of behavioral diversity is an essential ingredient in the classroom, and a skilled teacher can create activities that channel this diversity to enhance learning. This is because diversity in and of itself offers a context for learning to live, work, and get along with people who are different from ourselves within a democratic society (Gathercoal, 1998; Serow, 1983).

Second, schools provide access to a society's knowledge resources, such as the essential skills of reading and arithmetic, information on the sciences and humanities, and experiences with the arts and physical education. Certainly, as amply illustrated in discussions of literacy and reading (e.g., Au, 1997; Ball, 1997; Covington, 1996; Karp, 1997), what should constitute core curriculum remains very much a point of debate. It is reasonable to assume, however, that whatever is defined as the substance of a school's or district's curriculum is the body of knowledge that should be equitably offered to all citizens of a given age and grade level (Goodlad, Keating, & Bailey, 1990). Within this perspective on the purpose of education, tolerance for some level of behavioral diversity is perhaps necessitated to ensure that all learners have access to the same knowledge base. This, of course, means that exclusion, predicated on the need to enhance the learning opportunities of some students by removing those with fewer skills or apparent problems, or on the presumption that the knowledge needs of some students are different from those of the majority, should be subject to skepticism and increased scrutiny. This is because exclusion places these individuals at risk for marginalization and leaves them ill prepared for membership in the adult community. Put differently, as with enculturation, tolerance for some level of behavioral diversity in a class is an important indicator of the degree to which the classroom honors the ideals of a democratic society—mainly, the ideal of equity in educational opportunity.

Classroom teachers will, of course, have their own philosophies and styles of teaching that may differentially emphasize their roles as agents of enculturation versus purveyors of knowledge. Yet, based on the foregoing discussion, behavioral diversity, within some broad set of limits, would be expected to be part of any teacher's class if a community of learners is being equitably served by public education. Yet, studies of classroom life indicate that teachers overall are understandably deeply concerned with reducing "uncertainty" in their daily routines, and they accomplish this through utilizing crowd control and management techniques that are designed to reduce and eliminate behavioral diversity (Kennedy, 1997). As noted by Glasser, part of the problem rests with the often dismal nature of schoolwork and the need to motivate students to complete tasks and activities that are too frequently boring or hard: "In their frustration, almost all 'teachers' choose to use coercion, usually punishment, as the 'motivator'" (1992a, p. 63).

The need to experience certainty in the daily flow of activities is exacerbated by the fact that teachers are also under the sway of larger social and political forces that attempt to influence and redefine what is done with students. In reviewing the literature on school system stability, Kennedy (1997) noted that public schools are "extremely vulnerable" to the rise and fall of these public pressures. Hence, teachers intermittently feel pressure to realign their roles in relation to demands for curriculum changes, to respond to calls for "greater discipline" or "safer schools," and the outcries of various influential special interest groups (Kohn, 1998).

Taken together, the foregoing points indicate that discipline expectations may often assume proportions that can override the view that the classroom teacher accommodate a wide range of behaviors. Given the need for certainty in daily routines and the backdrop of changing public opinions on what teachers are to accomplish, the classroom teacher is likely to become preoccupied with reducing behavioral diversity. Therefore, instead of viewing behavioral diversity as something to be anticipated, to be allowed for and learned from, and to be prepared for by frequently rethinking teaching and discipline, classroom teachers feel pressured to develop discipline policies in which some students are "controllable," "willing to learn," or "compliant," and others are "unmanageable," "rebellious," or "noncompliant." Hence, the stage is set for intentional efforts to manage and eliminate any behavior patterns that fall outside of a narrowly defined band of acceptability (e.g., Winett & Winkler, 1972).

A perusal through any university library will reveal the staggering number of works written in the 20th century that characterize discipline problems and offer approaches that teachers can implement to maintain control over their classes (see especially Wolfgang, 1995). Some of these approaches have contributed to the development of knowledge about positive behavioral support, and these models are reviewed in Chapter 2. In the objective sense, however, it is not possible at the beginning of the 21st century to show with any degree of certainty that any one approach has an edge over any other. An examination of the literature on classroom discipline and behavior management suggests that much of the appeal of such works might rest less on a body of evidence showing sustained success in authentic classroom and school environments and more on the sheer level of need that teachers must often feel for a sense of control and certainty. To draw a parallel, as Skrtic insightfully observed, "We seek 'health' when we visit the hospital, but what we get is medical care. Although we are encouraged to see these outcomes as synonymous, there may be no relation between them, or the relation may be negative" (1995, p. 190). Likewise, teachers seek ways to enhance safety while promoting learning in their classes when they secure materials on how to more successfully maintain discipline; what they get are varying formulas for mixing what is known about instructional control with classroom management. Like medical care, teachers are encouraged to see these outcomes as synonymous, but "there may be no relation between them, or the relation may be negative."

There are two disturbing reasons why the popular knowledge base about working with discipline problems is especially incomplete. Both of these reasons exist precisely because of a preoccupation with control and discipline in public education. The first reason can best be understood by first noting the following observation: Approximately 90% of students in schools are not likely to present significant behavioral problems at all during a particular school year (Horner et al., 1995). For these students, experts call for basic prevention and early intervention measures (Dwyer, Osher, & Hoffman, 2000), usually including some form of explicit schoolwide system of expectations, rules, and consequences as the primary mechanism for ensuring order (Lewis & Sugai, 1999; Nelson, Martella, & Galand, 1998; Rosenberg, Wilson, Maheady, & Sindelar, 1997; Sugai, Sprague, Horner, & Walker, 2000). Yet, how is one to judge the effects of implementing certain discipline practices on these students who pose few problems? Some of these essentially compliant students might be responsive to *any* discipline model regardless of its features, and others largely respond to internal controls that are independent of a school's discipline policies. Hence, it is difficult to ascertain with any degree of certainty either from research or from the experiences of teachers and administrators whether these discipline "successes" are in any way connected with discipline practices. Yet, considering how success influences perceptions, it is easy to see how the successful 90% can mislead schools or professional communities into viewing their particular discipline models and policies as largely effective and therefore worthy of continuation and dissemination. Over time, what is likely created out of the dissemination of these kinds of experiences is a body of misinformation that "informs" the large-scale discipline practices that occur across public education (see also Miller, 1999).

The second reason why the knowledge base about working with students with challenging behavior is largely incomplete is that a typical response of teachers and administrators to students who have chronic or acute discipline problems is to try and remove them from their arena of responsibility by suspension or expulsion, placement in special education, or placement in some other alternative program. Horner and colleagues (1995) reviewed research indicating that the most likely reaction of schools to conduct disorders is some combination of punishment and removal (see also Walker et al., 1996). In a discussion of inclusive education with students with emotional and behavioral difficulties, Meadows commented that these students are often "the first group to leave the general education classroom and the last group to return" (1999, p. 176). Moreover, Reichle has noted that problem behavior is the "single, most common reason" for students with disabilities being removed from general education and other settings (cited in Lewis & Sugai, 1999, p. 1; see Display 1.2). Finally, as noted by Milofsky (1992), special education programs have often been used by public schools as repositories for students with discipline problems. The unintended consequence of reliance on removal as a primary reaction to problem behaviors is that systems of discipline within schools are never really put to the test of addressing problems posed by those students who are most apt to precipitate concerns for discipline in the first place.

There is no doubt that many educators are doing the best they can under often difficult conditions. As Barth noted, "Teachers are encountering times probably more difficult than at any period in American history" (1990, p. 13). Yet, this fact remains: When discipline practices are primarily applied to students with the least need and the option of removal is made amply available for students with the most need, educators are left with an incomplete knowledge base regarding the relationships among

DISPLAY 1.2—DISABILITY AND BEHAVIOR

A young woman with Down syndrome was at risk for removal from her middle-school classroom for reportedly screaming during class. A consultant observed the class and noted that several of the male students were very unruly, exhibiting an almost constant stream of misbehavior (e.g., sitting on the tables, talking while the teacher was talking, laughing inappropriately). The young woman, however, sat quietly throughout the entire class. The teacher reported that what the consultant observed was fairly typical of her day.

Confused, the consultant checked the records; he found that the frequency data indicated that the young woman only screamed one or two times per week. The consultant shared his findings with the principal, suggesting that the young woman was hardly a problem and that there were other discipline concerns of greater consequence. The principal responded by ignoring the other students with discipline problems and persisting in his recommendation that the young woman was disturbing others and did not belong in the classroom.

What is a likely reason for the principal's response in this situation?

If you were the consultant, what might you recommend or do if you were interested in helping this principal move beyond seeing removal as the best solution in this situation?

instruction, discipline practices, and behavior in general education settings. Consequently, any broad conclusions about the utility of particular strategies or discipline techniques or about the expected durability of change are at best tentative, potentially misleading, and possibly wrong.

Removal also unleashes repercussions for the removed students and for the larger school community. With respect to the removed students, there is the potential loss of the socialization and learning opportunities that represent the essential components of the purpose of public education, and these losses may only exacerbate their problems at later points in their school careers or adult lives. For the larger school community, using removal as the prevalent means for reacting to discipline concerns can significantly curtail certain types of learning opportunities for capacity building, professional development, and overall student growth. Put differently, removal 1) reduces the impetus for improving instruction and discipline because the responsible adults no longer experience circumstances that might encourage greater accountability and positive changes in practice (Skrtic, 1995) and 2) emulates for the remaining students the use of exclusion as a primary strategy for resolving problems when behavioral and learning difficulties challenge the status quo. More important, as the behaviors that prompted student removal may only be more obvious indicators of deeper and possibly systemic problems, student removal permits teachers and administrators to continue using discipline and instructional practices that may be ineffective, and sometimes even harmful, in their impact on the learning and behavior of the other pupils in the school (see Sapon-Shevin, 1996).

In sum, public education is charged with the dual role of offering opportunities for enculturation and equitably providing students access to a society's valued knowledge. Within a democratic society, both of these responsibilities are optimally realized when general educators can accept and productively channel a relatively wide latitude of behavioral diversity within their classes. Yet, it is not uncommon for general educators to be preoccupied with increasing the uniformity in the expressed behavior patterns of their students. These educators may employ a variety of discipline models and procedures depending on their needs and inclinations; however, the effectiveness of many of these systems of discipline remains very much an unknown quantity. Of even greater concern is the fact that the pervasive reliance on removal as a frontline procedure for dealing with behavioral issues may

- Create stasis in teaching practices when change might be desirable
- Impede the adaptive processes in which teachers and other school personnel become responsible and accountable for students expressing widely diverse needs, strengths, and concerns
- Model for the remaining students the deployment of exclusion as a viable means for addressing conflict and differences
- Mask problems in instruction and discipline that may be systemic and adversely affecting other students who are less likely to react to or to protest against a school's practices

Purpose of Education, Perceptions of Behavior, and Impact on Practices: Special Education

At the outset of this section, let us note that many special educators, like general educators, are to be lauded for their work, which is often performed under trying circumstances. For example, as inclusive education has increased in its appeal, some special educators have even placed their jobs on the line to increase the learning opportunities that their students have within general education. Yet, the struggle is an uphill one, and part of the reason for this rests in the history of special education services.

Skrtic (1995) noted that, for most of the 20th century, public education relied on a "decoupling" process whenever mandated to serve students who are perceived as not fitting traditional modes of service. That is, when faced with pressure to serve students whose needs could not "be accommodated within the standard practices of public education's prevailing paradigm" (Skrtic, 1995, p. 215), school systems generated separate tracks for these students. Skrtic presented the example of the growing use of self-contained special education classes in the early part of the 20th century when schools began to be required to serve students from working class and immigrant families. Fueled by belief systems such as those of the eugenics movement, pressured to serve students representing increasingly different nationalities and language backgrounds, faced with greater demand to prepare citizens to meet the changing requirements of industrial society, and given the school's historical roots in serving the privileged classes, public education has often selected a route that requires little change in traditional structure: developing special classes, then simply decoupling these "from the rest of the school organization" (Skrtic, 1995, p. 215; see also Oakes & Lipton, 1990; Richardson, 1994; Tomlinson, 1995b).

What is especially discouraging about the decoupling process is that it has its roots in a symbiotic relationship between general and special education in which the initial goal was to protect the "typical" students from individuals with learning and behavioral differences rather than to "do good" for the latter pupils (Tomlinson, 1995b). Historically, this has meant that special education—similar to its adult counterpart, rehabilitation (Albrecht, 1992)—has evolved into a provider of educational services to individuals with labels once they have been partially or fully removed from or denied access to general education. A corollary of this state of affairs is that the discontents among parents and advocates, not the discontents among special education professionals, are more likely to provide the impetus for change, especially when change involves fundamental civil rights. In fact, the enactment of some major laws that have enhanced educational benefit for people with disabilities has come about as a consequence of concerns over special education practice as much as over general education exclusion (e.g., Budoff, 1992).

A significant ramification of the way the relationship between special and general education has evolved is that, although "separate but equal" has been successfully challenged regarding students' race differences (e.g., Kluger, 1976), separate services remain well entrenched in law, policy, and special education practice (Kunc, 1992; Taylor, 1988; Woodward & Elliott, 1992). This paradox has also been noted by observers in the general education community (Banks, 2000; Serow, 1983). Serow (1983), for example, argued that special educators should be looking more at the race relations literature, and he commented that "there has been surprisingly little effort to apply interracial contact theory in issues around mainstreaming" (p. 88).

These patterns of separation, which have been endorsed for various reasons by large numbers of people in both professions, have influenced how special educators have come to define the overall purpose of education for their students. Given these patterns, the special education community itself has been largely outside the mainstream of education for close to a century; consequently, neither it nor its constituents have been major players in many of the large-scale discussions about educational purpose, quality, and reform (e.g., Slavin, 1997). What has emerged within this context of professional isolation is the notion that the primary guideposts for deciding what to teach students with learning and behavioral disabilities are their unique, individualized needs. In other words, in contrast to general education's emphasis on a broad curriculum for a community of learners, education within special education "is defined by teachers, related service and other professionals, and parents *for each individual child*" (Orelove & Sobsey, 1991, p. 446, emphasis in original; see also Chapter 5 in Serow, 1983). Since 1975, these prescribed outcomes of the educational process are legally documented in students' individualized education programs (IEPs).

Needless to say, the existence of a separate educational system—staffed by multiple disciplines and focused especially on individual needs—can have a critical impact on the schooling experiences that are offered to students with challenging behaviors. Certainly, the concept of individual needs is well intended and has an intuitive appeal. It is grounded in the belief that the outcomes of the educational process can be enhanced by thoughtful attention to the unique learning and management needs of students whose behaviors cause control or placement issues given the expectations of the mainstream.

Yet, the focus on individual needs also has its unintended consequences, and these must be balanced against the benefits of this approach. One of the unintended consequences is that the means and products of the educational process may sometimes be determined less by individual needs and more by the practices, beliefs, and values of the administrators, teachers, and other professionals who are responsible for services. Put differently, although the intended benefit of the interdisciplinary process is to ensure that the unique needs of the learner are appropriately addressed, what may actually transpire is that a student's IEP will be constructed in accordance with the unique professional culture that a particular mixture of traditions of practice, professions, and voices bring to educational planning. Depending on a district's customs of labeling and service provision, students who have challenging behaviors will have IEPs developed by very different combinations of professionals with training in any of the following areas: emotional and behavioral disorders, mental retardation, mild disabilities, severe disabilities, autism, early childhood education, psychology, school counseling, medicine, speech-language and occupational therapy, and/or mental health and social work. As these various professionals receive training that promotes contrasting views on what constitutes the likely and desirable outcomes of the educational process, and very different service provision protocols for realizing these outcomes, these views may influence the development of educational plans far more than the specific needs of the students. This means that students from different parts of the country who have similar behavioral issues—indeed, the same child when he or she moves from one school to another—can receive very different educational placements and experiences depending on the capacities and perceptions of the teams that are charged with planning their respective programs (see Display 1.3).

Another source of variation that casts doubt on the degree to which individual needs are really the driving force behind many students' educational programs is that there are a number of fundamental disagreements even within the same discipline on the origins of behavioral problems and how these origins predicate what constitutes "appropriate treatment." For example, with its roots in the emergence of biological explanations for "aberrant behavior" in the 19th century (Foley, 1995), medical model proponents seek explanations and treatments that are based largely on differential diagnosis of specific behavioral pathologies (see discussion in Hahn, 1993; Rosenberg et al., 1997). In contrast, a behavioral model is likely to view diagnostic processes as largely irrelevant to how education teams make their decisions. Instead, behaviorists are more likely to seek explanations and develop treatment protocols that focus on the environment—specifically, the antecedents that occasion behaviors and the consequences that change and maintain them (Alberto & Troutman, 1999).

These two issues alone bring into question whether an individualized approach to education, as it is frequently practiced at the beginning of the 21st century, unequivocally offers an advantage over what would be provided to these students if their educational experiences focus on the needs they hold in common with other students of the same age and grade level. Yet, perhaps the most striking consequence of the individual needs approach to education is not how individualization is compromised by complex disparities across teams and service models. Rather, it lies with a single commonalty that stretches across the experiences of children and youth who are defined as having major behavioral concerns: The specific behaviors themselves become the province of public education, and the need for their amelioration may assume the proportion of being the most important goal driving the educational experiences provided to these children and youth. In other words, IEPs for students with behavioral issues are likely to be configured in relation to specific behavioral difficulties, and the IEPs become the essential blueprint for delineating the educational opportunities that these students are offered, or are barred from, at any given point in

DISPLAY 1.3—MEETING INDIVIDUAL NEEDS?

A student with cognitive and emotional disabilities had been successful in an inclusive junior high school, and his parents wanted him to be placed in an inclusive high school so that his academic growth could continue. Despite his family's and junior high school teacher's advocacy efforts during the IEP meeting, it became clear that the high school had its own program that emphasized vocational skills. It was in this program that this young man would be placed, no matter what was written into his IEP.

What needs do you think the high school teachers identified in their evaluation of this student, and how do you think these differed from the needs identified by the junior high school teacher?

What might one find if one examined the needs of all of the children in the high school's "severe needs" vocational program?

Could problems emerge in this young man's behavior if he goes from an inclusive setting, in which he was successful, to a segregated program?

How will the high school special educators likely interpret these problems if they arise?

their educational careers. Moreover, because some of these students remain in the special education service system for large segments of their schooling, their behavior may serve a pivotal role in defining their educational experiences for much of their school careers. There are five especially critical concerns that can be raised about this practice.

First, the focus on changing behavior as a primary outcome of the educational process helps legitimize the long-standing practice of trying to "fix" behavioral concerns by suppressing their occurrence. As noted by Macht (1990), the "let's fix it" logic is, at best, questionable when it is applied to human beings:

> Regardless of manifested behavior, no matter how distasteful, disturbing, annoying, or unsettling the behavior might be to *someone else*, the individual manifesting the behavior is *doing the best he or she can to satisfy needs, to obtain what is perceived as valued or important.* (p. 7, emphasis in original)

This suggests that traditional practices, which are narrowly focused on behavioral suppression, are likely to be ineffective in the long run. They focus on eliminating behaviors—often within isolated settings—that are, in fact, functional and potentially robust for students in the real-world settings from which they came and to which they must return.

Second, the emphasis on behavioral change has contributed to the emergence of an entire industry of professionals who may assume primary, and sometimes exclusive, responsibility for the education of students with challenging behaviors by virtue of their "special training." Some of these teachers, for example, come out of programs designed to prepare them for working with students with emotional and behavioral disorders; others may come out of programs designed to prepare them to work with students who have severe disabilities. In some cases, these individuals may have received little or no preparation in general education curricula; in many cases, the focus of accountability for these teachers will not be on the delivery of instruction from grade-level general education curriculum. Suffice it to say that this places these students at risk for receiving a truncated educational experience that sacrifices what other children and youth learn so that "behaviors and related needs" can be extensively addressed.

Third, some of these students do not have chronic behavioral concerns per se but are experiencing dissonance because a teacher's or school's practices are insensitive to aspects of their cultural and family upbringing. For example, as noted by Webb-Johnson (1999), a disproportionate number of African American youth continue to be placed in special education. Webb-Johnson persuasively argued that, for some of these youth, the observed learning and behavioral problems that precipitate special education placement do not reflect a disability-based problem; rather, they are the student's adaptive reactions to inflexible educational and discipline practices that are themselves what need to be changed. This means that these students' behaviors are being inappropriately identified as individual needs that require treatment and amelioration. Aside from the impact that this action might have on their views of themselves in relation to society, it also places these students at risk for educational placements that interfere with their access to the valued educational experiences that are provided to other students within the same system.

Fourth, just as one can raise serious questions about the empirical validity of models of discipline used in general education, the same concern applies to the special education treatments that are used for the students with behavioral problems once they have been removed. There is a long and rich history of empirical research on working with specific behavioral problems in special education and related fields. Unfortunately, the majority of this research has been conducted in isolated special education "treatment" settings. Referring specifically to the movement toward educating students with behavioral challenges in regular education settings, Meyer and Evans noted,

> The eco-system of a regular education classroom or community job site is so dramatically different from a university laboratory school, institution, or sheltered workshop that it becomes difficult to imagine how any research findings based on segregated and specialized circumstances could be relevant to the new reality for the growing majority of individuals on whose behalf such research receives public and professional support. (1993, p. 228)

The implication of this point is that many students who have been labeled are removed for all or parts of their school day to participate in programs that, relative to what might occur if supported in general education, have uncertain value in facilitating the changes that such programs may promise. A good example of this concern is found in research on traditional social skills programs, which have often been assigned an important place in the educational experiences of students with behavioral difficulties. Using role playing, behavioral rehearsal, and other techniques, and often situated in special education settings in which all of the students have similar needs, such programs are designed to teach basic skills of effective interpersonal interaction, conflict resolution, and positive social control. Yet, reviews of the social skills instruction research raised serious questions about the efficacy and value of such training (Kavale, Mathur, Forness, Quinn, & Rutherford, 2000; Mathur, Kavale, Quinn, Forness, & Rutherford, 1998; Quinn, Kavale, Mathur, Rutherford, & Forness, 1999; Scott & Nelson, 1998; cf. Whiston & Sexton, 1998).

Fifth, many (e.g., Falvey, 1998) suspect that there are enduring negative psychological and social consequences for both the labeled person and the larger society when specific students are given special education labels that define their educational careers. For example, Van der Klift and Kunc (1994) cited the work of Dembo, Leviton, and Wright to note that most people tend to perceive an individual who has a disability primarily in terms of that disability and not as an individual with gifts, capabilities, desires, and needs. This phenomenon, referred to as *disability spread*, is shown in Figure 1.1. As this figure illustrates, the person with a disability may be assigned a variety of attributes and characteristics that reflect various stereotypes that people have about the disability, such as "all students with autism are non-communicative," "students with attention-deficit/hyperactivity disorder must have distraction-free environments in order to learn," and so forth. As noted by Van der Klift and Kunc, "These characteristics may not actually be true of any one individual" (p. 399). This process may be especially hurtful when the labels are based on a categorical assignment associated with behavioral difficulties (e.g., "conduct disorder") or

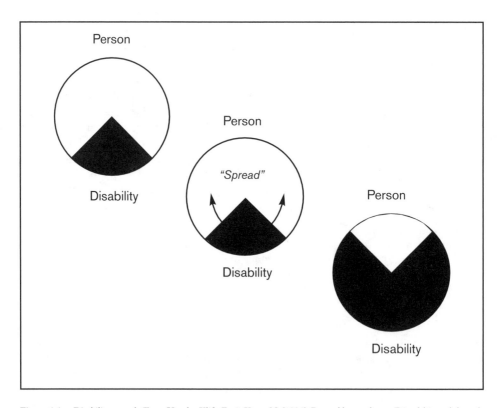

Figure 1.1.   Disability spread. (From Van der Klift, E., & Kunc, N. [1994]. Beyond benevolence: Friendship and the politics of help. In J.S. Thousand, R.A. Villa, & A.I. Nevin (Eds.), *Creativity and collaborative learning: A practical guide to empowering students and teachers* [p. 399]. Baltimore: Paul H. Brookes Publishing Co.; reprinted by permission.)

on the topographies of specific behaviors (e.g., "aggressive," "noncompliant," "hyperactive," "self-abusive," "socially withdrawn") (see also Cambone, 1995).

In sum, special education's role within the larger educational arena emerged as part of public education's reactions to both increasing student diversity and changing expectations about education. Partly as a consequence of how public education managed the transition to serving a broader population, special education has often attempted to serve students who are viewed as too disruptive or inappropriate for the mainstream within isolated settings, either through placement in self-contained facilities and classes or through long-term pull-out. Within a context of professional and physical isolation, the concept of individual needs, generated annually for a student by an interdisciplinary team and documented in the IEP, has come to represent a primary guidepost for deciding what needs to be taught to students in special education. Although intended to provide benefit by offering expertise-driven educational specialization, a number of unintended consequences have emerged. These give rise to concerns about the way this approach has been routinely used in making decisions about what to teach. First, questions can be raised about whether individual needs are really being addressed when 1) service systems and teams across the country differ widely in their placement and outcome prescriptions for students with similar needs and 2) there are major disagreements about feasible outcomes and useful treatment approaches even among members of the same discipline. Second, the individual needs approach to education has helped promote the view that "deviant behavior" is a legitimate target of the public education process for students who are designated as having this "need." This has helped maintain placement and treatment practices that

- Focus on behavioral suppression even when such a focus is unlikely to offer authentic benefit
- Require the services of specialists who are not necessarily prepared or expected to ensure that students receive opportunities to be part of the broader educational curriculum
- Inappropriately include students whose behaviors represent legitimate conflicts with insensitive and unyielding systems and not individual needs
- Have suspect empirical validity because they have been primarily used and validated in isolated treatment settings
- May have enduring negative effects on how people perceive the students and on the way that these students come to perceive themselves

TIDES OF CHANGE

Especially since the 1990s, many special education leaders have been calling for a shift in educational service provision so that 1) children with special needs receive the same general education experiences as their peers, 2) special educators serve as "intervention specialists" who provide professional support to general educators, and 3) general and special educators collaborate more fully in the education of all children and youth (Edyburn, 1997; Jackson, Ryndak, Keefe, & Kozleski, 2000; Lipsky & Gartner, 1997; Stainback & Stainback, 1996; Villa & Thousand, 1994). Reflecting this point of view, Graden noted, "It is more helpful to see special education as a support system to general education and to acknowledge that special educators will always have a helpful role to serve with regard to general education" (1989, p. 230).

This trend mirrors what some believe to be one intention of the Individuals with Disabilities Education Act (IDEA) Amendments of 1997 (PL 105-17): that is, to ensure that general education curriculum becomes the standard to which the outcomes of the special education process are held. This may seem contrary to the individual needs concept, which is deeply engrained in the same law; it is, however, more appropriate to say that it requires a reinterpretation of this concept.

The support concept truly places the individual in the center of educational decision making. It accomplishes this by asserting that what is done to assist a person with educational or behavioral concerns radiates not from a set of professionally defined problems or deficits but, rather, from an understanding of what the person and his or her family, teachers, and classmates wish to accomplish. Implementing a support perspective also requires understanding that achieving authentic educational outcomes involves removing barriers to school and community participation as much as it does fostering an individual's skill competence. The concept of support certainly does not mean that traditional skills training and discipline concerns are irrelevant. Yet, it does position these concerns within a larger context in which 1) long-term learning outcomes take some precedence over short-term behavior change outcomes and 2) greater equality exists between the people receiving plans and the people responsible for developing the plans.

It is reasonable to ask the following question: Given that the exclusion of students with behavioral challenges is so pervasive in general education, and given the overall complacency and active endorsement of this practice by many in special education, why would one anticipate that such reforms are likely? After all, look at the glum history of most, if not all, reform movements in education (Alexander, Murphy, & Woods, 1996; Elmore, 1996; Tyack & Tobin, 1994).

There are several reasons for believing that, by keeping our sights on a distant horizon, headway is possible toward conditions that can bring about needed change. First, certainly since the time of Dewey, public education has reflected the efforts of many to realize and to see expressed within our schools basic democratic principles (Apple & Beane, 1995; Darling-Hammond, 1996). Alexis de Tocqueville was one of the first to observe that in the United States a feature of democracy is the way that "traditional rules of order" inevitably give way to "new social compacts renegotiated so as to empower ordinary men and women" (Achenbaum, 1998, pp. 15–16; see also Friedman, 1999). Clearly, the realization of these principles has a bearing on the experiences of those most at risk for removal because of behavior. As noted by Gathercoal, "Educators who want to create a democratic environment must approach rules and consequences as a way of building community and keeping students in school, rather than using them as a means for pushing students out" (1998, p. 203).

Changes occurring in special education also give rise to hope. As indicated previously, changes in the way a profession describes behavior can represent changes in how that profession understands behavior. Texts in the late 1990s revealed both ethical and practical shifts in how special education and related disciplines are thinking about behavioral challenges (Koegel, Koegel, & Dunlap, 1996; Scotti & Meyer, 1999; see especially Evans, Scotti, & Hawkins, 1999). These changing views on behavior also require us to critically rethink the role and place of self-contained and residential facilities. For example, research has examined variables that influence the reintegration of students with behavioral problems back into their neighborhood schools and communities (e.g., Rock, Rosenberg, & Carran, 1995). Such research brings into

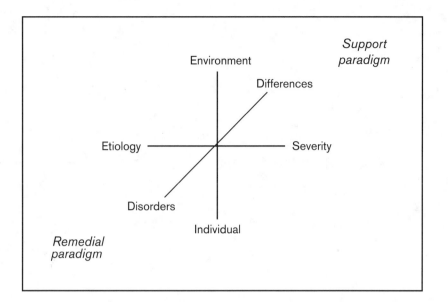

Figure 1.2.   The remedial paradigm versus the support paradigm. (*Source:* Hodapp & Dykens [1994]).

focus the need to more rigorously promote this transition as part of the services such facilities offer.

Especially encouraging is the emergence of the support paradigm within developmental disabilities and other fields of special education. This paradigm challenges the clinical, or *remedial*, treatment paradigm, which has long dominated services in special education. As shown in Figure 1.2, which was inspired by the work of Hodapp and Dykens (1994), the remedial treatment paradigm focuses on ameliorating conditions within an individual that are the product of etiologies and defined as disorders; in contrast, the support paradigm focuses on changing the environment so that individual differences are accepted and various adaptations are provided to match the severity of the support requirements. The growing appeal of the support paradigm is captured in Coulter's comment

> The field of developmental disabilities has undergone a shift in which the emphasis is away from categorical labels (e.g., mental retardation) and toward consideration of how individuals function in significant life activities. More recently, the treatment paradigm has shifted to emphasize supporting individuals to help them function in their desired environments, activities, and roles. (1996, p. 114)

Finally, change is promoted most effectively by making the needed tools readily available to practitioners, whether they are tools of argument or tools of action. The 1990s in particular witnessed the emergence of many research studies and practical manuals that provide both kinds of tools specific to positive behavioral support. In the chapters of this book, we examine these tools and comprehensively detail their applications within educational settings.

Chapter 2

Perspectives on the
Amelioration of Challenging Behavior

"What's past is prologue."
—William Shakespeare

Chapter 1 showed that professionals in general and special education approach behavioral concerns from different points of reference, reflecting differing perceptions of the purposes of education. Put simply, while general educators express concerns about how to control students with behavioral problems so that learning can occur, special educators are concerned with how to treat students with behavioral problems as one aspect of their learning. These differences in perspective may appear to unavoidably promote different educational processes and ends for students with behavioral difficulties, thereby justifying the continued professional isolation that is associated with these two educational systems. Nonetheless, the gap between these two approaches to challenging behavior can be narrowed through the development of a broad, shared understanding of the potential interrelationships between the discipline focus of general education and the treatment focus of special education. In different terms, the purposes of both professions can be met when educators treat the acquisition of general education knowledge, compliance with rules and adult expectations, and growth in personal skills for controlling one's own behavior as interdependent issues.

In general education, this point of view found expression in the work of Hoover and Kindsvatter (1997). They proposed that discipline is best viewed as consisting of three elements:

1. A formalized, "external social force" which establishes conformity and order so that schools can "accomplish their missions effectively" (p. 3)
2. The intrinsic processes within students that can promote positive responses to the expectations of others
3. The way that educators structure their learning experiences and communicate their expectations within classrooms and other settings

21

Roots for a broader conceptualization of "behavioral intervention" can also be found in special education in a number of works (Koegel, Koegel, & Dunlap, 1996; Scotti & Meyer, 1999). These authors all support the view that treatment should not exclusively focus on behavior reduction; rather, treatment must be an "educative process," promoting the growth of adaptive social and behavioral alternatives to problem behaviors through the provision of rich and rewarding learning experiences.

The development of a common understanding among educators regarding behavioral problems—one that is conducive to positive behavioral support—is probably more possible at the beginning of the 21st century than at any point in history. This is because current perceptions of people who have significant learning and behavioral difficulties, as well as emerging theories about human behavior and human differences, reflect substantial shifts. In fact, these changes have supported the creation of a number of discipline approaches and models that express in varying degrees a broader conceptualization of discipline.

This chapter reviews Western society's past and present approaches to challenging behavior. The chapter begins with a historical overview of the dual processes of discipline and treatment for individuals with challenging behaviors, exploring society's changing attitudes about and reactions to these individuals. Next, the chapter presents seven contemporary approaches to classroom management, which are representative of the changes that are occurring in the understanding of the interplay between discipline and treatment, as well as how this relationship relates to instruction. The chapter concludes with a summary of the historical trends and a review of selected points derived from the seven models. This summary shows how past and present approaches to addressing challenging behavior provide the seeds for the development of positive behavioral support.

HISTORICAL PERSPECTIVE

It is somewhat troubling to look closely at trends in discipline and treatment in relation to how Western society has dealt with "deviance." History is replete with the use of violence in the control of others, and neither discipline nor treatment practices have chronologies that are free from this very basic way of responding to conflict and human differences. With respect to discipline, as noted by Rich, stern and harsh measures have been "characteristic of much formal schooling in the past" (1982, p. 58). Practices of this nature have been grounded in two perspectives on behavior, as well as society's basic responsibility for its control. First, school discipline "has often been seen less specifically in terms of 'training for society' and more generally as a form of character training" (Docking, 1980, p. 19). Discipline practices in earlier times were guided by the belief that "consensual morality" should control the behavior of citizens and that schools were responsible for imposing these moral standards in accordance with a pupil's particular social class (Docking, 1980). Second, as expounded in Kant's *retribution theory*, "pain or loss should be caused to those who have done wrong," and this punishment is not "inflicted to achieve another good" but simply because a person has committed a wrongdoing (Rich, 1982, p. 165). Moreover, doling out punishment to wrongdoers is the "absolute duty of society if a system of justice is to be preserved" (p. 165).

Given this historical context, it is not surprising that corporal punishment has long been endorsed as a primary means for enforcing rigorous behavior standards in schools. Nevertheless, its use has also been questioned. In the first century A.D.,

Quintilian opposed the practice of flogging, common in his day, because he believed that young boys would be hardened by the experience, and he questioned the unlimited power that this practice gave the adults over the boys (Rich, 1982). Efforts in the United States to limit corporal punishment date back to the 1820s; however, even in recent times, only 27 states have enacted statewide legislation to abolish corporal punishment (Evans & Richardson, 1995). In fact, in a survey on disciplinary beliefs and practices completed in the 1980s, 75% of teachers still believed that corporal punishment was necessary to maintain discipline (Brown, 1988). These figures reflect the continuing acceptance by many within our schools that violence is a viable way to handle challenging behaviors.

The point of view that puzzling and challenging behaviors can be treated also has roots in the history of early Western society. Especially noteworthy during the Middle Ages, religious belief and civic law were closely aligned; hence, people attributed deviant behavior to supernatural or magical sources and sometimes invoked religious principles when prescribing treatments. Rockland (1989) described a number of early attempts to understand and treat behavior, which included 1) extraction of a pathogenic foreign body, 2) soul restoration, 3) exorcism, 4) confession, and 5) counter-magic. This thinking was slow to recede, especially when it could be used to reject individuals considered unsuited or dangerous. The Salem witch trials of the 1690s are a shocking illustration of how influential members of society can wantonly violate the basic human rights of others under the guise of ridding society of "challenges" to its basic safety and sense of order.

Coleman (1992) offered a historical chronology of mental health treatment practices consisting of a number of overlapping phases. A review and extension of these phases offers insights into not only the evolution of treatment approaches but also how the relationship between discipline and treatment has evolved over time. First, there was the *segregation phase* from the early Middle Ages to the 1600s. As the name implies, the emphasis during this phase was on ridding society of individuals whose behaviors were not understood. Mental hospitals and asylums were established during this era to segregate and punish people with mental disorders.

Second was the *transition phase*, which Coleman (1992) situated within the 18th and 19th centuries. During this phase, institutions were charged with the dual purpose of providing care *and* treatment to people with mental illness, mental retardation, or other disabilities. A number of these institutions were established in the United States in the 1800s on the grounds that such behavior was "curable" (Richardson, 1994). Nevertheless, for the most part, the very institutions that were designed to assist these individuals were replete with atrocities and/or neglect. More important, the impersonal nature of these institutions, either inadvertently or intentionally, worked against the very outcomes they sought to achieve. Equally tragic, intelligent, independent thinking—such as questioning an unfair practice—tended to confirm to those operating the facilities that a person indeed needed the treatment that such a placement offered.

Although the term *positive behavioral support* originated in the late 20th century, the practices associated with it have been invoked intermittently throughout history, usually but not always representing departures from prevailing standards and practices. An early example of humane treatment was a bold move by Pinel, a French physician in the 1880s. Pinel removed the chains from some of the patients at a mental hospital in Paris to test his theory that these patients would respond well when treated with kindness and respect rather than with cruelty and imprisonment. Some individuals showed "nearly miraculous improvement" (Coleman, 1992, p. 5). This account of Pinel's activities may be the first documented case of a large-scale treatment practice that expresses values similar to those of positive behavioral support.

Third, the *service phase* extended from about 1900 to the early 1990s. The focus of this phase was to help individuals become contributing members of society. During this phase, national policies were formulated and national organizations were formed (e.g., Council for Exceptional Children; National Association for Retarded Children) to address the educational and mental health needs of individuals with emotional, cognitive, and physical disabilities.

Psychodynamic theories also arose during this phase. In the late 1800s and early 1900s, Freud established the groundwork for the psychodynamic approach (Strachey, 1961). Freud proposed that there were psychic inner causes that directly regulated the way a person behaved, appropriately or otherwise, and uncovering these causes required an introspective exploration of the associated "conflicting, conscious and unconscious forces, motives, and fears" (May & Yalom, 1989, p. 375). Emphasis was placed on early life experiences, especially traumatic and stressful ones, because these were viewed as impeding healthy emotional and ego-identity development. In Freud's theoretical formulations, challenging behaviors could reflect an individual's inability to resolve a conflict at a specific stage of psychosexual development (Jones, 1959). In 1950, Erikson published *Childhood and Society*. This monumental work offered a reconceptualization of the origins of psychological conflict, suggesting that decisive and potentially enduring conflicts could emerge in any number of significant stages in ego-identity development, and these stages were dispersed throughout life. Of special significance for mental health was that if a conflict was not resolved while in the stage of origination, it could persist as an active dynamic that affected a person's essential happiness and well-being. Resolving the conflict required first uncovering the associated memories and emotions, then working through these by means of discovery and dialogue with a psychoanalyst. "Infantile fears" can accompany us "throughout life," but these can be partially alleviated through "gradual insight" (Erikson, 1963, p. 405).

Psychodynamic theories were revolutionary in their time, and despite questions about the effectiveness of psychoanalysis (Arlow, 1989), their contribution to the view of psychological problems as, to some extent, treatable are real and important. Because they provided explanations for behavior based on scientific constructs—constructs positing that a child's past experiences offer probable cause for today's problems—these theories, by their very nature, challenge discipline practices justified largely on society's obligation to instill moral character and exact retribution. At the same time, the educator may view the origins of challenging behavior as both distant and covert within psychodynamic perspectives. Thus, psychotherapy often does not seem to offer viable strategies for addressing challenging behaviors in typical school and community settings.

Coleman's chronology ended with the third phase. Yet, because the events of the later part of this phase represent significant and distinct developments in the field, it is useful to divide and expand Coleman's third phase into a separate fourth phase (1960–early 21st century). It can be said that, especially for people with disabilities, more progress has occurred during this phase than the other three phases combined. This phase may be variously called the *legislation and litigation phase* or the *model programs and research phase*, depending on what aspect of the change process one emphasizes. In the area of litigation and legislation, powerful and effective action was taken by citizens during this period on two fronts: 1) reforming and dismantling large residential institutions and 2) securing educational opportunities for people with disabilities. *Deinstitutionalization* became a politically charged word as families and advocates in the disability field, coupled with the media, accelerated their attack on placement, treatment, and abusive practices within large, state-operated residential facilities (Blatt & Kaplan, 1996; Larsen, 1976). Court decisions, such as *Wyatt v. Stickney* in 1972, not only contributed to the dismantling of institutions but also established due process safeguards and a basic right to rehabilitative treatment for people placed in residential facilities (Lakin & Bruininks, 1985).

Paralleling these developments were efforts by families and advocates to secure appropriate educational opportunities for their children in public schools (Budoff, 1992). Two major court decisions on this front were *Pennsylvania Association for Retarded Citizens v. Commonwealth of Pennsylvania* of 1971 and *Mills v. Board of Education of the District of Columbia* of 1972, which defined a basic right to a free appropriate public education (FAPE) for people with mental retardation and other disabilities. The single most important piece of legislation passed during this period, solidifying litigation gains, was the Education for All Handicapped Children Act of 1975 (PL 94-142). Coleman observed, "This law has had such a powerful effect that it has guided the direction of special education since its passage" (1992, p. 13). Many of the basic concepts that drive contemporary educational practices for people with disabilities—a FAPE, an IEP, use of the least restrictive environment (LRE), and transition services—are principles forwarded by this law or subsequent amendments.

The collective impact of the litigation and legislation across these two fronts is hard to fully comprehend because of its enormity. According to Lakin and Bruininks,

> Public schools systems expanded special education services from 2.1 million to 3.9 million handicapped children and youth in the fifteen years between 1966 and 1981 . . . during essentially the same period, 1967 to 1982, the total population of the traditional state institutions for developmentally disabled persons decreased from 194,650 to 119,335. (1985, p. 3)

It can even be argued that the inclusive education movement, a significant reform movement that originated in the 1990s (Lipsky & Gartner, 1997), represented the next generation of the efforts of families and advocates to secure social and educational inclusion through political action directed at public and residential school systems. Inclusive education firmly grounds the concept of FAPE with the provision of that education in natural communities, such as neighborhood schools and general education classrooms (Ryndak, Jackson, & Billingsley, 1999–2000).

As noted previously, this fourth phase can also be called the *model program and research phase*. This is because it is associated with applied research and model development activities that were directed at a variety of educational and treatment processes. Within this progressive research climate, many studies have been conducted on basic discipline practices, policies, and outcomes, and this research has nurtured the emergence of numerous discipline models. Many of the models have been well described in both the general and special education literatures; hence, a broad level of dissemination and replication in typical schools and other educational environments has occurred.

It can be argued that the research advances of the late 20th century have provided schools with the means for unifying discipline and treatment practices, and the discipline models developed during this period reflect this convergence. Because an examination of these models offers insights into early 21st-century theory and research on the amelioration of challenging behavior, the next section is devoted to a review of some influential models.

CONTEMPORARY APPROACHES TO ADDRESSING CHALLENGING BEHAVIORS

The seven models presented here are as follows: 1) social discipline model, 2) quality school model, 3) ecological model, 4) behavioral model, 5) cognitive-behavioral model, 6) multiple intelligences model, and 7) judicious discipline model. These approaches were selected from the numerous models that have arisen since the 1960s because they apply to all students, are used in public schools, and seem to have widespread appeal in education. In this discussion, each model is defined and described, selected essential practices are examined, illustrations of applications are provided, and certain limitations are conveyed.

It is important to note, however, that a brief review cannot do full justice to the richness of each model. Moreover, it is also important to note that our sequencing of these models is not intended to reflect either ranked importance or historical chronology. Rather, the models are ordered so that certain themes (e.g., recognition of motivational factors) unfold and become apparent to the reader in ways that highlight model similarities.

Social Discipline Model

As presented by Wolfgang and Glickman (1986), Dreikurs's social discipline model was based on the work of Adler, a noted social psychologist. Adler believed that the central motivation of all people is to belong and to be accepted by others. Likewise, Dreikurs contended that the purpose of misbehavior is to achieve social recognition and acceptance (Dreikurs, 1968). Dreikurs identified four goals that motivate students who misbehave: 1) attention, 2) power and control, 3) revenge, and 4) helplessness or inadequacy. A teacher can discover which goal motivates a student through a process of

- Observing and collecting data in social situations
- Generating hypotheses about the probable motivations that guide the student's behavior
- Examining the feelings the teacher has toward the student's behavior
- Interviewing the student with attention to his or her reactions

An appropriate intervention stems from a consideration and understanding of these results.

Essential Practices and Illustrations   Dreikurs's model departs from more traditional views of discipline in that it requires a teacher to engage in a reflective, self-examination process about his or her own feelings regarding a student's behavior. By asking questions such as "Do I feel annoyed?" "Do I feel beaten or intimidated?" "Do I feel wronged or hurt?" or "Do I feel incapable of reaching the child?", the teacher can derive an initial sense of whether a student's motive was attention getting, power, revenge, or helplessness (Wolfgang & Glickman, 1986, p. 88).

Dreikurs also proposed a variety of methods for assisting students in finding alternatives for their behaviors based on the motives served. For example, a student may hold a belief that acting out will get him or her the kinds of recognition that he or she seeks. Therefore, if a student disrupts the class to gain the teacher's attention, then the student might be counseled in ways to gain recognition more acceptably.

Dreikurs believed that, in a democracy, students must learn to be responsible for their behavior. Yet, he also believed that there was no place for "autocratic punishment," which he saw as counterproductive because it alienated and discouraged children. Dreikurs proposed instead that consequences to problems should either be natural or logical in nature. Natural consequences include a student's friends excluding a student from an after-school activity when he had bullied them earlier in the day. In contrast, logical consequences are arranged by the adults and are directly related to the student's behavior motivation. For example, a student who acts out for teacher attention but actually receives less attention from the teacher experiences a logical consequence because it directly affects his or her access to the attention he or she craves (Wolfgang & Glickman, 1986, pp. 95–96).

Limitations   According to Wolfgang and Glickman (1986) the student must have particular cognitive and verbal skills to engage in the type of interpersonal dialogue required of Dreikurs's model. Even then, it is sometimes difficult for the teacher to pinpoint the exact purpose that a behavior serves because a student may be unclear about his or her own motivations.

Another limitation derives from the fact that Dreikurs's model calls for the teacher to offer encouragement to the student through the provision of positive experiences of responsibility and belonging, including positive experiences immediately after an episode involving a problem behavior. This encouragement is intended to promote hope and maintain a focus on the positive. If used without careful consideration of other practices within the model, however, the encouraging act may become part of a regular pattern in which the student first behaves inappropriately, then experiences encouragement, later behaves inappropriately, then experiences encouragement, and so forth.

Finally, with respect to logical consequences, "logical" does not ensure that a consequence is right, ethical, or even effective given the teacher's behavior change expectations. In fact, a logical consequence could simply be an authoritative response from the teacher—related to the student's motive—which masks the teacher's own inadequacies in developing intrinsically motivating lessons or managing conflicts that may arise between groups of students.

Quality School Model

The quality school model has evolved since the mid-1960s from *reality therapy* to its present name. In its current form, the model also reflects the continuous improvement philosophy developed first for businesses by Deming (1986).

Glasser's (1965) reality therapy model represented a shift from the psychoanalytic focus on past events to a focus on assessing current reality. The core belief of the reality model is that human beings live in a world with other human beings and must take the needs of others into account when they make behavior choices. A related belief is that each person is responsible for his or her own actions and must bear the consequences for his or her behavior.

Based on the recognition that students need to accept the reality of classroom demands, this model offers a way to reverse illogical and irresponsible thinking. For example, a child may believe that his or her self-worth is measured by the degree to which he or she follows the lead of peers, who may not always be making good choices. A teacher in this situation may want to help the child think differently about what measures self-worth and how this relates to his or her relationships with peers.

This theory also posited that all people have five basic needs: 1) survival, 2) love, 3) power, 4) freedom, and 5) fun. Recognition of these needs by the teacher and others leads to a warm and supportive classroom, quality performances, and responsible self-evaluation by students of their own work (Glasser, 1992b).

Essential Practices and Illustrations   Glasser's model encourages fostering a personal and caring relationship with the student who is engaged in difficult or disruptive behaviors while seeking a resolution to the problem at hand. A key step in directing the student toward improvement is for the teacher to carefully assess the situation, especially as it relates to the teacher–student relationship. The teacher is asked to reflect on his or her past behavior with the student, start with a fresh approach, and expect a better tomorrow. Another key requirement is the individual student conference. The purpose of this meeting is to guide the student toward more responsible behavior by assisting him or her in developing a concrete action plan.

Glasser, like Dreikurs, believed in logical consequences—consequences that are teacher arranged but bear an interpretable relationship to the problem behavior. Glasser's model also clearly avoids punishment, especially physical intervention, which Glasser viewed as simply ineffective. Glasser's model does call for a form of isolation following relatively serious disruptions, but it is not used as punishment; rather, it is "for providing a place for the student to sit quietly and think about a plan for reentering the classroom milieu" (Wolfgang, 1995, p. 110). Usually, this place of isolation is somewhere in or near the class, but another room in the school could be used if the student becomes too disruptive while in the classroom isolation area. Out-of-school suspension can also be used when the second level of isolation fails. In all cases, reentry is always made possible by the student's development of a plan.

Because the concept of social interaction is also paramount in Glasser's work, he put major emphasis on classroom meetings. One purpose of these meetings is problem solving, in which the students and teacher focus on a problem or situation that affects all of them and generates a manageable plan that is both present and future oriented.

Limitations   Wolfgang (1995) provided what may be the most widely expressed concern about Glasser's quality school model: the time required for teachers to convene and maintain the classroom meetings. Related to this concern, children may sometimes need adult guidance in setting fair and ethical parameters for the classroom. Yet, some group decision-making processes may leave rule making solely in the hands of young children. In the worst case scenario, the resultant rules can actually violate students' rights (Butchart & McEwan, 1998).

Perhaps inadvertently, Glasser himself once offered a potential criticism of his own model. In a presentation at an inclusive education conference in Denver, Colorado (Glasser, 1993), Glasser was asked by a member of the audience how his model should be applied when a student in the class has "serious emotional disturbances." Glasser's response, much to the surprise of some in the audience, was that some children did not belong in the class in the first place because of the seriousness of their behavior. Such a response raises concerns as to whether his model has been tested in situations in which behavioral diversity is present.

Ecological Model

The central thesis of the ecological model is that the behavior of each human being must be studied in relation to relevant environments, which include both the physical and interpersonal settings that a person frequents (Barker, 1968; Bronfenbrenner, 1979). Hobbs (1966), Redl (1966), and Rhodes (1967) all described promising interventions for students identified with emotional and behavioral disorders based on this premise. For example, Hobbs directed Project Re ED, in which interventions directed at academic and adaptive behavioral objectives within residential schools were extended to the home, the school, and the broader community. Hence, in this project, the focus was not on changing the child in isolation but on working with the child toward adjusting to his or her natural ecological systems.

Essential Practices and Illustrations   Professionals who adhere to the ecological model follow the premise that the setting in and of itself is a powerful contributor to the origin and maintenance of challenging behavior; thus, in order for interventions to be effective, they must be implemented within and across multiple natural settings where the behaviors are probable. If the salient aspects of the setting that are related to the behavior can be identified and altered, then the child's behavior is likely to change. Sometimes, of course, the best way to identify useful setting alterations is to spend time with a person in a setting where a problem does not occur. In this way, one can identify positive features of this setting that, if present in other settings, could very well alleviate the concerns.

The inverse of this premise is that removing the child from the setting in which problem behaviors occur for treatment in a special setting, such as a self-contained classroom, school, or clinic, could prove counterproductive. This is because, although the behavior may improve in the treatment setting, the changes are unlikely to be maintained once the child or youth returns to the original setting. This is to be expected, as the individual is now faced with the same conditions and circumstances that initially elicited and maintained the problem behavior.

Teachers who follow an ecological approach typically examine a variety of factors that might affect behavior in their classrooms. For example, when one or more students seem to be easily distracted during particular lessons, a teacher may first examine his or her teaching style and the instructional materials. Sometimes even simple adjustments in these teaching processes, such as providing a peer tutor, can make a difference in terms of behavior. As another example, a teacher may examine a student's motivations in relation to an environment's specific conditions to identify simple contextual changes that could help meet the student's basic needs without disrupting learning. For example, a teacher might recognize that a student's sudden verbal outbursts, which occur during certain subjects but not others, reflect increasing stress for the student at these times of day, and he or she may offer the student more frequent breaks as a step in stress alleviation at these times.

The ecological perspective has been thoughtfully applied to the issue of choice in daily schedules within community residences (Brown, 1991; Oliva & Brown, 1994). Brown applied an antecedent analysis to scheduling daily events for people with challenging behaviors, and these schedules were revised according to what the analysis implied about preferences in the flow and structure of the daily routines. Initial results indicated that these schedule revisions had the effect of reducing problem behaviors.

Limitations   The primary disadvantage of the ecological model is the time and effort that it requires for gathering data from all parties in all relevant settings. Also, because one is sometimes working with large-scale social structures, the database for making intervention decisions may initially be somewhat ambiguous. Thus, it can sometimes require a resource-demanding trial-and-error process to determine the "true" antecedents to a problem behavior or its alternatives. Finally, related to the time issue, this model requires special coordination to implement interventions in multiple relevant settings, especially if a student's problems are manifested in complex ways across a variety of school and community environments.

Behavioral Model

Skinner (1953, 1968) developed a science of human behavior that has served as the basis for applications in many areas of human endeavor, including education. Applied behavior analysis (Baer, Wolf, & Risley, 1968) is probably the most widely used process for addressing a variety of learning and behavioral problems. There is no doubt that more data are available to support behaviorally based interventions for ameliorating behavioral problems than for all of the other models combined. For these reasons, this model is discussed in greater detail than the other models.

The basic assumption of applied behavior analysis is that behavior is a function of its consequences. The two major corollaries are 1) behaviors that are followed by reinforcers tend to occur more often in the future and 2) behaviors that are followed by punishing stimuli will occur less often in the future. After several early demonstrations of the effectiveness of interventions based on these premises (Hall, Panyan, Rabon, & Broden, 1968; Wolf, Risley, & Mees, 1964), the floodgates opened and widespread use of behavioral techniques in schools, homes, communities, and industry followed (Sulzer-Azaroff & Mayer, 1991).

Within applied behavior analysis, challenging behaviors are viewed as learned behaviors. Because they have been learned, they can be unlearned, and new adaptive responses can be learned in their place. A plethora of research studies have addressed the application of behaviorally based procedures for behaviors that interfere with an individual's participation in home, school, or community activities, and the studies have often demonstrated that these procedures are effective (for reviews see Didden, Duker, & Korzilius, 1997; Dunlap & Childs, 1996; and Scotti, Evans, Meyer, & Walker, 1991).

Essential Practices and Illustrations   The hallmark of the behavioral approach is precise and repeated measurement. Adherence to strict measurement standards allows educators to empirically examine the outcome(s) associated with procedures and make reasonable decisions about whether to retain or discontinue particular interventions.

Although an extensive array of academic, social, and self-advocacy behaviors have been taught using behavioral strategies, this section concentrates on procedures that are frequently applied to reducing behaviors that interfere with learning in schools. As indicated by Dunlap and Childs (1996), such programs often have a dual focus: increasing adaptive skills while simultaneously decreasing undesirable behaviors. Typically, planning involves targeting and defining the problem behaviors and skill alternatives, followed by generating strategies for positive behaviors, and, finally, delineating steps for reducing negative behaviors.

Reinforcement-based reductive procedures, such as differential reinforcement of other behavior (DRO) and differential reinforcement of alternative behavior (DRA), have successfully reduced a number of behaviors that typically interfere with learning in schools. When used appropriately, these techniques create an environment in which positive behaviors are strengthened through reinforcement, and specific negative behaviors diminish because they no longer result in the consequences that once maintained them. For example, DRO, in which reinforcement is provided differentially when the problem behavior is absent for a specific time period, has been used effectively for classroom disruptions (Allen, Gottselig, & Boylan, 1982), hyperactivity (Patterson, Jones, Whittier, & Wright, 1965), and the infliction of self-injury (Mazaleski, Iwata, Vollmer, Zarcone, & Smith, 1993).

Perhaps the most widely applied consequences used by teachers to reduce problem behaviors are time-out and response cost. Time-out involves removing the individual from the situation for a brief period of time contingent on the problem behavior. It has been used effectively in school (Wilson, Robertson, Herlong, & Haynes, 1979) and at home (Olson & Roberts, 1987). Response cost involves removing privileges or other reinforcers after an unacceptable behavior, and it has been used with a variety of different problem behaviors (Forman, 1980; Iwata & Bailey, 1974; Rapport, Murphy, & Bailey, 1982; Reynolds & Kelley, 1997; Sullivan & O'Leary, 1990).

Although the use of aversive forms of punishment—the infliction of pain or other noxious stimuli—is considered an option in the behavioral paradigm, its use has been highly disputed on moral and ethical grounds, as well as with respect to its efficacy (Brown, Pitz, Rosen, & Velez, 1997; Repp & Singh, 1990; Taylor & Bailey, 1996). It has, in fact, been questioned from the very inception of the behavioral paradigm when Skinner noted, "In the long run, punishment, unlike reinforcement, works both to the disadvantage of the punished organism and the punishing agency" (1953, p. 183).

Within the behavioral model, it is important to note that consequences are defined by their impact on the behavior rather than on an a priori basis. Indeed, paradoxical effects have been observed with both time-out (Solnick, Rincover, & Peterson, 1977) and restraint (Favell, McGimsey, & Jones, 1978; Singh, Winton, & Ball, 1984). As previously noted, the behavioral model mandates a process of carefully defining behaviors so that they can be measured, then using ongoing changes in these behaviors as evidence that a treatment has been effective.

The aforementioned practices focus on various consequence arrangements; however, behavior analysts have also addressed the role played by environmental antecedents. Bijou, Peterson, and Ault (1968) developed an antecedent-behavior-consequence (A-B-C) analysis that included noting the time and setting in which a behavior occurred. Several studies (Hall, Neuharth-Pritchett, & Belfiore, 1997; Kern, Childs, Dunlap, Clarke, & Falk, 1994; Weeks & Gaylord-Ross, 1981) have shown that varying antecedents, such as the length or the difficulty of a task or the place in which a child completes his or her studies, can reduce off-task behaviors. Similarly, Carr, Newsom, and Binkoff (1980) showed that, for certain children and youth, high-demand situations could be associated with high levels of self-destructive behavior and that these behaviors can be reduced by changing the nature of the demands. In the 1990s, antecedent analysis moved to the forefront of the procedures that behavior analysts use when generating ways to enhance learning and reduce behaviors that disrupt learning (Carr, Robinson, Taylor, & Carlson, 1990; Luiselli & Cameron, 1998).

Another innovation in applied behavior analysis is functional behavioral assessment (Carr, 1977; Iwata, Dorsey, Slifer, Bauman, & Richman, 1982). Functional, or motivational, assessment seeks to identify the purposes that a behavior serves for the individual engaged in it. Through observations, interviews, and other data-gathering processes, an educator uses functional behavioral assessment to generate hypotheses about the underlying reasons for a behavior (Lennox & Miltenberger, 1989; O'Neill, Horner, Albin, Storey, & Sprague, 1990). That is, *why* is an individual behaving in a particular way? Is it an attempt to communicate? Is it a way to gain attention? Is it a means to avoid a difficult task? Once the function of a behavior has been established, then appropriate behaviors that lead to the same function can be taught, thus reducing the student's need for the unacceptable pattern of behavior.

Limitations   Many criticisms have been levied at the behavioral approach. Kohn (1993) and Lepper and Greene (1978), for example, asserted that individuals should be encouraged to learn and perform for intrinsic satisfaction and not for artificial, extrinsic rewards. Kohn (1993, 1997), in particular, has been a leading critic of behavioral techniques. He has raised the following concerns about the use of rewards and punishers to induce learning: 1) problems transferring performance from the original learning situation to other, real-life situations; 2) the potential short-term duration of the change; and 3) issues about power and dependency in the relationships between the adults delivering consequences and the children receiving them.

Another criticism is the contention that behaviorally based interventions only deal with discrete target behaviors and not with the whole child (e.g., Freiberg, 1999; Lovett, 1996). This narrow focus on directly observable behavior can discourage practitioners from examining broader lifestyle and long-range outcome issues, which could form the basis for a more authentic and enduring plan of action (Jackson & Leon, 1998a). In fact, Meyer and Park (1999) argued that attention to preferred lifestyles should always precede the development of specific interventions.

Cognitive-Behavioral Model

By merging a number of important works (e.g., Beck, 1970; Ellis, 1984; Singer, 1974), Meichenbaum (1977) set the stage for conceptualizing an important role for cognitive events as major considerations in behavior change. His work has provided a theoretical and practical foundation for many school-based behavior change applications (Meichenbaum & Goodman, 1971; Rosenbaum & Drabman, 1979), as well as for the broader movement of self-determination (Wehmeyer, 1992). The basic premise of the cognitive-behavioral model is that cognitions (beliefs, thoughts, expectancies, and attitudes) drive behavior. This means that identifiable cognitive events underlie a behavioral problem and that behavior improves if these cognitions are altered. Cognitive-based changes can be accomplished through rational-emotive therapy (Ellis, 1984), self-instruction (Barkley, Copeland, & Sivage, 1980; O'Leary & Dubey, 1979), and various problem-solving strategies (D'Zurilla & Goldfried, 1971).

Essential Practices and Illustrations   Cognitive-behavioral training methods often teach individuals to use logical reasoning processes to realize improvements in how they respond to situations that tend to elicit distress and/or problem behaviors (D'Zurilla & Goldfried, 1971). Using these methods, an individual is encouraged to

- Recognize a problem when it occurs
- Define the problem in concrete terms

- Generate a set of possible alternative actions
- Select the most appropriate action
- Monitor the outcomes following engagement in that action

Cognitive-behavioral training programs have been used to improve the on-task behavior of students with learning disabilities (Rooney & Hallahan, 1985) and to reduce aggression and increase self-control in students with behavioral problems (Etscheidt, 1991).

The external processes used in teaching these logical reasoning steps are very similar to the processes that are used to teach self-management strategies. Forms and outgrowths of self-management include self-monitoring (Broden, Hall, & Mitts, 1971; Dunlap, Dunlap, Koegel, & Koegel, 1991; Prater, Hogan, & Miller, 1992); self-evaluation (Kern et al., 1995); and self-determination (Faw, Davis, & Peck, 1996; Wehmeyer & Schwartz, 1997). As with cognitive-behavioral training, self-management training has also been applied successfully to task-attendance problems in students with learning disabilities (Maag, Rutherford, & DiGangi, 1992; Rooney & Hallahan, 1985).

Limitations Cognitive-behavioral treatment has produced mixed results in assisting individuals to deal with emotional and behavioral challenges (Martin & Pear, 1999). Optimal results seem to occur when self-management or problem-solving approaches incorporate environmental consequences for the same behaviors that are the focus of the self-monitoring. Thus, at least in much of the research literature, the observed successes cannot be attributed to stand-alone cognitive behavioral treatment strategies; rather, successful behavior change seems to result from a combination of behavioral and cognitive-behavioral strategies.

Other problems relate to the tendency by some researchers to use isolated settings for training activities, with inadequate concern for whether the taught skills will transfer or have value in more authentic learning situations. As noted by Karoly, "A telling criticism of the published work to date in self-control and self-regulation training is the possibility that investigators may have provided children with clothes they will not likely wear outside the treatment context" (1984, p. 98).

On the practical side, it is self-evident that teaching individuals self-management or problem-solving skills can be time intensive. There is also the added difficulty of ensuring treatment integrity because the cognitive aspects of the intervention are, of course, not observable.

Multiple Intelligences Model

The theory of multiple intelligences (MI) was introduced to the public and professional worlds with the publication of *Frames of Mind: The Theory of Multiple Intelligences* (Gardner, 1983). Gardner stated that intellectual capacity is most fruitfully viewed as "the ability to solve problems, or fashion products that are valued in one or more cultural or community settings" (p. 7). Gardner (1995) proposed eight distinct intelligences: 1) linguistic, 2) logical-mathematical, 3) spatial, 4) musical, 5) bodily-kinesthetic, 6) intrapersonal, 7) interpersonal, and 8) naturalist.

The MI model was not originally intended for use as a specific model in education, much less for use in managing discipline concerns. Nonetheless, since Gardner's seminal work appeared, many publications have extended MI theory to a variety of educational applications (Armstrong, 1994; Boggeman, Hoerr, & Wallach, 1996;

Campbell, Campbell, & Dickinson, 1996; Gardner, 1993; Hoerr, 1992). In relation to discipline, MI can provide the basis for rethinking how educators perceive the role of diversity in lesson planning, which can be instrumental in resolving challenging behaviors that have their origins in the manner in which instruction is provided. This is because the very act of identifying more than one intelligence can have the effect of honoring and validating a wider variety of ways for demonstrating learning, and can give greater latitude to how teachers define what is acceptable in different learning and social situations.

Essential Practices and Illustrations   Schools in the United States tradition-ally have given substantially greater weight to two of the eight intelligences: linguis-tic and logical-mathematical. In fact, academic success is nearly synonymous with strengths in linguistic and logical-mathematical intelligence. The almost exclusive focus on these two intelligences in U.S. schools has left a legacy in which students who are differentially gifted in one or more of the other intelligences experience difficulty or may give up. Schenko (1994) noted that 90% of the students who drop out of high school seem to learn best through bodily-kinesthetic intelligence. Furthermore, post-school success has been shown to be linked to proficiencies in other forms of intelli-gence, such as interpersonal intelligence (Goleman, 1995).

Certain forms of instruction are especially noteworthy because of the way they incorporate modes of expression that require different intelligences. Long and Morse (1996) pointed out that the arts and other expressive media are especially valuable, noting that these should be included in programs for students with challenging behav-iors. Hileman (1985), for example, has provided evidence of the benefits of drama for students with emotional difficulties.

Another case in point is service learning, which involves arranging opportunities for students to participate in community experiences that are designed to benefit the community while promoting student learning. Although service learning projects may involve any of the intelligences, the bodily-kinesthetic, interpersonal, and intraper-sonal intelligences are especially well represented in many service learning tasks. For example, interpersonal intelligence is utilized when a student establishes community contacts and connections. Similarly, intrapersonal intelligence is evidenced in the reflective processes that may occur at the end of a service learning experience. Gent and Gurecka (1998) and Krystal (1999) documented the value of service learning for a variety of students with and without disabilities.

Armstrong (1994) advanced the view that the MI perspective represents a growth paradigm, which can eventually replace the deficit paradigm that is so widely used in educational placement and lesson planning decisions. As shown in Table 2.1, educa-tional decisions for students with behavioral challenges could assume a totally differ-ent character if the growth paradigm that is promoted by the MI perspective on stu-dent capacity were to become more commonplace in schools.

Limitations   From a theoretical perspective, Morgan (1996) questioned whether multiple intelligences are "true" intelligences or merely cognitive styles. He also argues that other researchers and theorists have advanced similar concepts and princi-ples and that MI does not really constitute a new or particularly noteworthy theory.

From a practical perspective, the design and implementation of a teaching-learn-ing environment based on this model is likely to be time and resource intensive. Moreover, it seems clear that teachers need administrative support and professional development because, like any innovative model that challenges traditional thinking,

Table 2.1. The deficit paradigm versus the growth paradigm in special education

Deficit paradigm	Growth paradigm
Labels the individual in terms of specific impairment(s) (e.g., ED, BD, EMR, LD)	Avoids labels; views the individual as an intact person who happens to have a special need
Diagnoses the specific impairment(s) using a battery of standardized tests; focuses on errors, low scores, and weaknesses in general	Assesses the needs of an individual using authentic assessment approaches within a naturalistic context; focuses on strengths
Remediates the impairment(s) using a number of specialized treatment strategies often removed from any real-life context	Assists the person in learning and growing through a rich and varied set of interactions with real-life activities and events
Separates the individual from the mainstream for specialized treatment in a segregated class, group, or program	Maintains the individual's connections with peers in pursuing as normal a life pattern as possible
Uses an esoteric collection of terms, tests, programs, kits, materials, and workbooks that are different from those found in a regular classroom	Uses materials, strategies, and activities that are good for *all* kids
Segments the individual's life into specific behavioral/educational objectives that are regularly monitored, measured, and modified	Maintains the individual's integrity as a whole human being when assessing progress toward goals
Creates special education programs that run on a track parallel with regular education programs; teachers from the two tracks rarely meeting except in IEP meetings	Establishes collaborative models that enable specialists and regular classroom teachers to work hand in hand

it will be implemented most effectively if given encouragement from leadership, tools and know-how for using them, and a community of like-minded practitioners.

Judicious Discipline Model

Some research evidence suggests that student attachment is strengthened and levels of disruption weakened when students have a voice in school governance and curriculum decisions (Holdsworth, 1988; Knight, 1988). Judicious discipline is one of a number of models (e.g., Hoover & Kindsvatter, 1997) that advocates shifting the balance in discipline practices so that students have both voice and more responsibility for establishing and implementing discipline policy within schools and classrooms. Similar to other models of discipline that advance democratic ideals, judicious discipline illustrates a classroom management approach that emphasizes prevention, tolerance for others, and self-regulated control.

The core belief of judicious discipline (Gathercoal, 1998; McEwan, Gathercoal, & Nimmo, 1999) is that the teaching-learning environment should respect the citizenship rights of all students. Furthermore, schools should actively create discipline practices that enhance community and promote keeping students in school rather than advocating for their removal when there are discipline concerns.

Essential Practices and Illustrations   As described by Gathercoal (1998), judicious discipline is a synthesis of the tenets of the U.S. Constitution, ideas from Kohlberg's moral development theory, cognitive management, and Dreikurs's approach to understanding reasons for challenging behaviors. Judicious discipline involves students participating in the classroom management processes, and as they do so, the relationships between their participation and the basic principles and procedures of democracy are identified and discussed.

Central to the judicious discipline approach to democratic classroom management is that it provides teachers with a framework for teaching citizenship every day through routine classroom interactions. For example, students learn to self-monitor their actions in terms of appropriateness of time, place, and manner and in consideration of their own rights and responsibilities, as well as those of their peers. Although its primary focus is on prevention, when behavioral problems do occur, teachers are encouraged to ask leading questions and carefully listen to a student's rationale. A typical consequence for misbehavior is restitution that relates to the misbehavior but still respects the offending student's self-esteem.

Limitations   Although the research results have been encouraging, especially with respect to the reduction of expulsion and suspension practices (Barr & Parrett, 1995), judicious discipline is a relatively new model. Hence, there is a need for more evaluative information on the processes and products associated with this approach.

Judicious discipline, like any approach that shifts discipline control to students, requires a major investment of start-up time and energy before it becomes fully operational (McEwan et al., 1999). For example, teachers report that judicious discipline requires a significant amount of time to simply establish and sustain the citizenship expectations in the students. This may, in part, reflect the fact that the model does not provide a simple "cookbook" for how teachers are to act in specific situations; rather, teachers must develop a thorough understanding of the democratic principles that underlie their decisions and their guidance of the students' decision-making processes. Nevertheless, as noted by McEwan and colleagues (1999), both the original and ongoing time investments are repaid with the reported increases in time available for instructional interactions and the decreases in time spent engaged in disciplinary procedures.

SEEDS OF POSITIVE BEHAVIORAL SUPPORT

This chapter has shown that, in early Western society, there was broad intolerance for behaviors that fell outside of very narrow standards of social conduct, and methods of discipline and treatment within and outside of schools communicated this intolerance in no uncertain terms. Unacceptable differences in behavior were viewed as an expression of something that, in some cases, might be extractable through exorcism or similar practices but could most readily be handled by isolation and punishment.

As treatment practices evolved in the 20th century, causes for challenging behaviors were reconceptualized as individual and treatable pathologies. Assisted by the emergence of advocacy organizations and increasing political action, treatment and discipline practices began to honor the right of citizens with challenging behaviors to greater due process regarding exclusion, to receive treatment in relation to their disabilities, and to participate in the broader community.

Two important shifts in thinking were signaled by Erikson's work in the mid-20th century. First, Erikson retained Freud's notion that behavior patterns can reflect persisting stresses experienced earlier in life but postulated that such events could occur at many points in life rather than only in the earliest periods. He also postulated that the character of the conflict could reflect a complex interaction between the effects of a person's earlier stressful events and present struggles. Erikson's (1963) particular stages of growth and predictions about what stresses and traumas are likely to emerge at each stage may or may not meet the tests of time. Yet, it is likely that the various professions concerned with behavioral issues in education have only begun to grasp the implications of stress and trauma across the life span for discipline practices in educational settings (Brendtro, Brokenleg, & van Bockern, 1990; see also Oseroff, Oseroff, Westling, & Gessner, 1999). The distinct possibility that some of the treatments used in schools and clinics have done little to ameliorate the influence of extreme and stressful life events or that such treatments may actually exacerbate a person's distress—or even be traumatizing events in and of themselves—is touched on in the Epilogue.

The second shift in thinking that Erikson heralded was addressed in a biography review by Edmundson (1999). Edmundson argued that one of the major shifts in thinking that Erikson's work forwarded was a movement away from equating mental health with sanity toward equating it with a state of happiness. When mental health is conceptualized in the latter manner, the status of a person's psychological condition is expressed not in a "degree of wellness" but rather in his or her genuine well-being. This insight, which has parallels in the field of medicine (Moberg & Cohn, 1991), remains largely dormant in education, as special educators and behavioral specialists continue to view their roles as ones of eliminating behavioral concerns with discrete skill training and management (see also Seligman, 1999). As proposed in Chapter 5, honoring and addressing broader lifestyle issues is a path that will likely yield authentic change for students with challenging behaviors, and this procedure implicitly recognizes the distinction between wellness and well-being.

During the late 20th century, professionals increasingly viewed challenging behavior as more of a systems issue than an indication of individual pathology—an issue that is best handled by ensuring access to educational opportunity, then developing effective teaching and discipline practices that alter how educators interact with students. From this point of view, the genesis of challenging behavior is not within the individual; rather, it resides within an ongoing and dynamic reciprocal interaction between the child's responses to the environment and the environment's reactions to the child. Bijou (1968), a behaviorist, was one of the earliest thinkers to advocate a shift in focus from "blaming the child" to examining other factors, such as the environment, the actions of adults and fellow students, and the contingencies of reinforcement that can promote and maintain challenging behaviors. Others who have contributed to this way of thinking include Blatt (1999), who suggested that the very existence of specializations such as abnormal psychology distort the essential nature of human psychology by misrepresenting many forms of diversity as pathology. Wayson and Pinnell also echoed these sentiments when they noted, "When discipline problems occur in school they can more often be traced to dysfunction in the interpersonal climate and organizational patterns of the school than to malfunctions in the individual" (1982, p. 117) (see Display 2.1).

Reviews were conducted in this chapter of a number of models that in different ways emphasize changing the quality of the learning environment to effectively ameliorate behavioral problems. Five promising themes are found in differing degrees across all models, and these should be incorporated into positive behavioral support.

DISPLAY 2.1—THE THREE WAVES OF COUNSELING

O'Hanlon (1994) described a series of three waves of change that have occurred in the field of counseling:

First Wave
Pathology-focused
Concerned with diagnosing and treating conditions that originate inside a person

Second Wave
Problem-focused
Concerned with identifying a person's problems and helping the person resolve them

Third Wave
Solution-focused/narrative
Concerned with defining a person's goals and how to rewrite a person's life so that he or she reaches these goals

Based on your experiences, where on this change continuum would you place special education services for students with challenging behaviors?

How might the language that is used by teachers, psychologists, and others (e.g., "deviant behavior," "inappropriate behavior") preserve pathology- and problem-focused thinking?

First, there is a recognition that addressing behavioral issues requires the collective actions of a community and that community membership, personal relationships, and belonging provide the essential bases for creating effective ways for addressing these issues. This concept is reflected especially in Dreikurs's social discipline model, which includes the premise that belonging is a basic human need and that discipline practices must flow from an understanding of the implications of this need. Some elements of the quality school approach, such as the classroom meetings focusing on collective problem solving, also reflect the idea of discipline being centered within a community rather than in a teacher or in the policies of a school. Judicious discipline's emphasis on giving voice in decisions to all students also reflects these basic ideas: Voice can enhance investment, and it is precisely investment in the purposes and processes of an institution that, in the end, promote adherence to rules and conventions. The multiple intelligences model has identified interpersonal intelligence as a key to success both during and after the school years. The latter model also postulates that, for certain students, this form of intelligence is a primary vehicle for the expression of their strengths and contributions to the school community.

Second, there is the recognition that problem prevention and amelioration require careful consideration of what is being taught, how it is being taught, the adaptations that are offered for those who are having difficulty, and the overall climate of the learning and interpersonal environments. The ecological, the behavioral, and the multiple intelligences models support the practice of examining teaching and curriculum when trying to understand behavioral issues, whether they apply to individual students or the class as a whole. Of course, one should be skeptical when this issue is framed as, "Is this the wrong curriculum for this particular student?" This question should be reframed as, "Is this curriculum relevant for all students, and, if so, what social and academic supports can we provide for the student who is exhibiting difficulty?"

Third, there is the recognition that self-direction and the experience of autonomy are important aspects of effective discipline practices. This is especially well represented in the cognitive-behavioral model, with its emphases on self-determination and taking charge of one's own change activities. It is also reflected in the quality school model's focus on the individual creating personal change plans and in the judicious discipline model's adherence to giving responsibility to students for the development of discipline policies and procedures. An activity that deeply reflects this principle but has not found adequate expression in any of the models is lifestyle or "person-centered" planning. In part, this is because, when professionals implement just about any discipline approach, they look for academic growth, instructional compliance, and conformity to social convention as the primary indicators of success. It is in lifestyle planning that positive behavioral support could offer something different from other discipline models, because it shifts attention from an exclusive concern for the adult's wish list to that of an individual student and his or her family.

Fourth, several of the models reflect an awareness that motivational factors—understood not as broad constructs but as specific relationships between the student's behavior and the way the environment responds to that behavior—provide a useful mechanism for 1) understanding behavior and 2) restructuring an environment for greater success. The social discipline model could be viewed as a precursor to this development because it includes a set of questions that a teacher must address to grasp the purposes behind a student's behavior. In its emphasis on the environment's complex and varying role in effecting challenging behavior, the ecological model is also congruent with the view that motivational factors must be considered when addressing behavioral problems. Yet, the behavioral model has perhaps contributed the most to this issue. As noted by Carr (1997), and Hendrickson, Gable, Conroy, Fox, and Smith (1999), many positive behavioral support concepts evolved from an empirical research base that was established over a 30-year period within applied behavior analysis. Nowhere is the connection more apparent than in the area of functional behavior assessment and hypotheses-based intervention, which are practices that were brought to the forefront largely through research in applied behavior analysis.

Fifth and finally, although the behavioral model routinely drew from a range of treatments that included aversives, in large measure, even within applied behavior analysis, many educators are expressing prudence regarding the use of punishment (Horner et al., 1990). Glasser in particular argued that there is no place for punishment in discipline, and even his various forms of suspension turn control over to the student as to when he or she can return to the natural learning setting. There is, of course, a place within crisis management for nonviolent, protective removal and restraint, and certainly there may be natural events that follow problem behavior that educators do not control. In addition, a team sometimes has to alter support plans to be consistent with consequences that are associated with what happens to other children in school, even if there is little agreement as to the soundness of those consequences. Nevertheless, there is no place for aversives within positive behavioral support. Moreover, the widespread use of time-out rooms and physical and mechanical restraints as routine procedures for dealing with children and youth is questionable, especially when such procedures are used exclusively for "consequating and managing" the behavior of children and youth with disabilities. The tools and procedures of positive behavioral support, when used in natural environments, can ultimately replace the archaic methods of control that evolved out of a history in which the conditions of self-containment may have made such methods seem necessary.

Chapter 1 showed that early 21st-century schools do not reflect the best of our knowledge about behavior and its causes and how to address it ethically. As Chapter 2 has shown, however, the long-term evolution of discipline and treatment practices indicates that streams of thought exist today, sometimes in latent forms, that have the potential to broadly effect how challenging behaviors are understood and treated. Approaches to teaching and learning are needed that can provide a foundation for these promising forms of action and thought. These kinds of approaches are explored in Chapter 3.

Chapter 3

Designing Theoretically Sound Classroom Practices to Guide Student Learning and Behavior

with Ginny Helwick

"He chose to include the things
That in each other are included, the whole,
The complicate, the amassing harmony."
—Wallace Stevens

As described in Chapter 1, the general education experience in its many forms has the potential to provide all students with critical opportunities for growth and learning through ongoing and cumulative contacts with society's knowledge base and socialization processes (Goodlad, 1990). Because one cannot predict a given student's adult outcomes, the "equality in educational opportunity" principle should govern the way that students are educated. This condition is made possible when each student is provided with equivalent educational experiences that are coupled with the necessary accommodations and modifications for addressing unique learning and behavioral support needs.

Many classroom teachers have a sincere desire to facilitate and enhance the growth of all of their students by providing each one with opportunities to access a society's knowledge base and opportunities for socialization. Individuals may enter the teaching profession with a desire to implement exciting new ideas about learning and instruction, or they may discover fresh ideas along the way that could improve their instructional methods. Somewhere during the course of their careers, however, many teachers lose sight of this desire for personal reflection and growth. Increasingly, they feel pressured to adapt to a school's culture and to conform to the political and social forces that are associated with school life. Influenced by these forces, which often focus on teacher performance, their love of teaching may give way to concerns for self-preservation. What was once the joy of watching a classroom of students learn and grow becomes instead a process of assigning privilege to those students who do well while unknowingly neglecting or depriving others. Within this framework of fear, the removal of students from classes because of seemingly unwieldy learning and behavioral problems—or because teachers are told that they lack the specific expertise to teach such students—becomes the accepted practice.

41

Such a practice is bound over time to erode public confidence in education. It promotes inappropriate reactions to cognitive and behavioral variation, it feeds discrimination based on ethnic and language differences, it casts doubt on the ability of public education to meet its responsibilities to educate all of its students, and it sows seeds of discontent in the students who are neglected and discarded by the system and in the teachers themselves. Feinberg observed,

> We are witnessing a remarkable change in the circumstances of public school teaching. The moral foundations of compulsory education are being questioned as people of many different political and educational persuasions challenge its legitimacy. Alternative schools grow more popular, proposals for vouchers and tuition tax credits receive sympathetic hearings, home schooling appeals to more people, and the public schools' moral authority continues to diminish. Unless a new moral conception of public education is developed, public schools may stand as meaningless institutional shells, reminders of once larger purposes. (1990, p. 155)

This reflection remains as true at the beginning of the 21st century as it was in 1990. Although the public's discontent has many causes, the splintering of public education through its dependency on removal, as well as its creation of learning tracks and special programs for students who are removed, likely exacerbates the overall fragmentation process that is occurring within the system.

Following Dewey's (1938) seminal work on the social aspects of education, there have been numerous efforts to define and innovate educational practice by linking classroom processes to theories about teaching, learning, and development. The essential idea is that a sound theory provides guidance for practice even as it offers a framework for the empirical examination of advancing methodologies. This chapter raises questions regarding the role of learning theories in guiding and sustaining educational practice. Then, drawing from the work of a number of contemporary theorists and thinkers, five general principles of learning are developed that offer a cohesive view of optimal student placement and instruction. Next, the chapter briefly reiterates the point that a number of pervasive, deeply entrenched student placement and teaching practices that affect students with behavioral challenges are contrary to these principles. The chapter then explores the scientific paradigm that underlies and helps create the division between what is and what should be regarding the placement and instruction of students with behavioral challenges. Finally, this paradigm is reformulated into one that is more consistent with the principles of learning that are developed in this chapter.

THEORY IN EDUCATIONAL PRACTICE

As previously noted, the field of education is replete with efforts to improve teaching practices by finding and developing links between theory and practice. This section situates learning theories within the broader context of teacher belief systems, teaching pedagogies, and personal philosophies, and it confirms the importance of using theories of learning as guideposts for practice. Five principles are then developed from a number of theoretical works that, when used to guide instructional practices, provide benefits for both learning and discipline in the classroom of the 21st century.

Belief Systems, Teaching Pedagogies, Personal Philosophies, and Learning Theories

Discussions about how teachers should instruct or respond to behavior are often framed in terms of educators' theories about learning, pedagogies for instruction, and/or personal philosophies about education. In reality, however, it is more accurate to say a teacher's entire belief system—which includes what he or she understands about learning (theory); endorses about teaching (pedagogy); embraces about education (philosophy); and many other perceptions, observations, mental categories, and attitudes—drives the teaching process. Moreover, it does so regardless of whether the teacher is conscious of all or portions of the beliefs that comprise his or her system.

In ecological theory (Bronfenbrenner, 1979; see Chapter 2 of this book) and other theories that focus on the role of the environment in human behavior (Kozulin, 1996), an *activity* is a central unit of analysis for understanding the development of consciousness, identity, and behavior patterns. Following Leontiev's activity theory (Kozulin, 1996), beliefs themselves emerge out of the teacher's ongoing and historical experiences, including carrying out, reading about, thinking about, and talking about different teaching and learning activities in relation to specific motives, actions, and conditions. Put differently, classroom instruction and interpersonal interaction with students are guided by the teacher's implicit and explicit beliefs about self, people, learning, and instruction. These beliefs evolve directly out of the complex array of teaching activities in which the teacher has engaged over time.

In practice, however, a teacher's beliefs are frequently overridden by specific expectations and standards that administrators and other influential members of the school community impose on classroom teachers. Ayers (1993) argued that such systemic practices turn teachers into "functionaries," requiring that they "implement the initiatives of others," which simultaneously "disempowers" and "deskills" them, as well as institutionalizes "a system that prespecifies each teacher's thoughts and oversees and constrains our activities" (pp. 18–19). In some situations, these systemic pressures can dominate how a specific teacher interprets his or her role and how he or she performs various classroom responsibilities. Yet, it is important to realize that the domination of imposed expectations over other aspects of teaching and learning seldom alter the belief system that underlie the teaching process. Rather, they tend to force expression of the underlying beliefs in different ways, and these expressions may become distorted versions of what the teacher would do in the absence of such pressures.

Preventing the foregoing situation requires that teachers have a foundation that helps them properly incorporate into their belief system the predetermined expectations and standards that they are being asked to implement. This foundation can be laid with the presence of strongly felt theoretical principles that can guide teachers through the quagmire of imposed standards and expectations. Yet, teachers are surrounded by numerous myths and fictions that parade as truths and theories within the popular literature and culture of the teaching trade. For example, Ayers (1993) asserted that a dominant myth in education is that "teaching is little more than the simple and efficient delivery of curriculum," and "there is little need for adjustment" and "no need for dialogue" (p. 17). Aoki (2000) noted that much of the so-called "art-of teaching" has been conceptualized as a kind of dentistry, in which teachers and students are asked to extract something concrete from material at hand, much as a dentist extracts a tooth. As Aoki noted, however, "a good teacher differs from a competent dentist. Extraction, by definition, leaves something behind . . ." (p. 352).

Clearly, teaching is considerably more than curriculum delivery or the extraction of essential information from assigned readings. A sound theory of learning can assist the teacher in sorting through the plethora of recommended teaching methods and materials to find those that are consistent with the vastly more complex processes that a teacher encounters when instructing students and maintaining a social environment that is conducive to learning. Teaching consists of discovering new ways to engage students in the ongoing, dynamic, and collaborative construction of the material to be learned. Authentic learning, then, is situated within the learner's culture and group; it is contextual rather than abstract. A material's boundaries grow and shrink for the group as a whole and for individual learners as new material is encountered, examined, and internalized. As Tomasello, Kruger, and Ratner aptly put it, "What is internalized in instructed learning is . . . a dialogue" (1993, p. 500).

Given the perspective that learning and behavior are conceptualized as complex and interactive processes, theories addressing intergroup dynamics and discourse processes have much to offer the practitioner, as they provide tenets and principles that can guide instructional design to optimize learning. Theories of observational and sociocultural learning are also of value because they frame learning as a developing product of the individual's learning history, given certain basic mechanisms that govern and regulate the way that both skill acquisition and cultural learning occur. Returning once again to Goodlad's (1990) framework, the former theories are of value when one is thinking about the internalization of knowledge, and the latter are important when one is considering the socialization processes that are associated with enculturation.

Learning theories and their relationship with instruction and discipline are especially significant because, when their essential principles become enmeshed in a teacher's belief system, they provide understanding and guidance to instructional design that can enhance the purpose and utility of a teacher's classroom discourse and lessons. Teachers who immerse themselves in well-founded learning theories and allow these theories to inform their practice move beyond the arbitrary and the expedient to the grounded and the coherent. This makes them more able to weather the political forces that attempt to place the interests of the school's organization over those of students. The next section offers a series of such theoretical principles and presents some details about their meaning and application.

Five Principles of Learning

Whether the issue is academic learning or appropriate social expression in the classroom, understanding should be the desired outcome of the educational process (Gardner, 1999; Wiggins & McTighe, 1998). Understanding does not involve simply learning about what is viewed as "true" or "right" within a discipline or culture. Rather, it involves acquiring frames for thinking and dialoguing about information that promote active problem solving and discourse across a variety of situational and interpersonal contexts. In this process, the recall and rethinking of previously acquired information constitutes a significant activity. Hence, the following five principles of learning are those that are most useful for elucidating how understanding in students emerges and blossoms in relation to the teacher's activities.

Learning occurs in a medium of group norms. These norms are acquired through ongoing observational learning processes in which the models that one repeatedly sees and hears strongly influence and enhance what one does and becomes.

All classrooms have norms that control, channel, and guide student and teacher behavior. Class norms, arising from within the class or imported from outside of it, create the social and behavioral fabric in which various forms of thinking, learning, and acting are facilitated or not facilitated within the routine discourse of members of a class. As a set of attitudes and expectations that are shared by members of the group, Schmuck and Schmuck asserted that

[Norms] help to guide the psychological and behavioral processes of the group members. They influence *perception*—how members view their physical and social worlds; *cognition*—how they think about things, other people, and themselves; *evaluation*—how they feel about things, other people, and themselves; and *behavior*—how the members overtly act. (1988, p. 185, emphasis in original)

As described by Schmuck and Schmuck, Goffman (1959) depicted the development of norms as being on a stage without the necessary script and gradually learning the play's lines and actions through interacting across time with the other actors. Norms are often implicit rather than explicit; they emerge out of ongoing and everyday inter-actions between members of the group, and they are the products of incidental, rather than direct, instructional procedures.

As noted by Schmuck and Schmuck (1988), classrooms will have a variety of norms that support different social and academic activities. Norms can be perceived as positive when they provide support for learning or prosocial behaviors among class members. Negative norms can also develop in a class that interfere with academic learning, such as those that support "talking at the same time and not feeling obliged to listen, students interrupting one another in disrespectful ways, students using sar-casm, ridicule, or put downs to express insulting disapproval of other students, and students pushing and shoving one another" (p. 183). Another class norm that can cre-ate problems is one that discourages students from taking risks in their social and aca-demic learning, which establishes a very narrow range of behaviors that fall within the realm of what is viewed as "safe."

Schmuck and Schmuck (1988) posited that one especially positive behavioral norm is the norm of reciprocity. This type of norm promotes and preserves among students the kinds of assistive, supportive, and conflict-resolution behaviors that can help the teacher achieve his or her classroom goals and expectations. Left to develop on their own, strong norms of reciprocity may not arise within the class social milieu. Schmuck and Schmuck noted that for this norm "to take hold," group members have to share two types of understanding: "(1) that members should help those who have helped them; and (2) that members should not injure (or ridicule) those who have helped them" (p. 190). They remarked that a teacher can help generate norms of rec-iprocity by "finding avenues for increasing the amounts of positive social reinforce-ment that are initiated from one student to another" (p. 190).

Although ecological theory (see Chapter 2) can be applied to understanding norms, social learning theory (Bandura, 1963; Rotter, 1982) offers an especially strong basis for understanding how behavioral consensus and commonalties emerge. One proponent, Rotter (1982), first noted that context, or the "psychological situation," was an important determinant of behavior. In contrast to psychological theories that stress the role of personality in predicting behavior, Rotter proposed that "behavior varies as the situation does" (p. 303). Rotter relied mostly on reinforcement processes for explaining the development of such behaviors, emphasizing the value assigned to the reinforcer by the learner. Conversely, Bandura (1963) argued that modeling and imitation play powerful roles, especially noting the impact on the learner of observ-ing others enjoy the production and outcomes of their behaviors. Commenting on how earlier theories relied mostly on reinforcement processes, Bandura asserted,

There is considerable evidence, however, that learning may occur through observation of the behavior of others even when the observer does not reproduce the model's responses during acquisition and therefore receives no reinforcement . . . an adequate social-learning theory must take account of the role of *vicarious reinforcement*. (p. 4, emphasis in original)

Schmuck and Schmuck (1988) pointed out that a student may exhibit a state of *normlessness*, in which the individual honors few rules and recognizes few group development standards for self-monitoring personal behavior. They indicated that normlessness refers to "the emotional condition of the individual for whom there are few guidelines and few expectations shared with others" (pp. 184–185). Normlessness can emerge from a sense of alienation, in which the individual student feels socially isolated from the group.

Norms can change or stay constant across time within a particular social group. In either case, continuous immersion and ongoing observational learning within the social system sustains these norms, which help maintain behaviors that are deemed acceptable to all participants. Of course, there is no guarantee that all students in a class will invariably respond in ways that are consistent with the norms, and certain individuals will be resistant to particular norms. Nevertheless, it appears unlikely that removing an offending student from the classroom and placing him or her with other students who have similar problems is a helpful step, as resistance to accepted norms or alternative potentially maladaptive norms are likely to be influential pressures in many self-contained environments. Instead, the first step that should be taken is to work on group membership and developing norms of reciprocity within the general education class.

Learning is co-constructed within a social context, and what is learned defines social membership and connects learners with each other and with the culture as a whole.

Dewey (1938), an early spokesman for learning as an inevitable social process, emphasized that academic subject matter can only be effectively communicated by designing experiences that convey the material in its fullness to the students. Dewey further proposed that such experiences only come about through interaction among all of the learning participants, implying that "education is essentially a social process," and that "this quality is realized in the degree in which individuals form a community group" (p. 58). Dewey also proposed that one-sided processes of teaching and controlling students in classes essentially deny the social nature of learning. He proposed that when teachers "deliver" the curriculum to students, who are treated as passive recipients of knowledge, such instruction actively interferes with the development of learning habits needed later in life when situations arise that require self-directed learning.

Perhaps Vygotsky (1962, 1978) is the most well-known theorist who examined learning as an essentially social phenomenon. In contrast to many theorists in psychology, Vygotsky viewed all mental processes as "entirely social," originating in social interaction, organized by social relations, and consisting of constituents that are "social artifacts such as linguistic symbols" (Ratner, n.d., p. 1). Vygotsky strongly believed that development is the medium for acquiring the skills needed to master the world around us and that development involves the internalization of action, particularly verbal action that occurs in external dialogue with others. Although Vygotsky's theories are largely about development, Bruner noted in his introduction to *Thought and Language* (1962) that Vygotsky's "conception of development is at the same time a theory of education" (p. v).

John-Steiner and Mahn asserted that the "power of Vygotsky's ideas lies in his explanation of the dynamic interdependence of social and individual processes. *Vygotsky conceptualized development as the transformation of socially shared activities into internalized processes*" (1996, p. 192, emphasis in original). They noted that a common misunderstanding about Vygotksy's theories is the presumption that Vygotksy meant the transfer of an external activity from one source (i.e., an adult or another more advanced learner) into the mental schema of another (i.e., the student). According to John-Steiner and Mahn, however, the correct interpretation of Vygotky's theories requires recognizing that the learner plays an active role in both constructing knowledge and in contributing to the constructions formed by others. When viewed from an educational perspective, this means that the internalization of learned information that leads to a deep understanding—which is the desired outcome of the educational process—first happens within interpersonal exchanges, such as those that occur in an "interactive classroom" (Fogarty, 1999). Such interchanges "awaken" the mental activities that lead to the learner's internalization of the knowledge as being active and meaningful (Englert & Palincsar, 1991). Moreover, it means that learning is less the transfer of knowledge and information from one who is knowledgeable to one who is not and more the active and ongoing co-construction of information by a community of learners.

This point of view also has implications for how knowledge itself is conceptualized. Although it is not uncommon for people to view knowledge as being fixed, constant, and independent of the observer, co-construction implies that knowledge is changeable, fluid, and social. Knowledge exists and is fully comprehended by understanding the contexts and discourses within which it is used and applied. This is an especially apt description of the nature of knowledge within literacy and literacy development. Literacy knowledge is deeply embedded in the immediate sociohistorical and cultural contexts that define its character and use (Englert & Palincsar, 1991). Literacy and those skills that make literacy possible are acquired through dialogic processes in which the activities of literacy are inseparable from the processes of understanding, interpretation, and transformation that learners bring to bear on these activities.

In sum, the social nature of academic learning can be viewed from two dimensions. The first dimension is that learning is optimized and the quality of what is learned is enriched when learning occurs within a social-interactional context. Learning is of a higher quality when individuals who are participants in the learning process actively examine facts and ideas from the multiple perspectives that are made possible by group discourse. Inversely, as illustrated in relation to literacy instruction, when learning is relegated to "rigid instructional routines" that do not allow for "student–student interactions around texts," teachers in effect "silence students' oral and written voices within the literacy community" (Englert & Palincsar, 1991, p. 225). The second dimension is that the nature of knowledge is essentially social and changeable. It emerges out of collaborative processes in which the many voices of students and the teacher come together in ways that express both resonance and dissonance; knowledge is not distinct from the interpretations and personal experiences that participants in an exchange bring to the learning situation.

The movement from social construction to internalization within the learner also has a bearing on how students come to define themselves as individuals and in relation to others. When knowledge construction is both interpersonal and intrapersonal, students find themselves confronting who they are in relation to their peers and teachers and in relation to the material that they are learning. This is a recursive process in that students are continually required to revisit themselves as players in the dramas of the classroom life and as learners in the culture at large. For students who express behavioral problems that arise out of experiences of alienation and disconnectedness, knowledge co-construction could help them redefine themselves in ways that are, over extended periods of time, more conducive to adherence to the norms and expectations of their schools and communities.

A final step in this analysis of the social nature of learning and knowledge is to consider the impact that knowledge construction has on the individuals who are part of—or not part of—the process. Co-construction of a shared discourse creates cohesion among the individuals who participate in the knowledge construction process, and group members are those who possess the knowledge by virtue of contributing to its construction. Inversely, those who are not part of the exchange come to be viewed as outsiders, not as members of the cultural discourse that carries the knowledge shared by the participants. Hence, equality in educational opportunity may be less about access to the same information that others receive and more about participation in the construction of that information. This point has relevance for tracking and for relatively restrictive forms of special education services for students with disabilities. These topics are tackled next.

Learning that truly promotes understanding occurs in a social context that is heterogeneous; inversely, learning within largely homogeneous contexts restricts skill and knowledge acquisition in adverse ways for many learners.

Chapter 1 describes how public education has used removal and the creation of alternative educational experiences as primary mechanisms for dealing with diversity within the classroom. Students with major behavioral issues and all students who are served by the IEP process are especially prone to being placed in special programs for all or part of their school day. These programs can vary in the amount of pull-out services or self-containment used. Regardless, students who are subject to these programs are at greater risk than their peers for experiencing 1) fewer opportunities to be part of social groups of peers without disabilities and 2) curtailed access to the general education curriculum.

Yet, special education programs are simply one of many means that schools employ to separate students based on performance and perceived ability differences. The practices of tracking and ability grouping, for example, are also ways that students are separated into different settings and groups. These practices are presumably based on ability or future career goals, but they are often affected by factors such as ethnic and language differences, cultural distinctions, family background, social and behavioral concerns, and social status.

Tracking refers to students being grouped for their educational experiences based on either different curricular needs or on the need for the same content at different levels. It has a long history in the United States and in other Western countries, especially at the secondary level. In fact, Lucas pointed out that "a policy of *explicit* allocation to different curricula is followed in the majority of western nations" (1999, p. 2, emphasis in original).

In the United States, many of the more institutionalized and rigid tracking programs were dismantled in the mid- to late-20th century. Nevertheless, as noted by Lucas (1999), since the dismantling of these program tracks in the United States, the logic of tracking has not disappeared but has only become submerged, and the patterns of tracking have become more difficult to ascertain. The primary vehicles for tracking in high schools at the beginning of the 21st century are the courses that students choose or are encouraged to take by their teachers and school counselors. Although it is less likely to find students grouped together because all of their courses are prescribed as a package, course selection that is based on general criteria such as "college preparatory," "general," or "vocational" remains a powerful determinant of student grouping and stratification patterns in the "comprehensive high school" (Lucas, 1999; Oakes, Selvin, Karoly, & Guiton, 1992).

Sometimes, the mechanisms for tracking are so well submerged that students are unaware of the impact of their course selection decisions. Mehan, Hertweck, and Meihls (1986) described how, in one case, a particular seventh-grade foreign language course effectively determined the other courses that students took. On one hand, students who took the foreign language course were in other top courses. On the other hand, students who chose a different course—perhaps because of other interests, the interests of friends, or because of family or cultural factors—were in inferior classes. Mehan and colleagues stated, "As a result, some students who chose a certain course of study in junior-high school did not realize they had, for all intents and purposes, predetermined their later-life career options" (p. 24).

Ability grouping is a term that is often interchanged with *tracking* (Gamoran, 1992), perhaps because tracking represents a version of ability grouping. Nonetheless, the term *ability grouping* can also be applied to common practices such as grouping students based on similar skills or abilities, removing specific students from their classes for certain periods of the day for placement in lower or higher grades, and sorting all students at a given grade level into ability-configured groups for reading instruction. These practices are not limited to the secondary level; they occur with great regularity and frequency in the lower grades as well.

Reasons for tracking and ability grouping (e.g., differential career goals and aspirations, a need for intense skill practice, offering access to academic materials "at a student's level") do not outweigh the reasons for not using tracking and ability grouping. Some of the more apparent problems include the following (Braddock & Slavin, 1995; Gamoran, Nystrand, Berends, & LaPore, 1995; Oakes, 1985; Oakes et al., 1992; Webb, Nemer, Chizhik, & Sugrue, 1998):

- The logic of allocating differential curriculum opportunities on the basis of student characteristics does not account for the possibility that a student's abilities and motivations are altered by their curriculum opportunities.
- Irregularities in the distribution of curriculum opportunities often favor students who have more advantages and often hurt students who have fewer advantages.
- Students tend to learn what they are taught, and they cannot learn something that they are never exposed to in their school careers.
- The quality of instruction is often poorer for groups of students placed in lower-ability groups as compared with both higher-ability groups and mixed-ability groups.
- Academic achievement is, on average, higher for students when they are not tracked than when they are tracked if they are individuals who are frequently placed in lower tracks.
- Although there may be some problems for students with high ability who are placed in mixed-ability groups, mixed-ability groups "provide a greater benefit for below-average students than they impose a detriment on high-ability students" (Webb et al., 1998, p. 607).
- Students on low tracks with low achievement levels have poorer self-esteem scores than students with low achievement levels who are not tracked.

- Tracking and ability grouping exacerbate patterns of racial and ethnic segregation, and they impede the development of positive, intergroup relations among people with different cultural backgrounds.

In terms of social affiliation patterns at the secondary level, it is useful to think about the impact of special programs, tracking, and ability grouping on students in terms of scope (Lucas, 1999). *Scope* is the degree to which students spend their class time in school with the same or different students. If students are with the same peers all of the time, such as in a self-contained program, scope is high. If students attend many different classes in which there are often different groups of students, scope is low. For students who have marginal social status in school, low scope can be viewed as positive because it ensures contact and the potential for relationships with a wider range of peers. The degree to which these students experience a restricted range of contacts increases with ability grouping, tracking, and special programming.

Tracking, ability grouping, and isolated special education programs present long-standing concerns that can take years for a school to resolve. In the long run, individual teachers can make a difference in their school's reliance on these practices (see Chapter 6). Yet, there are limits to what a teacher can do in the short run. The foregoing literature was reviewed mainly to raise questions among teachers about any practices that place students together for extended periods of time because of a narrowly defined concept of ability. Being aware that these practices pose problems for both equity and excellence is an important first step in finding alternatives.

It is also important to capitalize on the inherent value of heterogeneity. Because diversity is a major feature of U.S. culture—and because democracies require people to live, learn, and work together—classrooms should provide for the socialization and norm-development processes that these lifelong activities require. As noted by Schmuck and Schmuck (1988), Dewey was an early theorist to recognize the classroom as a microcosm of the broader democratic community. It provides a basis for individuals to learn how to get along and work with others who live in the same system, who may differ in relation to individual, family, and cultural patterns (Schmuck & Schmuck, 1988; Sharan & Sharan, 1992).

It is equally important to bear in mind that academic learning, when conceptualized as a co-constructive process, is enhanced when different and diverse voices are brought into the learning equation. As noted in Chapter 1, students with disabilities, including students with emotional and behavioral disorders, tend to be perceived largely and unfairly in terms of their disability rather than in terms of their skills and personalities. Of course, the simple fact is that any individual, regardless of perceived characteristics, can contribute something unique to others' learning experiences. Nevertheless, significant differences in life experiences, such as those associated with having a disability, can make for especially unique perspectives on life and school; this speaks strongly for including these individuals in the shared learning experiences that are provided to others.

The following question can be raised: How does the teacher manage learning in heterogeneous classes and group situations? Part of the answer lies in simply using different kinds of grouping arrangements. Examples include mixed-ability literature circles; same-interest groups; flexible partner reading arrangements; flexible groups for brief strategy instruction; and student committees to complete certain classroom jobs, such as planning a field trip (Crafton, 1994). Yet, a large factor is how the natural classroom group dynamics are used to optimize students' learning. This topic is discussed next.

Learning that truly promotes understanding occurs in a social context that is purposefully designed by the teacher to optimize positive and engaging group dynamics and processes.

Schmuck and Schmuck described a group as a "collection of interacting persons with some degree of reciprocal influence over one another" (1988, p. 20). They noted that classrooms vary in their degree of "groupness," but it is to the teacher's advantage to cultivate this quality early in the school year. Stanford (1977) identified three benefits that are associated with enhancing group processes in the classroom: 1) improved subject matter acquisition, 2) improved manageability of the class, and 3) improved social skills. Schmuck and Schmuck also reviewed evidence indicating that "when students are taught to work interdependently and cooperatively on learning tasks, they can learn the material faster and retain it longer than when they are given mass instruction with no attention to collaboration and helping" (1988, p. 32).

Three properties of group learning that are fostered when a class works as a group are cooperative learning, collaborative information sharing, and problem solving. Stanford (1977) suggested that there are two primary methods for turning a class of students into a well-functioning group. The first method is modeling the necessary group interaction processes, such as turning over and sharing leadership and listening respectfully to others. The second method is providing and practicing specific group development activities, such as jigsaw learning (Aronson, Blaney, Stephan, Sikes, & Snapp, 1978), reciprocal teaching (Fahey, 2000; Palincsar & Brown, 1986), and various learning games in class lessons (Silberman, 1996). Stanford remarked,

> Whenever possible . . . group development can be fostered using the subject matter of the course as a basis. By adapting the format of structured experiences to the course content, you can achieve group development goals at the same time that you are teaching subject matter. (p. 41)

Encouraging learning in groups that are heterogeneous in terms of their learning and behavioral needs requires knowing how to broadly conceptualize the curriculum (Sapon-Shevin, 1999). Small-group cooperative learning activities are especially useful. This is because tasks can be designed and outcomes conceptualized for learners who are at various places in their knowledge construction and acquisition capabilities, in their present knowledge levels, and in their favored learning styles. Sapon-Shevin (1999) identified two different approaches that can be used by a general educator and a special educator who are working together to design multilevel cooperative learning tasks. In the first approach, the general education teacher designs in advance a cooperative learning task for a lesson or unit. Sapon-Shevin gave three steps for making the task applicable to a variety of learners: 1) "think about the cooperative learning lesson"; 2) "consider individual children, including those with IEP goals"; and 3) "design modifications and adaptations that allow *all* to participate" (p. 131, emphasis in original). In the second approach, the teachers collaboratively design the cooperative learning lesson from the start. Sapon-Shevin's three steps for this collaboration are 1) "think about the individual students (all of them, including, but not limited to, those with IEP objectives)"; 2) "think about the academic content of the lesson and the social skills objectives"; and 3) "design the cooperative learning task" (p. 132). The first approach is useful for integrating a student or students with diverse learning or behavioral needs into a class with preexisting curriculum-based activities; however, the second approach typically produces the best results in terms of learning and participation for all students.

Methods associated with differentiating instruction are also useful for thinking broadly about the curriculum to accommodate learners with diverse and varying learning needs. It is beyond the range of this book to describe how these methods can transform a curriculum's content into multiple levels and the variety of instructional processes that can be used to communicate it. The interested reader is encouraged to read Tomlinson for details (1995a, 1999).

Of course, the processes of developing effective groups and differentiating the curriculum for diverse learners take time. Stanford asserted, "Group development activities are best undertaken as an integral part of the class program, not as a gimmick tacked on as an afterthought" (1977, p. 41). A number of stages have been identified regarding how groups grow in maturity and competence, and specific activities exist for enhancing positive group processes in each stage (see Display 3.1).

It is important to emphasize that although various small-group and cooperative learning formats are useful group instruction formats (e.g., Johnson, Johnson, Holubec, & Roy, 1984), the principle at hand refers more to strengthening group cohesion and capitalizing on group dynamics at the whole class level. Various grouping practices (e.g., pairs of peers, whole class discussion) assume a new level of productivity when the teacher develops group cohesiveness first at the class level and then regularly uses the specific interpersonal dynamics and co-constructive processes within the larger group to both strengthen the social network and convey intended learning.

Finally, it is also worth pointing out that there is a place for direct, individualized instruction and practice in which a student works with a single adult or with a peer tutor. The forms of learning described previously can sometimes be augmented with direct methods of instruction (e.g., one-to-one instruction, peer tutoring). Nevertheless, certain conditions should guide decisions about the use of these practices. First, direct instruction should not replace or interfere with mainstream learning opportunities. Second, direct instruction, especially with a single adult, should not effectively reorder a person's social membership by making the student's primary or only peers other students with a disability label (e.g., "handicapped," "at risk," "behaviorally disordered"). Third, the outcomes of direct instruction should be assessed in relation to the broader intentions of the general education curriculum and setting, not simply to the mechanics of the skills that are being directly taught (e.g., isolated vowel sounds, behaviorally rehearsed anger control).

Learning is enhanced for all students when educators express genuine and nonjudgmental respect and acceptance for each learner as well as for the products and processes of learning that each brings to the classroom.

In a thought-provoking discussion of how teachers should perceive their students, Ayers commented,

> When teachers look over their classrooms, what do they see? Half-civilized barbarians? Savages? A collection of deficits, or IQ's, or averages? Do they see fellow creatures? We see students in our classrooms, of course, but who are they? What dreams do they bring? What experiences have they had, and where do they want to go? What interests or concerns them, how have they been hurt, what are they frightened of, what will they fight for, and what and whom do they care about? (1993, p. 28)

DISPLAY 3.1—STAGES IN GROUP DEVELOPMENT

Groups pass through stages as students get to know each other and mature. Stanford (1977) identified five stages through which a group of students typically moves at various rates and how active teacher intervention optimizes group development so that academic and social learning are enhanced:

Orientation Stage: The students and the teacher become acquainted and begin acquiring the information that they need for the class. Group development interventions during this stage include helping students get to know each other, establishing expectations, and modeling appropriate behaviors. The students should be comfortable with each other and begin to feel like they can communicate freely with others before moving on to norm establishment.

Establishing Norms Stage: The students develop norms among themselves and in relation to the teacher. The group begins learning how to work together and respectfully listen to each other, to work in small groups, to be independent of the teacher, to cooperate rather than compete with each other, and to face and solve problems. Membership patterns, leadership issues, tolerance for dissent, methods and rules for speaking, and consensus decision making processes are also developed. Group development interventions include helping the students move from teacher-oriented to task-oriented performance, work in small group patterns, develop seating arrangements that are conducive to working together, and listen to each other. The teacher uses redirection to help students stay focused on each other, encourages and models behaviors (e.g., cooperative behavior, consensus seeking), frames activities to encourage consensus seeking, offers suggestions when groups "get stuck" or face a problem, and carefully defines group and academic outcomes for group work. During this period, the teacher must be active as a resource and an observer but not as a leader. A teacher should also be cognizant of his or her own style of teaching and the strategies with which he or she is comfortable.

Coping with Conflict Stage: As students begin to work more intensely and more closely with each other, anticipate a period of conflict in which students feel more free to disagree. They may bicker among themselves and criticize the teacher. Group development interventions include helping students learn that conflict is okay, supporting students who find conflict difficult, and helping students develop ways to express and work through conflict. The teacher should accept the conflict processes and avoid becoming authoritarian.

Productivity Stage: Group identity and cohesiveness emerge, so group work is especially effective during this stage. Students know that they are truly a group and can solve most problems that arise. The teacher's attention should alternate between the tasks at hand and the interpersonal and relationship needs of individual members. Group development interventions include helping members of the group maintain skills and working through regressions when they occur.

Termination Stage: Students may become upset with the pending dissolution of the group, and they must cope with the emotional attachments that they have formed. Symptoms of termination may include increased conflict, anger at the teacher, a breakdown of collaborative skills, lethargic responses, and/or frantic work on ongoing and new projects. Group development interventions include helping students directly address their feelings regarding the termination, modeling personal reactions to the breakup, helping the group review and reflect on their experiences and successes (e.g., "remember when . . ."), assisting them in thinking ahead to future experiences, and tying up loose ends.

If a student is increasing his or her interactions with peers through these processes of group development, how might this positively affect his or her social and academic behavior?

If a student has challenging behaviors, how might these behaviors be exhibited differently during the various stages of group development?

What strategies can a teacher identify at each of the different stages to help this student channel these behaviors into more productive avenues?

Ayers also noted that when teachers see students in relation to disability categories, this will invariably "lower our sights, misdirect our vision, and mislead our intentions" (p. 29). He suggested that, along with concealing more than they reveal, labels focus the teacher's attention on a child's problems. This only draws more attention from peers and other teachers regarding what could become an endless list of weaknesses.

Similarly, Falvey (1998) commented on how focusing on labels can have debilitating effects on student self-esteem and motivation. She added that a label's stigmatizing effects can increase as segregation increases, as she reported situations in which children who were in self-contained classes were viewed more negatively than children who spent more time in general education classes. Rodis, Garrod, and Boscardin's (2000) analysis of the lives of young adults with learning disabilities also provided descriptive accounts of the emotional difficulties that people with labeled disabilities experienced in public education. Commenting on the experiences of some of these students, Rodis and colleagues asserted that numerous children who attend schools that are "unable to accommodate any behavior or learning style outside of a narrow range" learn a "lifelong lesson": that they are "incompetent, inadequate, damaged" (p. 159).

Kunc (1992) commented that schools often view the quality of "giftedness" as being a special attribute of a minority of students. He noted that this minority has been "artificially created to a large degree" in that only a narrow range of domains or life interests are considered relevant to giftedness (e.g., athletics, science). Kunc suggested that students with gifts in other areas (e.g., auto mechanics, love of nature, strong nurturing capabilities) "are relegated to the world of the normal and mediocre" (p. 32).

These points by Ayers (1993), Falvey (1998), Rodis and colleagues (2000), and Kunc (1992) draw attention to the commonsense but often missed human dimension: viewing each student as whole, as worthwhile, as possessing gifts worthy of celebration, and as a contributor to the class and the teacher's life. As noted by Henderson, "The first characteristic of reflective teaching is the ethic of caring" (1992, p. 2). For Ayers, this meant "attending to the details of one child at a time" to fully get to know each student and the promises that each brings to the classroom (1993, p. 37). For Henderson, quoting Noddings, this meant that when a teacher "asks a question in class and a student responds, she receives not just the 'response' but the student" (p. 2).

Kunc (1992) conducted an influential analysis of the application of Maslow's (1970) hierarchy of needs to schools. He described how the basic emotions of safety, belonging, and love are essential for students' academic and social success. Kunc also noted that, in Maslow's theory, the self-esteem that is associated with achievement, mastery, and recognition depends on having a foundation of safety and belonging. He then remarked that educators often "work from the premise that *achievement and mastery rather than belonging are the primary if not sole precursors for self-esteem*" (p. 31, emphasis in original). In other words, educators may make belonging contingent on the achievement and mastery of academic content and other skills. This actively interferes with developing a sense of belonging which, in turn, is needed for the risk taking associated with learning and growth.

Kunc (1992) linked the teacher's ongoing expressions of respect and caring for individual students to the impact on learning and behavior; thus, he showed that respect and concern are not simply good moral qualities for teachers. Rather, even when a teacher is unaware of these emotions in his or her interactions with students, expressing them is directly relevant to student learning and behavior. Certainly, respect and concern need to be coupled with content and pedagogy. It is worth asking, however, if solid pedagogy and dedication to content could truly be present if respect and concern are absent. For that matter, could authentic concern and respect exist for students if solid pedagogy and dedication to content are absent?

The Gap Between Theory and Practice

These five principles, which are derived from several theoretical frameworks, connect student learning and behavior with broad classroom practices. When teachers actively consider these principles for designing, implementing, and revising their instruction, they enhance the quality of their pedagogical decisions for ensuring student learning and understanding. To assist the reader in thinking about and remembering these principles, they are recast in the following summary:

1. *Setting:* Norms provide the underlying basis for activity and social intercourse within the classroom, and they define its climate.
2. *Workings:* Group processes and co-construction define how knowledge is communicated, how knowledge is defined, and how membership is influenced.
3. *Players:* All students can and should be included, which requires heterogeneity in the way students are placed and grouped.
4. *Orchestrating:* Ensuring that the foregoing principles are productively employed requires enhancing group development, effectively using groups for instruction, and selecting and presenting curriculum content so that it is differentiated and multilevel.

5. *Permeating Characteristics:* All of the previous processes must be infused with respect, dignity, and concern as the teacher interacts with students.

At this point, one may ask, "Why are practices based on these principles not more commonplace in today's schools?" After all, much of this knowledge has been available for years, so one would expect these ideas to be routinely reflected in the activities of teachers. Yet, anyone who has recently spent time in public schools knows that a teacher who routinely uses these principles is more the exception than the rule.

Any adequate answer to this question will be complex, requiring a discussion that goes beyond the scope of this book. Part of the answer lies with historical practices in schools, and part of the answer rests squarely on the shoulders of the social discrimination and prejudice in the communities from which schools derive their values. A piece of the puzzle also lies in the changing roles of the classroom teacher, however, which partially derives from the proliferation of distinct, separate service specializations in schools. Methods based on the five principles assume that teachers feel responsible for all students who enter their classrooms, regardless of learning needs, and that removal is only used as a last resort. Soo Hoo (1990) expressed the belief that teachers were once more likely "to accommodate the diverse needs of students without question"; however, teachers at the beginning of the 21st century more commonly relinquish teaching responsibilities to numerous specialists when certain learning or behavioral problems are present (p. 210). Soo Hoo argued that this "collision of multiple programs with the basic curriculum" ultimately reduces teacher confidence in designing the kinds of differentiated instructional contexts that are needed to serve students with diverse needs (p. 211).

There is another reason for the discrepancy between the foregoing theoretical principles and classroom practices. Its source lies in the scientific paradigm that guides and directs much of the thinking, research, and innovation development within the education field. This paradigm is also the framework of the remedial model described in Chapter 1, and it impedes the shift to the support perspective. This paradigm is described next, and the chapter closes with an alternative paradigm that is consistent with the five learning principles.

THE DOMINANT RESEARCH PARADIGM AND ITS REPERCUSSIONS

Educational research has borrowed much from the physical sciences over the years, so it is not surprising that underlying paradigms that control research in the physical sciences bear a strong resemblance to those that guide educational research. Figure 3.1 is a paradigm that was drawn from materials science and engineering (Olson, 2000). It is an apt representation of one kind of thinking that has been prevalent in theory, research, and practice in education, psychology, and special education.

As illustrated in Figure 3.1, this paradigm is essentially reductionistic. It models causality (i.e., cause–effect) as a flow-through process that originates from an elemental processing core, extends outward and upward through the basic structure of the system into its properties, and finally influences the system's external performance. The means for changing the system's performance lie in altering earlier system components, and more profound changes occur when the system's processing activities are altered. Hence, the goals associated with system change, although often motivated by a desire to change performance, are connected with making alterations within the deeper levels of the system.

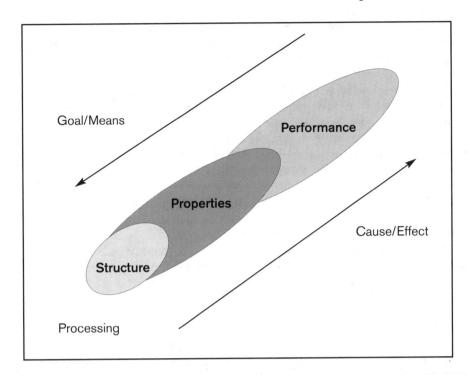

Figure 3.1. The "four-element" paradigm from the materials science and engineering. (From Olson, G.B. [2000]. Pathways of discovery: Designing a new material world. *Science, 288* [p. 996]; reprinted by permission.)

Applied to education, the model in Figure 3.1 would typically be used to characterize how students' different levels of cognitive and emotional activity influence their performance. *Performance* is the outcome, characterized in a variety of ways, that is associated with a student's completing or struggling to complete a particular academic or social activity. Examples include writing an English essay, answering the teacher's questions about a chapter that was assigned for homework, dissecting a frog with a group of students in biology class, informally interacting with others, asking for help or assistance from peers, reading aloud for miscue analysis, completing a spelling test, or simply writing the alphabet on the chalkboard. Properties and structure will, of course, differ depending on the performance being considered. *Properties* may represent the learner's traits or characteristics that can be observed in the natural environment or derived by clinical means. A *structure* is often an underlying cognitive, social, or emotional classification of the learner, such as "conduct disorder," "moderate mental retardation," "learning disability," "gifted," or even "normal learner." Processing represents the mental activities that the person must complete to produce the performance, which filters through and is influenced by the student's classification (structure) and related traits and characteristics (properties). Thus, a student with dyslexia who faces a difficult reading task first processes the information during a demand for performance that is constrained by the disability (structure). Then, he exhibits some variability compared with others who have dyslexia based on his particular configuration of learning characteristics (properties). These operations define the student's performance, which may then be consistent with the hypothesized structure and properties for the learner. As another example, a student with the IEP-identified label "emotional/behavioral disorder" processes taunts and threats from peers so that her final "performance" (uncontrolled rage) reflects to the adult observers the social and emotional constitution that was first defined by the label (structure). Then she demonstrates the characteristics that are specific to her personal history and repertoire of skills (properties).

It is almost impossible to understate the pervasive use of this paradigm to measure and explain human variation in performance, to help justify differential educational placements for students with labels (including "normal"), and to design specialized educational activities that affect "processing." This paradigm characterizes the core of the multiple and complex labeling systems that drive the way that educators categorize students, then use inferences about underlying structures to define differentiated educational needs and treatments. Student performance on reading tasks is especially prone to models of classification and instruction that first differentiate learners based on specific skill and processing deficits, then propose intense instructional procedures (e.g., specialized instruction in isolated phonics) for "remediating" these deficits. As Bartoli remarked about U.S. education since the mid-1980s, "The number of students given labels of reading and learning disability or deficiency . . . has tripled, and the number of those failing or at risk for failure who eventually drop out of school has risen sharply as well" (1995, p. 29). If present trends in labeling were to continue, then "the projected rate of disability/deficiency labeling for the next century" would be about one out of every four students (p. 30).

The influence of the thinking represented by this paradigm is both profound and disconcerting because it so completely drives the research and practice methods by which many special educators and others in related fields perceive their subject matter, their roles as educators, and the very functions of their fields. Equally disconcerting, it provides one inadequately examined rationale for the legal and educational device known as the "continuum of services." This concept encourages educators to define differentiated human potentials, then to use this information to place students in a descending hierarchy of classes. These classes are at risk for setting increasingly lower academic expectations, paradoxically coupling them with more intense and specialized services (see Display 3.2).

Finally, the paradigm assigns primary causation for performance variations to deep-seated differences between students as learners. Therefore, the model tends to place accountability for learning not on the teacher's actions but on the learner's presumed capabilities. This promotes deficit correction and alternative curriculums as the primary means and goals of the educational process. In effect, the thinking that is reflected in this paradigm tends to limit the vision and the activities of both teachers and researchers to teaching and facilitating compensatory skills; prerequisite skills; or, worse, skills that are entirely unrelated to the experiences of same-age students (e.g., "functional skills"). Inversely, it does little to encourage teachers or researchers to consider multilevel curriculum design or to differentiate instruction as preferred solutions when there are marked differences in student performance. Finally, the paradigm tends to absolve teachers from being truly accountable for their instruction because it permits "handicaps" to bear the brunt of the blame when the education process is not working.

AN ALTERNATIVE PARADIGM AND ITS IMPLICATIONS

One could say that the foregoing criticisms fail to give justice to the paradigm's apparent productivity. After all, many effective educational methods seem to have arisen out

DISPLAY 3.2—THE CHANGING ROLES OF THE SPECIAL EDUCATOR

Increasing concerns about the deleterious impact of segregation on both the social and academic outcomes for students with special needs means that new and innovative ways for educating students with IEPs in general education classrooms will likely become more the rule than the exception. When students with special needs spend more of their school day in general education, the special educator's role dramatically changes. The emphasis shifts from teaching a separate curriculum to ensuring access to the general curriculum; to providing needed academic, behavioral, and medical supports that are jointly determined by the general educator and the special educator; and to orchestrating the provision of services and materials to students who may be served in a variety of general education settings. Jackson and colleagues (2000) identified 21 different roles and responsibilities for special educators who are supporting students in general education. Many of these roles differ substantially from those traditionally associated with special education services. Here are six of the new roles:

- Using the general education lecture notes to solo teach the general education class so that a classroom teacher can work with a student or group of students
- Team-teaching with the general educators, including planning and preparing material and lessons, grading work, and assisting with general education classroom management
- Directly training and supervising educational assistants/educational support professionals in their respective support activities (e.g., on-the-spot modifications, modifications prepared in advance)
- Modifying and accommodating curriculum, materials, and assessment processes prior to using them in class
- Scheduling and reliably delivering in-class supports and consultation to a number of general education teachers
- Planning for and assisting in resolving short-term emergencies, conflicts, and crises (e.g., behavioral issues that disrupt class instruction)

How do the training needs of special educators in inclusive settings differ from the training needs of special educators in traditional special education settings?

Some special educators are responsible for students who are included for all or most of the day and also must teach a special life skills or social skills class for their students. What dilemmas does this situation create for general education teachers and special education teachers?

What do administrators need to know when evaluating a special education teacher's job performance when the educator's roles are inclusive?

of the paradigm's applications in the past. Yet, as Goodman commented on the observed successes associated with specialized phonics programs in reading, "No one has yet been able to devise an instructional program so bad that it has succeeded in keeping the majority of pupils from learning" (Goodman, 1993, p. 107). Put differently, a vast body of research perpetuates the paradigm by showing learning changes that are confined to the understandings that the paradigm promotes. If a different paradigm were to become available for research and practice in education and related fields, however, a very different picture could emerge—one that would require reassessing the generality and authenticity of these learning changes. Such a paradigm could provide educators with new ways to perceive disability, define educational research activities, and generate practices that are conducive to learning and growth. For these reasons, it is fitting to end this chapter with the construction of such a paradigm.

Although this book's authors seriously question the value and utility of the classification system that is used with students who are "exceptional learners" (structure), the new paradigm still reflects all of the first paradigm's basic concepts. Nonetheless, the authors want a paradigm that permits greater latitude in conceptualizing the relationship between structure and processing so that questions about the value and utility of these constructs can be fruitfully explored. Hence, the new paradigm reconfigures the layout of these concepts. It is hoped that the new paradigm, which is shown in Figure 3.2, will assist researchers and practitioners in rethinking sources of causation and the origins, nature, and purposes of educational activity.

This paradigm proposes that 1) the relationship among structure, processing, properties of the learner, and actual performance is neither hierarchical nor linear but one of complex and multiple overlaps and 2) these characteristics of the learner are embedded within a larger social context, which includes the interpersonal and activity networks of the classroom. The model also proposes that both the sources of causation and the goal/means of the educational process lie in the interaction between the social context developed by educators and the hypothetical characteristics of the learner. It suggests that performance can be influenced by—but is not dependent on—hypothetical structural and processing factors, and it is immutably determined at least in part by environmental variables. Thus, researchers and practitioners can redistribute their attention so that a broader range of issues is considered in the design and application of new teaching practices. Not surprisingly, many of the issues that will come up when applying this paradigm will likely mirror considerations that arise from the five theoretical principles presented in this chapter.

Of special significance for students with behavioral challenges is the fact that, unlike the traditional paradigm, the revised paradigm is also consistent with the support model that was first introduced at the end of Chapter 1. The traditional paradigm primarily drives research for the remedial approach to problem behavior. In contrast, the second paradigm's emphasis on environmental processes promotes a research platform for creating social and educational supports for learning and behavioral concerns.

CONCLUSION AND A LOOK AHEAD

This chapter has primarily focused on the development of five theory-derived principles that offer guidance for teachers in the design, implementation, and revision of their instructional activities. When a teacher's belief system is infused with these principles, they provide a basis not only for sound educational practice but also for suc-

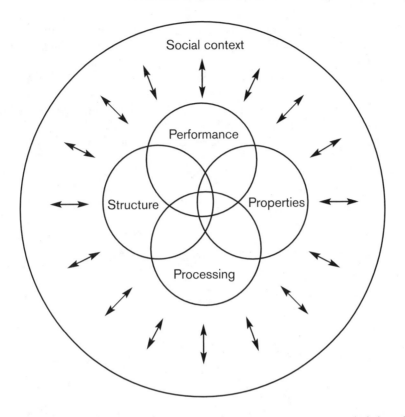

Figure 3.2. An alternative version of the "four-element" paradigm. (Key: The arrows represent both the goals/means and the cause/effect dimensions.)

cessfully adapting to mandates to adopt specific, often untested, programs and standards. These principles encapsulate much that is known about how social norms are developed and are communicated, how tolerance and acceptance of diversity can be engendered in others, and how engagement in learning can be enhanced; thus, practices based on these principles form the first line of defense against discipline problems. In other words, maintaining the well-ordered classroom does not begin with applying specialized methods and procedures for controlling behavioral problems. Rather, it begins with using teaching methods and activities that are based on the social dynamics that are naturally present in the class; celebrating students' diversity; and awakening within students a desire to learn, grow, and participate in the community of the classroom and the school-at-large.

As previously noted, however, these principles probably will not fall on fertile ground at the beginning of the 21st century. As Reid indicated, the theories that a teacher "chooses to embrace" typically reflect, among other things, "the dominant paradigms of the current historical period" (1996, p. 214). Because the dominant paradigm in contemporary education, especially in relation to disability and behavioral problems, emphasizes internal processes and their remediation, any theoretical principles that emphasize the sociocultural features and products of learning could have less appeal. Hence, this chapter offers a new paradigm that includes all of the old paradigm's components, reconfigured so that the model is more conducive to research and practice that are consistent with the five principles proposed in this chapter.

Although good teaching is the basis for sound classroom discipline, a very large management technology has been operative for many years within public education. This has often been presented to teachers as the primary means by which classroom order is maintained and learning occurs. The emerging perspective of positive behavioral support challenges some of these practices' underlying assumptions. In addition, a good working knowledge of this perspective is required to develop more varied and complex methods for handling chronic and acute discipline concerns, which may sometimes seem untouched by simply good teaching practice. Chapter 4 covers these topics.

Section II

Understanding
and Characterizing
the Support Process

Chapter 4

General Considerations
for Positive Behavioral Support

*"I am always doing that which I cannot
do, in order that I may learn how to do it."*
—*Pablo Picasso*

Chapter 2 described seven influential discipline models that predated and seemed to anticipate the emergence of positive behavioral support. Five themes were derived from these models. Because these themes reflect qualities that are essential for any positive behavioral support effort, they provide a good starting point for this discussion of general considerations in support planning. The first theme was that addressing behavioral challenges requires educators and students to interact as a community and for good relationships to be established among and between peers and educators. The second theme was that prevention and amelioration of problem behaviors begins with careful consideration of what is being taught, how it is being taught, where it is being taught, and with what adaptations for students who have learning and behavioral difficulties. The third theme was that if discipline policies and procedures are to be effective, students must be given some latitude and control over them. The fourth theme was that understanding the motivations that underlie the relationship between a specific student's behavior and environmental conditions helps educators restructure their activities and classrooms for greater success. Finally, the fifth theme was that a nonaversive approach to behavioral problems should guide the development of discipline policies and procedures to realize a learning environment that is free of punishment's unintended side effects.

Chapter 2 also mentioned an important historical trend with the emergence of these five themes: the merging of processes meant for the general control of conduct with processes designed for the individualized treatment of problem behaviors. In real-world school settings, of course, the merger of these two streams of thought cannot be described as smooth. Although the desired end of fewer behavioral problems may seem to provide a common framework, the multitude of competing attitudes and ideologies that flow from these two concepts impedes their unification.

Chapter 4 continues this book's development of the positive behavioral support concept by describing many of its essential features while grappling with these two contrasting streams of thought. The chapter begins by elaborating on the breadth and depth of the gap between ideologies of discipline and treatment in many school settings. Next, the discussion shifts to three sets of issues that affect the interplay between approaches to discipline and approaches to treatment. Infused in this discussion are qualities that must be expressed if a positive behavioral support effort is to enhance the growth of a learner with troubling behaviors and adhere to a school's discipline concerns. The chapter's closing discussion presents a mission for ensuing chapters in this book: to demonstrate by analysis and example how positive behavioral support offers educators a viable means for meeting both the learning needs of individual students and the discipline concerns of the school as a whole.

WHEN DISCIPLINE AND TREATMENT APPROACHES COME TOGETHER

An astute observer might note that this merger—or collision—often creates for students a volley of mixed messages. A classroom teacher might begin class with "treatment," by consistently displaying concern and reinforcing the "good behavior" of his or her more challenging students. Then, as the teacher's stress level increases, he or she shifts to discipline, by giving repeated, ineffectual verbal warnings and arbitrarily imposed consequences.

As described in Chapter 3, teachers are guided in their activities by their belief systems. These belief systems may embody disparate perceptions, derived from experience, about a teacher's functions regarding student discipline needs and student treatment needs. These disparities may then be expressed as alternating patterns of treatment and discipline when teachers struggle with their own conflicting needs to assist a student with problems, get through the day with minimal stress, and maintain a classroom atmosphere that honors the rights of all students.

Of equal importance in explaining these mixed messages is the simple fact that treatment ideologies are relatively new. The longer and more enduring patterns of responding to behavior in schools are associated with discipline. In fact, some treatment models have practices, such as the use of aversives within behavioral psychology, which reflect ambivalence between assisting individuals with behavioral needs to become socially and behaviorally more mature and assisting the larger society in ridding itself of problems that impede others' comfort.

In some ways, the latter comments provide the keys to understanding what must be accomplished with positive behavioral support to reconcile ideologies of control and suppression with those of treatment and resolution. There will, of course, always be gray areas when questions of treatment collide with questions of discipline. To survive as a set of classroom practices, however, positive behavioral support concepts should provide effective ways for educators to assist individual students with both mild and excessive behavioral problems to become more mature and valued members of their school communities. Yet, educators must accomplish this feat without sacrificing the needs of the other students or the safety and order of classrooms and other school environments.

Part of the solution lies in educators learning to apply—and having the latitude to use—the five principles described in Chapter 3. Natural heterogeneity, positive social norms, group cohesiveness, instructional processes that capitalize on the contributions of all students, and a classroom teacher who accepts all of his or her

DISPLAY 4.1—AN UNRULY CLASS

A project specialist was asked to follow Darren, a student with Down syndrome who was included all day in a variety of sixth-grade classes (e.g., social studies, language arts, science). He moved between classes mostly with the same group of students. It did not take long for the project specialist to realize that Darren was in a "low track" group, in which most of the 26 students had IEPs, were minimally proficient in English, and/or were considered at risk.

In his classes, social studies, language arts, and science instruction mostly consisted of large group work and individual seat work (e.g., worksheets). In science, small group work was expressly prohibited; in social studies and language arts, students were allowed to pair up to complete their individual assignments but with minimal supervision and no effort to coordinate the group work. In terms of managing behavior, all three teachers used tangible rewards, verbal warnings and reprimands, and response cost procedures to control behavior.

In effect, the situations in these classes violated most, if not all, of the five principles described in Chapter 3. The project specialist observed the following things throughout the day:

- The students continuously reacted to each other's behavior by pushing; shoving; running around the room; and engaging in social chatter about their friends, sports, and other nonacademic issues.
- Noise that was not associated with learning was extreme throughout the day. This noise reflected the students' boisterous play, interrupting the teacher and others, calling out answers to questions with or without knowledge of correct answers, teasing, and talking among themselves, as well as the teachers' verbal threats and reprimands.
- Most students failed to complete their individual assignments, or the assignments were very poorly completed and contained numerous wrong answers.
- "Co-construction" occurred, but it was often wrong information that circulated among the students (e.g., an "estuary" is a product that Sweden exports to other countries).
- A disproportionate number of students exhibited more serious behavioral problems, and they often interacted with the teachers in ways that slowed down or stopped instruction.
- All three teachers became tired and frustrated long before their class periods ended. They began to issue increased reprimands and response cost measures, or they simply retreated to their desks and let the class "run itself" for the remainder of the period.

- Quieter and better behaved students simply withdrew from the class activities and discourse. Darren was among these students.

Describe what might happen if these classes included a student who had his or her own comprehensive, individualized behavior intervention plan and was described as being

- *Delinquent, with good leadership skills*
- *Depressed and withdrawn, with few friends*
- *Highly distractible in academic work but very athletic*

students can provide the "social umbrella" under which the more individualized behavioral support needs of specific students can be addressed with greater comfort for all involved. Inversely, classrooms that do not approximate these principles present problems for students who are likely to react with fear or anger when corrected or are on the margins of the social aggregate of "successful students" (see Display 4.1).

Another part of the solution lies with changing the expectations that are placed on special educators so that their primary responsibilities increasingly become problem solving with general educators and supporting students with behavior and learning needs in general education (e.g., Bahr, Whitten, Dieker, Kocarek, & Manson, 1999; Snell & Janney, 2000). Experience suggests that many special educators still perceive themselves and are perceived by others as being tied to special education locations, such as resource rooms or self-contained classrooms. In addition, many special educators and general educators express discomfort when special education services, especially for students with behavioral issues, are to be provided in general education through joint planning, co-teaching, and service coordination. Moreover, although children with disabilities are increasingly educated in general education classes (Gallagher, 1997; McLeskey, Henry, & Hodges, 1998), state education agencies, professional organizations, and public schools have been slow to incorporate these trends into their definitions of special educators' service roles and responsibilities (Jackson et al., 2000; Jackson, Ryndak, Keefe, & Kozleski, 2000).

Yet, another important part of the solution lies in how treatment practices are perceived and conceptualized by teachers, administrators, and parents, and how these contrast or blend with a school's ongoing discipline practices. As is true at the class level, there are mixed messages at the building level when the behavioral treatment needs of individual students collide with community demands for increased discipline. Many schools respond to political pressures for greater safety in schools by implementing zero tolerance policies (Leone, Mayer, Malmgren, & Meisel, 2000; Skiba & Peterson, 2000). Such policies can only reduce the organization's overall ability to handle diversity even as the policies negatively affect the socialization activities of those who most need appropriate peer relationships and models (see Chapter 1).

Walking the thin line between meeting the needs of students who have behavioral problems and honoring a school's discipline concerns is probably one of the most difficult responsibilities of the educator who believes in inclusive education. Successfully fulfilling this responsibility requires a clear knowledge of three sets of issues that influence how to address problem behaviors from a positive behavioral support perspective: 1) outcome issues, 2) practice issues, and 3) community rights and needs issues. Outcome issues are the desired results of a positive behavioral support effort for students and teachers. Practice issues are the desired characteristics of a positive behavioral support effort. Community rights and needs issues are limits that schools and society impose on services for a specific student given other students' need for safety and access to a school's curriculum and routine experiences. Each set of issues is reviewed in turn.

OUTCOME ISSUES

Winett and Winkler (1972) publicly questioned the use of treatment target outcomes that mainly conform to the status quo and to classroom rules regarding the absence of negative behaviors. Despite their plea to researchers and practitioners to focus on long-term benefits (e.g., discharge rates from treatment programs) and positive forms of active engagement (e.g., interpersonal interactions, creativity), the literature remains replete with studies that disproportionately focus on the same outcomes that Winett and Winkler questioned (e.g., Bachman & Fuqua, 1983; Kamps, Kravits, Stolze, & Swaggart, 1999; Neef, Shafer, Egel, Cataldo, & Parrish, 1983; Nelson et al., 1998; and Schulman, Suran, Stevens, & Kupst, 1979). Such studies build on the findings of earlier research by showing how emerging and newly conceptualized treatment procedures yield desirable changes in the rates of different problem behaviors; however, these studies still leave unaddressed many important questions that are reminiscent of the concerns originally posed by Winett and Winkler. These questions are explored in the next section.

Unaddressed Outcomes

Doubtless, such studies intuitively appeal to educators in their suggestions that discipline needs can be met by a teacher's use of identifiable, specific strategies and procedures. Consistent with Winett and Winkler's (1972) thinking, however, it is what is not described and not measured in many of these studies that should be defining the desired post-intervention outcomes. Consider the following often unanswered questions:

- What kinds of academic learning were experienced by students who received intervention, and did academic learning change as a result of the intervention?
- If some of the students were in self-contained schools or classes, were the academic curricula and learning expectations comparable to those of the students who received the intervention in age-appropriate, general education settings? How did rates and types of learning for students in the self-contained facilities compare before and after intervention with rates and types of learning among the students who were in typical classrooms?
- If some or all of the students were in self-contained schools or classes, did reported positive behavioral changes result in placement changes for any of the students? For example, did any students return to general education as a result of changes in their behavior?

- If the students were in general education classes, how did both those who received intervention and those who did not feel about the intervention? How was class membership affected for students who received intervention?
- Did students feel that they were learning more as a result of an intervention?
- How did the discipline climate in classes change, and what impressions did the classroom teachers and students have about these changes?
- Did an intervention affect the teaching practices so that better instruction resulted for all students?
- Did general education teachers express a renewed readiness to accept and serve students with behavioral problems in their classes because of growth in their classroom management skills?

Obviously, no single research study would ever be expected to provide answers to all of these questions. Yet, research is largely silent on these questions, which should give those in the field pause to reflect on the still-present Winett and Winkler dilemma: Outcomes continue to be conceptualized as child-change measures that reflect the behavior reduction and compliance needs of classroom teachers. There is insufficient consideration of more authentic forms of learning for students or improved teacher communication of the curriculum (or lack thereof) as a result of improved discipline. Moreover, student placement issues, including changes in placement, are usually not addressed when a study's results are offered.

Outcomes from an Educative Perspective

It is important to acknowledge that many behavior reduction studies do contribute to the education field by offering alternatives to the punitive discipline practices that are found in some schools and classrooms. Nevertheless, such studies also show how many treatment approaches still rely on a remedial model of services. Such approaches focus on eliminating behavioral problems instead of enhancing students' authentic social and academic growth (see Chapter 1).

Vittimberga, Scotti, and Weigle (1999) argued that positive behavioral support must move beyond this "eliminative" approach to behavior and toward what they described as an "educative" approach, in which the focus shifts to "skill building and proactive support strategies" (p. 48). From this perspective, the outcomes that reflect students' growth and lifestyle changes are especially critical and should become the focus of any intervention effort. For example, Janney and Meyer (1990) worked with 33 students with severe disabilities and challenging behaviors over a 3-year period. Janney and Meyer reported data on specific challenging behaviors, but they also reported findings as to whether the students were placed in and were successful in an inclusive environment at follow-up. Turnbull and Turnbull (1999) also offered another example of addressing and sometimes achieving a full range of meaningful outcomes for an individual. Their account reflected some creative approaches for helping their 31-year-old son gain access to activities, people, and services—aspects which were then continually evaluated for their contribution toward achieving desired lifestyle outcomes. Risley also captured the intent of the educative approach when he suggested questions such as, "Is the person continuing to develop new interests, new friends, and new skills?" to assess long-range outcomes (1996, p. 428).

PRACTICE ISSUES

At the heart of behavioral support efforts are its practices, which are "the application of positive behavioral interventions and systems to achieve socially important change" (Sugai et al., 2000, p. 133). Because positive behavioral support is often defined in relation to intervention practices, principles of practice are often conceptualized in terms of the specific properties that are desirable for strategies and techniques that are to be used in an intervention (e.g., Horner et al., 1990; Sugai et al., 2000; Vittimberga et al., 1999). Yet, positive behavioral support also has important, if somewhat neglected, roots in advocacy, social justice, and legal rights (e.g., Lohrmann-O'Rourke & Zirkel, 1998; Lovett, 1996; Turnbull, Wilcox, Stowe, Raper, & Hedges, 2000). Hence, this discussion of basic considerations for practice offers principles that represent methodological considerations and principles that represent advocacy, social justice, and legal rights considerations.

Methodological Considerations

Vittimberga and colleagues (1999), along with Horner and colleagues (1990), identified a number of educative-based principles that show how to configure positive behavioral support practices. Many of these principles find expression in the remaining chapters of this book. Nevertheless, three are introduced in this chapter because they represent especially definitive aspects of the educative approach to problem behaviors. These are 1) use functional behavioral assessment, 2) enhance generalization, and 3) avoid the use of punishers.

Use Functional Behavioral Assessment A basic assumption in positive behavioral support is that, although challenging behaviors have physical characteristics that may be disturbing to others, these behaviors also have adaptive, often complex underlying functions (Vittimberga et al., 1999). Functional behavioral assessment, which is extensively addressed and readdressed throughout this book, is a set of assessment procedures that help identify the purpose(s) of a challenging behavior(s) (Iwata et al., 1982; Repp & Horner, 1999). Once the purposes of a behavior are understood, interventions can be developed that take into account these purposes for the student.

As of the end of the 20th century, schools are legally required to address the relationship between problem behavior and the learning environment. The 1997 IDEA Amendments state the following:

> In response to certain disciplinary actions by school personnel, the IEP team must, within 10 days, meet to formulate a functional behavioral assessment plan to collect data for developing a behavior intervention plan; or, if a behavior intervention plan already exists, the team must review and revise it (as necessary), to ensure that it addresses the behavior upon which disciplinary action is predicated. (§ 615[k][1][B])

Enhance Generalization Research has demonstrated the value of intentionally making provisions for the generalization of new learning across settings, individuals, and time (Stokes & Baer, 1977). When new behaviors are taught to replace problem behaviors in the very environments in which the problem behaviors occur, the need for specific training for generalization is lessened. Conversely, if a student is removed from his or her natural environment for training to occur in a special setting, there is no assurance that the problems that precipitated removal will not reappear. Thus, a critical practice is to place students in natural settings. Vittimberga and colleagues described students in natural settings as "... living fully inclusive lives in typical environments, with typical peers, and doing typical activities and routines" (1999, p. 60).

In addition, when a student has been placed in a more restrictive setting, the real measure of success is the degree to which new learning is exhibited when he or she is returned to the natural environment. Sometimes, as described in Chapter 8 and elsewhere in this book, this requires deliberate planning by educators during the reintegration process in both environments to ensure that the desired responses will occur and will be supported in the less restrictive environment.

Avoid the Use of Punishers   Avoiding the use of punishers was already addressed in Chapter 2, and it is discussed in even greater detail in Chapter 5. Yet, it is a principle that deserves repeating, and it cannot be overstressed. Sadly, there are so many instances of the antithesis of this principle in U.S. schools and society. As Sidman stated, "The application of noncoercive forms of control has been insignificant in comparison to humanity's habitual recourse to coercion" (1989, p. 2). He noted the long-term deleterious effects of the coercive model (e.g., hostility, isolation), the most critical one being that coercive control prevents positive reciprocal interactions from developing. Such practices have no place in positive behavioral support.

Even a seemingly innocuous procedure, such as the use of frequent verbal reprimands, can have unexpected repercussions. When publicly reprimanding, the teacher may be communicating marginalization of a particular child. The way the teacher treats the child is the way that child is perceived by the other students in the class, at least within that setting. Thus, teachers who are not role models for accepting students with behavioral differences may make peer estrangement more likely.

Punishment systems, unfortunately, sometimes serve a similar function. The student who is punished by the teacher may experience rejection or disapproval from peers, as association with the punished child may be perceived as going against the will of the teacher. Of course, as discussed in Chapter 5, avoiding the use of punishment does not mean that serious behavioral crises can be left unchecked in the classroom. Yet, responses to behavioral crises when safety and management—not punishment—guide one's actions assume a very different quality (see Display 4.2).

Social Justice Considerations

Those who have been in the special education field for some time likely recall the fervor surrounding the discovery of the power and possibilities that were associated with behavior modification (Evans et al., 1999). In the interest of science and/or rehabilitation, some highly questionable procedures and processes were developed and then used with students who had little voice in the decisions that were made about them.

Experience suggests that although most educators mean well, schools and residential institutions continue to place students with behavioral concerns at risk when it comes to honoring principles of human dignity. Two principles that are especially important from a social justice perspective are 1) respect personal needs, preferences, and the dignity of the individual; and 2) consider equality of educational opportunity in placement decisions for students in special education. These are both large issues that can only briefly be discussed in this book.

Respect Personal Needs, Preferences, and the Dignity of the Individual   As Knoster asserted, "Effective support plans are person-centered in that they respect personal preferences and goals and are tailored to the student's typical daily routines at school, home, and community" (1998, p. 1). Vittimberga and colleagues (1999)

DISPLAY 4.2—IS A BEHAVIORAL
CRISIS A GOOD TIME FOR LEARNING?

There is disagreement in the field regarding whether a crisis (e.g., rage, loss of control, serious aggression, screaming) can be used as a time for learning new and more appropriate behaviors or learning to avoid future crises. On one hand, Wood and Long (1991) developed life space intervention for facilitating learning during a time of crisis. They contend that it is helpful for the individual to see connections between feelings and behavior. Life space intervention is a therapeutic verbal strategy that enables a person to 1) recognize his or her feelings, 2) see how these feelings do not necessarily need to lead to improper behavior, and 3) find other ways to express difficult feelings. Life space intervention is based on one of the principles of a therapeutic milieu, namely that crises can be converted to memorable learning occasions (Long & Morse, 1996).

On the other hand, Kunc and Van der Klift (1995b) asserted that there is an important relationship between quality of judgment and emotional state. They suggested that it is during the peak of a crisis that judgment is most impaired and irrational. Therefore, once the person's behavior is out of control, any teaching attempts are thwarted and receptivity to new ideas is dulled. Thus, it would be of questionable value to advance arguments or explanations for alternative and more rational forms of behavior when a crisis is occurring. Rather, during a crisis, the focus should be on ensuring the safety of other students and finding ways to calm or comfort the individual to return to a state in which class participation can be rewarded.

Are these points of view necessarily incompatible?

Are there perhaps different points in the course of a crisis in which learning is possible or not likely?

argued that "choice and control" must be built directly into practice so that students with behavioral support plans have ample, ongoing opportunities to select from activities, responses, and incentives. Such a process makes sense purely from a procedural point of view, but it also constitutes best practice in terms of showing respect and positive regard for the individual student.

An indirect benefit of giving a student more control over his or her learning and recreation options is that doing so necessitates listening to the student. As stressed by Lovett (1996), the problems and issues of individuals with difficult behaviors become more understandable and less insurmountable when educators actively listen to the messages that are inherent in the actions, choices, and verbalizations of the people with whom they work. Many times, problem behaviors may simply reflect an individual's need but inability to connect with others "in socially ordinary ways" (Lovett, 1996, p. 25).

The selection of intervention techniques for responding to problem behaviors when they occur should also be guided by this principle. This is especially true for people who have disabilities that affect their capacity to communicate desires and needs. Based on the earlier work of Wolf (1978), Horner and colleagues (1990) reiterated that any procedure that we find offensive for ourselves should not be considered for people with disabilities.

Consider Equality of Educational Opportunity in Special Education Placement Decisions   Dworkin (2000) argued that a primary function of government is to ensure equality in the opportunities that are provided to its citizens. At the risk of simplifying often complex ideas, he suggested that there are two ethical principles that help shape his arguments for equality. The first is the principle of equal importance, which asserts that it is important that "human lives be successful rather than wasted" and that this is true for "for each human life" (p. 5). The second principle is that of special responsibility. This principle states that, given the choices that are made available to all individuals, a specific individual has responsibility for making his or her own life choices. Dworkin argued that these two principles must both be operative in governmental and service system affairs and that equality of opportunity ensures this.

As pointed out in Chapters 1 and 3, whenever a student with behavioral challenges is removed from the educational environment of his or her peers—either indirectly through tracking or intentionally through special program placement—he or she is at risk for receiving lower quality socialization opportunities and academic curriculum. As shown in Chapter 1, although it is well intended, when the concept of individualized needs comes to prescribe a significant proportion of the student's educational experiences, it introduces the possibility that the individual's larger potentials will go unfulfilled.

It is helpful to remember that the legal concept of LRE does not mean that one should place the student in the environment that seems less restrictive educationally because of the services that it might entail. The notion of *restrictiveness* refers to curtailment of liberty, presumably to promote some valued end, such as educational attainment or "therapeutic purpose" (Turnbull et al., 2000; see also Thomas & Rapport, 1998). When a restriction of liberties is being considered, such as placing a student in a self-contained program for emotional or behavioral concerns, educational teams should explore five issues:

1. Whether the use of supports (e.g., learning accommodations, behavioral supports) has been adequately tried in the general education settings
2. The comparability of the curriculum used in the general education and special education placements
3. The likely benefits of the placement relative to those associated with remaining in the general education setting
4. The time interval for the placement
5. How a transition back to general education (reintegration) will occur

Yet, the reality is that given the availability and ease of the removal option in schools, teams are unlikely to fully explore these issues when making such decisions.

Part of the reason may be lack of knowledge about dealing with the student's behaviors and needs in the general education environment, an issue that this book is designed to address. Another reason relates to the issues of safety and security for other students, and this can represent a legitimate concern for the educational team. This issue is examined in the next section.

COMMUNITY RIGHTS AND NEEDS ISSUES

The availability of positive behavioral support procedures makes possible serving many more students in general education than are being served at the beginning of the 21st century, and all students should have the right to be part of their school communities. Nonetheless, there are times when the individual's rights run headfirst into the other community members' rights to educational services that are unimpeded by serious threats to their safety or ability to learn. These issues are explored in this section.

Individual Rights versus the Rights of Others

Gathercoal (1998) addressed the balance between individual rights and the rights of the state to curtail individual liberties in the interest of the common good. He used the phrase *compelling state interests* to describe public interest arguments that are grounded in legal principle and history. According to Gathercoal, individual rights may be denied when the exercise of those rights results in 1) property loss or damage, 2) legitimate educational purpose, 3) threat to health and safety, and 4) serious disruption of the educational process. Thus, Gathercoal stated, "School rules and decisions intended to protect these four compelling state interest arguments will, in all probability, withstand the test of today's court rulings despite the fact that they deny students their individual rights" (p. 202).

Yell and Rozalski (2000) reviewed two Supreme Court decisions that were related to the rights of individuals in schools. In summarizing these cases involving drug use and drug testing, the authors noted, "The high court clearly stated that when the rights of students and those of school officials seem to conflict, the law favors the duties of school officials" (p. 191). Therefore, although the issue of violence was not directly reviewed, the role of the school in providing a safe and orderly learning environment for all students was affirmed. Yell and Rozalski concluded by offering 10 recommendations for developing legally sound school district policies and procedures related to violence and violence prevention:

1. Know the law.
2. Make prevention of violence a publicly announced priority.
3. Involve the community.
4. Assess the physical safety of district schools and implement correction procedures.
5. Form school district and individual school teams.
6. Conduct districtwide training of all staff.
7. Implement prevention programs.
8. Develop crisis procedures for responding to violent incidents.
9. Use law enforcement and the courts to address violence when it occurs.
10. Formatively evaluate school district policies and procedures.

What Research Says

Although legal rulings provide critical information for school districts, findings from educational research and practice sometimes offer a different perspective. According to Mayer (1995) and Mayer and Leone (1999), the use of punitive and restrictive measures to manage student behavior in schools is often associated with increased disorder and problems. Alternatively, if positive behavioral support is implemented schoolwide, a school could experience significantly fewer problems and safer schools (Lewis & Daniels, 2000). Dwyer and Osher (2000) and Dwyer, Osher, and Warger (1998) offered comprehensive overviews of a wide range of positive strategies that are available for prevention, intervention, and crisis management in schools. (See Chapter 12 of this book, which is devoted to this topic.)

It is likely that the reactions of a community, whether it is the school community or the larger community, toward behavioral issues is related to its members' perceptions of a specific behavioral problem. If a behavior is perceived as an intentional violation of the codes of a culture, community members may view the behavior differently than if it is perceived to be a function of frustration due to unfair, unclear, or inflexible academic work. Moreover, community members may accept minor violations of school rules and codes of conduct, but when it comes to weapons and drugs, many hold fast to a zero tolerance position. Reflecting society's view, schools

> Have instituted policies that suspend students from schools for a wide range of rule infractions that range from threats of violence to possession of weapons to use or possession of drugs on school property. Zero tolerance has created situations in which principals have no latitude or discretion in administering disciplinary sanctions. (Leone et al., 2000, p. 4)

As noted previously in this chapter, zero tolerance policies can be problematic. Reports show that students with disabilities (Leone et al., 2000) and African American students (Townsend, 2000) often receive disproportionate numbers of exclusionary consequences. Concerns can also be raised about the real impact that zero tolerance–driven consequences have on students, such as automatic suspensions and exclusions. As Skiba and Peterson (2000) observed, "Suspension may simply accelerate the course of delinquency by providing a troubled youth with little parental supervision a few extra days with deviant peers" (p. 339). They also noted that the net effect of such consequences is to weaken or break the school social bond. For these reasons, practices that are based on zero tolerance policies are often detrimental to students.

Skiba and Peterson (2000) offered an early response model as an alternative to the zero tolerance approach. Their early response model is meant to be preventive, and it is designed to encourage a positive, safe school community. The model is multidimensional and takes into account many proactive approaches to discipline, such as conflict resolution, parent involvement, and functional behavioral assessment. Leone and colleagues (2000) also presented a case for adopting alternative approaches in lieu of punishment-driven systems. They suggested approaches that focus on engaging the students in the school and promoting their behavioral and academic success.

THE TASK AHEAD

It was noted at the beginning of this chapter that an important historical trend was the merging of streams of thought focused on discipline with streams of thought focused on treatment. What brings these disparate concepts together is a common goal: to prevent and to respond to behavioral problems so that they are significantly less likely to affect society. Treatment processes can be made palatable to those who are primarily concerned with discipline by showing that the long-term goal of reducing discipline concerns might be attained if particular treatment practices are incorporated into a school's discipline activities.

This chapter has recommended that a first step in reconciling these streams of thought is to reconceptualize a treatment approach to problem behaviors as an educative approach. This has implications for conceptions of positive behavioral support practices and for the outcomes of positive behavioral support efforts. Yet, this is complicated by tensions between the rights and needs of the individual to experience an authentic educative intervention and those of other students to experience reasonable levels of safety and comfort. A balance between these issues must be struck when constructing support plans that attempt to realize both educative and discipline ends.

The survival value of positive behavioral support depends on its ability—relative to other approaches—to address the issues and meet the concerns that are summarized in the foregoing paragraph. This, then, defines an essential mission for the remaining chapters in this book: to describe and illustrate a coherent set of principles, procedures, and practices that can effect change in individual learners, realize broader discipline goals of the school, and simultaneously honor the rights and needs of individual students and those of the broader school community. Accomplishing this mission requires something more than a cookbook of strategies or methods for responding to behavioral problems. To be skilled in positive behavioral support, an educator must have a firm grasp of its essential principles and processes (Chapter 5), and he or she must also understand how to work with larger systems issues within schools to effect change (Chapter 6). The educator must be equipped with a protocol that sketches the sequence of events that are associated with generating positive outcomes and developing support plans (Chapter 7), and he or she must also know how to use assessment tools to define concerns and suggest courses of action (Chapter 8). The educator must have practices and procedures for working with individual problem behaviors that vary in severity and persistence (Chapters 5–11), and he or she must also be able to effectively implement these within the complex social and professional environments of schools (Chapters 9, 10, and 11). Finally, the educator needs information on how to nurture building environments that facilitate and sustain positive behavioral support practices and procedures (Chapter 12).

Chapter 5

Critical Processes
within Behavioral Support

"Where there is no vision, the people perish. . . ."
—Proverbs 29:18

Chapter 4 explored how positive behavioral support offers an approach to challenging behavior that shifts the emphasis of intervention from an eliminative to an educative stance. Moreover, the values that underlie positive behavioral support presuppose that students with behavior challenges can and should be instructed in natural communities and that educators' efforts achieve a higher level of authenticity when directed at either finding ways to support students in typical environments or returning them to these environments after removal.

As the term *positive behavioral support* becomes widespread in the vocabularies of people who are responsible for students with behavioral challenges, a risk emerges. Rather than recognizing that behavioral support values signal a need for a shift in the education of children and youth with behavioral difficulties and how their behaviors are addressed, agencies and educators may simply relabel their traditional behavior management practices as "support." What has to be established in education is a clear recognition that the values and processes of support are neither honored nor implemented when children and youth with behavioral difficulties are "micro-managed" through systems of rewards and punishers that support little more than adults' comfort levels. In fact, it can be argued that calling classroom management activities in self-contained settings "support" is misleading unless there are explicit steps within a plan for educators to reintegrate a student into his or her community.

While Chapter 4 focused on principles, values, and the governing parameters of the support process, this chapter describes, both conceptually and procedurally, four critical processes associated with positive behavioral support. These processes are

1. Person-centered planning
2. Relationship development

3. Hypothesis-based intervention
4. Crisis intervention

The following sections illustrate that natural school communities optimize the power and value of the specific strategies and tools that these processes represent.

PERSON-CENTERED PLANNING

Person-centered planning is used in this book to encompass a variety of procedures and techniques that have two common purposes. Applied to students with behavioral challenges, the first purpose is to provide educators with a way to identify authentic outcomes for students, which can assist them in formulating goals for the behavioral support process. *Authentic* means that the identified outcomes exhibit one or both of two qualities: 1) they reflect the individual's or family's desires and wishes regarding a meaningful life and 2) they reflect appropriate options given what the student's age- and grade-level peers are doing in school and in related communities.

The second of the two purposes is to provide educators with a step-by-step and detailed planning process for developing formal, concrete plans for achieving the identified outcomes. Some of the different systems of person-centered planning that are considered in this discussion include

- Life-Style Planning (O'Brien, 1987)
- Personal Futures Planning (Mount & Zwernik, 1988)
- Lifestyle Development Process (Malette et al., 1992)
- Whole Life Planning (Butterworth, Hagner, Heikkinen, De Mello, & McDonough, 1993)
- MAPS (Making Action Plans [formerly known as the McGill Action Planning System]; Forest & Lusthaus, 1990; Pearpoint, Forest, & O'Brien, 1996; Vandercook, York, & Forest, 1989)
- PATH (Planning Alternative Tomorrows with Hope; Pearpoint, O'Brien, & Forest, 1993)

In all cases, person-centered planning represents a way of thinking about the development and implementation of supports that is consistent with the principles and values articulated in Chapter 4.

Five Distinguishing Features of Person-Centered Planning

The literature (Anderson, Bahl, & Kincaid, 1999; Gaylord, Abery, McBride, Pearpoint, & Forest, 1998; Morningstar, Kleinhammer-Tramill, & Lattin, 1999) indicates that person-centered planning models share five features, which give them form and substance. The first feature is that they are designed to encourage the collaborative involvement of educators, family, and friends in the initial planning and subsequent implementation steps. A common scenario for the initial planning stage is that the student, family members, educators, and friends gather as a small group, and a facilitator leads them through a sequence of steps that defines outcomes and delineates the supports that will make the outcomes achievable. At the implementation stage, the process relies on the social network that is created by those involved in planning to ensure that the proposed supports are put into place. For example, a parent may share with the teacher strategies for preventing a certain behavior from occurring in the classroom, and the parent may then intermittently brainstorm with the teacher if the behavior continues. As another example, an administrator may agree to provide a special education teacher with a walkie-talkie so that the special educator will be available as needed when called by the general education teacher in the event of a crisis.

The collaborative aspect of the planning process is absolutely essential. To illustrate this point, Lovett (1996) described how two paid helpers assisted a young boy, who had a reputation for striking others, to become more successful in school. The helpers accomplished this by assisting the educational team in generating ways to replace their time-out procedures with choice provision strategies. Lovett noted that "only when everyone involved in this boy's life used their heads and hearts to collaborate" could a "practical and respectful alternative to time-out" be developed (p. 109).

The second feature of person-centered planning is that it focuses on a person's strengths. The team members who gather together place their energies on the capacities, assets, and preferences of the individual who is the center of the planning process, rather than belaboring the student's deficits, limitations, and difficulties. This is aptly illustrated in the way that the MAPS process (Vandercook et al., 1989) directs the planning team's attention toward a student's strengths by posing a question such as, "What are the student's strengths, gifts, and talents?" and giving each team member a chance to respond. Similarly, the PATH process focuses on a person's likely capabilities, with the objective being "to build sufficient common understanding and mutual support so that people can focus their wisdom and their energy on developing the hopeful potentials in difficult situations" (Pearpoint, O'Brien, & Forest, 1993, p. 5).

The third feature of person-centered planning is that it calls for the creation of a *vision* for the student—that is, an assembly of broadly stated outcomes that represents the hopes and desires of the student and his or her friends, family, and teachers. The MAPS process, for example, poses the following question to the team regarding planning, "What is your dream for the individual?" (Vandercook et al., 1989, p. 207).

Based on years of work with students who have significant behavioral problems (see Jackson, Dobson, Wimberley, & Shepler, 1993; Jackson & Leon, 1995; Jackson & Leon, 1996a; Jackson & Leon, 1997a; Jackson, Shepler, & Dobson, 1991; Leon & Jackson, 1995; Leon & Jackson, 1996), Jackson and Leon (1998a) identified three characteristics of a vision that can enhance the vision's value as a guide for support planning. First, a vision statement is most useful if it includes between three and eight succinct, positively stated, broad outcomes. Vision statements of this nature are especially helpful for channeling the development of goals and objectives toward worthwhile ends and for gauging the student's growth over time. Second, the long-term aspirations of the student and family can and should be acknowledged in a vision statement, but the statement should also focus on the student's potential progress in 6 months to 1 year if the proposed behavioral support processes work. Jackson and Leon (1996a) reported that vision statements that are primarily focused on outcomes too far in the future (e.g., "Become a welder after I graduate" or "Live independently in an apartment" for a ninth-grade student) offer little real guidance for defining the supports or the skills required for realizing the vision. Moreover, using long-range community outcomes for a young student who is still in school can sometimes place the child at risk for placement in "life skills" or "community" programs that deny or severely restrict access to the general education curriculum. School districts that continue to preserve segregated life skills programs will sometimes try to steer families toward these programs by encouraging them to consider adult outcomes for their child's IEP goals. Third, especially useful visions address each of the following three areas:

1. Membership in a community of typical peers who are themselves invested in the school community
2. Participation in activities in which same-age typical peers regularly engage and that add value and worth to a student in his or her eyes and in the eyes of peers and adults
3. Autonomy and control over events that are important to the student and constitute school-day activities for other age- and grade-level children (see Display 5.1).

The vision process can be critical for a student who has been removed from the general education classroom because it provides direction for the development of authentic reintegration outcomes within the school community. Designating these

DISPLAY 5.1—DANIEL'S VISION

District personnel believed that Daniel, a kindergartner, had intense learning and behavioral support needs that required a self-contained "center-based" program. Despite district resistance, Daniel's parents requested that their son attend his neighborhood school and attend only general education classes. To help the new educational team frame educational planning and goal development, the family offered the following vision:

1. Learn what the other age-level children are learning, even if Daniel does not learn it all or as quickly as the other students
2. Have a valued role with the other same-age students, including leading the other children in activities (he enjoys instructing others) and helping others during morning routines (he likes to be in charge)
3. Be part of the storytelling experiences of his peers
4. Have access to a variety of places in his home community so that he can participate in a variety of peer social activities at school and in his neighborhood
5. Respond more effectively to the demands of people in authority (e.g., responding with less melodrama to corrections and to redirects)

Which of these vision statements addresses activity participation? Membership and belonging? Personal control and autonomy?

For several years now, Daniel has been in a general education classroom with direct special education support provided only during routines in which extensive reading is required. How often should the educational team revisit and revise this vision statement?

outcomes can guide intervention efforts toward what is desirable and beneficial for the student and for others in the school community. Moreover, this process can help prevent the team from becoming overwhelmed with disconcerting or potentially frightening aspects of the student's behavior. Of course, for a student who presents minor concerns or conflicts and is already included in his or her age- and grade-level classes, all that may be required for the vision is a simple "agreement" that support planning will emphasize 1) affiliation and friendship with peers, 2) involvement in the content and activities of the classroom and curriculum, and 3) ways for the student to exercise choice. At the same time, especially for students who have IEPs, some sort of vision planning is strongly recommended. This is because the IEP planning process, which may occur in conjunction with positive behavioral support planning, tends to focus the team's attention more on what needs to be remedied than on what new growth is possible. For example, IEP goals and objectives are often based on needs lists, which frequently reflect the things that seem "most wrong" about the child or youth. Operating from a vision can assist the team in generating a list of needs that is consistent with the vision, or it can help the team organize and select vision-correlated, priority needs from a more traditional needs list.

The fourth feature of person-centered planning is an action plan, or a *behavioral support plan*, for reaching the vision. Jackson and Leon (1998a) argued that a truly successful behavioral support plan includes steps for translating a vision's statements into outcomes that address the previously mentioned areas of membership, activity participation, and autonomy. For example, if a student's vision statement includes the goal "a group of classmates who like her and regularly support her in her classes," then the behavioral support plan must include steps that educators can take for incorporating this into the student's regular school day. After Meyer and Evans (1989), Jackson and Leon (1998a) referred to these aspects of support planning as *long-term prevention*, reporting that the best way to ensure that behavior change will occur and endure is by planning for the outcomes prescribed in a vision to happen in the here and now. Conversely, failure to construct a plan in which outcomes prescribed in the vision are implemented as part of the educational team's activities weakens a plan's chances for achieving its intended purpose. For self-contained programs, this can pose a serious dilemma, as illustrated in the following situation: A student is moved to a restrictive setting (e.g., residential school, day treatment program) and is expected to work within a levels system (Scheuermann, Webber, Partin, & Knies, 1994) to earn the right to move back to his or her neighborhood school, but he or she is not provided with a plan from educators in the two settings that details how such a transition is to be enacted. There is the risk that the student will not trust nor be willing to invest in a program's expectations when outcomes of membership, activity participation, and autonomy in the nonrestrictive setting are remotely imaginable but not experienced as unfolding realities of daily life.

Malette and colleagues (1992) identified steps that should guide the plan development process. Along with vision setting, these include the following:

1. Describe ways to remove "barriers to participation"
2. Assemble meaningful schedules and routines
3. Develop specific instructional and behavioral intervention strategies

It is important to note how the sequence of these three steps deviates from the usual rationale behind the construction of many behavior management plans. Management plans commonly start with instructional and behavioral intervention strategies (Step 3) and may or may not identify ways to remove barriers (Step 1) or to assemble meaningful schedules and routines (Step 2). For a student who is already in general education classrooms and for one who has a planned outcome of reintegration, it is crucial to first conceptualize how to remove barriers to participation, then create a schedule that describes a typical day in those settings. Brown (1991) showed, for example, that the construction of an appropriate schedule can be one of the most significant steps that a team can take toward successfully solving behavioral problems. Only once barriers to participation have been mitigated and meaningful schedules have been created does it make sense to develop the additional instructional and behavioral supports for immersion in the school community when participation in that community is either in place or pending.

As this discussion illustrates, person-centered planning places a premium on the use of *natural supports*—supports that are available in the community rather than supports that are specifically construed and contrived for people with disability labels. Uditsky (1993) used the term *natural pathways* and commented that it is especially important to explore informal and ordinary processes that contribute to friendships. In fact, he has argued against formal strategies for promoting friendship. An example of a natural pathway is children being near one another on the school playground enjoying the same activity. Of course, adults can model playing together, but the focus is on modeling this for all of the children rather than modeling specifically for the child who has a disability.

The fifth and final feature of person-centered planning is that anticipated behavioral and learning outcomes are defined not only for the learner but also for all members of the student's community. As stressed by Anderson and colleagues, effective person-centered planning creates environments "where everyone involved is a learner" (1999, p. 388). This is illustrated in focus group research (Carr, Turnbull, & Turnbull, 1997; Ruef, Turnbull, Turnbull, & Poston, 1999) in which peers and friends of people with behavioral challenges spoke of the need to learn more about supporting these individuals. Peers and friends commented that they needed general support information and mentoring from "veteran" friends, as well as information on understanding and resolving their own reactions to behavioral events and issues.

Additional Characteristics of Person-Centered Planning

There are three additional characteristics that are not common to all planning, but they are still important considerations for professionals who use person-centered planning in a behavioral support effort. First, in some situations, the individual for whom the plan is designed takes the initiative in facilitating the planning process. His or her activities may include but are not limited to issuing invitations, naming the location for the meeting, and identifying major issues to be discussed. This approach has been used mainly with high school students (Hagner, Helm, & Butterworth, 1996; Morningstar et al., 1999).

A second characteristic associated with some person-centered planning processes is the use of graphic organizers for recording the ideas, suggestions, and recommendations that are proposed in a meeting. The PATH approach, Personal Profiling (Kincaid, 1996), and Personal Futures Planning use graphic organizers. The purpose of graphic recording is to capture words and images on paper, offer a timely summary of the group's work, and provide a permanent record to view and share with everyone who participated in the meeting.

A third characteristic that is sometimes present is a recognition of the importance of outcome measures. Hagner and colleagues (1996) provided an example of how to measure outcomes in a qualitative study of a person-centered planning process for six individuals who were making the transition from school to adult life. Five of the six individuals reported that they were satisfied with the outcomes and wanted to continue the process, and these participants cited a closer social connection as a common benefit. The authors noted that this type of planning tends to encourage the individuals themselves to seize opportunities (sometimes afforded through social networks) that otherwise may have been overlooked. This heightened awareness for new options, the authors pointed out, is reminiscent of Cabral and Salomone's (1990) notion of the role of "chance" in career development. These findings also supported the work of Malette and colleagues (1992) who reported increases in community involvement, social relationships, and functional skills for individuals who participated in a similar process called *lifestyle development.*

Although person-centered planning can incorporate outcome measures to evaluate changes in the individual's environmental arrangements and behavioral patterns, some may argue that explicit measurement of behavior is not appropriate. One reason for not measuring behavior is the opinion that the person's change experiences should be treated as personal and subjective and not as public information. From this point of view, all that needs to be ascertained is whether behavior support planning resulted in the long-term prevention outcomes being realized and sustained, because these represent indicators that often correlate with other aspects of the plan, including changes in challenging behavior.

The Person-Centered Planning Advantage

What does person-centered planning offer over and above the more typical team meetings, such as those convened for IEP purposes? Kincaid (1996) identified five outcomes specifically associated with person-centered planning. For the student who is at the center of the planning process, these include

1. Participating in community life
2. Developing satisfying relationships
3. Making decisions in everyday life
4. Having opportunities for respected roles
5. Having opportunities for lifelong learning

Although it can be argued that these should be intended results of IEP meetings, the reality is that IEP meetings often lack the structure for directing the team's thinking toward such outcomes.

In conclusion, person-centered planning is not simply about rethinking who attends a planning meeting for a student with behavioral concerns and how the agenda of the meeting is structured. Rather, person-centered planning represents a significant shift in philosophy, principles, and practices regarding the realization of solutions to behavioral concerns, and it leads to outcomes that potentially impact a person's entire lifestyle, as well as the lifestyles of friends, teachers, and family. It accomplishes this by first establishing an authentic direction for the planning process, then developing a plan that focuses on success in the natural community as the most important outcome of the behavior support process, regardless of where the student is receiving services when the process is initiated. As Lovett wrote, "If we faithfully attend to what people need, want, and wish for, then we will find them more amenable to change, and they will change in the direction of more ordinary behavior" (1996, pp. 136–137).

THE ROLE OF RELATIONSHIPS IN THE SUPPORT PROCESS

One of the reasons that person-centered planning works is because existing and newly formed relationships become catalysts in the provision of the supports that a student experiences in his or her daily life. There are opportunities for the individual to develop emotionally satisfying personal and mentoring relationships with educators, community members, and, especially, peers.

Vandercook and colleagues noted, "Relationships are not only one of the most valid markers for measuring a person's quality of life, they are also viewed as serving a function in social and cognitive development" (1989, p. 206). Similarly, Ayres, Hedeen, and Meyer (1996) asserted that a relationship with another child is far more likely to result in positive outcomes than any kind of behavior management plan or program. The latter is an especially poignant observation, as an examination of behavior change plans in many schools would probably reveal that the majority focus on expectations of the child and on mechanics of instruction and control, with less consideration for long-term relationship issues (e.g., Lovett, 1996). Yet, clearly, relationships with others represent potent vehicles for change because relationships can provide the *raison d'être* for behavioral change and learning, as well as the sustenance necessary for change to endure.

Relationships as Factors in Behavioral Change and Learning

Caine and Caine (1994) examined findings of brain research and models of brain functioning for their implications for educational reform. They contended that "the brain does not naturally separate emotions from cognition, either anatomically or perceptually" (p. vii). Thus, feelings may enhance or constrict learning just as cognition may enhance or constrict one's emotional state. Their observations underscore the importance of teachers creating classroom environments in which belonging is nurtured and positive interpersonal relationships with all student(s) are encouraged so that each student's potential for growth and learning is optimized.

Bronfenbrenner's (1979) seminal work on relationships in human development provided a model that shows how interpersonal relationships can incrementally affect learning and human behavior in daily life. Bronfenbrenner described how interpersonal relationships undergo a course of development just as individuals do. Individuals may begin a relationship by simply having opportunities to participate in joint activities, which facilitate reciprocity and response similarity among the involved individuals during these activities. As a relationship evolves, however, processes of imitation become more likely, and the one individual's patterns are more likely to be adopted by others within the relationship, first when the person is present, then in his or her absence. At later stages, a relationship may assume an important role in guiding self-monitoring processes: People within a close and extended relationship are more likely to use each other as mental models for making decisions about how to respond in various situations. As Bronfenbrenner postulated, a key consideration with respect to whether a relationship can reach these latter stages of development is the degree of *positive affect* that is invested by partners in a relationship. Brofenbrenner stated, "To the extent that they [relationships] are positive and reciprocal to begin with and become more so as interaction proceeds, they are likely to enhance the pace and the probability of occurrence of developmental processes" (p. 58).

Bronfenbrenner's concept that relationships serve as foundations for learning and socialization is consistent with Maslow's hierarchy, in which the need to belong is more basic than the need for mastery and achievement (Maslow, 1970). As described in Chapter 3, Kunc (1992) persuasively argued that the mastery of social competence should not be viewed as a prerequisite for the development of relationships; rather, specific social skills will follow when a student experiences membership and belonging in a community of peers. Knowlton (1998) took this argument another step by asserting that a genuine sense of belonging in the school's culture is a prerequisite to benefiting from the academic curriculum. Despite a growing knowledge of the connections between belonging and achievement, Kunc and others (e.g., Overton, 1997) have noted that schools often focus on needs such as skill mastery while neglecting the influence that social membership has on the successful realization of such higher order needs.

It is self-evident that if relationships and belonging are catalysts for learning and growth, then there are likely connections between a student's affiliation patterns and challenging behaviors. If a student's peer group or close friends value patterns of behavior that are troubling, disruptive, or dangerous, then the association between interpersonal relationships and development will promote the opposite of what is best for the student (e.g., Xie, Cairns, & Cairns, 1999). It is clearly up to us—teachers, administrators, and classroom peers—to make overtures that can alter the course in the relationships that these individuals develop and sustain during their formative school years. Accordingly, educational placement is a disturbing issue that must be squarely faced when considering our impact on a student who turns to us for personal values and behaviors. Despite the best intentions, placing youth in self-contained classes and facilities in which all peer group members have behavioral problems may be detrimental to these students and, by extension, others when these youth return to their classrooms and natural communities (see Display 5.2).

Fortunately, as Brendtro and colleagues noted, education professionals (e.g., Farmer, Farmer, & Gut, 1999) are becoming aware of the role played by positive interpersonal relationships, and they suggest that educators are increasingly seeking new ways to "rekindle a shared sense of community" (1990, p. 38). The following three types of activities for enhancing supportive relationships among peers are partially based on Stainback, Stainback, Raschke, and Anderson (1981): 1) activities that educators can use to provide opportunities for peer relationships to develop, 2) activities that peers can use to enhance respectful and appropriate behaviors among each other so that relationships can form and prosper, and 3) activities that teachers can use to promote the acquisition of relationship-sustaining social skills.

The first set of activities includes ways that classroom teachers and others can increase opportunities for relationship formation through how students are grouped and how learning activities are organized and presented. Opportunity begins with proximity, and initial classroom assignment processes must not overrule mixed-ability groupings and natural heterogeneity (see Chapter 3). Then, instruction can be delivered through activities that inherently provide opportunities for the development of supportive relationships and a sense of belonging. Cooperative groups, peer pairing

DISPLAY 5.2—WHAT THE D.A.R.E. OFFICER RECOMMENDED

The local police station sent an officer to a seventh-grade class to discuss responsibility, drug use, and staying out of trouble. In an opening exercise, the students were given a multiple-choice test that included the question, "What should you do if your parents ask you to stop seeing a favorite friend because he or she has repeatedly gotten in trouble with the law?" The answers included a) stand by your friend and tell your parents that you plan to see your friend regardless of their views; b) say that you will stop seeing your friend but then see him or her anyway; c) agree to stop spending time with this friend. The correct answer was "c."

If a student is actively rejected by most of his or her classroom peers, how likely is it that he or she will truly choose answer "c" in this situation?

How might a teacher's actions facilitate or impede a student who is seeking to make the right decision in this situation?

How meaningful would this question be if all of these students were all in a self-contained, special education classroom or program in which most individuals fit the description of this hypothetical student's friend?

for projects, and peer tutoring relationships can be excellent vehicles for both enhancing learning and promoting relationship formation.

It is important that peer tutoring is not used in a one-sided fashion, in which "help" is always given by students without labels to those with labels. Helwick and Jackson (1999) described how a boy who was silly and disruptive in his third-grade class but was a skilled athlete became more appropriate in that class when, among other things, he was given the responsibility to help younger children participate in their physical education class. This illustrates how activities should be selected for enhancing relationships: Choose activities that capitalize on the strengths and capabilities of students with challenging behaviors to enhance their esteem in the eyes of others.

Rogers, Ludington, and Graham (1999) offered an extensive array of relationship-building exercises for students in K–12 settings. For example, an interest poll can be used to explore connections among students by asking questions such as, "What is something that you would like to do more often?" and "What movies have you really enjoyed?" Ice breakers enable all students to feel welcomed and accepted in the classroom.

The second set of activities includes ways that peers can encourage in each other the kinds of social interaction patterns that enhance their mutual comfort level so that relationships can develop and flourish. The classroom meeting concept, introduced in the discussion of the quality school model in Chapter 2, is one way in which students can help regulate how they treat each other and how difficult situations are handled so that the social norms that emerge among the students enhance mutual respect and caring. Janney and Snell (1996) offered another way that students can create a milieu in which relationships are enhanced. They examined how students with severe disabilities are supported by peers in general education classrooms. Their study focused on how implicit and explicit "rules for helping" are formed so that the assistance to classmates with disabilities does not encroach on the formation of more reciprocal relationships. Janney and Snell's findings apply to any situation in which a student has significant behavioral concerns and difficulty communicating wants and needs. Working with the teacher(s), peers can develop simple, individually tailored guidelines for giving space, honoring communications, and handling conflict, thereby increasing their comfort level with the student who has behavioral difficulties.

The third set of activities includes ways for educators to teach and facilitate social skills that enhance the formation of positive, supportive relationships within educational environments. Scott and Nelson (1998) reasoned that students with behavioral difficulties do not acquire many critical social skills in natural environments because either their good behavior is not reinforced or it is being actively punished. These authors suggest two approaches for encouraging the development of critical social skills: 1) contextual intervention and 2) environmental manipulation. In contextual intervention, a student with behavioral challenges is taught skills in the natural school environment that he or she can use to meet needs that were originally sought by inappropriate behaviors. In environmental manipulation, the environment is altered so that the student with behavioral challenges does not experience the needs that evoked the problem behaviors in the first place. Scott and Nelson illustrated these procedures with the example of a student who is often verbally harassed during sporting events and games for making errors, so the student reacts by hitting and kicking his or her peers. This problem can be handled by both encouraging the student to walk away or to call on an adult for assistance (contextual intervention) and using strategies such as peer mediation to reduce the teasing in the first place (environmental manipulation). According to Scott and Nelson, the goal of these processes is to establish a situation in which "both the student and those in her environment can begin to develop a new history of positive interactions" (p. 270).

Relationships as Factors in Sustaining Change

Lovett (1996) commented that ongoing mutual affection and positive regard are indispensable elements of all healthy relationships. He also suggested that experiencing continued commitment through "thick and thin" instills such value in relationships. This insight rings especially true with students who have behavioral difficulties. Although part of what educators must seek is the amelioration of problems, they must also recognize that a potentially more powerful outcome is that a student experiences support so that he or she can learn, over a longer period of time, how to manage his or her own crises and difficulties. In any case, there is reason to believe that ongoing interpersonal relationships can sustain and promote growth and change in all areas of a person's life.

Probably one of the most widely known strategies for maintaining long-term supports for a student is Circles of Friends (Forest & Lusthaus, 1990; Perske, 1988). According to Leyden, Newton, and Wilson, this is a

> Group of people, including age-peers, who respond to a request for involvement in the life of an individual who needs the friendship and participation of others. . . . They may also be a network of people willing to befriend a person, get to know them, spend time with and care about them, and share activities and interests. (1998, p. 14)

Circles of Friends activities usually include 1) short, informal meetings in which the friends and the student discuss new ways to promote the student's membership and involvement in classes and in other activities in school and in the community and 2) direct support in school activities throughout the day by one or more of the friends. Typically, peers choose to move in and out of the circle so that there is always a group of students who are part of the circle while others are not.

The Circles of Friends concept has been criticized by Van der Klift and Kunc (1995), who pointed out that the process can model demeaning and counterproductive values regarding "helping the handicapped." Van der Klift and Kunc suggested that it may be more appropriate to conceptualize these circles as "circles of support," in which the goal is not that of friendship but that of finding ways to include a student with learning or behavioral difficulties in activities from which he or she might otherwise be excluded (see also Van der Klift & Kunc, 1994). Such a process, of course, provides an opportunity for sustained relationships to develop, but it does so without presupposing that friendship must be an outcome as well. Similarly, Kozleski and Jackson (1993) found that Circles of Friends for a particular student can evolve from being a circle around the specific individual to a circle that can support social and other needs for all of its members. This happens as the student with the disability becomes a more natural member of the school community because, for several years, he or she has experienced all educational services within grade- and age-appropriate classes with typical peers.

Promoting Relationships Between Educators and Students

Student–educator relationships are affected by the educator's need to impart skills and knowledge within a fixed time frame. Hence, the kinds of relationships that develop between students and teachers are different from those that students form among themselves. Yet, relationships between students and teachers are of equal importance; not only do they affect the educator's ability to accomplish his or her objectives but such relationships also may influence student self-esteem, self-efficacy, and overall competence (Hartup, 1985). Jones and Jones (1998), summarizing research on student–teacher relationships, noted that the quality of the relationship between the teacher and the student appears to affect academic achievement and classroom behavior (Glasser, 1992b; Noddings, 1992).

Rogers and Renard (1999) also emphasized the importance of relationship-driven teaching and how it can enhance the student's motivation to learn. They contended that students are motivated "when they believe that teachers treat them like people and care about *them personally and educationally*" (p. 34, italics added). They suggested that when teachers and students are engaged in quality learning, inappropriate behavior may simply become a nonissue. Citing Covey (1989), these authors pointed out that seeking to understand students with difficulties and discovering what motivates them can be keys to success.

The nature of the student–teacher relationship can be especially important when the student has a history of disrupting or threatening others' learning and/or safety. If it can be said that a good peer relationship affects outcomes for a student with challenging behavior better than a "program" can (Ayres et al., 1996), perhaps the same is sometimes true for the student–teacher relationship. Significant disruptions may be less likely, and dispelling them more easily accomplished, when there is mutual respect and trust between the teacher and the student.

When a student is in a self-contained classroom or school for students with emotional or behavioral labels or a correctional facility, the student–teacher relationship assumes a new level of importance. Nowhere else does one find such a concentration of significant emotional and behavioral difficulties, without the benefit of a diverse, changing, and constantly present range of natural opportunities to see and model the typical behaviors of responsible peers and adults. Hence, the teacher plays a pivotal role in whether the student chooses to live according to lessons learned during experiences with the teacher or according to experiences with other students who are struggling with their own issues. The authors' experiences working in residential and correctional facilities suggest that the key to student success often lies less with what is taught than what is modeled in the teacher's spontaneous decisions and activities. If the teacher's daily behavior expresses caring, understanding, respect, goal directedness, reasonable conflict resolution, and decision-making skills, then there is a chance that a positive relationship between the teacher and a student will develop that can be a basis for similar patterns in the student. This is because the kinds of advanced social relationships described by Bronfenbrenner (1979) can occur, in which individuals spontaneously emulate the values and practices of other individuals with whom they share a deep and potentially abiding relationship.

Although the focus here has been on how the teacher influences the student, it is important to bear in mind the concept of *reciprocity*. Not only does the teacher affect the student's behavior, but the student's behavior, in turn, affects and changes the teacher's behavior. Carr, Taylor, and Robinson (1991), for example, studied the impact of severe behavioral problems in children on the instructional activities of teachers. They found that teachers responded more to students who did not display problem behaviors. Hence, as the previous discussion of person-centered planning showed, the way that relationships form and develop across time is very much a two-way process, each person affecting and being affected by the other. This reciprocity establishes a recurring need for educators to examine their personal expressions of respect for individual students and to closely monitor equity in the way that they distribute instructional attention, contingent recognition, and positive regard.

HYPOTHESIS-BASED INTERVENTION

Several promising themes shared by many contemporary educational discipline models were identified in Chapters 2 and 4. One was that educators should view motivational factors as important considerations when developing interventions for students who have challenging behavior. As suggested in Chapter 2, this means examining a range of variables that may contribute to a behavior's presence or absence in different situations, then using this information when constructing the intervention steps and strategies. The first of these processes, *functional behavioral assessment*, examines a range of variables to ascertain which seem correlated in useful ways with the behavior. This approach, which is described in Chapter 8, provides the data for generating one or more working hypotheses "about the purpose (function) of the problem behavior being examined," which then leads to "ideas about what would constitute a plausible intervention" (Carr, Langdon, & Yarbrough, 1999, p. 24). The second of these two processes, *hypothesis-based intervention*, uses the information gathered through functional behavioral assessment to develop the steps and strategies of a plausible intervention.

The emergence of hypothesis-based intervention and its corollary, functional behavioral assessment, in applied behavior analysis signaled an important conceptual shift in how problem behaviors should be addressed when developing practical interventions in schools and other settings. As noted by Carr, before this shift occurred, "technology took precedence over understanding" (1994, p. 393; see also Repp, 1999; Vittimberga et al., 1999). That is, prior to the emergence of these concepts and practices, positive and negative intervention strategies and techniques were used with children and youth without consideration of the specific, unique needs and desires that might be functionally associated with the behaviors. In fact, in reviewing findings from Scotti and colleagues (1991), Vittimberga and colleagues noted that only 22% of the reviewed behavioral intervention studies reported between 1976 and 1987 attempted to use functional behavioral assessments as part of their intervention planning.

As noted by Carr (1994), this purely technical approach can fall short of success precisely because it fails to incorporate the functions served by the behaviors. As an illustration of the phrase *technology taking precedence over understanding*, consider the situation of a young girl who is nonverbal and who frequently reaches out and touches her classmates during class. When understanding is not a factor in intervention decisions, this behavior might be defined by a teacher and a participating psychologist as inappropriate because it interferes with her learning and that of her classmates. The fact that the girl might use this behavior to communicate interest in or affection for others would not be relevant when these educators designed their intervention plan. Rather, selecting an intervention would primarily involve choosing from a menu of consequence-based strategies that have a proven track record for reducing inappropriate behaviors while encouraging appropriate forms of classroom participation. The strategies of choice for these educators might be differential reinforcement of other behavior, so that the child is being systematically reinforced when she keeps her hands to herself and stays on task, plus verbal reprimands (e.g., "No touching!") so that the child is consistently discouraged from inappropriate touching. These procedures, of course, might prove to be effective; the child could, for example, perceive the reinforcers (e.g., candy, stickers, adult attention) as adequate replacements for the social attention that she received when she touched her classmates. Yet, it is also possible that these procedures might prove ineffective because the child may not be willing to relinquish this form of physical contact with her peers, or her behavior may even become more problematic because of the interference in the student's efforts to meet her affiliation and peer relationship needs. In either case, this intervention neither honors the child's needs nor does it build on her strengths as a willing communicator and potential friend to her classmates. Of even greater concern is the next step that these educators might take if their program does not prove to be effective: They might switch to more restrictive procedures, such as isolating the child from her peers or even using a more potent negative consequence, such as time-out, contingent upon occurrences of the behavior.

This example, which is a composite of several real incidents, compellingly speaks to the rationale that underlies hypothesis-based intervention. Educators should use interventions that are based on developing an understanding of probable causes for behavior because the courses taken by such interventions can honor the student's needs even as they address educators' needs. Of course, one's understanding of student behavior is always hypothetical, as knowledge gained through observations and interviews is inevitably limited. It is only through testing hypotheses during the actual intervention that educators can experience some level of confirmation regarding the informed judgments that they make to guide their activities.

The Coming of Age of Hypothesis-Based Intervention

Since its inception, the knowledge base about hypothesis-based intervention has increased in a number of important ways, which have contributed to its value and effectiveness for educators (e.g., Carr, 1994; Carr, Carlson, Langdon, Magito-McLaughlin, & Yarbrough, 1998; Horner, 1994). As indicated by Carr (1994), much of the early work on the association between problem behaviors and the design of intervention procedures focused principally on four motivations that seemed to underlie many of the problem behaviors observed: 1) securing attention, 2) task avoidance, 3) desiring tangibles, and 4) seeking sensory reinforcement (e.g., Durand, 1990). In much of this early work, which was often conducted with children and youth who had significant disabilities and were in clinical or self-contained settings, educators found that they could construct hypotheses about underlying motivations, such as "task avoidance" or "attention," that could guide them in selecting effective consequences for behavior. For example, hypothesizing that a student acts out to avoid doing particular tasks may lead a special educator to decide that time-out contingent upon acting out probably would not work. Alternately, hypothesizing that a student acts out to receive attention from a teacher may suggest providing attention whenever the student is appropriately engaged in an instructional task.

An important expansion that has occurred in hypothesis-based intervention is the emergence of larger and more varied sets of motivational factors that should be considered when educators develop hypotheses about what is controlling and maintaining particular behaviors. For example, Horner and Carr (1997) spoke of six underlying motivations that may explain why an individual acts in a particular way in particular situations: 1) attention, 2) escape/avoidance, 3) tangible items, 4) automatic (sensory) reinforcement, 5) social avoidance, and 6) biological reinforcement (self-addiction). Borrowing from other systems (e.g., Carr, 1994; Dreikurs, 1968; Jackson et al., 1991; Jackson & Leon, 1998a; Maag, 1999), additional sources of motivation can include the need for power and control, a sense of helplessness, emotions of fear and terror, communicative frustration, affiliation/friendship needs, pleasure in taking risks, and needs associated with physiological variables such as medications. Although this expansion makes creating useful hypotheses a somewhat more complicated process, greater precision in hypotheses formation allows for better interventions and more successful problem solving when things go awry.

Another area of expansion in hypothesis-based intervention is the increasing use of two types of contextual information in the development of behavioral hypotheses: antecedent and setting information. *Antecedent information* typically refers to events that immediately precede and seem to occasion a behavior (e.g., peer teasing, adult directives). Especially fruitful interventions can be developed when it is highly probable that particular antecedent circumstances trigger specific behaviors (e.g., Kennedy, 1994). For example, hypothesizing that a student acts out when spurred on by classmates could lead an educator to change seating patterns, more effectively engage the other students so that they are less likely to seek a diversion, or discuss with classmates how their actions affect this student's right to be part of their instructional experiences. Alternately, hypothesizing that a student acts out because a particular task is too hard can result in developing accommodations or modifications for the task, regularly providing access to peer assistance, or rethinking how prompts and explanations are given to the student and to others.

Setting information refers to the broader contextual features of situations that correlate with a behavior's presence or absence. Setting information can include

- Immediate setting events, such as the curriculum content, peers who are present or absent, classroom arrangements, and other broad ecological properties of environments
- Preceding setting events, such as whether a student argued with his or her parents in the morning before school
- Biological setting events, such as illness or lack of sleep
- Prolonged setting events, such as parents divorcing, difficulties in a newly formed intimate relationship, or a family's eviction from its apartment

With respect to immediate context, knowing in which settings behaviors are more likely to occur can guide educators when they are formulating their hypotheses. For instance, if a child demonstrates high task participation in physical education but variable participation in math, more specific hypotheses can be developed, by using information from both settings, that focus on supporting student learning and reducing problems occurring in math. Regarding preceding and biological setting events, a growing body of research has established that patterns of behavior can correlate with things that have happened in the recent past or pressing biobehavioral conditions (Gardner, Cole, Davidson, & Karan, 1986; Kennedy & Itkonen, 1993; Kennedy & Meyer, 1996; O'Reilly, 1995, 1997; Wacker et al., 1996). Knowing, for example, that a student's behavior strongly correlates with migraine headaches can promote educational planning that accounts for the student's different levels of pain and stress and may cause the team to seek additional medical interventions. Finally, a body of behavioral research that examines how to employ information about prolonged setting events in hypothesis development is not available as we enter the 21st century. Yet, the authors' own school-based experiences indicate that such events can have pronounced effects on day-to-day behavior and that behavioral interventions should take these effects into account.

A third and final area of expansion that has occurred in hypothesis-based intervention is the emergence of intervention approaches that focus on the especially powerful connection among behavior, consequences, and interpersonal communication (e.g., Carr et al., 1994; Reichle & Johnston, 1993). For instance, consider a student who acts out when he is interrupted working alone at the computer and is redirected to a new task. Teaching him a communicative response for indicating that he wishes to finish his work before moving on not only alleviates a problem but also teaches a functional behavior that can give the student more appropriate ways to control his surroundings. What is especially important about the addition of communication to the hypothesis-based intervention approach is that it represents a shift from solely developing interventions that focus on using student motivations to meet adult ends to developing interventions that honor the student's needs as well. Consider, as an illustration, the example used previously in this section in which a special educator recognized that time-out as a consequence is contraindicated when a student's motivation is task avoidance. From the vantage point that teaching communication skills should be a large part of hypothesis-based intervention, the issue shifts from rejecting time-out as impractical to honoring the student's need to experience a break from educational routines. In addition it is not too big of a step for educators to begin reflecting on what they are offering to *all* of the students in a school or class and whether the message from the student with a disability is simply a more overt communication of needs being experienced by many within the class.

Developing Support-Oriented Hypotheses for Behavior

The specific hypotheses that educators create to drive their interventions are the pivotal points in hypothesis-based intervention. The previous section illustrated the knowledge base expansion regarding the kinds of information that can be used in developing hypotheses, as well as how educators can apply information that connects behavior to its consequences, motivations, antecedents, setting conditions, and communication needs. Complicating this picture, however, is the fact that challenging behavior is usually a complex function of an interaction among different variables, some of which are proximal (e.g., immediate classroom events) and some of which are distal (e.g., something that occurred at home a day ago). In addition, motivational factors are seldom as clear cut as the terms *escape* or *attention* imply. A student may use the same behavior to realize one motivation (the need to escape) in one situation and a second motivation (the need for attention) in another, or a behavior may be a function of various motivations simultaneously, or there may even be a sequence of different motivations as an episode unfolds (Jackson et al., 1993). These possibilities can complicate the design of hypothesis-based interventions, such as when one teaches a student to voluntarily take a break instead of becoming violent, and it turns out that escape is the motivation for rage in only one of several settings in which rage occurs.

Jackson and Leon (1998a) believed that hypotheses are more enlightening and prescriptive when they are written in the vernacular, when each provides sufficient detail for relating behaviors to specific sets of conditions, and when various hypotheses are written to cover the multitude of situations that are of concern or interest to the educators. They stress that an individual hypothesis is most adequate when it

- Identifies contextual circumstances (e.g., classrooms, times of day)
- Delineates the specific behavior patterns and whether they are more or less likely to occur under the delineated conditions (e.g., striking out at other students is most likely to occur when . . . , refusing to leave the room is less likely to happen when . . .)
- Specifies the reason or motivation that is believed to underlie the behavior (e.g., difficulty understanding the material, fatigue from overexertion)

As an illustration, consider a special educator who is concerned that Susan, a high school student, is becoming increasingly agitated (e.g., audibly groaning, fussing and complaining) in her general education classes as the school year progresses. The problem is approaching the point of being severe enough to remove Susan from the classroom for being "disruptive." Through observations and dialogues with Susan and her teachers, the special educator finds that the behavior occurs mostly in science class, usually when Susan is reading required materials that she describes as "too hard for me and everybody else," and its occurrence is sometimes followed by the teacher letting Susan do something different. The special educator also finds that this problem occurs much less frequently in English class, as the reading materials appear to be more interesting for Susan. Finally, the special educator notes that in English class, the students are often paired or placed in groups to discuss, interpret, and critique the materials and that Susan responds exceptionally well to this instructional arrangement. This leads this particular special educator to generate two hypotheses: 1) "In science class, Susan is more likely to become agitated when she is engaged in reading material that she finds too difficult" and 2) "In English class, agitation is largely absent during reading activities because the materials are more interesting for her and because she enjoys working with her peers." These two hypotheses—the second of which could be subdivided into two, if helpful—could then lead to the following changes:

- Allowing accommodations that alleviate stress during reading science materials (e.g., listening to sections on audiotape when content is critical)
- Providing more opportunities in science class to read in pairs with friends or peers
- Giving Susan greater guidance when she is expected to show evidence that she understands what she has read
- Initially honoring agitation as a communication by promptly offering understanding and assistance, then encouraging and giving Susan reason to use more appropriate communications to express her need for help

In addition to illustrating a particularly useful style for constructing individual hypotheses, this example illustrates a number of conditions that should be met when hypothesis-based intervention techniques are used as part of a positive behavioral support effort (e.g., Carr, Langdon, et al., 1999; Meyer & Park, 1999; O'Neill et al., 1990; Vittimberga et al., 1999). First, the intervention is based on information gathered in multiple situations in which the problems are both present and absent. Second, the purpose of the intervention is to support the student's continued involvement in, rather than removal from, the educational activities of his or her peers. Third, intervention steps and procedures are deliberately designed to accomplish three ends: 1) promote the student's success and continued educational growth, 2) give educators effective ways to prevent and respond to the individual's behavior that do not rely on suppression techniques, and 3) equip the student with alternative ways to meet the real needs that often underlie challenging behaviors.

Components of Effective Hypothesis-Based Interventions

The major components of an intervention that is largely premised on hypotheses is aptly illustrated by an example of an individual who had frequent outbursts of "verbal aggression." Gardner and colleagues (1986) described a young man, John, who lived in a small group home and attended a specialized vocational program in the community, a situation not unlike what is occurring in many district-sponsored transition programs across the United States at the beginning of the 21st century. His verbal outbursts had resulted in removal from other vocational programs, so this young man needed assistance in curbing these behaviors. Functional behavioral assessment was used to identify a number of antecedent events that had either low or high associations with John's verbal outbursts at work. For example, of 115 incidents of receiving praise, only 2 were correlated incidents of verbal aggression (1%); of 48 incidents of being reminded of an upcoming event on the schedule, 4 were correlated incidents of verbal aggression (8%); of 25 incidents of experiencing repeated prompts to complete an expected activity, 5 were correlated incidents of verbal aggression (25%); and of 55 incidents of being teased by peers, 18 were correlated incidents of verbal aggression (32%). There were also a number of setting events—occurring earlier in the day—that had relatively high associations with incidences of verbal outbursts at work. These included the presence of a particular staff person during morning routines in his home who was especially direct and forceful and arguments with peers at the bus stop before work.

Creating an effective and potentially enduring intervention for this young man would require integrating processes designed to lead to an envisioned lifestyle with processes designed to resolve behavioral issues. The former processes are drawn especially from person-centered planning and relationship development; the latter processes are drawn primarily from relationship development and the construction of informed hypotheses about the behaviors. Based on the work of Meyer and Evans (1989), Jackson and Leon (1998a) found that the syntheses of these processes can be attained by ensuring that an intervention includes steps associated with four interrelated components of support planning. These components—long-term prevention, short-term prevention, adaptive alternatives, and handling crises—are described next.

First, as mentioned in a previous section, steps must be taken to enhance long-term prevention. These steps include facilitating the individual's access to and development of relationships with others; access to meaningful activities; and opportunities for greater choice and control. For John, long-term prevention could involve his service provider's working with the professionals in the vocational setting, John's peers, and John himself to broadly alter their social and interpersonal relationships. It is also possible and even likely that John does not particularly value his work situation, and that self-control could be more easily fostered if he were in a job situation that represented an integrated placement and was more to his liking. Hence, a more substantial and enduring long-term prevention effort may first require developing a lifestyle plan and vision that delineates his desired work and residential changes, then establishing steps for reintegration into the community. Long-term prevention may also involve giving John greater control over who is present in his home during morning routines, as there was a person in his home who was a stimulus for his problems.

Second, steps for short-term prevention must be taken. These steps, which rely on hypotheses development, usually involve finding ways to attenuate triggering antecedents, to enhance comfort, and to make more immediately rewarding the individual's experiences within environments in which problems are likely. For example, because teasing was an antecedent that was associated with verbal aggression, reducing teasing from John's peers could help prevent the behavior in the short run. Another short-term measure would be to create neutralizing routines—such as time in the morning to talk about his feelings with a staff person before starting work—that could be used on the days that John had an argument with peers at the bus stop (Gardner et al., 1986; Horner, Day, & Day, 1997).

Third, steps must be taken to provide the individual with adaptive alternatives. Typically, this involves teaching and encouraging an individual to use communicative or adaptive responses that achieve the same outcomes as the problem behaviors but are more acceptable to others. The process of identifying potential adaptation alternatives relies heavily on behavioral hypotheses. Because being teased seems associated with verbal aggression, providing John with a different set of reactions to teasing (e.g., walking away, cracking a joke, using a scripted phrase) and encouraging him to use them could represent potentially effective adaptive alternatives.

Fourth and finally, there should be steps that others follow for handling a crisis when it arises. These steps may be different for different people because supervisors, peers, friends, and family members have different relationships with the person who exhibits the challenges. Moreover, these steps should be exclusively designed to "interrupt the behavior for the safety of the individual" and others, and "not for the specific purpose of causing an overall reduction in a particular challenging behavior" (Vittimberga et al., 1999, p. 58). Depending on what additional data reveal about John's responses to others' reactions to his verbal outbursts, peers may be taught to use scripted expressions (e.g., "John, it's okay; I didn't mean to upset you") or to walk away from John while saying, "Let's talk later," if an outburst continues. Adults may be encouraged to 1) briefly sympathize with John, then redirect him and expect him to get back to work, possibly providing help if necessary or 2) suggest to John that he may need to take a short break to compose himself before getting back to work (see Display 5.3).

It should be clear from this example that developing an effective behavioral support plan requires more than simply translating hypotheses about behaviors into intervention steps. These processes must be embedded within steps for addressing long-term change needs associated with a student's lifestyle and relationships, which were the topics of previous sections in this chapter. Moreover, as this example further illustrates, sometimes there is a need to address a student's emotional and behavioral crisis events when they occur. This is discussed in detail in the next section.

CRISIS SUPPORT: RESPONDING TO CHALLENGING BEHAVIORS

Educators, consultants, and other professionals often express understandable figure–ground difficulties when they grapple with problem behaviors exhibited by a student. That is, when developing ways to cope with the behaviors of a student, they are inclined to see the challenging behavior in the foreground and to place all else (e.g., environmental circumstances, the student's positive qualities, the times when there are no problems, the student's point of view) into a hazy background. Their interventions may be doomed to short-term success or even abject failure, because preoccupation with managing the problem behavior serves as a barrier to accurately perceiving how the student's behavior connects with history and context.

Much remains to be described and discussed about how to create positive behavioral support plans using the critical processes associated with person-centered planning, nurturing peer and adult relationships, and hypothesis-based intervention. Ensuing chapters, especially Chapters 9–11, explore in depth how interventions that are developed to reflect lifestyle issues, relationship needs, and specific behavioral hypotheses can prevent problem behavior. In fact, many behavioral problems can be reduced through the intentional use of procedures associated with these three components alone. Nonetheless, when the behaviors are dangerous or especially disruptive, explicit crisis management procedures must be included in the positive behavioral support plan (Janney & Meyer, 1990).

In the broadest sense, *crisis* is defined in this section as a behavioral episode that directly and significantly disrupts other students' learning, threatens or affects the safety and well-being of the student and others, and/or causes injury or property destruction. The student in crisis may seem to appear out of control or "out of it," and escalation from mildly disruptive to more extreme behavior is a common pattern. Crises defined in this way demand immediate action by educators so that the safety of all students and adults is ensured or reestablished and the teacher can expeditiously return to his or her instructional activities.

Note what is *not* being treated as a crisis by this definition: the child who is experiencing depression or more tumultuous emotions, sometimes connected to trauma, and lives with these feelings and fears without expressly making them known to others. Because such events do not visibly affect delivery of instruction, educators seldom categorize them as events that disrupt learning or endanger adults or students. Of course, when a teacher suspects that a student is experiencing an internal crisis, the

DISPLAY 5.3—BEING ON THE OTHER END

Some professionals may take exception to these recommendations for managing John's verbal outbursts. They may point out that these consequences are too mild to offer effective suppression and that they may reinforce the very behaviors that need to be modified. How is this criticism addressed from a support perspective?

Behavioral research indicates that student behavior communicates messages that, if listened to, can guide intervention planning. What has not been examined at the same level of depth or detail are the messages that adults send when implementing response cost consequences. On the surface, the message should be "Don't behave in this way." Yet, other messages are communicated, intended or otherwise, and these can affect future behavior. The student may end up with the following thoughts: "If this person cared for me, would he or she be doing this?" "I can't trust this person anymore," "I never get it right anyway in this person's view, so why try?" or "Doesn't this person understand how I am feeling and what I am experiencing?"

Incidences such as John's verbal outbursts require ensuring the safety of others, but they also represent opportunities for adults to communicate acceptance of the student, confidence in his or her eventual success, and availability to assist the individual. Moreover, the support paradigm posits that desired behavioral changes are best realized not through behavioral suppression but rather through the careful design of the long-term prevention, short-term prevention, and adaptive alternative aspects of the intervention.

Consider, for a minute, which consequence would be most helpful for you if you were having a bad day at work and got into a heated argument with a co-worker in which your behavior might be described as "ranting and raving":

1. *Having your point of view acknowledged and honored, then being encouraged to get back to what you were both doing before your outburst*
2. *Being told that you were being inappropriate, then being planfully ignored*

teacher should attempt to provide emotional and instructional supports for the student in the classroom and other school environments, to connect the student with counseling and related services within the school, and/or to assemble a team of individuals to explore additional support options both within the school and in the broader community. For this book's purposes, however, the upcoming discussion focuses on crises that have an immediate and deleterious impact on the student, others, and the environment. The discussion explores the crisis cycle first, then guidelines for using temporary removal if the student is in a general education classroom.

The Crisis Cycle

A useful way to understand the crisis experience and to forge strategies for effectively managing it is to analyze the sequence of behaviors and contextual circumstances associated with it for a particular student. Many serious behavioral outbursts—characterized by yelling and cursing, verbal abuse, assault, tantrums, and/or property destruction—have a distinguishable acceleration and deceleration process. Walker, Colvin, and Ramsey (1995) provided one of the earliest models of this crisis cycle. Their model of the crisis cycle, which focuses on "acting-out" behavior, has seven qualitatively different phases that also vary in severity: 1) calm, 2) triggers, 3) agitation, 4) acceleration, 5) peak, 6) de-escalation, and 7) recovery. The authors identified behavioral indicators for each phase and offered strategies for managing behavior during respective phases.

Kunc and Van der Klift (1995b) also offered a model of the crisis cycle, which they developed from a model that was created by the Crisis Prevention Institute. Kunc and Van der Klift's model seems especially appropriate when used within a support approach to crisis. Their model, shown in Table 5.1, has five stages: 1) anxiety, 2) trigger, 3) crisis, 4) recovery, and 5) resolution. As the table shows, patterns of behavior that are associated with the five stages begin with relatively mild disagreements and disruptions during the anxiety and trigger stages; progress to the serious and potentially dangerous patterns of the crisis proper; and finally move into the aftermath emotions of guilt and shame and the restoration of calm, which are associated with the recovery and resolution stages, respectively.

Table 5.1 also identifies responses that educators can use for a student who is at various points in the crisis cycle. The table shows responses that can be helpful during each stage, as well as those that would likely prove counterproductive. In general, an educator's best chance to restore order early in the crisis cycle and to prevent movement into later stages lies in the sincere use of productive responses during the anxiety and trigger stages of the cycle.

The importance of discovering and then using productive responses early in the crisis cycle to prevent escalation cannot be overstated. Crises often arise out of differences between what the student wants to do and what is immediately required by the teacher, the class routine, or the school's discipline code. When the person in authority is bent on compliance and fails to weigh in the repercussions of a power struggle with a student, then both the student and the adult are hurt in the long run. As noted by Colvin, Ainge, and Nelson (1997), an educator often can defuse behavior early in the cycle simply by presenting a series of mutually acceptable options from which the student can choose. For example, a student who is caught taking food on the bus despite a "no eating on the bus" rule could be given the option of quickly finishing his snack before he gets on the bus or having the bus driver hold the snack for him until

Table 5.1. The arousal cycle

Crisis development	Unproductive response	Productive response
Anxiety		
Noncompliance	Directive	Listening
Disruptive	Set limits	Curious
Any action that is out of the ordinary for that person	Establish consequences	Supportive
	Labeling	Partnering
		Healthy expectations
Trigger		
Questioning	Demand compliance	Self-efficacy
Refusal	Apply consequences	Self-reflection, answer
Emotional outburst	Threat/intimidation	Self-reflection, negotiate
		Listen/anchor (if necessary)
		Self-discipline
Crisis		
Intimidation/threat	Anger	Protective/protection
Violence	Move in	Move back/keep contact
	Retaliation/expulsion	Follow established plan
	Punishment	
Recovery		
Embarrassment	Placing blame	Listening and support
Guilt, shame	Retaliatory instruction	Normalize the crisis
		Sense of perspective
		Collaboration
Resolution		
Calm	Reminding of crisis	Analysis
	Avoidance	Problem solving
	Expectation of recurrence	

From Kunc, N., & Van der Klift, E. (1995b, March). *Learning to stand still: Supporting individuals with puzzling behavior* (p. 3). Paper presented at the Council for Exceptional Children Courage to Risk Seventh Annual State Conference, Colorado Springs, CO; adapted by permission.

he arrives at his destination. As another illustration, a student who enjoys reading and is absorbed in a story when the class activity changes, could be given options such as finding a good stopping point before she joins the group, finishing the story at another identified time, or taking the book home for the evening. In both of these cases, showing some latitude early in the crisis cycle could prevent more serious incidents that could only hurt all who are involved.

A useful procedure for assisting educational teams in developing appropriate and effective ways to react to a specific student at the different stages in the cycle is to first develop hypotheses for the behaviors at each point within the cycle, then brainstorm possible adult responses using the Kunc and Van der Klift suggestions (Table 5.1) as a guide. Table 5.2 is an example of a worksheet that can be used during these brainstorming sessions, which has been partially completed for a first-grade student named Carlos. As this table shows, Carlos's behavior at various points in the crisis cycle are described, Kunc and Van der Klift's "unproductive" and "productive" responses are presented, and a column for recording educator responses to Carlos's behavior is provided. (In Table 5.2, this column has been completed.)

Although educators may be predisposed to focus on the earlier stages of the crisis cycle because of the potential for prevention, it is also important to create adult responses to the later stages. Chapter 9 offers more details about *debriefing*, a strategy that can be used when calm has been restored (Sugai & Colvin, 1997). The purpose of debriefing is to provide a transition back to the routine events that were underway

Table 5.2. Worksheet for brainstorming crisis cycle responses

Crisis cycle component	Unproductive response	Productive response	Responses to Carlos
Anxiety			
Noncompliance Putting head down Disengaging Moving faster Looking around Touching others Gibberish Crawling or running around	Directive Set limits Establish consequences	Listening Supportive Partnering Healthy expectations	*Try to maintain:* Encourage Carlos to remain in the classroom, using the provided choice negotiation script. Yet, honor any of Carlos's requests to take a break or work somewhere else (no power struggles). The classroom teacher could ask him to do a job or run an errand.
Trigger			
Physical resistance Running around	Demand compliance Apply consequences Threat/intimidation	Self-reflection, answer Self-reflection, negotiate Listen/anchor (if necessary) Self-discipline	*Change of setting:* If Carlos is still in the classroom, quickly guide him out of the room. Verbally encourage his moving into either a setting where he takes breaks or an approved alternate learning setting.
Crisis			
Accelerated physical resistance and running around Rage	Anger Move in Retaliation/expulsion Punishment	Protective/protection Move back/keep contact Follow established plan	*Protective removal:* If Carlos is still in the classroom, calmly move him to the hallway, then to Room #45. Use two people for the move if possible, but only one person should stay with him in Room #45. Movement should involve a combination of comforting, leading, and using protective physical holds, as needed. Monitoring should occur outside of the door because Carlos prefers to be alone, but he should not be allowed to hurt himself. Get assistance from other adults as needed, using the approved list.
Recovery			
Game playing Getting a blanket Shedding tears Asking for hugs	Placing blame Retaliatory instruction	Listening and support Normalize the crisis Sense of perspective Collaboration	*Return to calm and normalcy:* When Carlos is calm or he signals an adult to enter Room #45, the adult can go in and provide emotional support. Make eye contact, listen, and answer his comments, stressing collaboration. Also discuss the fun things that are going on in class to which he can soon return. Change the setting when Carlos is fully calm and after he indicates his readiness to leave.
Resolution			
Tears and hugs usually signal authentic recovery Cycle repeats itself if control issues are still present	Reminding of crisis Avoidance Expectation of recurrence	Analysis Problem solving	*Return without stigma:* Try to get Carlos back with his classmates, but honor his choice if he chooses another setting. The classroom teacher and students should welcome Carlos back to class, and they can say things such as, "Are you all right now?"

From Kunc, N., & Van der Klift, E. (1995b, March). *Learning to stand still: Supporting individuals with puzzling behavior* (p. 3). Paper presented at the Council for Exceptional Children Courage to Risk Seventh Annual State Conference, Colorado Springs, CO; adapted by permission.

before the crisis. During a typical 3- to 5-minute debriefing session, the teacher may give reminders to the student regarding what he or she can do in the future when the same triggers occur. Of course, a student may sometimes need help in identifying the conditions that tend to occasion the challenging behavior.

Jackson and Leon (1998a) stressed that a student's return to the classroom after a crisis event may prompt feelings of shame, fear, and/or despair. They suggested that a positive behavioral support plan should include steps that can be taken for the student to return to good standing with peers and adults. It may include apologies or simple restitution (e.g., helping the teacher pick up thrown objects), but it is the act of being welcomed back by classmates and educators that truly helps alleviate emotions that could carry over into other situations and set off similar chains of events. Anthropological perspectives on human interaction when power, threats, and social acceptance are major emotions (Brown & Levinson, 1978) point to "saving face" as an important psychological mechanism operating here. Acts of restitution, reacceptance, and being given another chance are powerful ways for all members of the class to "save face," thereby potentially decreasing the long-term probability of crisis.

Guidelines When Using Removal

It cannot be stressed enough that a viable support effort largely rests in how behavioral hypotheses are used in planning, how existing interpersonal relationships are nurtured and new relationships made possible, and how person-centered planning processes are reflected in the final plan. Moreover, for some students, analysis of the crisis cycle and generating responses to the student's behavior at early points in the cycle can make intense problems less likely to occur. Nevertheless, despite an educator's best efforts, there will be times when efforts to reestablish order falter and there is a need to remove a student from the classroom for safety reasons and/or to permit the normal resumption of instruction.

The following six guidelines come from the authors' work in schools. They address procedures and precautions for the temporary removal of a student from a general education classroom when the student needs supports that go beyond the school's discipline policies, the removal steps are part of a written positive behavioral support plan, and removal occurs during a disruption (not in anticipation of one). These guidelines should be considered only if a teacher or educational team is working with one or more students for whom some form of removal is highly probable because of the severity of their behavioral problems. Keep in mind that each student with serious behavioral issues must be treated as an individual. As shown in ensuing chapters, solutions to behavioral concerns are best generated by a team of people who are committed to keeping the student in the school and in his or her classes and who are well informed about the student's daily routines, participation patterns, and needs.

First, the criteria for removal should be set in advance through a consensus among the general education teacher, special education support professionals, and, often, the student, family members, and a building administrator. A decision that a student must leave or be removed at a particular moment in time should be made and communicated by the classroom teacher and not by support personnel, as this affects the student's perception of who is in charge of the classroom and who is really concerned about the outbursts.

Second, although the decision for removal is in the classroom teacher's hands, the person who actually removes the child during a particular incident depends on the severity of the behavior, interpersonal relationship considerations, and on who has been trained to use specialized removal procedures. For less serious disruptions, one school reversed the roles of the special and general educators when disruptions occurred with students who had IEPs: The general educator took the offending student into the hall to "process" while the special educator briefly took over instruction in the class. For more serious crises, it may be helpful if someone other than the classroom teacher removes the student. School crisis teams sometimes include teachers whose classrooms are near the classroom in which a student who is prone to crisis receives instruction. Other possibilities are having a hall monitor positioned nearby during certain times of the day or having a special education support person assume responsibility for the removal.

Third, removal processes should be for a short duration, especially when the student's behavior is disruptive but does not result in damage or injury. In addition, the return to the classroom should be based on the student's readiness to resume his or her place, not a fixed time interval. Unfortunately, when students with IEPs in general education classes act out, they too often spend the remainder of the class period, or even the entire day, in the special education room or another room in the building. The latter actions are often problematic and can even increase future incidents of crisis in some situations.

Fourth, whenever possible, the removal should be to a place that reminds the student that he or she is expected to return to the classroom. Removal that extends no further than the hallway is often best, but other possibilities include a nearby empty classroom or an office in the building. Taking the student to an in-use special education class or resource room usually is not an acceptable option. Not only is this often counterproductive, it is also unfair to and sometimes endangers a group of students who are potentially vulnerable. In addition, both the use of exclusionary time-out within specially designed time-out rooms and the common practice of sending the student home are not usually good ideas. In the former case, the negative side effects may outweigh the possible benefits of problem behavior reduction. In the latter case, although there are exceptions, the underlying message of "washing our hands of this student" is far too clear to the student, to other students, and to other educators to make such an action beneficial.

Fifth, although protective restraint processes are sometimes required to prevent injury, they should be used sparingly and only as a measure to ensure the safety of the student and others. Restraint can adversely affect the relationship between two people by lessening the value and regard of the person doing the restraining in the eyes of the person being restrained and vice versa. Rather, when initially developing the support plan, the team should carefully consider and adopt any alternative removal strategies that might serve in place of physical restraint (e.g., a person known to be effective gently guides the student out of the classroom). Moreover, release from restraint should always be based on a judgment of student readiness and never on a time interval requirement.

Sixth and finally, the issue of whether to apply consequences when the student's behavior is perceived as disruptive or dangerous is a sticky one. Often, this matter needs to be approached on a case-by-case and school-by-school basis. Part of the dilemma rests with whether a time of crisis is really a time of learning (see Chapter 4), and part of the dilemma derives from the feelings and needs of the people who are experiencing the effects of the crisis. In terms of learning, a consequence might be helpful if it serves as a "wake-up call" rather than as a punisher. In terms of honoring the feelings and needs of others, educators may consider applying the natural outcomes that the school would impose on any other student, sometimes in an abbreviated form, when others have been hurt or there is damage to property. Of course, in some cases (e.g., drug use, serious assault), the consequences are inevitable and lie outside the jurisdiction of the educator (see Chapter 4).

In any case, decisions about consequences often require a negotiation process in which building administrators, classroom teachers, special education support personnel, and often the student and his or her family are involved. Although certain realities must be accepted, the goal should be to ensure that when consequences are used, they will not in and of themselves negatively affect the long-term goal of helping the student become a participating and contributing member of the school and the broader community. Most certainly, consequences should never be routinely written into behavior plans as if they were invariably necessary for learning to occur.

The preceding point is especially important. Too often, when teachers are new to a situation or a group of students and behavioral problems become evident, their thoughts turn to consequences (e.g., time-out, response cost). The authors have seen this situation spin out of control in too many occasions because the teacher's first response was to consequate rather than create prevention steps by using the message contained in the child's behavior. This may be in part a natural tendency to react protectively when confronted with things that are disruptive, disconcerting, or dangerous. Yet, part of the responsibility for this pattern rests with those in universities and in positions of responsibility in schools (e.g., building administrators) who have, in the past, encouraged teachers to focus more on control than on understanding when faced with such situations.

SYNCHRONIZING THE FOUR BEHAVIORAL SUPPORT PROCESSES

The educative approach, which was discussed in Chapter 4, emphasizes that interventions should focus on "meaningful outcomes," incorporate information about the functions that behaviors serve; and promote "maintenance and generalization" (Vittimberga et al., 1999, p. 52). Chapter 5 has defined, reviewed, and described processes that can be considered the actual substance or essential ingredients of such an approach to behavior challenges. This chapter suggests that to fulfill the requirements of an educative approach to challenging behavior, an intervention must reflect a synthesis of processes that are designed to promote a fulfilling and contributing lifestyle, with processes that are designed to address the behavioral concerns. The former processes are largely derived from person-centered planning and relationship development; the latter processes are drawn from relationship development and the design of hypotheses about the behaviors. Depending on the severity of the behaviors in question, these processes may need to be augmented with individually tailored supports for crisis, with *crisis* being defined as a situation in which the challenging behavior significantly interferes with the safety and instructional activities provided to the student and/or others.

Figure 5.1 is a conceptualization of the relationship among the four processes that have been detailed in this chapter. This figure suggests that person-centered planning (including vision development), hypothesis-based intervention, and relationship development are processes of the larger, more pervasive outer circle, and crisis support represents a smaller but critical center of the positive behavioral support effort. As suggested by the arrows in Figure 5.1, the three support processes repre-

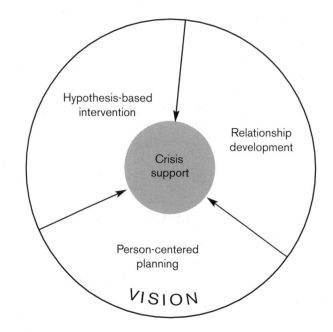

Figure 5.1.   The four critical support processes.

sented in the outer circle affect a student's crisis support needs, and these processes must be designed and implemented as a first step in defining the student's true crisis support needs. Put differently, without the development and synchronization of person-centered planning, hypothesis-based intervention procedures, and relationship development, formulating crisis support steps—no matter how well they are designed—largely becomes an exercise in futility.

This chapter shows that positive behavioral support stresses the use of natural school communities as the stage for conducting interventions and that activities that occur within more restrictive placements should be directed toward reintegration. What may be evident to the reader by this point in the book is that the described processes are not being widely used in many public schools today. In Chapter 6, the issues of change and change processes are examined because the widespread adoption of the positive behavioral support model ultimately depends on an appreciation of the dynamics involved in facilitating change in schools.

Chapter 6

Facilitating Change to
Enhance Behavioral Support
for Students and the Community

with Ginny Helwick

*"If we want to change the world, we must
begin by changing ourselves; if we
change ourselves, we will indeed change the world."*
—Burton Blatt

Chapter 1 discussed how many general educators first use removal when dealing with problem behaviors, as well as how this process is complemented by the clinical intervention practices of special educators. Chapter 1 and other chapters in Section I also examined the origins of these patterns, considered why these processes are ultimately self-defeating in terms of public education's mission, and explored new and emerging approaches for addressing discipline issues that do not rely on removal. Previous chapters in Section II have delineated some of the major properties of behavioral support. The task of this chapter is to consider the larger issue of change and how change processes can benefit the implementation of the behavioral support paradigm at the individual, classroom, school, or broader systems level. The discussion opens with a reconsideration of the issues that general education teachers face in classrooms in which disruptive or dangerous incidences occur.

As discussed in Chapter 1, when confronted with challenging behaviors, classroom teachers are often motivated to act by their need to reduce uncertainty in their classrooms (Kennedy, 1997). In other words, educators attempt to reestablish stability within their school or classroom, a state in which things "remain more or less unchanged in the face of various disturbances acting upon it" (Casti, 1990, p. 61).

For many educators, the goal of achieving stability translates for them into a return to the state of affairs in the class or school that existed before there was a problem. Yet, what these educators may be failing to consider is that a return to this state of affairs may not resolve their problems. It was from this state of affairs that their problems first emerged; hence, efforts to return conditions to this state could prove to be both counterproductive and discouraging. Perhaps what should be sought when trying to resolve problems—such as recurring behavioral problems—is not a return to the way things were but, rather, the creation of a different set of conditions in which the origins of the problems and alternative ways to address them become evident.

From this point of view, the overall outcome shifts from returning to a previous state of affairs to generating a new state of affairs that redefines what the educators are doing and even who they are. This thinking parallels ideas that are being proposed within the new sciences of chaos and complexity (Crutchfield, Farmer, Packard, & Shaw, 1986), in which the actions of living systems are viewed as being most adaptive not when they are seeking equilibrium but, rather, when they are sensitive to the natural and invariable dynamics of changing environments (Beardsley, 1992). This way of thinking stresses that people are most successful when they are on "the edge of chaos" (Kauffman, 1991), poised for the next set of events and experiences that will challenge them and promote change in them and in others.

To return for a moment to a central thesis of this book, public education's purposes are most adequately realized when schools find ways to educate all students together, using instructional and disciplinary practices that capitalize on, rather than constrict, the natural diversity that exists among students. This implies that systems change, developing teacher and student capacity in schools, and the reintegration of removed students must guide the efforts of those who work with children and youth who exhibit persistent behavioral concerns. Given that flux—not stability—is the more pervasive parameter of adaptive systems, then educators must turn to the processes and tools of *change* when addressing challenging behaviors if schools are to approach the degree of inclusivity that is advocated in this book.

This chapter discusses some important features of change and how institutions and people are affected by change. The chapter offers some basic premises that serve as foundations for how change processes can be conceptualized, understood, and used in positive behavioral support. The discussion of these premises culminates with the presentation of a process called *guided inquiry*, which is a major theme for subsequent discussions of planning and assessment for positive behavioral support. This chapter is critical at this juncture because, although more theoretical than other chapters in the book, it provides direction for later chapters. In addition, the direction that it provides departs in important ways from many of the planning and intervention procedures that are routinely used by educators at the beginning of the 21st century.

UNDERLYING PREMISES FOR WORKING WITH CHANGE

Three underlying premises guide how educators work with change: 1) viewing systems as complex, dynamic entities; 2) overcoming barriers to understanding; and 3) recognizing positive behavioral support as innovation. Because of their descriptive power, metaphors from chaos theory are used in the ensuing discussions of these three underlying premises. Yet, it should be recognized that their usage in this book differs from that associated with chaos theory proper, which is largely concerned with mathematically representing the underlying order of phenomena that do not appear to be governed by known laws or principles (Krippner, 1994).

Viewing Systems as Complex, Dynamic Entities

Bronfenbrenner's (1979) eloquent theory applies systems logic to growth and human behavior and characterizes human development from an ecological perspective. As noted in Chapters 2 and 5, Bronfenbrenner proposed that people and social environments represent evolving, interdependent systems; thus, monitoring, understanding, and promoting change requires attending to the complexity of relationships among and between the activity, interpersonal, and intrapersonal variables that constitute these systems. Put differently, phenomena such as subcultures, neighborhoods, households, schools, classrooms, and the individuals themselves are *complex, dynamic systems*; hence, facilitating change requires knowledge of the parameters of such systems and how these operate in real time.

A system, such as a school, is described as being complex because of the magnitude of variables that determine how it operates. Dörner defined *complexity* as a property of any system in which there are "many interdependent variables" that are continuously defining the state of the system from moment to moment across time (1996, p. 38). Dörner also noted that, in relation to problem solving and decision making, "complexity is not an objective factor but a subjective one" (p. 39). That is, an educator can grasp and, in effect, simplify the complexities of a system by understanding the variables operating within it and how they interact with each other, and this understanding comes from active experiences via immersion within the system. One of the ways that an educator can simplify the complexity of a system is through creating, from experience, "supersignals," which effectively collapse "a number of features [of a complex situation] into one" (Dörner, 1996, p. 39). In other words, supersignals reflect the experience- and intuition-driven integration of many different signals into a unitary signal, which can then be used to guide problem solving or decision making (see Display 6.1).

Dynamic is used to describe a system that expresses three properties (Dörner, 1996). First, the system is subject to continuous change across time. Second, the ongoing occurrence of this change is not dependent on the actions of those trying to guide it, but these individuals can influence the course of change. Third, the variables that control change can have intricate, nonlinear relationships with each other. These three properties operate at different levels in the system (e.g., classroom, building), and changes at different levels are sometimes correlated with, and at other times independent of, events at other levels. The pace of change can also vary at different levels, accelerating and decelerating across time in complicated ways.

Within complex, dynamic systems, there are two forms of change (Ruelle, 1994). First, some changes have a recurrent quality. Examples of changes that are recurrent include

- Regular changes throughout the year regarding the amount of time that a teacher spends reviewing class rules, correlated with increasing student awareness of these rules
- Routine changes in a teacher's discipline style, correlated with whether the teacher is in the classroom or serving as a playground or hallway monitor
- Anticipated changes in a student body's activity level, correlated with time of the school year and proximity to holidays
- Expected deterioration of a specific student's behavior, correlated with whether he or she spent the weekend with his or her father or mother

Second, some changes have a chaotic quality. Examples of changes that are chaotic include

- A major revision in a school's discipline policy, precipitated by the arrival of a new principal in a school
- A major change in a teacher's discipline style, precipitated by his or her discovery of a new system for managing the classroom
- Events associated with a period of emotional and physical upheaval, precipitated by the injury of several students by a disgruntled former student
- Events associated with a student whose home life is in crisis, precipitated by the marital breakup of his or her parents

Within complex, dynamic systems, what differentiates recurrent from chaotic change is the degree to which the events that are going through change are *sensitive to initial conditions*. Recurrent changes reflect less sensitivity to initial conditions: They follow a predictable course over time, and they tend to rise and fall in expected ways regardless of day-to-day perturbations in environmental, interpersonal, and intrapersonal conditions. Because they are predictable, experienced educators can use fore-

DISPLAY 6.1—PREDICTING TANTRUMS

Larry, a fourth-grade student, sometimes has major tantrums, in which he yells, hits, kicks, bites, and throws himself on the floor. During the morning hours, when a particular paraeducator is present, tantrums are rare. They are also rare on the playground. However, Larry is much more likely to have a tantrum during the following times:

- During social studies class
- When he is not given adequate cues about what his teacher expects of him
- When he is egged on by other students
- When his teacher tells him to behave
- When his teacher asks him to leave the classroom until he can calm down and get back to work
- When he is physically removed from the room by the special educator

These various precipitating circumstances are complexly related to each other and to the likelihood of tantrums. Certain combinations of these circumstances often occur together, and such patterns of co-occurrence make tantrums more likely and easier to predict.

How might Larry's special and general education teachers develop "supersignals" to predict Larry's tantrums?

What role does ongoing experience with a student play in the teacher's ability to develop these signals?

sight to anticipate them and hindsight to confirm them, and new learning is generally not required because the change patterns have established habits associated with them. Conversely, chaotic changes reflect more sensitivity to initial conditions: They do not follow an anticipated path precisely because they are occasioned by environmental, interpersonal, or intrapersonal disturbances that were unexpected and possibly dramatic. Because they are unpredictable, experienced educators can use hindsight to understand them, but they cannot use foresight to fully predict them. Moreover, new learning will be required of people within the system if the changed conditions are sustained over time.

Although the inevitability of chaotic change may seem disturbing, it is important to recognize that it is precisely the chaotic aspect of complex, dynamic systems that permits individuals and teams to make a difference in large, seemingly immovable systems. Citing the work of Crutchfield and colleagues (1986), Krippner noted that it is the "amplification of small fluctuations" that provide "natural systems access to novelty" (1994, pp. 52–53). In more practical terms, reminiscent of the work of Hord, Rutherford, Huling-Austin, and Hall (1987), the possibility for chaotic change ensures that anyone holding any position can effect change across levels within an organization. When educators institute and follow through, even with small changes, there is the potential to promote larger innovations because what is accomplished reverberates through a system. Crutchfield and colleagues (1986) provided a useful metaphor for the notion that small events can influence large systems: Place a drop of blue food coloring in a mound of bread dough, then knead it. The coloring will gradually spread so that what was once tan becomes a bluish color throughout.

Implications   Whether implementing a change plan for moving a school team from a remedial to a support orientation in its services or implementing a behavioral support plan for a student who is in conflict with most adults in a building, the fact that educators are working in complex, dynamic systems has important implications for initial and ongoing decision making. The three implications discussed in the following paragraphs are primarily based on two properties of complex, dynamic systems: 1) the essential instability of the flow of events within such systems and 2) the inability for a single person to have ready access to all of the information that is necessary for optimizing his or her decisions. Note that these properties are inherent to complex, dynamic systems; that is, they cannot be "corrected" no matter how rational, comprehensive, proactive, and/or diligent decision makers might be.

The first implication is that, although facilitating a change process sometimes requires a sequential step-by-step plan at start-up, the actual change process "unfolds" rather than follows a predictable course. There are simply too many unforeseen ways that variables can interact, and although some of these interactions will be of little consequence to the change process, others may veer the process off course. This realization gives new meaning to Fullan's notion that "change is a journey, not a blueprint" (1993, p. 21). As change facilitation affects the observable events and their underlying patterns of interaction, decision makers must be prepared to constantly rewrite and rethink the prescriptions of their plans.

This implication is supported by findings in studies of good and poor decision makers who tried to make improvements within computer simulations of complex, dynamic social and economic systems (Dörner, 1996). Poor decision making was associated with a pattern in which inquiry and reflection occurred initially in plan development but then fell off across time, even as the rate of decision making necessarily increased in response to unanticipated changes in conditions. As noted by Dörner, these participants "thought, mistakenly, that they already had the knowledge they needed to cope" with emerging problems (p. 17).

This way of thinking also calls for a reevaluation of how *success* is defined in complex change processes. There are no successful or unsuccessful plans, and one should not be preoccupied with whether a "terminal goal" will be achieved in the end. Rather, there are successfully and unsuccessfully implemented change processes, and one must be concerned with the degree to which the resulting outcomes—some originally defined by the plan and some surprises—are acceptable to all parties at different points in time. Likewise, in terms of assessing the integrity of the intervention, the much touted concept "consistency of implementation" carries less weight when what is done inevitably (and often for the best) changes as the plan unfolds. Instead, integrity of implementation is most usefully characterized by indices of flexibility and persistence in the evaluation of intervention activities (Jackson & Leon, 1998a).

The second implication is that it can sometimes be counterproductive to create behavioral support plans that prescribe small, fixed sets of logic- or theory-driven rules that link specific behaviors to precise adult responses or consequences (e.g., "When Johnny does [behavior], the adult always does [response]," "Always reinforce [desired behavior] while consistently ignoring [problem behavior]," "When any student becomes unruly on the playground, the adult does [response]"). In complex, dynamic systems, although the desired end results are always kept in mind, it may often be best to allow for a more *heuristic decision making process* (Gigerenzer & Todd, 1999), in which one or more of several options may be employed depending on both the immediate circumstances surrounding an incident and the objectives that define the purpose of the plan (see Display 6.2). For example, running in a commons area may reflect a number of interacting considerations that go beyond the student's physical action, such as whether he is racing another student, is delivering an emergency message, is excited about an "A" on an exam, has just been corrected by the same teacher for the same behavior, or is imitating the behavior of a higher status friend who did the same thing moments before. The goals of preventing injury and discouraging future running may be more productively realized in the future if teachers 1) have the flexibility to openly use immediate considerations when they decide how to respond and 2) are permitted to respond in one or more of a number of approved ways, instead of being required to deliver fixed consequences that are preestablished by a schoolwide committee. Likewise, if a teacher is not successful in handling a specific problem, he or she can use heuristic decision making to create improved ways for achieving an intended result—ways that may not emerge if creativity is obstructed by an inflexible discipline code.

As these examples suggest, not only does heuristic decision making more adequately match the realities of complex, dynamic systems, it is also beneficial because it reduces the ineffective and sometimes counterproductive rigidity that can accompany the unexamined use of simplistic, "either/or" rule-based systems; promotes positive growth and change in the adults; and models decision-making processes that the students themselves will also face in life, when difficult choices must be made under circumstances for which the consequences for various options are mixed, ill defined, and/or variable.

The third implication is that the unpredictable aspects of the change process, whether beneficial or problematic, are most easily monitored and managed when behavioral support plan development and implementation occur through a collaborative process in which all stakeholders are represented and most or all of the planning

DISPLAY 6.2—HEURISTIC DECISION MAKING

Gerald, a middle school student who was nonverbal, was subjected for years to various forms of restraint and time-out. By eighth grade, his rage and aggressive behavior had reached a point that he was maintained in a special education classroom by himself throughout the school day with a single teacher, who kept him busy with various age-inappropriate tasks. When a new teacher started working with Gerald, she began a process in which agitation, a reliable precursor to rage and aggression, was honored as a communication. The teacher used a symbol-based approach to ask Gerald about his needs and how they could be met whenever he became agitated. The new teacher also began introducing more age-appropriate activities for Gerald, including events outside of the special education classroom. This gave her more options to use when Gerald became agitated. In an especially notable success, Gerald began taking a general education social studies class. Yet, it was agreed that serious agitation would result in Gerald's leaving the room for a fixed period of time.

One day, when Gerald became especially agitated and began pounding on his desk, the general educator summoned the special educator. The general educator believed that Gerald needed to be removed from the class. Yet, when the special educator approached his desk, Gerald suddenly looked at her with an imploring look that seemed to mean, "I am okay now. Can I please stay if I pull myself together?" The general educator and the special educator agreed to keep Gerald in the classroom and to see how he would do during the rest of class. Much to their satisfaction, he was able to make it through the entire class without further incident.

Some people would argue that a strict rule of removal should have been used to communicate the importance of consistency and accepting responsibility for one's actions and to avoid teaching Gerald to manipulate adults. Other people would argue that the decision made by these two teachers, which was based on momentary circumstances and teacher intuitions about what was best in the long run, communicated trust, respect, willingness to listen, and flexibility in decision making. What do you think?

and implementation participants are experienced members of the system to be changed. This implication assumes major importance when it is recognized that the initial and ongoing decisions that must be made by the participants are not highly prescribed formulas but, rather, are heuristic decisions. Heuristic decision making requires that all stakeholders not only fully understand and commit to the goals and general guidelines of a plan but also have past and ongoing experience with the contexts and situations in which the plan must have an effect. This is because heuristic decision making often occurs in the heat of school and classroom life, and such decisions are often embedded within other instructional decisions and ongoing actions that constitute the craft of teaching. These decisions require the competent use of supersignals (Dörner, 1996). Educators rely on condensed factual and intuitive knowledge of a pattern and its variations to interpret what is occurring at a given moment, then make an action decision configured to the unique properties of the situation and the long-term learning and discipline objectives. This, of course, means that expertise must be (or become) more of a property possessed by people within a system and less of a commodity purchased from the outside.

Overcoming Barriers to Understanding

Consider the following all-too-familiar situation described by Jones and Nisbett:

> When a student who is doing poorly in school discusses his problem with a faculty advisor, there is often a fundamental difference of opinion between the two. The student, in attempting to understand and explain his inadequate performance, is usually able to point to environmental obstacles such as a particularly onerous course load, to temporary emotional stress such as worry about his draft status, or to transitory confusion about life goals that is now resolved. The faculty advisor may nod and may wish to believe, but in his heart of hearts he usually disagrees. The advisor is convinced that the poor performance is due neither to the student's environment nor to transient emotional states. He believes instead that the failure is due to enduring qualities of the student—to lack of ability, to irremediable laziness, to neurotic ineptitude. (1979, p. 82)

This example illustrates a major tenet of attribution theory: *"There is a pervasive tendency for actors to attribute their actions to situational requirements, whereas observers tend to attribute the same actions to stable personal dispositions"* (Jones & Nisbett, 1979, p. 83, emphasis in original).

Perhaps the first thing that comes to mind when one reads this passage is the implication of this tenet for the actor, the student with a ready answer whenever asked why he or she continues to behave in certain ways. Yet, because the balance of power invariably favors the educational system, the importance of attribution theory for the observer is of greater concern. This passage is an apt description of the troubling way that many educators misassign causation when a student's behavior places him or her in conflict with the norms or routines of the educational setting. Educators often perceive a student to be predisposed to behave in particular ways, regardless of correlated and potentially relevant short- and long-term environmental circumstances. By acting on the initial assumption that the student bears the brunt of responsibility for an ongoing behavioral problem, educators often fail to consider the contributions of possibly amendable ecological circumstances, medication reactions, peer relationships, family situations, interpersonal communication breakdowns, poor instructional procedures, ill-considered removal and segregated placement decisions, and inflexible and poorly thought-out discipline policies and procedures. In effect, change facilitation decisions that are based on incomplete and misleading perceptions of the origins, causes, and best solutions for problems are regularly made, and these decisions broadly and significantly affect the lives of children and youth with behavioral challenges and their families. Along with missed opportunities for creating educational plans that would actually benefit students and their schools, misplaced causation sometimes has a larger, more far-reaching consequence: Students may feel blamed for circumstances that were neither of their creation nor under their control, which will assuredly exacerbate the behavioral problem and the student's future interactions with the school and society at large.

Of course, any analyses of the circumstances and motivations that seem to contribute to a particular situation or conflict are subject to human error. Dörner (1996) used the term *intransparence* to denote that, in complex systems, decision makers cannot know about certain critical links when they first make decisions, which injects an unavoidable "element of uncertainty into planning and decision making" (p. 40). Yet, what is being emphasized here is not human error but the relegation of blame by those with power and influence onto those without power and influence.

Misrepresentation of causation can be a major barrier to the development of the kinds of understandings of behavior that promote effective interventions. Yet, underlying misrepresented causation is another, deeper barrier to understanding, and this barrier is entrenched within the way that schools conceptualize and implement discipline policy. Grasping this concern requires an in-depth examination of the way that schoolwide discipline codes are frequently implemented and how removal and principles of individualization are then applied when behavioral diversity poses problems for such codes.

As discussed in Chapter 1, schools often employ some form of schoolwide discipline code—complete with simple, prescriptive consequences for code violations—as a primary means for encouraging order. A set of expectations for students is certainly an important component of a school's policies. Nevertheless, the following two extreme cases reveal shortcomings in how such either/or discipline codes actually work.

At one extreme, a schoolwide discipline code may be variably enforced, depending on whether educators' personal discipline codes routinely supersede the school's code; whether adults are predisposed to be authoritarian, authoritative, or permissive in style; a transgressing student's specific friendship status with an adult; the student's social status in school; and/or whether a student has been labeled as having a behavioral problem. When discipline enforcement is largely arbitrary, the message sent to the more capable students is that principles of conduct can never rise above the potential for their corruption and that personal autonomy is mainly a matter of knowing how to manipulate others so that there are no binding distinctions between being in or out of compliance with a particular rule. Students who have the disadvantages of labels, low social status, or even a lack of knowledge about "the game" may derive from their discipline experiences a sense of learned helplessness, which then contributes to viewing themselves as outsiders who cannot benefit from school.

At the other extreme, schools may insist that all adults adhere to the discipline code without regard to teachers' philosophies, styles, or specific circumstances. In the latter case, the pressure on educators to enforce discipline codes can mean that prescribed consequences can take precedence over accommodating a disciplinary action to extenuating circumstances, even when prudence suggests that the consequences will do more harm than good for both the student and his or her community. Implementing a discipline code at this extreme level places teachers into enforcer rather than educator roles which, in turn, negatively affects how the students feel about themselves, their teachers, and the learning process. Moreover, strictly enforced, adult-driven discipline codes can effectively disempower students as they enter adult society, contributing to their belief that they are subservient to rather than co-contributors in the formation and enforcement of law within democratic institutions.

Experiences in schools suggest that students must often adapt to enforcement processes (sometimes products of politically inspired discipline campaigns) that vacillate between these two extremes at different scales and at different levels within the building. For students who are inclined to behave well, this inherent uncertainty can create consternation, and it can reduce their respect for the school and its codes of conduct. Yet, these students are also likely to adjust to the complexities that such systems impose either by selectively violating school rules or a lack of inclination to deviate from the rules. For students with behavioral issues, the uncertain and arbitrary nature of these enforcement patterns may challenge their already tenuous views of schools as caring and equitable institutions. Moreover, such code applications do not assist these students in developing personal discipline codes that could help them succeed in a democratic society. Although some professionals may view these troubling patterns as potentially remediable products of poor staff training or uneven policy enforcement, these patterns may be more a function of the nature of either/or rule systems themselves when applied within complex, dynamic systems.

As discussed in Chapters 1 and 2, the Education for All Handicapped Children Act of 1975 (PL 94-142), the Individuals with Disabilities Education Act (IDEA) Amendments of 1997 (PL 105-17), and similar laws require a public education for students who express diversity in behavior and learning. Increases in behavioral diversity within a school can bring into sharp relief the shortcomings of a school's discipline codes. Theoretically, this should help schools better understand the inadequacies of their policies even as it provides them with insights into how to improve their systems to better serve all students. As noted in Chapter 1, however, when faced with student diversity, schools are inclined to rely on removal and/or processes of individualization that are less defined by student needs and more by system needs. For example, a student with an IEP who violates one or more school rules may be placed on a behavior contract in lieu of full enforcement of the discipline code. Such contracts are often constructed to simply reiterate the compliance requirements of the school, with little consideration for the voice of the student or for the complexity of issues that surround the behavioral problem. Moreover, it is not uncommon for a contract to be imposed *after* partial or full removal from general education, with the idea being that the student must now earn his or her way back into general education.

Although some professionals may view these practices as regrettable but not unsolvable, such practices may be explicitly and implicitly encouraged in schools precisely because they help preserve traditional discipline codes and powers of removal even in the face of laws, such as IDEA '97, that potentially threaten these powers. In other words, by developing policies that mirror the larger body of discipline policies but are separate and distinct from them, schools can avoid making the kinds of changes that might be necessary to meaningfully implement the individualization obligations of the law, the LRE requirements of the law, and discipline policies that are better suited for serving all students.

In all fairness, it must be said that principals or teachers who intentionally and systematically try to rid their schools and classrooms of any and all students who represent diversity are probably few and far between. Nevertheless, the practices that are described here are widespread, because they are so deeply entrenched in the culture of schools and their application simply seems right and justified by the circumstances that a principal or teacher faces when he or she is making a specific discipline decision. Yet, the unexamined use of either/or discipline codes, coupled with practices that treat students with behavioral problems as exceptions, are significant barriers to developing a deeper understanding of the nature and causes of behavior—an understanding that could promote more effective ways for dealing with such problems in all children.

Implications   This discussion of barriers to understanding has indicated that the development of understanding is impeded by educators' tendency to assign causation to the students, with less than adequate consideration of other factors. It has also been noted that another barrier is the unexamined use of either/or discipline codes, which foster decisions that can unacceptably vacillate between strictly adhering to rules and relaxing rules on the basis of spurious and irrelevant factors. Prescriptive codes tend to encourage decision making that—although designed to be fair as a result of its "blindness" to the person of the transgressor—can be counterproductive in effect because of the way that various other human factors come into play within complex, dynamic systems.

Dörner (1996) asserted that it is imperative to create and update a "reality model" that characterizes the many parts of situations in which change is required. An adequate reality model improves the chance that decision making will be effective because it permits configuring decisions to the unique conditions presented by sets of problems or circumstances. Thus, critical to the long-term survival of any behavioral support effort is using continuous assessment and reflection to construct an evolving understanding of the challenges and possibilities posed by specific students with behavioral challenges—or posed by the discipline structures of a classroom or building.

It was suggested previously in this chapter that schools should adopt heuristic decision making for all students because it is especially adaptive for use in complex, dynamic systems. Heuristic decision making also helps overcome barriers to understanding because of its emphasis on gathering information as a prerequisite to action. Heuristic decision making gives educators some latitude in how they approach discipline and behavioral support situations, but it also requires thoughtful, concurrent consideration of the nature and consequences of the infringement, the student's knowledge of the educational environment and its rules, immediate or extenuating circumstances that are related to the observed behaviors, and the implications that different decisions have for the student's future success.

The basic principle-centered values of positive behavioral support (see Chapter 4) must, of course, provide boundaries for heuristic decision making, and these values place clear restrictions on the indiscriminate use of removal. Equally important, however, is that such decision making requires adults to handle discipline situations by gathering information about the behavior and the situation before or when taking action, in accordance with the severity of the problem. Minor transgressions, such as a loud argument, may require something as simple as briefly asking the students about their problem; more severe transgressions, such as persistent fighting with peers, usually require careful and deliberative information-gathering strategies before taking action. In all cases, heuristic decision-making activities can foster a fair and equitable understanding that precedes or accompanies action.

A key word in the preceding discussion is *understanding*, which is a much broader concept than *knowing the facts*, *being familiar with the student*, or *identifying the applicable discipline policy*. Wiggins and McTighe (1998) offered a multifaceted view of what constitutes *understanding*. Their view, which identifies six different facets of understanding, can be holistically applied to subject matter mastery, learning and transfer, classroom management, and the behavioral concerns that are associated with specific students. These differing facets of understanding are relevant to how information is gathered, analyzed, and understood when teams make behavioral support decisions on the basis of heuristic decision-making requirements. Wiggins and McTighe's six facets of understanding—explanation, interpretation, application, perspective, empathy, and self-knowledge—are discussed next.

Explanation entails developing hypotheses and theories that propose why, how, when, and where certain behaviors (as well as peer and adult reactions to those behaviors) happen or do not happen in relation to precipitating conditions, possible motivational factors, and associated interpersonal dynamics. Explanatory understanding promotes the development of warranted opinions—that is, opinions that go beyond the simple facts and their policy implications and into areas of analysis that are characterized by words such as *"explain, justify, generalize, predict, support, verify, prove,* and *substantiate"* (Wiggins & McTighe, 1998, p. 47, emphasis in original). When a team's goal of understanding includes explanation, there must also be analysis and dialogue processes that encourage educators to develop a useful "balance" between fact acquisition and "theory building and testing" (p. 47).

Interpretation has been aptly described by the philosopher Wittgenstein, who proposed, "We understand the behavior of an individual when we grasp the meanings that are informing that person's activity" (quoted in Harré & Gillett, 1994, p. 18). According to Wiggins and McTighe (1998), interpretation involves assigning significance, proportion, and connectedness to the incidences and experiences that a team of educators is trying to understand. This is accomplished by examining the different participants' perceptions of the meaning behind the events. In this way, interpretative understanding provides a basis for going beyond explanation and into how the invested players (e.g., teachers, students, family members, counselors) perceive, feel about, comprehend, and assign value and purpose to the events that precipitated the onset of behavioral support activities. When a goal of understanding includes interpretation, there must be times for ongoing, shared dialogue among the parties, which emphasize listening to others' stories, recognizing and valuing the feelings and beliefs that guide others' actions, and avoiding the assignment of "right" or "wrong" judgments as individuals share their stories.

Application expresses the fundamental notion that "to understand is to be able to use knowledge" (Wiggins & McTighe, 1998, p. 51). Wiggins and McTighe stated,

> We show our understanding of something by using it, adapting it, and customizing it. When we must negotiate different constraints, social context, purposes, and audiences, understanding is revealed as performance know-how, the ability to accomplish tasks successfully with grace, under pressure, and with tact. (p. 52)

Psychologist William James was referring to application understanding when he distinguished theoretical knowledge from the concrete knowledge that is required for teaching (Wiggins & McTighe, 1998). It is knowledge that is firmly grounded in the classroom and in other building contexts in which decisions are to be made and actions taken. When a goal of understanding includes application, there must be evidence that the information gathered via observations, interviews, and dialogues results in interventions that blend well with already present, "proven" instructional and discipline-related practices and are likely to yield the expected results.

Perspective is how things look from different vantage points, and it represents an especially developed form of understanding. Wiggins and McTighe (1998) indicated that when team members show perspective in their understanding of an issue or concern, they are able to "expose questionable and unexamined assumptions, conclusions, and implications" and "gain a critical distance from the habitual or knee-jerk beliefs, feelings, theories, and appeals that characterize less careful and circumspect" problem-solvers and decision makers (p. 53). Perspective understanding promotes something similar to what Schwab referred to as the art of "eclectic" (see Wiggins & McTighe, 1998, p. 55): deliberately ensuring that participants in the change process see and hear different points of view and alternative solutions for the problems at hand. When a goal of understanding includes perspective, team members have opportunities to openly and explicitly confront alternative explanations and feelings about behavioral concerns and to explore the complex and diverse relationships and response patterns that constitute the history of these concerns. The ability to explore different perspectives on problems and challenges allows participants to acquire the kinds of information that foster heuristic decision-making processes.

Empathy is the ability to see the world from another person's point of view. As noted by Wiggins and McTighe, empathetic understanding involves

[The] deliberate act of finding what is plausible, sensible, or meaningful in the ideas and actions of others, even if they are puzzling or off-putting. Empathy can lead us not only to rethink a situation but to have a change of heart as we come to understand what formerly seemed odd or alien. (1998, p. 56)

Empathic understanding of a situation requires acquiring a level of respect for the individuals involved, including students, so that resulting decisions reflect an open-mindedness that is not possible in the absence of such respect. When a goal of understanding includes empathy, participants have planned opportunities to reflect on questions such as: "How does it seem to you? What do you see that I don't? What do I need to experience if I am to understand?" (p. 55).

Self-knowledge, the sixth and final facet of understanding, is derived from the idea that understanding the circumstances and events that surround and perplex one requires an understanding of oneself. As Wiggins and McTighe stated,

It asks us to have the discipline to seek and find the *inevitable* blind spots or oversights in our thinking and to have the courage to face the uncertainty and inconsistencies lurking underneath effective habits, naive confidence, strong beliefs, and world views that only seem complete and final. (1998, p. 59)

Self-knowledge as a component of understanding requires becoming aware of the limits of one's present knowledge and how everyone is prone to misunderstanding because of preexisting habits, prejudices, and styles of thinking. Self-knowledge as understanding requires not only being aware of what one does not know but also understanding 1) what one does know, 2) how thinking processes influence what one knows, 3) what influences thinking, and 4) how these processes affect one's understanding of present situations and problems. It may also involve perceiving, then rising above, habits of relying on categorical labels (e.g., Down syndrome) for explanation and/or direction instead of using the specifics of a situation when making decisions. Sometimes, participants may acquire the necessary self-knowledge for a particular situation by laying bare interfering thought processes and attitudes. When a goal of understanding includes self-knowledge, participants have opportunities and a wide latitude for engaging in self-reflection. In this process, they are encouraged to distinguish between what they actually know about a situation and what represents preconceived points of view or entrenched patterns of thinking.

Just as is the case with either/or discipline practices, there can be a thin line between heuristic decision making that is based on presenting facts and arbitrary decision making that is based on adult inclinations. To maintain fairness and promote prevention when discipline policies encourage teachers to make discipline decisions that are fitted to immediate circumstances, a richer understanding of the following must evolve among all members of the school community: 1) the nature and causes of behavior, both with respect to specific students and in the broader student population and 2) how specific discipline policies and practices can unintentionally contribute to problems when they are used inappropriately. For schools to give their best to all students, such knowledge should not be compartmentalized within special education. Instead, Wiggins and McTighe's (1998) six facets of understanding should be collaboratively developed by all educators who have a stake in either solving specific discipline concerns or enhancing a school's basic discipline practices.

Positive Behavioral Support as Innovation

Previously in this chapter, schools were described as complex, dynamic systems. This suggests that schools should be open to "chaotic" change, provided that it can be shown to be beneficial and given that there is sufficient determination and persistence on the part of those who wish to see change. Along with chaotic change, however, the other form of change in dynamic systems is recurrent change, in which a system repeatedly experiences the same states intermittently and in different combinations. Both the authors' experience and the research literature (e.g., Elmore, 1996) indicate the obvious: Although recurrent change can be readily observed in many schools, change that occurs concurrently with a substantial rethinking and revising of ongoing practice happens on a smaller scale. School communities, similar to people in general, tend to behave in a self-preserving fashion, cycling and recycling through variations of the known and familiar, regardless of actual outcomes or value.

Some of the reasons for this inertia were discussed previously in this book. In practical terms, however, positive behavioral support poses a dilemma similar to that of inclusive education: Educators are reluctant to adopt, and may feel threatened by, support practices mainly because they have never used or experienced these practices. Continuing with the inclusion analogy, research on educator perceptions of inclusive education during the 1990s (Giangreco, Dennis, Cloninger, Edelman, & Schattman, 1993; Goessling, 1998; Jackson, Ryndak, & Billingsley, 2000; Waldron, McLaskey, & Pacchiano, 1999) suggests that commitment and positive attitudes toward inclusive schooling—coupled with skepticism toward traditional, segregated alternatives—are much more likely when educators have experienced in their own practice the successes that inclusive education make possible. Conversely, educators are more prone to express negative opinions about inclusion when they are steeped in older service delivery models and have never taken part in an authentic inclusive education experience.

Because support processes are an inherent part of educational activities within inclusive schools, attempts to implement positive behavioral support policies and procedures are more likely to be successful in environments that are already inclusive. This is because the educators are more likely to be familiar with support processes and their benefits (see also Weigle, 1997). In the absence of the ongoing support experiences associated with inclusive education, these ideas may be viewed with skepticism by general and special educators who have always relied on removal and clinical intervention as solutions for behavioral challenges. Because most public schools practice the latter model, a robust behavioral support process must often be implemented against doubt and resistance that is sustained more by a lack of experience than by rational understanding. In a sense, it is a situation similar to what Skinner once called the "problem of the first instance" (1968, p. 210). People are fearful of taking the first step because they have never seen what the supports look like or how they could benefit either themselves or their students. Thus, implementing positive behavioral support at the building, class, or individual student level is usually an *innovation*, an "idea, practice, or object that is perceived as new by an individual or other unit of adoption" (Rogers, 1995, p. 11).

Implications   A number of important works (Fullan, 1993; Hord et al., 1987; Roberts, Becker, & Seay, 1997; Rogers, 1995) describe how educators at all levels within a school can foster the diffusion of innovation. According to Rogers, *diffusion of innovation* is "the process by which an *innovation* is *communicated* through certain *channels* over *time* among members of a *social system*" (p. 10, emphasis in original). Because space constraints do not allow for comprehensive coverage of all of these ideas, readers are encouraged to explore for themselves the growing field of change technology that is associated with the diffusion of innovation (see the suggested readings list at the end of this book). Also, as conflict often occurs in conjunction with efforts to bring about change, readers should also familiarize themselves with key elements of conflict resolution (Fisher & Ury, 1992; Giannetti & Sagarese, 1998; Yankelovich, 1999). For our purposes, three especially critical implications from the innovation and conflict literatures are discussed next. The first implication is that innovation acceptance and use requires an active recruitment process on the part of those who seek change. As Fullan (1993) noted, change, especially complex change, cannot be mandated. Individuals must use their own relationships with other educators to begin recruiting a network of people who will assist each other in the support of students with behavioral challenges in general education classrooms. The objectives of recruitment can vary depending on the needs of the person or team leading the change process, but they can include recruiting people to support a particular student at a grade level or during a transition, recruiting a cadre of general education teachers to support a number of students with behavioral challenges in general education, and/or recruiting a "critical mass" of administrators, teachers, related services providers, and family members so that support becomes a pervasive part of the school's climate.

Of course, the rate of adoption of innovation will vary across people within the educational community (Rogers, 1995), and efforts should initially be directed at those who are already open and sympathetic to the support process. In a study that examined a tool for evaluating the adoption of the support paradigm among community agencies, Roberts and colleagues (1997) identified three factors that may be useful when trying to ascertain who might be most open to an innovation:

1. The degree to which the support innovation matches the philosophies of the potential adopter (value)
2. The degree to which the potential adopter feels that the support innovation is needed and important (obligation)
3. The degree to which an innovation will result in a payoff that benefits the adopter of the innovation (yield)

The latter point, yield, can be especially important because authentic successful experiences can initially be so critical. Success builds confidence, such that general educators become less inclined to seek alternative placements, and special educators become less inclined to feel the need to "protect" or "change" the child before reentry into general education.

With respect to recruitment efforts among classroom and special education teachers, both diplomacy and perseverance are required to establish a pattern in which the classroom teacher relies less on removal and more on inner resources or assistance from others to resolve behavioral problems. If the special educator is working in a self-contained classroom or facility, the recruitment process can be especially time intensive. School personnel may not feel inclined to change their service delivery processes simply to accommodate a group of children or youth with behavioral problems who are now seemingly no longer a problem for them. Yet, bridges can be slowly constructed when special education teachers who work in self-contained settings set as one of their professional priorities the recruitment of general educators, principals, and related service professionals who are sympathetic to a reintegration process. As a result, some students will return to the schools and classes that they would have attended had they not been labeled and perceived as needing a more restrictive placement. Of course, ensuring that there is a successful reintegration experience (yield) for the receiving teachers assumes critical strategic importance when a teacher works in a self-contained setting, and this may often affect which students are first chosen to return to the general education community. This is, indeed, regrettable; yet, it is a stark reality when school systems depend on removal as a primary intervention procedure for students who are viewed as having significant behavioral problems.

There is no doubt that leadership support is crucial for these types of changes (Jackson et al., 2000; Mamlin, 1999). Unfortunately, educators are not always blessed with administrators who are willing to endorse even well-founded innovations that are both new to them and to the many practitioners with whom they communicate throughout the school day. This means that the educators who champion innovations must also actively recruit administrators even as they recruit fellow teachers, families, and related services personnel. This requires ensuring that administrators are kept informed of innovation efforts, that their advice is sought and listened to as changes are made, and that successes and difficulties are documented and reported to administrators on a regular basis.

The second implication is that innovation acceptance and use—especially in situations in which participants hold conflicting values, goals, and methodological perspectives—necessitates the strategic use of both dialogue and relationship by those seeking change. Yankelovich (1999) noted that dialogue means moving beyond superficial conversation and the "face-saving" defenses that hold communication at bay so that authentic decision making can occur. It requires participants to refrain from simply declaring positions or stands and to instead express the specific concerns and interests that underlie these various positions. Placing these underlying concerns and interests on the table, such as a concern for the safety of the other children in the classroom, can forge the way for decisions that are acceptable to all participants, because they often contain the seeds of common ground (Kunc, 1996; Skovron, 1999).

Yankelovich (1999) and others (Covey, 1990; Cramer, 1998; Senge, 1990) identified a number of different preconditions that need to be satisfied before meaningful dialogue can occur. Yankelovich asserted that dialogue depends on the presence of three factors: 1) meeting as equals, with no "coercive influences" present (p. 41); 2) active and empathetic listening to each other's perspectives; and 3) examination of each and every participant's basic assumptions without value judgements. The authors' experiences in schools indicate that IEP teams in particular often do not reflect these three qualities. In fact, it is not uncommon for such teams to consist of groups of individuals who are clustered around positions, and these individuals tend to blame and place responsibility on others with different points of view. For example, school professionals may come into a meeting with the view that the parents are "unreasonable" and hold to this stance regardless of the degree of accommodation that a family offers to reach a middle ground. As noted by Cramer, team members are often challenged by the need to move "from focusing on the other person as the problem source to yourself as the potential problem solver" (1998, p. 169). Part of the reason why this shift is so difficult is because there is often so little trust between the team members from the outset. Senge (1990) noted that trust usually develops best not in formal meetings but under conditions such as social events, casual conversations, and informal meetings at various school and nonschool environments. Regrettably, this type of informal exchange between professionals and family members is relatively rare.

Goleman commented that "dialogue is no substitute for genuine social bonds" (1999, p. 24), and this succinctly states the case for the role of relationships in the diffusion of innovation, especially when conflict is likely. The authors' experiences in facilitating both inclusive and positive behavioral support practices within schools indicate that building solid relationships that cross discipline lines and extend into families is often a crucial step, and this should precede the introduction of innovations when possible. Skovron (1999) stressed that when conflict is probable or ongoing, preserving existing relationships should be the first priority. She noted that parties that work toward common understanding and mutually acceptable decisions must always bear in mind what she termed "the shadow of the future"; that is, participants must consider that all that is said and done can have unintended repercussions in the future. The preservation or disruption of a critical social relationship between participants is clearly one of these "shadows," so maintaining relationships should be in the forefront as dialogue proceeds and subsequent decisions are made.

Although dialogue and relationships are important considerations in supporting the adoption of innovation, especially when there is controversy, Kunc (1996) made an especially critical point: It is important to show consideration and respect for others who have differing points of view, but it is equally important to firmly seek resolution to the issues that initially led to the meeting. Kunc aptly described this as being "soft" on the person while being "hard" on the issue. Put differently, whether seeking ways to construct supports for an individual student or a shift in the paradigm that drives a school's practices, one certainly should not let his or her position impede efforts to resolve shared concerns and realize common interests in safety and comfort. At the same time, it is self-defeating if one forgets that the primary issue is the education of the student with challenging behaviors, and this goal may be inalterably compromised when final decisions result in the student's removal and placement in a more restrictive setting. Within the support paradigm educators ideally seek a resolution in which both the students and the adults are assisted in succeeding with minimal or no removal of the students from the general education setting.

Of course, educators are not always successful in securing or maintaining an inclusive placement. When this happens, educators must not let the planning process stop with the alternative placement. Instead, the process of reintegration then takes priority for educators and family members who want a district, school, or group of educators to eventually adopt positive behavioral support. This reintegration process cannot and should not focus exclusively on what is required of the student, such as when the student is held responsible for "earning" the right to return to the general education classroom. Instead, reintegration planning focuses on enhancing the capacity of the educators and the other students in general education to provide supports so that all parties experience success and growth as the student becomes reacclimated to general education.

The third implication is that innovation acceptance and use is optimized when the participants feel that the adopted innovations are of their own invention. It is a simple truth that people are more likely to do something if it emerges from their own design or from that of people with whom they have a positive relationship. Innovative practices are less likely to be implemented when they are espoused by professionals from outside of the system who claim specialized expertise.

The challenge this third implication creates has previously surfaced in this discussion: How do educators ensure that behavioral support expertise becomes something inherent within the members of educational team and not something that must be routinely secured from outside of the system? The next section of this chapter presents a model of collaborative inquiry that offers a way for teams to build and use behavioral support expertise.

SYNTHESIS: THE CO-CONSTRUCTION OF UNDERSTANDING AND INNOVATION IN COMPLEX SYSTEMS

Yankelovich exclaimed, "Astonishingly, the idea of knowledge as a hierarchy has persisted for 2,500 years" (1999, p. 195), and this statement captures the heart of the problem. In the many-tiered world of school professionals, educators have presumed that there are certain kinds of knowledge that are acquired much less through patterns of experience and much more through years of study within professional disciplines. They often conclude that this "clinical and theoretical knowledge" is of higher value than practical knowledge for generating solutions to discipline concerns and behavioral challenges. From this perspective, schools heavily depend on the informed judgments of trained experts in psychology, special education, and counseling to address behavioral concerns. These experts are expected to use their special knowledge and analytical tools to cut through the myriad patterns of events and circumstances to produce unfettered diagnostic and prescriptive understandings of the student with behavioral issues. These individuals are then expected to use these understandings to provide innovative strategies and tools, which are drawn from their stores of professional knowledge that represent current empirical research.

There is certainly a place for outside expertise in the development of positive behavioral support activities in schools. Experts with professional training, knowledge of the literature, and experience with positive behavioral support can facilitate processes of support planning and implementation. In particular, experts can guide a school in developing its capacity for constructing behavioral and other supports. Yet, the critical role of practical experience has been underrepresented in the popular equation of *understanding*. Practical experience is derived from the actual situations and problems that require change. Developing and effectively using the necessary skills for negotiating complex, dynamic systems and establishing the six facets of understanding comes largely through investment and daily immersion in the actual environments and situations that call for action and innovation.

The situation that schools and professionals face regarding support is not unlike Huberman's (1999) description of what needs to happen for practitioners and researchers who work together to mutually learn from each other. Researchers must adjust their conceptual models to real-world patterns of understanding, and practitioners must value researchers' offerings, which can provide unique perspectives on teaching and learning. Huberman described two phenomena that make these changes possible. First, there must be sustained interactivity, in which practitioners and researchers are immersed together for prolonged periods of time in the common pursuit of solutions to practical problems. Second, the participants must confront anomalies, events that pose discrepancies between what happens at a practical level and the mental maps that participants hold to guide their understandings of particular issues and situations. Huberman suggested that *dialogue* between researchers and practitioners provides the necessary linkage for sustained interactivity to occur and for anomalies to be confronted. He also added, "Unidirectional flow has a short shelf life . . . conversations that produce thinking devices (exchanges, arguments, and batting back and forth of examples and evidence) rather than authoritative commentary are more likely to be readily and durably appropriated" (p. 310).

The parallel with enhancing change in relation to positive behavioral support is as follows. Those with a vested interest in creating change need to enact solutions that move individuals who are affected by a situation or problem into a different state, a state in which enhanced understanding and productive innovation are both possible. All of the participants in planning, including those with and without specialized knowledge, possess distinct abilities and perspectives, some of which will be useful in particular situations, some of which will have no value, and some of which will be counterproductive. To overcome the inertia of history, there must be a vehicle for bringing out these different perspectives such that all six facets of understanding can emerge and evolve in all participants. There must also be a vehicle for creating innovation out of the voices of the people who are engaged in the planning process.

As noted by Huberman (1999), dialogue over sustained periods is a critical vehicle for these processes. However, dialogue seems insufficient in and of itself to ensure that understanding and innovation will be emergent properties of the planning process.

To ensure that both understanding and innovation are products of dialogue, there must be an additional vehicle for ensuring that participants confront anomalies (Huberman, 1999)—that is, counterevidence between their existing understandings and tools of intervention for behavioral problems and the real-world situations that they are now confronting. In other words, participants must face discrepancies that can emerge from the realization that solutions to current problems require something different from solutions that were used to address past problems.

Research (Helwick & Jackson, 1999, 2000; Jackson, Barnes, Padilla, McClure, & Anson, 1998; Jackson & Leon, 1997b) suggests that understanding and innovation are both promoted when practitioners use what this chapter calls *guided inquiry*. In this process, educators, family members, and others use a series of carefully framed questions to examine interactions and relationships between student behavioral concerns and the educators' teaching, interpersonal, and discipline practices. Guided inquiry goes beyond traditional assessment activities because it recognizes that the necessary expertise for solving problems requires both gathering behavioral information and questioning one's practices to uncover anomalies between present practices and desired outcomes. Moreover, one cannot partial out values in this process because values are essential for constructing authentic understandings of problems and potential solutions. Guided inquiry begins with a group of individuals who commit themselves to the ends and means of positive behavioral support; then, it uses sets of questions to guide both the dialogue process and correlated information gathering activities (assessment).

Figure 6.1 depicts how guided inquiry generates innovation (Helwick & Jackson, 1999). As this figure shows, the dialogue of guided inquiry occurs within a context that includes the decision-relevant factors of interpersonal climate, teacher decisions, student and family patterns of interaction and behavior, and content standards/curriculum. Solutions to both routine discipline concerns and chronic behavioral problems will often be drawn from the solution space labeled *current solutions* (see left side of Figure 6.1), even when there is little proof that the chosen solutions are actually effective. Movement between current solutions and innovations (labeled *emergent solutions*; see right side of Figure 6.1) requires a process of inquiry in which the questions that are used as the basis for gathering information and exploring understandings prompt participants to think in new ways about the issues. The arrows in this diagram represent the questions that the team uses to create understanding and construct their solutions.

Helwick and Jackson (1999, 2000) found that when given sets of questions that promote the exploration of the six facets of understanding developed by Wiggins and McTighe (1998), teams tend to move from their existing solutions into the emergent solution space, then move back into the current solution space as the dialogue continues. That is, guided inquiry inevitably leads participants to innovations (i.e., strategies that are new to them given their past experiences), but they also invariably drift back and forth so that their final product (e.g., a behavioral support plan) contains a mixture of traditional and new strategies and practices. Helwick and Jackson also suggested that there is a "chaotic" quality to this process. Both teams and individuals will shift back and forth over time between traditional and innovative solutions in unpredictable ways, until a time is reached when the "emergent" becomes the "current" and these

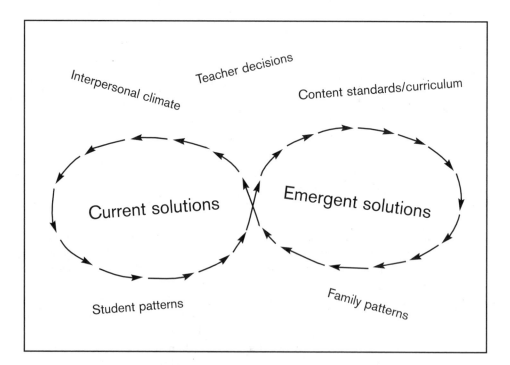

Figure 6.1.   Generating innovation through guided inquiry. Arrows represent the process of asking pertinent questions.

formerly novel ways of thinking assume a more predominant role in how an educator or group of educators routinely respond to discipline and behavioral concerns.

As indicated by the preceding discussion of the arrows in Figure 6.1, the critical component of guided inquiry is the set of questions that are used to conceptualize the nature of the concerns at hand, guide the selection and use of assessment procedures, and generate solutions. Upcoming chapters, especially Chapters 8 and 10, present detailed descriptions of the kinds of questions that educators can use and how these questions drive assessment processes in relation to individual students.

Planning and Assessment for Positive Behavioral Support

Chapter 7

Planning for
Positive Behavioral Support

*"One jumps into the fray,
then figures out what to do next!"*
—*Napoleon Bonaparte*

From discussions in previous chapters, it is clear that an intervention can fail to achieve sustainable and valued results if its objectives and processes focus on either behavior reduction or trying to reinstate once-familiar environmental conditions. Students can be motivated to change if the possibility of something better than the present conditions exists for them. This is made possible when educators steer the inevitable change processes associated with complex, dynamic systems through steps that include the 1) specification of outcomes, 2) design of steps leading toward the specified outcomes, 3) implementation of interventions that address challenges while honoring the realities and traditions of a system's culture, and 4) ongoing evaluation of change. These steps are the topic of this chapter.

Dörner (1996) described in detail how to develop and implement interventions in complicated, difficult situations in which plans are likely to go awry if the interventions are not carefully formulated and scrupulously monitored. Dörner focused on large-scale interventions, in which entire social systems are affected by innovation plans that are intended to reform conditions within the systems. Nevertheless, his ideas about planning and managing change are equally applicable to the smaller scales represented by schools, classrooms, and interpersonal relationships. A major point derived from Dörner's work is that educators' actions when designing and conducting positive behavioral support efforts involve creating and constantly updating a reality model (see Chapter 6 of this book). A *reality model* consists of one's structural and intuitive knowledge, both implicit and explicit, about the one-way and reciprocal linkages between events and how they influence each other. A well-constructed reality model can guide the use of student-specific and situation-specific knowledge in the creation of an intervention process and meaningful outcomes. Two points Dörner made about reality models are that 1) individuals always use a mental model, regardless of whether it is deliberately and consciously constructed, to interpret what is happening and

2) reality models are often "incomplete" or "wrong," and "one would do well to keep that probability in mind" (p. 42).

Knowledge about positive behavioral support (see Chapter 5), when combined with knowledge of system and system change issues (see Chapter 6), well equips one to begin translating reality models into positive behavioral support plans, even within difficult situations. Yet, failure can result if explicit procedures for generating well-conceived initial plans and for making change decisions along the way are absent. Put differently, a protocol is needed for constructing and revising plans, understanding the inevitable limits of any such plans, and knowing how to gather and use information to enhance initial and subsequent intervention decisions.

Dörner (1996) illustrated some of the decision processes that can make or break an intervention. In computer simulation research on decision making that is associated with social and economic reform, patterns of "making decisions," "reflecting," and "asking questions" were examined as participants used a continuous flow of data to make, execute, and revise their innovation plans. Participants initially displayed a helpful pattern of high levels of reflecting and asking questions and correspondingly low levels of decision making. Nonetheless, a common failure among the participants was to increasingly make more decisions while engaging less in reflection and questioning as their reforms unfolded and began affecting their simulated societies. Dörner commented that once the participants' initial assessments of the situation were completed, they "mistakenly" thought that they "already had the knowledge that they needed to cope with" the problems they were attempting to solve (p. 17). Teachers and building administrators also sometimes tackle concerns with behavioral problems this way. They may make an effort to collect data and to initiate their interventions based on these data. Nonetheless, the actual interventions may then be progressively conducted in the absence of the reflecting and questioning activities that are necessary for ongoing informed decision making (see Display 7.1).

As a prelude to the upcoming chapter on assessment (Chapter 8) and as a structural guide for subsequent chapters on intervention (Chapters 9–11), this chapter offers an overview of critical planning activities for developing positive behavioral support plans and outlines pitfalls to avoid. The chapter organization resembles the chronology of events associated with support planning:

- Determine the degree of concern
- Plan the intervention
- Initiate the intervention
- Implement the intervention
- Revise the intervention

The chapter ends with a flowchart of this planning sequence, which was inspired by Dörner's (1996) version. This flowchart is then referenced in subsequent chapter discussions on the organization of assessment and intervention activities.

DETERMINE THE DEGREE OF CONCERN

Positive behavioral support processes can be applied by using different combinations of time, energy, and personnel, depending on the nature, complexity, and severity of the behavioral concern. Whether, for example, a concern is emerging between a teacher and a student, intermittent within a particular class of students, or persistent between the larger school community and a particular student can and should define the scope and types of resources that are used to address it.

Tilly and colleagues (1998) described how one support resource, functional behavioral assessment, can be differentially applied depending on need. As shown in Figure 7.1, when "behavior becomes an issue that impedes the individual's learning or the learning of others" (p. 24), there should be a match between the severity, intensity, and durability of the behavioral problem and the amount of assessment resources deployed to understand it. In other words, as the degree of concern increases, the need for precision in the analysis of the problem increases; hence, there is a corresponding need to increase the resources brought to bear on the problem so that efficacious solutions are identified.

Figure 7.2 offers another yardstick for measuring the relationship between the degree of concern and the use of resources. The figure's column headings identify different levels of disruptiveness that may be associated with a particular behavior pattern. Perceptions of disruptiveness could be from a single individual; alternately, they could represent a consensus reached within a school about different types of disruptions and how their effects are defined. *Disengaged* refers to mild inattentiveness and to various forms of self-stimulation. The forms of these behaviors will vary among students; however, they have the same effect: A student is not, at a given moment, participating in learning or in the class routine. The next behavior, *self-expression*, may seem out of place on a table that identifies behavioral concerns. Yet, educators may be less inclined to interpret certain behaviors (e.g., being the class clown, answering out of turn) as serious "problems" if they reframe the behaviors as types of communication. An educator who views such disruptions as communicative expressions of excite-

DISPLAY 7.1—MORE CHARACTERISTICS OF POOR DECISIONS

A number of Dörner's (1996) insights into decision making confirm that knowing how to construct plans and make decisions is as important as knowing the substance to include in one's plans and decisions.

Have you seen any of the following features of poor decision making in behavior intervention planning?

1. *Acting without substantial prior knowledge of a situation*
2. *Creating and being guided by goals that are intended to repair what is wrong rather than goals that are intended to reach authentic outcomes*
3. *Focusing on problems for which solutions are known rather than problems for which solutions are needed*
4. *Mistakenly presuming that immediate and obvious improvements mean that the correct procedures were implemented*
5. *Becoming preoccupied with side projects so that neither the original goals nor newly emerging concerns are being addressed*

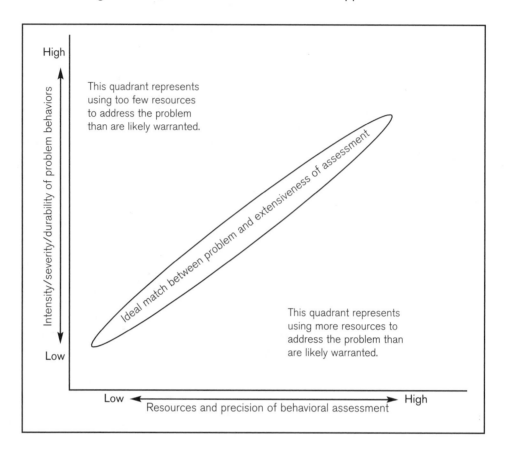

High

This quadrant represents using too few resources to address the problem than are likely warranted.

Ideal match between problem and extensiveness of assessment

This quadrant represents using more resources to address the problem than are likely warranted.

Intensity/severity/durability of problem behaviors

Low

Low ← Resources and precision of behavioral assessment → High

Figure 7.1. Conceptual relationship between degree of behavioral problem and the behavioral assessment resources required. (From Tilly, W.D., Knoster, T.P., Kovaleski, J., Bambara, L., Dunlap, G., & Kincaid, D. [1998]. *Functional behavioral assessment: Policy development in light of emerging research and practice* [p. 24]. Alexandria, VA: National Association of State Directors of Special Education; reprinted by permission.)

ment, exuberance, social membership, or independence may be more inclined to deal with them in a way that both the student's and the teacher's needs are met. The concepts of *minor disruptions, severe disruptions,* and *dangerous behaviors* will sound familiar to most teachers. Although definitions of these terms will vary from educator to educator, they represent a progression from nuisance and interruptive behaviors (e.g., throwing a paper wad, a minor altercation) to behaviors that significantly interfere with learning (e.g., yelling, verbal abuse) to, finally, behaviors that threaten the safety of others (e.g., fighting, throwing desks).

The left side of Figure 7.2 shows a progression of planning and support activities that require different levels of resource investment. The first three activities represent informal activities that educators can use and improve on in their work. *Supporting relationships* refers to activities that encourage and nurture positive interpersonal relationships among students and among students and educators. *Reflecting on teaching in relation to behavior* consists of activities in which the teacher examines his or her practices to strengthen problem-prevention skills and better address problems when they arise. Examples of *processing with the student* include actively listening to and dialoguing with a student when a disruption occurs to enhance understanding and achieve a better balance between teacher and student needs. These activities can be used for any behavior, but they are especially helpful for reducing disengaged behaviors; channeling student self-expression; and addressing minor, intermittent disruptions.

Functional behavioral assessment is the fourth type of planning and support activity that is suggested in Figure 7.2. It is the basis for hypothesis-based intervention (see Chapter 5), a useful means for addressing intermittent minor disruptions, and an essential tool for managing more intensely disruptive behavior (Gable, Hendrickson, & Smith, 1999).

The next activity is *recruiting other adults.* This includes both seeking 1) the *advice* of other adults who know the student or have experienced similar concerns when addressing minor intermittent disruptions and 2) the *assistance* of other adults when minor disruptions are persistent (i.e., chronic).

When minor disruptions persist, informal efforts may give way to a formal *behavior intervention plan.* Although this activity may be needed earlier, it is definitely warranted when disruptions are severe. At this juncture, a student is especially at risk for long-term removal, and resources must be mobilized quickly to resolve the issues for the teacher(s), the peers, and the student.

When disruptions are severe and persistent or dangerous, more resources are required. At this point, the final type of activity, a *comprehensive behavior intervention plan,* is usually needed. If the student has been removed from general education either temporarily (e.g., suspended) or through placement (e.g., self-contained room), *reintegration* is emphasized. The latter in particular requires greater resources and skilled resource coordination to ensure the student's successful and safe return to the general education environment.

As Figure 7.2 suggests, the degree of concern rises with behavioral disruptiveness. Sprick, Sprick, and Garrison (1993) and others (e.g., Dwyer et al., 2000; Gable et al., 1999; Meyer & Evans, 1989; Sprague & Walker, 2000; Sugai et al., 2000) recognized that assessment and intervention activities must match the degree of concern that accompanies a particular situation. Consistent with this principle, positive behavioral support assessment and intervention activities are conceptualized in this book as falling within three overlapping categories, which correspond to increasing degrees of concern:

1. *Enhance practices* covers assessment and intervention activities that are appropriate when concerns are minor, general, and primarily related to improving day-to-day support for preventing and minimizing problems.
2. *Develop a behavior intervention plan* covers assessment and intervention activities that are appropriate for persistent or severe behavioral disruptions.
3. *Develop a comprehensive behavior intervention plan* covers assessment and intervention activities that are appropriate when concerns are especially critical, problems are entrenched, and/or removal via suspension or special placement has occurred or is imminent.

Chapter 8 and particularly Chapters 9, 10, and 11 present assessment and intervention options that reflect these three categories of support activities.

Ascertaining the degree of concern is an important first step in the development of the reality model that can guide decision making during intervention. At the same time, knowing the degree of concern only signals the need for an intervention with a particular level of resource investment. It gives no substantial information on what the

Planning and support activities	Disengaged	Self-expression	Minor disruptions		Severe disruptions		Dangerous behaviors	
			Intermittent	Persistent	Intermittent	Persistent	Intermittent	Persistent
Supporting relationships	X	X	X	X	X	X	X	X
Reflection on teaching in relation to behavior	X	X	X	X	X	X	X	X
Processing with the student	X	X	X	X	X	X	X	X
Functional behavioral assessment			X	X	X	X	X	X
Recruiting other adults — Advice			X	X	X	X	X	X
Recruiting other adults — Assistance				X	X	X	X	X
Behavior intervention plan					X	X	X	X
Comprehensive behavior intervention plan						X	X	X
Reintegration						X	X	X

Figure 7.2. Matrix for planning and support activities in relation to the degree of concern.

intervention needs to look like. Ceasing to gather information at this point is all too common among some educators. Once a need is established for an intervention of a certain intensity, some professionals immediately create their intervention plan, deriving its components from a limited toolbox that largely consists of knowledge about specific disability labels, some management tools (e.g., positive reinforcement, providing choices, time-out), and informal reflection on the factors that seem most responsible for the behavior.

These actions can have tragic consequences. For example, some well-intentioned programs have imposed periods of isolation on children who cherish being with peers because someone has provided the following label-derived (mis)information: *This student, who has (label; e.g., autism), becomes overstimulated and behaves a certain way (e.g., striking others) when around the noise and activities of other children.* Using this information, the educators then implement positive reinforcement programs within isolated settings in which food and praise are used to reward the student for good behavior (e.g., "hands in lap") on tasks of questionable usefulness (e.g., worksheets, sorting tasks). Yet, having taken away what represents the very essence of the quality of life for the child, the positive reinforcement program fails. In turn, the involved educators may then reach the appalling conclusion that a particular child is "still not ready" to be returned to the natural environment. This scenario may seem far fetched, but it and others like it have been observed far too often to dismiss them as the extreme cases of poor intervention design. Educators need to be equipped to engage in a systematic planning process that, although geared to the degree of concern, accurately informs their emerging reality model about the nature and best approaches for addressing a particular behavioral problem.

PLAN THE INTERVENTION

An intervention for behavior is a deliberate, arranged set of alterations in environmental conditions (e.g., instructional, interpersonal) that is designed around a student (or a group of students) with challenging behaviors. An intervention is intended to accomplish three purposes: 1) promote the student's growth and learning; 2) enhance the student's and others' comfort by alleviating the behavioral challenges through support and instruction; and/or 3) create understanding among everyone involved, including the student(s). A fruitful intervention can affect not only behavior but also others' perceptions about the student. In addition, an especially well-conceived intervention can indirectly affect an educator's ability to adapt to future situations in which student conflicts are present and/or unfamiliar patterns of behavior are encountered.

As noted in Chapter 5, interventions should have both short-and long-term consequences for all parties. In the short run, they should promote immediate learning and bring into balance the behavioral excesses that prompted the intervention; in the long run, they should affect the student's potential for future success and participating educators' and peers' responses to similar situations in the future. Especially if the degree of concern mandates a formal plan, as described in Chapter 5, an intervention should include steps and procedures to

- Create and implement a person-centered vision, which addresses age- and grade-level activity participation, membership, and autonomy needs

- Enhance adult and peer relationships, which can support student growth and performance
- Formulate and enact hypotheses about the behavior, which can help prevent problems and provide the student with more adaptive ways to meet needs and interact with others
- Handle crisis situations, which can facilitate the return to stability and alleviate the student's and others' discomfort

A well-designed intervention also acknowledges and works with what is realistic given the province and control of those responsible for its design. However, an intervention grounded in vision setting, relationship enhancement, hypothesis-based intervention, and appropriate crisis support can have far-reaching benefits for all involved, even as it meets the parameters of being "realistic."

Especially if a formal intervention plan is needed, there can be a need for considerable breadth and depth of understanding of the student, his or her relationships with others, and his or her responses to the school's learning and behavioral expectations. Generating this understanding is accomplished through a decision analysis process consisting of four, largely inseparable subprocesses: 1) gather information, 2) formulate outcomes, 3) delineate hypotheses, and 4) generate forecasts. The relationship among these four processes is shown in Figure 7.3, and highlights are presented in the following four subsections.

Gather Information

When planning and conducting an intervention, data gathering must be continuous. It also should be guided by the information needs associated with making initial and ongoing decisions about intervention outcomes, behavioral hypotheses, and the forecasts that link outcomes and behavioral hypotheses with the intervention's steps and procedures. Particularly within special education, the emphasis has been on quantitative as opposed to qualitative data and on formal data collection processes instead of informal reflective processes. Nevertheless, both the type of data and the data collection process should depend on the degree of concern. In general, informal and qualitative procedures make the most sense when the degree of concern is at the "enhance practices" level. Maintaining a journal, engaging in self-reflection, and dialoguing with others can often yield sufficient descriptions of activity and behavior associations, as well as new ways to engage and interact with the student.

As the degree of concern rises, both greater formality and more quantitative measures may be required. At the same time, risks are associated with both formality and quantification. Formality may inadvertently support rigidity: Once decisions are made, people sometimes have difficulty changing direction when the data do not adequately mirror all of a situation's relevant facets. Because quantitative measures are so highly valued in U.S. culture, they sometimes engender a false sense of understanding and accountability. They may even obscure subtle but more important knowledge about a behavior that could be discerned via qualitative methodologies. Finally, a risk with both lies in the message that they send to the young person who is the center of attention, to his or her peers, and to other educators. The act of gathering formal, especially quantitative, information that is focused on behavior can sometimes stigmatize the young person and exacerbate the problem behavior.

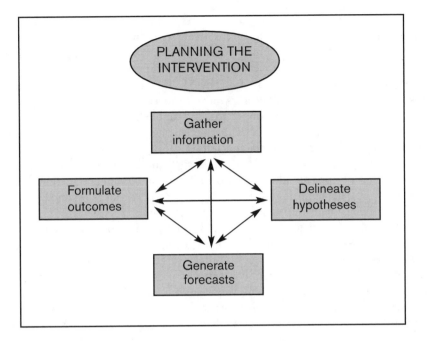

Figure 7.3.   Relationships among the essential processes for planning an intervention.

A first step in the information-gathering process is to characterize the circumstances that appear to necessitate a behavioral intervention. These are *precipitating circumstances*, the behavioral and situational conditions that, when examined in relationship to each other

- Evidence the necessity for an intervention of a particular scope and magnitude within and across different environments
- Provide perspective on the gap between what presently exists within different situations and what is desirable for the student and for the adults
- Explain the relationships among various behavior patterns and contexts so that certain interventions are anticipated
- Shed light on the interim and final outcomes that might be acceptable to all parties

Descriptions of precipitating circumstances can include accounts of the various behavior patterns that are of concern and frequency, duration, and severity information might be included if truly helpful. Yet, descriptions of behavior and accompanying data must be embedded within 1) information about correlated setting, antecedent, consequent, and motivational factors; 2) patterns of student participation in different settings and activities throughout the day, analyzed in relation to what other students are doing in those situations; 3) "good day" and "bad day" patterns, if prominent and likely to establish day-to-day differences in the intervention; 4) the feelings of other people who are associated with the student in various roles and capacities (e.g., teachers, coaches, educational assistants, fellow students, tutors, friends, hall monitors); and 5) the student's personal feelings and levels of investment in the social and academic activities of his or her age- and grade-level peers.

Thinking in terms of precipitating circumstances rather than in terms of behavioral problems helps instill the view that an intervention is needed not because of a behavior but, rather, because of a behavior situated in identifiable conditions. Thinking in this way can help educators move from a blame posture toward an understanding posture in their perceptions of students and behavioral concerns. It also facilitates intervention designs that focus less on management procedures for reducing behavior and more on instructional and setting supports that reduce problem behaviors because they enhance school success. As such thinking is more likely to achieve meaningful results for the adults, it also builds their confidence in their ability to resolve difficult behavioral issues. In the long run, this reduces reliance on removal strategies and placement into more restrictive settings.

Along with the judicious use of existing records, data on precipitating circumstances can be assembled by using informant-based assessments, in which interviews are conducted with parents, teachers, or others; direct observations, in which the student is observed within a variety of contexts and particular behaviors are recorded in relation to time, activities, and other events; and functional (experimental) analysis, in which structural and functional aspects of the student's environment are systematically manipulated to determine factors related to the behavior (Jackson & Leon, 1998a; Lennox & Miltenberger, 1989).

The research literature often emphasizes functional (experimental) analysis because of its power to confirm descriptive findings (e.g., Wacker, Cooper, Peck, Derby, & Berg, 1999). The assessment tools and techniques offered in Chapter 8, however, depend more on existing records, informant-based assessments, and direct observations, because these techniques are generally more appropriate and practical within schools.

Formulate Outcomes

An intervention may falter because it is not grounded in an authentic sense of direction and purpose. A poorly designed plan often begins with ill-conceived outcomes, and there are four prominent signs that a plan's proposed outcomes are short-sighted and likely to contribute to the plan's demise:

1. The proposed intervention outcomes are limited to simply the absence of the problem behavior.
2. The proposed intervention outcomes are difficult to achieve, and potentially attainable intermediate outcomes are not delineated.
3. The proposed intervention outcomes represent the adult's point of view but do not reflect the student's or the family's desires and needs.
4. The proposed intervention outcomes define student change expectations but not expectations related to the skills, feelings, behaviors, and needs of the adults and peers who interact with the student.

Avoiding these pitfalls requires having a grasp of three principles of goal development, which are described next (see also Display 7.2).

The first principle is that the long-term, primary goals of the plan should identify positive, valued outcomes for the student. Dörner (1996) made a distinction between positive and negative goals, suggesting that although this distinction may "sound academic," it is actually a critical one for designing interventions (p. 50). Positive goals describe conditions "that we want to achieve"; negative goals focus on conditions that we wish did not exist (p. 50). Intervention efforts must be driven by the desire to achieve positive goals rather than by the desire to "change, abolish, or avoid conditions" that seem difficult or intolerable (p. 50). Similarly, Dörner also warned against "repair service" behavior, in which the focus of the intervention shifts from working toward desired positive outcomes to trying to correct the numerous things that are wrong with a situation.

Maintaining a positive focus when developing and implementing behavior intervention plans can be difficult because the problems can sometimes seem so insurmountable. It is not uncommon to see teams of educators whose best attempt at a positive goal is not an outcome that reflects what would be valued by the student and others, but rather an outcome in which the negative behavior is simply reversed (e.g., focusing on on-task behavior when the problem is off-task behavior). Whenever an intervention's goals are offshoots of the student's vision, it is more probable that a positive focus will be expressed in those goals. Some strategies for conceptualizing positive outcomes are presented in Chapter 5 in the discussion of vision setting and lifestyle planning. Another technique for envisioning positive outcomes is offered in

DISPLAY 7.2—RECOGNIZING UNPRODUCTIVE AGENDAS

Consider the following two situations:

1. During a school faculty workshop on using support rather than removal procedures to handle behavioral crises, the trainer emphasized outcomes such as the safety and protection of all students, the return to normalcy following a crisis, and the long-term reduction of crisis incidents. Although most of the educators agreed with the trainer regarding the long- and short-term objectives for crisis support, one teacher persistently asked, "How many times do I have to do these things before I can get rid of a student?"

2. During a meeting about the reintegration of a student with behavioral concerns into her neighborhood school, an administrator first instructed the team to define the point at which the plan could be viewed as a clear failure and the child could be immediately moved to another placement.

If an individual team member's agenda for defining conditions for permanent removal is adopted by the full team early in the planning process, what effect does this have on how adults who are new to the situation view the student? Also, what outcomes become increasingly probable for the behavior intervention plan?

What can be said or done to help such individuals view things from a more positive perspective?

Chapter 10, in which solution-focused concepts are introduced as a way for creating behavior intervention plans with a positive outlook.

For students in special education, IEP goals and objectives should optimally focus on educational outcomes and not behavior reduction, with the proposed behavior intervention plan being developed as a related document. Nonetheless, when members of the team insist that behavioral concerns be represented in the IEP's goals and objectives, positive rather than negative objectives should be developed. For example, a student whose precipitating circumstances include acting-out behaviors, making noises, and disturbing others by grabbing their materials, may have the following IEP objective:

> While participating in large group activities in gym and during weight class, Calvin will 1) maintain noise levels at the same volume as the rest of the group, 2) partially complete the activities that are performed by others, 3) follow the example of nearby students for the use of his hands, and 4) stay with the class. (Measurement and criteria: Behavior checklist— receive teacher ratings of "satisfactory" or better for each behavior every day for 3 weeks.)

For a student who is participating in gym and weight classes, this objective provides a stronger footing for achieving the desired results than would an objective that focuses on the behaviors that educators find intolerable and want to eliminate.

The second principle is that formal plans, especially comprehensive plans, should identify a series of responsible short-term expectations in addition to long-term goals. A source of frustration for teachers and students is the tendency of some educational teams to develop behavior reduction plans that delineate difficult-to-achieve long-term outcomes yet provide no reasonable expectations for the short term that could lend a sense of accomplishment. In this situation, the plan's failure is very likely to be announced within a few weeks, an outcome that might even be hurried along by sabotage from a teacher who has a reputation to preserve.

Jackson and Leon (1998a) reported that a way to construct short-term expectations begins as follows: The planning team collaboratively reflects on the discrepancy between outcomes that are proposed for the long term, which should be derived from the vision statement, and the student's present situation in terms of participation in general education, membership in a community of students, and responsible autonomy. These reflections are then used to create a set of between five and seven short-term expectations that might be achievable within one or several months, depending on the time frame set for the long-term outcomes. Short-term expectations are best when they are positive and potentially measurable (e.g., "Asking for a break when she becomes agitated in her general education class"), and they should be focused on authentic participation in age-appropriate activities, membership in peer groups consisting of typical students, and autonomy regarding participation in the school and other communities.

The third and final principle is that the visualized outcomes of the plan should also include outcomes that have value and meaning for others (e.g., teachers, peers, parents). Most people are more willing to invest in a plan if the consequences of success or failure affect their own lives and situations. During the plan design process, it is helpful to define outcomes of the support process that are positive and useful for the participants who must carry out the plan, whether this is addressed as part of the dialogue during team meetings or explicitly written into a plan. For example, a special education teacher who was spending inordinate amounts of time monitoring a student in time-out before the support plan was developed might hope that the plan results in his no longer spending time and energy on this activity. As another example, a general education teacher might wish that the plan results in her being able to spend more time teaching and less time handling disruptions from the student and others. More often than not, the results desired by such individuals are short term in nature; a successful plan will, in the long run, take care of their concerns. Nevertheless, because these short-term outcomes are critical for their ongoing responsibilities as teachers, short-term solutions should be found that can help resolve these issues so that the student's placement in general education is not jeopardized.

When an education team views these as important outcomes of the support process, it also helps involve reluctant members of the school community. Of course, there are times when troublesome discrepancies exist between the student's educational and behavioral needs and the educators' immediate safety and security issues. This is when a negotiation process is required and a consensus is sought in which the short-term issues of particular educators and the long-term needs of the student are balanced in the development of the plan.

Adhering to the previous three principles during plan development establishes a foundation for thinking long term rather than short term when behavior intervention plans are developed and implemented. Moreover, well-designed positive outcomes should in and of themselves give rise to intervention ideas and procedures. For example, providing an artistic high school student with alternative media to complete class projects might arise naturally out of a planned outcome that states, "The student experiences more choice and autonomy over what is learned and how learning is expressed within his general education classes." It must be remembered, however, that such authentic goals and outcomes are best achieved when the person with challenges has access to the settings and experiences afforded to other students who are achieving these and similar outcomes without special supports. Especially productive intervention ideas and procedures can emerge by placing the student within the settings in which the desired outcomes are to be realized, then building into these settings behavioral, social, and academic accommodations as needed. Generating hypotheses about the functions served by the behaviors can help define more precisely the nature of the accommodations that are needed.

Delineate Hypotheses

In hypothesis-based intervention, the educator uses student assessment information to develop hypotheses about how the student's motivational and communication needs may be driving the behaviors, how existing contingencies of consequation might be related to problems in some situations and helpful in others, and/or how antecedent and setting events may be occasioning the presence or absence of particular behaviors. These hypotheses can then be directly translated into two types of action steps within the behavior intervention plan: 1) steps that alter the ecological and interpersonal conditions of the environment to prevent or attenuate problems and 2) steps that provide the student with adaptive alternative responses (replacement behaviors) so that he or she can successfully meet needs without using the behaviors that others view as inappropriate or difficult.

As noted in Chapter 5, the specific hypotheses that educators construct to guide their selection of intervention strategies represent the pivotal points in hypothesis-based intervention. A hypothesis is most enlightening and prescriptive when, written in a common language, it correlates specific and prevalent conditions with the presence or absence of particular behavioral concerns. Moreover, although different situations may require different wording, it is useful for a hypothesis to identify setting and/or task conditions, correlated behavioral patterns, and probable motivational factors.

In some situations, developing clusters of hypotheses that describe the same scenario from different angles can help create understanding and solutions that focus on prevention. In the following two examples, the first hypothesis provides the primary information about the situation, the problem, and potential underlying causes. The second hypothesis piggybacks on the first, focusing on plausible strategies for the adults to use to avoid problems and secure positive responses to their directives.

1. "When asked to complete a worksheet during writing instruction, Julie is more likely to have a tantrum if she indicates "no" and the adult keeps applying pressure, because Julie would rather continue working on—or finish—whatever she was doing prior to the directive."
2. "When asked to complete a worksheet during writing instruction, Julie is more likely to eventually comply if the adult briefly backs off and lets Julie finish what she is doing or offers Julie an alternative time to complete her present work."

As most human behavior is complexly influenced by numerous variables, behavior intervention plans are more likely to be successful if a variety of different hypotheses are developed. These should collectively address

- The different behavioral patterns that are part of the precipitating circumstances (e.g., transition problems on the playground, not completing instructions during academics, acting out during class lectures)
- Situations in which certain problems are both more or less likely to occur (e.g., transition difficulties to social studies but not to lunch, difficulty with work completion during science but not during social studies, acting out during class lectures except in math class)
- The factors within situations that seem to explain a behavior's presence or absence (e.g., transitions off the playground after recess are difficult because social studies follows, and this class is difficult for this student in the absence of accommodations; the student does not act out during science lectures because Mr. Green treats the student as a star pupil, which is very different from how he is treated in many other classes).

Because they can suggest different and sometimes distinctive procedures for addressing behavioral issues, multiple sets of hypotheses can also help educators realize a major property of a well-constructed behavior intervention plan: the incorporation of multiple intervention components, simultaneously and differentially addressing a variety of setting, task, outcome, and student preference issues (e.g., Horner et al., 1990). For example, Kern, Childs, Dunlap, Clarke, and Falk (1994) combined a variety of assessment activities to derive the following five key hypotheses about a particular student's levels of academic task engagement within three elementary classrooms: 1) engagement as a function of the task's handwriting demands, 2) engagement as a function of problem solving versus drill and practice expectations, 3) engagement as a function of whether the task was broken down into smaller units or required one long episode, 4) engagement as a function of the teacher providing reminders versus leaving the student to him- or herself, and 5) engagement as a function of being able to choose to work in a study carrel. Each of the student's three teachers were then given the freedom to construct their own multicomponent intervention plans based on one or more of the five hypotheses, which they could tailor to their own curricular demands and teaching styles. The overall intervention package, which consisted of these differential applications of the five hypotheses across the three classrooms, proved effective in increasing this student's overall academic engagement.

There are two especially useful principles for constructing hypotheses. First, several works (e.g., Jackson & Leon, 1998b; Moes & Frea, 2000) indicate that the conditions and situations of the natural communities in which the student participates should be used in hypothesis development. Put differently, a student should not be moved into a clinical setting for the initial generation of either the specific hypotheses or intervention steps and procedures. Such settings cannot simulate the interaction of the ecological and interpersonal variables that are typically associated with real-life patterns of positive and problematic behavior. Moreover, when possible, educators should examine the full range of situations that characterize the student's day in school and in various community settings.

Second, although hypotheses at many different levels of detail may be helpful, if an intervention does not suggest itself when a specific hypothesis' information is examined, then a deeper level of analysis may be required. For example, a teacher may hypothesize that a student who exhibits many behavioral problems at school in contrast to few behavioral problems at home does so because he or she would rather be at home than at school. Despite its lack of specificity, such an hypothesis is useful because it raises further questions about the conditions of life at school versus at home, the answers to which may prove to be important for understanding this student's behavior. At the same time, a deeper level of analysis is clearly needed for developing actual intervention procedures. This deeper analysis may show that the student experiences a sense of caring and belonging at home but not in his or her school relationships. The development of hypotheses about the specific affective relationships between the student and members of her home versus her school environments can then provide the level of detail necessary for creating interventions that address the student's emotional and affiliation needs even as they help ameliorate behavioral problems and conflicts.

In solving especially complex and difficult problems, it can sometimes be helpful to create visual representations of the pertinent antecedent, behavioral, and consequent events associated with a given hypothesis. Sugai, Lewis-Palmer, and Hagan (1998) offered an exceptionally useful tool for analyzing competing pathways, which is provided in blank form in the appendix. Figure 7.4, a filled-out version of this tool, shows that a specific problem behavior is first situated between the setting and antecedent events that are believed to be occasioning the behavior and the consequences that are believed to be maintaining it. For Cary, talking out loud and not working tend to be occasioned by headaches and sitting near peers, and these behaviors seem to be maintained by adult and peer attention. Next, the involved educators envision what change in the student they would like to see (desired alternative) and what they are willing to live with (acceptable alternative). For Cary, sitting quietly and working are desired alternatives, and helping at the front of the classroom or sitting in the back of the room are acceptable alternatives. Because the desired alternative may require the student to come to value a different set of consequences than those that maintain the problem behavior, the involved educators must also generate a prediction of what will

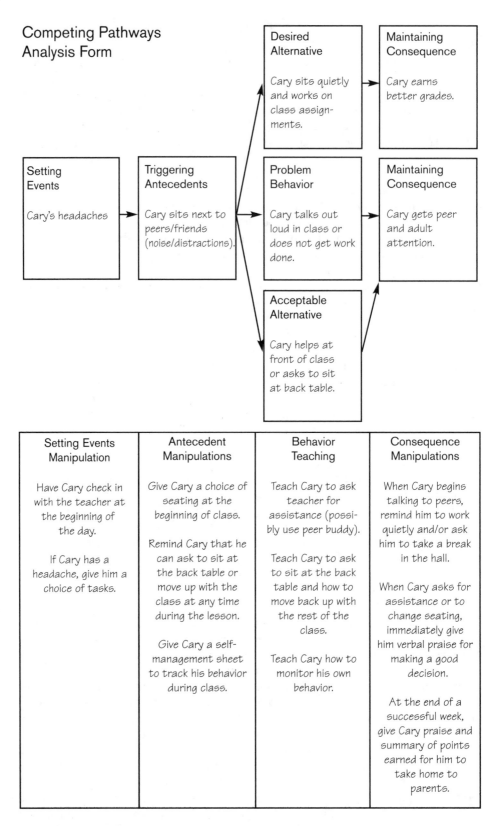

Figure 7.4. Illustration of a competing pathways analysis. (From Sugai, G., Lewis-Palmer, T., & Hagan, S. [1998]. Using functional assessments to develop behavior support plans. *Preventing School Failure, 43*[1], 11. Adapted with permission of the Helen Dwight Reid Educational Foundation. Published by Heldref Publications, 1319 Eighteenth Street, NW, Washington, DC 20036-1802. Copyright © 1998.)

maintain the new behaviors once they begin to occur. It is believed that better grades will provide sufficient reward to help Cary continue to use his newly developed behaviors. Finally, as shown in the four boxes at the bottom of Figure 7.4, the involved educators must develop intervention steps for prevention (first two boxes), instruction (third box), and handling the behaviors when they occur (fourth box).

Another example of a useful visual representation of key events is shown in Figure 7.5. Unlike Figure 7.4, this diagram focuses on the specific behaviors of a student (Andrea) in relation to adult commands at school, as well as the team's estimates of the conditional probabilities associated with Andrea's likely responses (see Repp, 1999). When an adult communicates an expectation to Andrea, her four possible responses are that 1) she goes into "escape mode" (e.g., looks away, drops to floor), 2) she grabs in anger (e.g., an "anger grab" at the adult's shirt or hair), 3) she complies with the directive, or 4) she complies if another option is quickly made available. The probabilities, which appear within the arrows, report expectations for known likes (e.g., listening to a story read by an adult) and known dislikes (e.g., doing math work). The line that connects "escape mode" with "complies when given another option" provides a clue about an activity that became part of Andrea's intervention plan: When Andrea's behavior indicates that she is actively trying to escape the situation, offering the choice of a desired activity is one way to give compliance a higher probability. This finding was an innovation for Andrea's team, because adults had typically reacted to her escape mode behaviors by trying to force agreement with their selections, then consequating the escape behaviors by removing her from the setting.

Finally, labels (e.g., autism, conduct disorders) are not helpful in developing hypotheses designed to assist a team of educators in better understanding behavioral problems. Labels may even be counterproductive or hurtful if they are used in initial hypothesis delineation and subsequent behavioral intervention decisions. In his trea-

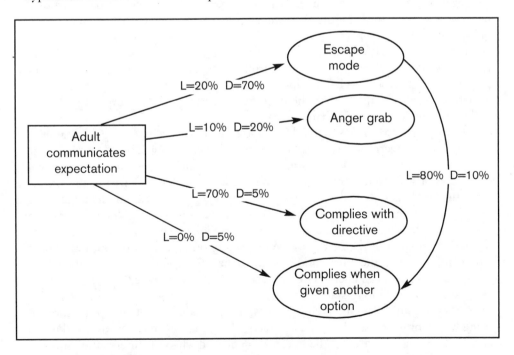

Figure 7.5.   Andrea's different responses to adult expectations. (Key: L = likes activity, D = dislikes activity.)

tise on large-scale decision making, Dörner commented, "By labeling a bundle of problems with a single conceptual label, we make dealing with it easier—provided we're not interested in solving it" (1996, p. 55). Labels are easy to use when one is not expected to do anything about the concerns that they represent. As Dörner's noted, "A simple label can't make the complex nature of a problem go away, but it can so obscure complexity that we lose sight of it. And that, of course, we find a great relief" (p. 55).

Generate Forecasts

Dörner stated, "The essence of planning is to think through consequences of certain actions and see whether those actions will bring us closer to our desired goal" (1996, pp. 136–137). This statement captures the heart of what is described in this book as *forecasting*. Especially in the case of formal behavior interventions, support planning must include efforts to conceptualize the possible effects of different intervention steps and procedures on student growth and progress, problem prevention, the management of crises, and resource utilization. Forecasting involves juxtaposing information about desired outcomes and behavioral hypotheses with the intervention options that arise out of the analysis of these issues to generate descriptions and projections of how different intervention procedures will likely affect learning, behavior, and resource allocation.

Forecasting can be implicit, in which unstated assumptions are used to anticipate the results of an intervention. For example, a team may simply feel that giving a particular student more voice in how his assignments are completed will improve assignment completion. Forecasting can also be explicit, in which the analytical activities associated with formulating outcomes and delineating hypotheses are used to describe and project various possible futures. For example, a team may know from functional behavioral assessment that if the same student is given more voice in assignment completion, he will probably complete more assignments. Forecasting can also vary in comprehensiveness. It may involve little more than making a series of "If we do . . . then the student will . . ." statements during a meeting, or it may involve complex flowcharts that express relationships between various behaviors and intervention activities. Obviously, the greater the degree of concern, the more explicit and comprehensive the forecasting activities must be.

It was suggested previously in this chapter that one's reality model about a set of problems and concerns is very likely to be incomplete or wrong. This is especially true when a team of educators faces a student with long-standing and chronic behavioral difficulties or when reintegration to a general education setting is part of the agenda for a student. Although it is always best to bear this point in mind, this dilemma never gives intervention planners license to skip the forecasting process. Not attempting to envision relationships between actions and results violates the very point of developing an intervention in the first place. When acting on a person's behalf, one should have confidence that the intervention can prove beneficial, and confidence of this sort evolves out of careful and deliberate forecasting. At the same time, when a problem is especially difficult or long-standing, educators must be prepared to adjust their forecasts, then rethink their intervention steps and procedures. It is not a question of being wrong or unprepared; rather, it is recognizing that one did not have, and probably could not have had, all of the information needed when the intervention was initially planned.

When preparing formal behavior intervention plans, forecasting can take several different forms, some of which are detailed in Chapters 10 and 11. One particular forecasting sequence is illustrated next in the case of a high school student named Kendra. Precipitating circumstances for Kendra's problem behavior include transition difficulties when she is enjoying an activity or has no desire to participate in an upcoming activity. A possible long-term outcome identified for Kendra might be that she will successfully participate each day in at least some of the activities that occur in each of her classes. The team may also set short-term expectations for Kendra, delineating reasonable expectations for her in 1 month regarding her participation in various classes.

Using information about what Kendra enjoys and what she finds unpleasant (some of which may have come from the behavioral hypotheses), forecasting begins with visualizing steps and procedures that can enhance Kendra's enjoyment of and participation in her classes as a valued member. Then, bearing in mind these steps and procedures, the team considers the impact of transition problems on the realization of class participation outcomes. The team then makes decisions about how much to emphasize these transition concerns, as well as what resources are needed. (It is possible that the solutions developed for realizing class participation outcomes will preclude the need for further work on transition problems.) Next, if needed, the team utilizes the hypothesis-based knowledge of how, when, and under what conditions transition problems are likely to focus on finding ways to help Kendra reach closure on present activities, rethinking what happens during and who is involved in the activities that presently occur as part of her class schedule, developing ways to enhance positive anticipation of upcoming events, and/or planning ways to handle inevitable transition difficulties. The team then generates different tactics for facilitating transitions and for handling problem situations and considers the likelihood that each tactic can make a difference within particular situations. To be effective, the tactics selected for facilitating transitions and for handling transition problems may often need to assume different forms across situations (e.g., transitions from reading to math classes versus from math class to lunch), people (e.g., specific teachers), and activities (e.g., a social studies lesson on African culture versus a lesson on reading maps). As tactics are considered, certain staff training and resource needs become apparent, and it is during forecasting that the team must begin projecting how to meet these needs. Finally, the team reconsiders behavior change expectations for both class participation and transition activities in light of the proposed intervention activities, and the behavior change expectations are adjusted as necessary.

Inherent within this example are five phases of forecasting when it is relatively comprehensive and explicit in form. First, begin with positive long-term goals and short-term expectations, and develop steps and procedures for the realization of these outcomes. Second, consider the problem behaviors as they affect progress toward these outcomes, and decide how much emphasis and what kinds of resources are needed both to prevent these problems and to handle them when they occur. Third, use behavioral hypotheses to generate prevention and skill acquisition tactics for these problems, then specify guidelines and tactics for handling problems when they occur. Fourth, consider the resource and training needs that are required as different tactics are developed and selected for inclusion in the plan. Fifth and finally, reexamine the desired change expectations with respect to the long-term outcomes and the anticipated problem behaviors in light of the proposed support activities, and adjust these expectations as needed.

It is important to emphasize that forecasting should be applied more toward developing a variety of tactical options and recommendations and less toward generating one-step solutions. For example, if a team's information suggests that Josh's disruptive talking in his high school classes will decrease if he believes that the class material is more connected with his interests, then intervention planning could include a combination of the following options: 1) assisting Josh in creating a personal vision and related learning goals, 2) reconfiguring Josh's schedule of classes in relation to his goals and interests, and 3) helping teachers plan class or homework projects that address Josh's interests and are consistent with curricular and learning expectations.

Of course, forecasting can lead to new problems, such as, in Josh's case, how to handle a required course in which the teacher's instructional activities are relatively fixed or a course in which a teacher has strict and unbending expectations for student performance. At this point, the team should examine other knowledge about Josh to generate separate forecasts that offer intervention strategies for these very specific situations. For example, if the team knows that Josh is less likely to talk disruptively in class when he is confident in his ability to perform the class's required activities, his intervention plan might include peer or adult tutoring during a study hall for difficult, required subject matter. Finally, it is possible that forecasting will partially or completely miss the target, and Josh will continue his disruptive talking in certain classes. At this point, another analysis may be needed, and a whole new set of conditions that were not initially anticipated might be uncovered. For instance, peers in his new classes may tease or reject Josh. This would require Josh's team to rethink parts of the intervention plan and develop new planning forecasts that address these emerging issues.

Forecasting may seem complex and time consuming. Yet, when long-term outcomes and short-term expectations are well developed and the behavioral hypotheses are either well-constructed or self-evident, forecasting becomes an emergent property of these activities. This is especially the case for relatively simple plans, in which forecasting can be more implicit. Nevertheless, even in more complex planning processes, the key to making explicit forecasting work is the quality and detail present in the formulated outcomes and the delineated hypotheses.

INITIATE THE INTERVENTION

Intervention initiation is the process of using the information that was gathered and organized during planning to design and propose to others a plan of action that relates to behavior change. Of course, the degree of concern determines how much effort, formality, and description go into the plan. When the degree of concern about a student's behavior is minimal, the plan could be nothing more than a teacher using data about the student in different situations to develop better ways to interact with him or her. As the severity of the behavior increases and the degree of concern rises, plan initiation may involve using the information that was gathered during planning to write a formal behavior intervention plan.

In all cases, as mentioned previously in this chapter, a plan that is designed to change the behavior of another should provide evidence that it is accomplishing three purposes: 1) It should promote the *growth and learning* of the student and that of others who come into contact with the student, 2) it should enhance the *comfort* of the student and those who come into contact with the student, and 3) it should foster in others an *understanding* of the student while also helping the student gain an understanding of the issues and needs of the school. These three intervention purposes have a greater probability of being met when an intervention's components reflect the quality of richness. *Richness* refers to the degree to which a plan's specifications and guidelines branch beyond the specifics of the behavioral conflicts and into related areas, such as the evolution of student–student and student–adult relationships within the school community; the communication and control needs of a student who is in conflict with the school; and changing the effectiveness of the school community in its work with learners who have diverse needs.

Richness communicates the quintessential idea that good interventions are less about behavior and more about the long-term growth of the student with challenging behaviors *and* those who work with the student. As noted by Dörner (1996), richness is a quality of good decision making when people are seriously concerned with resolving problems. Dörner asserted that good decision makers address problems by using multiple decisions, which branch into various areas that are connected to the problem at hand. The richer and more varied the intervention, the more likely it will provide a robust base for success as the intervention progresses.

Richness can be viewed as a lateral expansion of "multicomponent interventions" (Horner et al., 1990). A particular student's intervention plan possesses multicomponent properties when it provides different hypothesis-based prescriptions for different situations and different sets of behaviors. Such an intervention plan would also be considered rich if it addresses a variety of long-term change and quality of life indicators for the student in addition to problem amelioration and hypothesis-based prevention.

When initiating a behavior intervention plan, team members need to construct the plan and recruit resources. These two activities are defined next.

Construct the Plan

As noted by Albin, Lucyshyn, Horner, and Flannery, a support plan is "actually a prescription, or set of directions, for those people involved in implementing the plan" (1996, p. 86). In other words, it is a guide for the decision-making activities of those who interact with the student. In addressing the aforementioned issues of growth, comfort, and understanding, plans should provide guidelines and information for making three types of decisions: 1) fixed decisions, such as decisions to place a child in a particular first grade class or to create a daily schedule with built-in activity options and transition processes; 2) fluid decisions, such as the delineation of three teacher options to be used when a child reacts negatively after being given a directive (e.g., ask the child if he or she needs a break, offer another activity choice, explain the task in more detail); and 3) recommendations, such as five to seven general suggestions for enhancing learning within a particular class to prevent problems.

Fluid decisions can be especially important when the challenging behaviors are disruptive or dangerous. They are often associated with threshold points, in which the right decision can make the difference between preserving order or having a prolonged period of disorder, as well as possible injury. Fluid decisions are similar to recommendations in that they usually contain several options. Yet, fluid decisions resemble fixed decisions in that, although several options are available, the options are often narrowed to a range of best choices.

Depending on how they are constructed and used, all three types of decisions can be consistent with the notion of heuristic decision making. Recommendations clearly meet the criteria of heuristic decision making because the choices that a teacher has available are open, as long as he or she keeps in mind the three major purposes for the intervention (i.e., promote growth and learning, enhance comfort, create understanding). Fluid decisions are also very much in line with heuristic decision making because they encourage on-the-spot thinking about the best procedures, given immediate circumstances and the pending likelihood of something desirable or undesirable happening. Also, over the course of an intervention, if conditions improve, the options contained within a particular fluid decision can become recommendations to be used when needed. Finally, although fixed decisions do possess a certain permanency, they can be subject to change depending on the progress that occurs or fails to materialize during the course of an intervention. Fixed decisions are consistent with heuristic decision making if they are viewed as appropriate only within specific contexts and time periods and they are subject to deletion or modification in relation to the outcomes of the intervention activities. The latter point is important when one considers how behavior support efforts are sometimes inappropriately construed by educators: An apparent lack of student progress is viewed as the student's failure in relation to a well-designed plan, as opposed to the failure of a plan in its present form in relation to the student.

Selecting an appropriate documentation format for recording plan components is a necessary step when a behavior intervention plan is being initiated. Buck, Polloway, Kirkpatrick, Patton, and Fad (2000) offered a suggested behavior intervention form with headings that include specific goals, proposed interventions, people responsible, and evaluation methods and criteria. Yet, many districts have their own formats for completing behavior intervention plans, and educators will usually need to configure their planning documents in relation to the constraints set by a school district's documentation guidelines. Formats that have proven useful in the authors' work are discussed in Chapters 10 and 11 and typically include the following: descriptions of precipitating circumstances, including hypotheses about behaviors; vision statements and long-term outcomes and how they are to be achieved; short-term expectations; decision steps and procedures for prevention, skill instruction, and handling crisis; and selected supervision, evaluation, and training issues.

Recruit Resources

Behavior intervention plans may require designating and securing a number of different kinds of resources, including specialized training for staff and peers; people or teams of people who will be available to provide a plan's learning, prevention, and crisis supports in the classroom and other environments; materials, such as communication and schedule boards, self-monitoring data sheets, or video cameras; and experienced personnel and appropriate materials for problem solving and progress evaluation. As discussed previously, many resource recruitment decisions should be made as forecasting proceeds because resource decisions must be tied to a plan's specific intervention activities.

Typically, resources trickle into situations at about the same speed as people learn to conduct the intervention procedures; thus, it is always important to take the long view when engaged in deliberate behavior support efforts with a student who has behavioral challenges. This means that it is important to avoid making premature judgments about a plan's effectiveness, such as concluding that a plan is a failure when the facts show that the required picture communication schedule was never designed for the student.

IMPLEMENT THE INTERVENTION

The implementation of a viable behavior support effort depends on strategy as much as planning. Planning provides the initial forecasts that allow educators to act in a responsible manner; strategy makes possible the necessary movement through the murky social and political realities of schools.

Dörner noted that von Moltke, a 19th-century Prussian field marshal, defined *strategy* as a "system of makeshifts" that provides for the

> Further elaboration of an original guiding idea under constantly changing circumstances. It is the art of acting under the most demanding conditions . . . that is why general principles, rules derived from them, and systems based on these rules cannot possibly have any value for strategy. (1996, pp. 97–98)

When the behavioral issues are severe and the degree of concern is high, effective strategic action often requires the presence of positive relationships with the other participating educators and the key administrators in the building. These relationships become the cornerstone of the successful plan when bumps and hardships occur along the way. People are generally more willing to pass through difficulties with a student if they have a positive relationship with those who have instigated action on behalf of the student. Part of what creates such a relationship for special educators is demonstrating over time a willingness to provide the necessary supports for the classroom teachers, paraprofessionals, and others who carry out an intervention. This can involve regularly making accommodations for the special requests of classroom teachers and others, such as agreeing to co-develop specific lessons and activities for a classroom teacher or teaching the class on a day when the general educator has an emergency. It can also involve graciously accepting a setback with a particular student, such as when the student's behavior becomes sufficiently out of control that the classroom teacher demands some form of relief through removal. The process of taking a loss must be viewed as a temporary setback, however, and not the final outcome of a failed plan.

The student's day-to-day movements and activities within classrooms and other environments are the data that lay the foundation for strategic action. Of course, behavioral data only tell a small part of the story. For example, a source for especially important data could be how certain team members feel about and react to an intervention that is in progress. In other words, closely monitoring stressors, which can include the anxiety or fears of the people who are implementing a plan (Albin et al., 1996), often provide a better indication of how a plan is faring than the behavioral data.

Based in part on the work of Jackson and Leon (1998a), six key activities associated with implementing an intervention are described in the following subsections. Certainly, if the primary purpose of an intervention is to simply enhance one's practices or if the degree of concern about the behavior is minimal, then the activities described next may occur informally and in a substantially abbreviated form. To provide clear and useful explanations of the underlying processes and issues, however, the following descriptions reflect more serious behavioral concerns.

Put in Place Educational and Environmental Changes

The fixed decisions, fluid decisions, and recommendations that are related to educational placement, instructional activities, and prevention must be communicated to the people who will enact them. Even with the best of plans, it can take weeks to get these processes started and have them occur regularly. This period is especially critical for the student. Not only is he or she operating under new expectations and experiencing potentially novel activities, the student is also likely feeling the effects of the inconsistencies and errors made by the educators who are still learning the plan. It is not uncommon for even very good plans to fail during these early weeks because people do not allow for mistakes during the start-up process.

Put in Place Professional Development

Schools sometimes encourage educators who need a particular kind of information to attend an in-service training session. The training may use real-life examples that fit the content of the training, but these examples may not match the complex and varied situations that the participants face with specific students. Especially for highly motivated teachers, certain kinds of information can be acquired through workshops of this type; certainly, protective restraint procedures have been taught in this format for years. For behavior support efforts to be most effective, however, the training that is provided should be tailored to the steps and procedures prescribed within a particular behavior intervention plan.

Put in Place Incident Response and Crisis Procedures

Decisions about the proper management of crisis situations must be communicated to everyone who is a part of the student's education. If crisis issues are addressed as part of the support process, all of the involved educators must have a clear knowledge of their options and the steps for returning normalcy to a classroom.

Although this book emphasizes the long-term goals of the support effort, a negative undercurrent will likely appear in the school community if incident response and crisis support fail. Members of the broader school community may be glad to hear that a student is attending more classes and has made a friend, but they can turn against the support process quickly and without warning if they believe that behavioral incidences are not being handled properly or are jeopardizing the learning or safety of others. Hence, particularly during the early weeks, the ways that adults handle problem behaviors—especially crisis situations—must be carefully monitored, frequently revisited, and collaboratively discussed.

Effective crisis support requires a school to behave as a community rather than as an aggregate of classrooms and individuals. If only a single person is trained in crisis support, such as the paraprofessional who works with a student, the crisis support process is in jeopardy from the start. Effective crisis support requires a coordinated effort in which a variety of individuals are trained to play a variety of roles in the support process. Moreover, keeping the larger school community informed—at least with respect to knowing that a plan does exist and that proper crisis management processes are in place—can be useful for containing the rumor spreading that is bound to emerge in any human community.

Ensure Critical Communications

A complex support process requires a network of participants, each having specific information needs in order to carry out their part of the plan. Mechanisms for ensuring the initial communication of the plan's steps and procedures, plan revisions, and information on progress can include regular meetings between specific participants, written communications, and informal contacts initiated relatively frequently by the educator most responsible for plan conduct (e.g., special education teacher, psychologist, counselor).

Ensure On-Demand Problem Solving

In a complex behavior support effort, two types of situations that evoke discomfort in those implementing the plan are bound to arise: 1) when the educator did something not identified in the plan and 2) when the educator did what the plan required, but the results were not as anticipated. Both of these situations are remedied by opportunities to reflect and problem solve with others, either immediately or at the end of the school day.

It is useful to have a specific format that all participants follow for quick, on-the-spot reflection and problem solving. The team could agree on using the following three-step process, which is partially based on the six facets of understanding discussed in Chapter 6 (Wiggins & McTighe, 1998):

- Describe and characterize what happened.
- Use questions to organize reflections about explanation, interpretation, perspective, and empathy (see Chapter 8 for questions that can be used in this process).
- End the session with reflections that center on application and self-knowledge.

Evaluate Change in the Learner and the Community

Although no one would seriously question the importance of keeping data on progress, the format and focus of measures remain critical, unresolved issues in education (e.g., Singer, 2000). The dilemma has two parts. First, as previously mentioned, past classroom management practices have often emphasized quantitative data, and this has been translated by educators as frequency counts of problem behaviors, coupled with sometimes superficial reports of learning progress. Relying on these types of data can pose a serious threat to behavioral support. Teachers should instead rely on rich descriptions of behavioral incidents, embedded within a sustained focus on progress toward the long- and short-term goals of the intervention. Second, many educators use their data exclusively to assess whether the student is improving and not as a mechanism for evaluating the support process. It is common to find situations in which the available data emphasize student noncompliance with the plan but there are no data on the integrity of plan implementation. Instead, educators should treat data that show continuing problems as evidence that the behavior intervention plan needs revision, and they should also keep data on intervention processes.

REVISE THE INTERVENTION

The quality of richness, when built into a behavior intervention plan, provides a robustness that can contribute to the plan's initial success. If there are a number of different options from which to choose, such as when a plan includes a number of recommendations and/or fluid decisions, the line separating "appropriate" and "inappropriate" for on-the-spot decisions is not so stringent that adults find themselves making more wrong than right decisions. Also, because of the range of "correct" possibilities for different situations, it is more likely that different adults can find at least a few approved strategies that fit their own styles of interaction and the contexts in which they operate. Finally, a buffer exists against the natural patterns of error that inevitably occur in real-world situations, because parts of the plan are often in effect even if the educators falter in their implementation of other plan components. For example, a group of educators may be having difficulty appropriately implementing designated crisis management steps but may still be encouraging peer relationships as intended by the plan. Thus, a movement toward success, albeit not always evident, could be occurring that would not even be possible in a more sparse plan that only prescribed steps and procedures for behavioral crises.

At the same time, as already indicated, people who initiate problem solving for complex problems usually operate with a mental model that is incomplete or wrong (Dörner, 1996). Hence, although plan richness can help, the processes of analysis and forecasting, described earlier, should be viewed as necessary and ongoing throughout an intervention. Dörner's research also revealed an important distinction between good and poor decision makers regarding how each approaches (or avoids) the task of revising an intervention. He noted that poor decision makers view the initial fact-finding process (e.g., gathering information) as a search for absolute truths rather than a search for testable hypotheses that will be confirmed or rejected when an intervention is implemented. Hence, it is not surprising that poor decision makers' post-intervention reflections about their decisions tend to focus on recapitulation rather than critical analysis and increased understanding. People who are rigid and unwilling to rethink a behavior intervention plan in the face of discrepant facts are likely to experience failure in their behavior support efforts. Conversely, decision makers who realize from the outset that their plan will need revision improve a plan's chances for success.

One of the dilemmas that a team of educators faces is achieving an appropriate balance between stability and innovation when revising a behavior intervention plan—that is, how much a plan should be changed and how much of it should stay the same at any given point in time. This problem is often complicated by the emotional reactions of particular adults, who may not clearly understand the support plan's goals or may have personal agendas that are inconsistent with the goals of the support process. This problem may also be exasperated by the student's seeming lack of progress, especially if measurement efforts solely focus on a prominent target behavior.

In terms of innovation, Dörner's (1996) findings indicated that a major difference between good and poor decision makers during the revision process is that poor decision makers make more drastic innovations across all intervals of time. That is, each time decisions are made, poor decision makers are more likely than good decision makers to introduce elements to their plans that significantly deviate from their previous decisions. Poor decision makers also do not properly evaluate the positive qualities of what already exists. In other words, in their efforts to correct a problem, they are more likely than good decision makers to discard aspects of an intervention that, in fact, were working in some way. Finally, when under pressure, poor decision makers are likely to call for overdoses of already established measures rather than examine what most clearly needs changing.

One of the ways that these signs of poor decision making are evident during the course of an intervention is in the way poor decision makers oversteer in their revision decisions. They interpret an observed problem as evidence that a major change in the plan is absolutely required. Dörner (1996) noted that oversteering reflects a tendency to make decisions based on the immediate and pressing circumstances at one point in time, as opposed to considering present circumstances in relation to the intervention's history. For instance, poor decision makers who observe that a student is "still yelling" on day 11 of an intervention might drastically reduce the student's already small amount of time spent in general education classes. In contrast, good decision makers in this same situation would express concern about the yelling but would try to explain its continued presence and look for signs that some solutions are actually working. They may find, for example, that the adults are becoming more adept at prevention, the peers are becoming more skilled at redirecting the student, and the student is more comfortable in the general education setting. Good decision makers may then discover that the student's requests for breaks, which were once honored, are now being dismissed by a paraprofessional who is engaged in a personal struggle between honoring communications and establishing firm boundaries. In contrast to poor decision makers in this situation, good decision makers are likely to propose that certain things remain (e.g., keep the general education schedule) and that emerging concerns (e.g., the student's break requests now being ignored) be addressed with specific measures. As this example shows, good decision makers use "*differentials* between sequential stages" and not "the *situation* in each stage" to consider the changes that might be needed in an ongoing intervention (Dörner, 1996, p. 30, emphasis in original).

These findings provide simple and direct guidelines for navigating the revision process. Even if an intervention seems to have major implementation problems, it is best to think conservatively about the revision process. This involves first evaluating all of the plan's components to decide what needs to be retained (as opposed to changed), then making small changes that directly address specific concerns. Finally, far from complicating revision decisions, rich interventions—which contain numerous diverging branches—are an asset. This is because a rich plan provides a broad base of activities in which change decisions can be made. Hence, even when certain revisions are substantial, stability is assured by the broader range of elements that remain essentially unchanged.

Plan revision activities sometimes falter when a narrow focus on the problem behaviors obscures the school's failure to fully implement steps that promote the support plan's long-term goals. This problem can sometimes be avoided by creating an agenda for problem solving and plan revision meetings, in which the long-term issues are examined before crisis management concerns. Table 7.1 provides a recommended sequence of topics for a team meeting to consider behavior intervention plan revisions.

Finally, the continued existence of the long-term removal from general education option can negatively affect a team's willingness to revise an existing plan. First of all, the availability of this option allows poor decision makers to use situational lack of progress as a vehicle for removal. Moreover, even good decision makers are less likely to take the time and effort to revise a plan for a difficult situation when they know that it is relatively easy to shift the problem to another setting. The latter observations reflect another insight that Dörner (1996) offered about decision making in complex situations. Sometimes, it is not the lack of knowledge that causes the problem. The mistake lies less with "not knowing than not wanting to know" the information that, if sought, could produce viable solutions in difficult situations (p. 58). Until schools are expected to take responsibility for all students who can legitimately enter their

Table 7.1. Recommended sequence of meeting topics for behavior intervention plan revisions

Step	Action	Important questions
1	Review the student's vision and long-term activity participation, relationship, and self-autonomy goals.	Have we lost sight of the long-term objectives of this student's support plan? Do the in-place activities really address the long-term outcomes? Is the student developing relationships?
2	Review (and revise as necesary) the short-term expectations.	Are the immediate behavior change expectations for this student unreasonable? Has the student made progress in certain areas that can help us rethink our expectations at this juncture in the program?
3	Review (and revise as necessary) the short-term prevention steps and procedures and the proposed adaptive alternatives.	Are the prevention steps and procedures difficult to implement? What could ease implementation? Are our hypotheses holding true? Are we working with the most relevant hypotheses? Are there more effective ways to teach this student appropriate ways to meet his or her personal needs?
4	Review (and revise as necessary) educator responses to challenging behavior.	Are we having difficulties implementing responses to problem behaviors? If so, what could help? What is the student's present response to these steps and procedures?

doors and special education resources are reallocated so that they more adequately address student success in general education, teams of educators will continue to express understandable reluctance to engage in lengthy plan revision processes. It is always easier to pass a persisting problem on to someone else than to solve it.

REFLECTIONS AND REVIEW OF THE PROTOCOL

Calne (1999) proposed that the ability to use reasoning processes during reflection and decision making needs to be resurrected from obscurity. Calne pointed out that what distinguishes the scientist from the charlatan is not specialized knowledge, because both lay claim to something called "expertise." Rather, the difference lies in the way that scientists develop exacting and coherent systems of principles, which over time yield consistent results when used in decision making. Calne argued that such systems result from the rigorous application of reasoning tools to the human problems of survival and adaptation.

Nowhere are these issues more pronounced than in the education of students with behavioral challenges. Although a variety of proven concepts and tools have emerged since the 1970s (see Chapter 2), public education relentlessly falls back on reactive strategies when addressing behavioral concerns. In fact, given the outcome data for students who have behavioral disorders (McLaughlin, Leone, Meisel, & Henderson, 1997), public education appears to be falling seriously short in meeting its responsibilities with these young people. The reasons for this failure are complex, but they may include a reliance on behavior intervention decisions that resemble the decisions of poor decision makers more than good decision makers. Hence, a good starting point for reform is to examine how behavior intervention decisions are made and then improve the decision makers' skills.

At the same time, the reliance on rational reasoning processes must be tempered with two fundamental realities. The first is that decisions about behavioral problems are invariably affected by one's emotions. The emotions that erupt in educators when reacting to violence and disruptions cannot be discounted. These reactions must be incorporated, rather than denied or ignored, in any proposal to resolve the issues that are posed by students with significant behavioral concerns. This is one reason why it is important to fully use Wiggins and McTighe's (1998) six facets of understanding when facing behavioral issues.

The second reality, based on late 20th-century studies of human decision making and noted by Todd (1999) in his review of Calne, is that logical reasoning processes are themselves constrained by cognitive and environmental limitations when decision makers work within complicated systems of human action and interaction. Indeed, this growing recognition of the limits that complex, dynamic systems pose for human decision making challenges the very notion that rigorous and coherent systems of principles can be reliably constructed and trusted for making intervention decisions in real-world settings.

The need for rationality and the realities of difficult emotions and complex environments are reconciled within the concept of heuristic decision making. The position that behavioral issues are best addressed through heuristic decision making does not preclude rationality, but it does require rethinking what it means to be "rational." Decision making that is grounded in classical concepts of rationality stresses the need for well-reasoned solutions that are based on sound theoretical principles. In contrast, heuristic decision making seeks solutions that are based on "ecological rationality"—that is, rationality that is "defined by its fit with reality" (Gigerenzer & Todd, 1999, p. 5).

This chapter has offered a problem-solving and decision-making protocol for defining and clarifying behavioral concerns where and when they occur and then generating, administering, and revising heuristics-based solutions to these concerns. Again, the major activities of this protocol for behavior support planning are

- Determine the degree of concern
- Plan the intervention
- Initiate the intervention
- Implement the intervention
- Revise the intervention

The entire protocol is shown in Figure 7.6. As shown in this figure, determining the degree of concern is a critical point in the process, and it has implications for the requirements in all subsequent steps. Activities across the three degrees of concern are distinguished from each other by the nature and extensiveness of the step completion process and the professional skills that are required. Regarding the nature of the step completion process, when the degree of concern is low, formulating outcomes may require simply reiterating the outcomes that are desired of all students in a class or a school. Intervention planning and actually initiating and implementing the plan may then occur simultaneously. Inversely, when the degree of concern is high, outcome designation may be quite specialized and an extended planning period may be necessary. Moreover, there may be long periods during which intervention components are tried, found wanting, and revised. In addition, it may be necessary to implement an

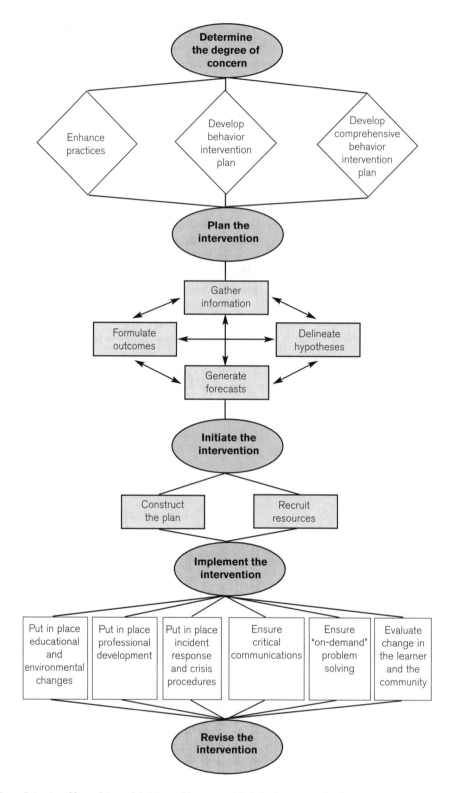

Figure 7.6. A problem-solving and decision-making protocol for behavior support planning.

intermediate plan until a more complete plan can be developed. What remains to be accomplished in this book is the description of these processes at practical levels and illustrations of these processes in schools. Chapters 8, 9, 10, and 11 address these issues.

Chapter 8

Support-Based Assessment

*"People only see
what they are prepared to see."*
—*Ralph Waldo Emerson*

Chapter 7 offered a protocol that sequenced the decision-making processes for developing and implementing behavior intervention plans. It is self-evident that dutifully following the protocol does not in and of itself ensure that educators will make *informed* decisions at each step. What differentiates informed decisions from uninformed decisions is the investment in assessment activities that can characterize present circumstances and provide future prognoses. Well-conceived assessment activities offer confidence that some decisions make more sense than others and credibility in the eyes of administrators, family members, and others. As recommended in Chapter 7, assessment activities can be aligned to the critical decisions that need to be made at the key points in planning, initiating, implementing, and revising an intervention.

According to Cohen and Spenciner (1998), assessment is the process of "observing, gathering, recording, and interpreting information to answer questions and make legal and instructional decisions about students" (p. 8). Following that definition, *behavioral assessment* consists of a variety of formal and informal data gathering, documenting, and interpreting activities that are used to assess conflicts between one or more students' actions and the norms and expectations of specific school or community settings. Behavioral assessment is very much "an exploratory, hypothesis-testing process in which a range of specific procedures are used to understand a given child, group, or social ecology and to formulate and evaluate specific intervention strategies" (Ollendick & Hersen, 1984, p. 6). Behavioral assessment 1) assists educators in characterizing and understanding behavioral concerns in relation to situations of occurrence and nonoccurrence; 2) permits educators to situate their concerns within the student's social and educational activities, needs, and aspirations; and 3) supports educators in contextualizing their concerns in relation to the "social, disciplinary, and interpersonal contexts" of the school community (Jackson & Leon, 1998a, p. 11).

Especially in the psychology and special education fields, behavioral assessment traditions emphasize data gathering and interpretation activities that focus on diagnostic and descriptive measurement for purposes of placement and problem elimination. In contrast to this remediation-based approach to assessment, the tenets and purposes of positive behavioral support suggest a different direction for assessment. Table 8.1 summarizes the major distinctions between these two approaches. As shown in the table, these two assessment approaches vary in their purposes, scope and focus, settings, instrumentation, and consequences for the student. For example, the purposes of remediation-based assessment range from classifying a student as eligible for special education services and determining placement, to collecting baseline on problem behaviors, and recommending the least restrictive interventions for eliminating the behavior. As the name implies, remediation-based assessment focuses on using data to make placement and programming decisions that are designed to "fix" a behavioral problem. In contrast, the purposes of support-based assessment are to address how behavioral concerns interface with socioecological factors such that an intervention is needed, to generate hypotheses for designing prevention and instruction steps and procedures, and to recommend specific supports to help the individual and others handle crises and reach their goals within natural communities. As the

Table 8.1.   Important distinctions between remediation-based assessment and support-based assessment

Parameters	Remediation-based assessment	Support-based assessment
Purposes	Conduct initial assessment in relation to specific criteria, then retest in relation to the same criteria.	Conduct initial assessment to build a feasible reality model, then reassess intermittently to update the model.
	Conduct assessment to select the least restrictive intervention.	Conduct assessment to select hypotheses-based intervention.
	Determine diagnosis and baseline levels of problem behaviors.	Understand why an individual behaves in certain ways.
	Recommend and select from various placement options.	Recommend and design appropriate, individual supports.
Scope and focus	Assess a person's abilities, aptitudes, and problems in relation to age-peer expectations.	Assess a person's participation and behavior in relation to others at home, at school, and in classroom situations.
	Conduct assessment to ascertain the individual's degree of adaptive and maladaptive behaviors.	Assess the features of the environment and the actions of others that trigger behavioral challenges or support more appropriate alternatives.
Settings	Conduct assessments in available settings, which might be apart from natural communities (e.g., clinics, special education rooms).	Conduct assessments in natural communities (e.g., typical home, school, work, and other community settings).
	Use established protocols and predefined activities.	Use natural activities and routines.
Instrumentation	Rely on norm-referenced tests and direct observations of behavioral frequency and duration.	Rely on informant-based procedures (e.g., interviews, dialogues, questionnaires) and direct observations of behavior in context.
	Use more standardized procedures.	Use more informal procedures.
Consequences	Determine what opportunities to offer or withhold from the individual (i.e., gatekeeping function).	Determine how to include and support the individual in the opportunities that are offered to age-peers (i.e., invitational function).

name implies, support-based assessment focuses on using information to better understand the student and to identify natural and introduced supports, which can help preserve and enhance the student's place in the community.

As suggested in Table 8.1, the major consequences of the remediation-based assessment approach are that the student who qualifies gains access to certain services but may also lose access to the social and learning opportunities provided to others. In contrast, the consequences of a support-based assessment approach are that a student with behavioral issues gains access to services that support continued involvement in the social and learning opportunities provided to others. In other words, remediation-based assessment serves a gatekeeping function that is a dual-edged sword: It defines how educational experiences are provided to and withheld from students who are defined in particular ways. Support-based assessment serves an invitational function because it attempts to identify ways to help the student, regardless of labels, remain with others but with learning assistance and support through times of crisis.

It is worth noting that support-based assessment may be less likely to result in the inappropriate labeling and removal of students from diverse cultures and ethnic backgrounds. Culturally diverse students are often misdiagnosed, and the diagnosis of differences as a disability can result in the inappropriate removal of these students from general education settings (see McIntyre, 1996; Sugai & Maheady, 1988; Webb-Johnson, 1999). In some cases, this has even contributed to a student's academic, social, and/or behavioral difficulties. A discussion of cultural diversity in relation to special education placement is beyond the scope of this book. However, the support model may help circumvent these problems because both the labeling process and removal decisions must be based on cumulative evidence that a variety of supports have been tried and have failed. Although there are vestiges of remediation-based assessment in many schools at the beginning of the 21st century, other schools are moving toward a support-based assessment approach. It is difficult for the two approaches to coexist within a school because of their differing assumptions, practices, and—in particular—the way that each drives resource allocation. Because this book's authors are committed to the support model, the remainder of this chapter focuses only on promising support-based assessment practices. The chapter begins with a discussion of four considerations for assessment within a positive behavioral support paradigm, some of which are based on guidelines that have already been established in this book. The sections "Assessment for Creating the Intervention" and "Assessment for Implementing the Intervention" follow the decision model presented in Figure 7.6. These two steps represent major junctures in the positive behavioral support process in which critical information is needed to make decisions about what type of intervention should be used and how well it is working, what is working, and how it should be revised. The chapter closes with some reflections on how educators within schools that have vastly different social and academic climates perceive and use behavioral data, which provides a transition to Section IV of this book.

FOUR CONSIDERATIONS IN SUPPORT-BASED ASSESSMENT

Assessment activities should define the behavioral support needs of the student(s) and prescribe the adults' decision processes and guidelines so that the conceived supports become real supports within the school and other environments. Conducting assessments to realize these purposes requires that educators consider a school's cultural context, the degree of concern, assessment and intervention to be an ongoing cyclical process, and the concept of social validity. These four points are discussed next.

The Cultural Context of the School

All assessment and intervention activities occur within a school's social and political culture, which consists of numerous implicit and sometimes conflicting attitudes and perceptions. These attitudes and perceptions frame how different educators view a particular child's behaviors and what interventions should be used for them. These attitudes and perceptions spring from each educator's definitions of the functions and limitations of the educational process, the fundamental nature of behavioral problems, and the roles of various adults in addressing different kinds of educational needs. This means that an individual educator's assessment activities must be embedded in larger processes of immersion in the school community, continuous and respectful dialogue with colleagues and others, and self-reflection on one's practices as they affect others.

From this perspective, the key to developing responsive solutions to problem behaviors lies in forming a reality model that consists of deep understandings of the relationships among the people who are involved in a situation, the interpretations of the events that these people hold, and an understanding of oneself as a participant in the circumstances surrounding a problem. Creating an understanding of this type requires that educators regularly ask questions about what they see and why they are seeing it, then base their data-gathering activities on these questions.

This is the essence of the guided inquiry process described in Chapter 6: Broad sets of questions frame the way that behavioral issues are examined and handled, and these questions are fielded not by a single "responsible educator" but by all educators who are participants in the process. When such inquiry processes guide data-gathering activities, then the adequacy of the data depends on the kinds of questions that are being asked when an intervention is planned.

Guidance in deciding what questions to ask can come from reexamining Wiggins and McTighe's (1998) six areas of understanding, which were presented in Chapter 6:

1. What is happening and why (explanation)
2. Knowing the meaning of different behavior patterns and related events as they affect the actions of others (interpretation)
3. Knowing how to translate explanation and interpretation into action (application)
4. Viewing the progression of events and processes from different angles as an integral part of assessment and plan design (perspective)
5. Seeing the progression of events and processes from the others' points of view (empathy)
6. Forming and applying a realistic view of oneself and how one's intervention design and implementation affects others (self-knowledge)

Table 8.2 presents questions that are related to these six facets of understanding. Questions such as these should be used to guide assessment activities; however, the level of precision and detail in which these questions are explored can vary depending on the degree of concern that is associated with a student's problem behaviors.

Educators would do well to remember that most traditional behavioral assessment activities, whether associated with informant interviews or observational procedures, primarily address questions that are related to explanation, interpretation, and application. Yet, informant-interview processes can be reframed by using questions

Table 8.2. Using the six facets of understanding to guide inquiry: Suggested questions for educators

Explanation

What different and distinctive patterns of behavior (both challenging and acceptable) are occurring? Within which activities, situations, and relationships are these patterns more likely?

What conditions in the environment seem to anticipate particular problem behavior patterns or seem to ensure their absence?

How do we treat this individual when he or she seeks affiliation, is actively engaged in learning activities, or is passive but not problematic? How might these responses affect the future probability of either the desired or the challenging behavior patterns?

How do we treat this individual when he or she is "on the edge," agitated, experiencing stress, or in conflict with others? How might these responses affect the future probability of the challenging behavior or its resolution?

What is the typical aftermath of a problem episode for the individual and for others in terms of feelings, consequences, and social interaction patterns? How might these factors affect the future probability of either the challenging behavior or its resolution?

Interpretation

How do specific behavior patterns (both challenging and acceptable) affect our feelings and behavior and those of our colleagues? What words might we use to indicate our feelings (e.g., fear, relief, helpful, glad, inadequate)?

What does the student achieve by engaging in the problem behaviors that might be maintaining these behaviors? What do others think he or she is achieving?

How do the other students feel about this student and what he or she is doing? What messages do we send to these other students by the way that we interact with this student and how we respond to his or her challenges?

What possible reasons are there for the student to meet our expectations of him or her? How would he or she benefit by doing so?

Application

How can we enhance the learning opportunities that we offer and the instructional procedures that we use to better ensure that this student will be more apt to participate in learning activities?

How can we develop ways to include this individual in the social and emotional life of the school and class?

How do we use hypotheses about where, when, and why problems arise to generate prevention strategies?

How do we use hypotheses about why the student engages in particular problem behaviors to identify adaptive alternative behaviors?

If we are significantly changing the conditions of the student's educational environment (e.g., reintegration), how might our knowledge of explanation, interpretation, and application be applied within the new conditions?

Perspective

How are the behavioral issues being differentially defined, described, and understood by various key participants (e.g., students, family members, building administrators)?

Now that an intervention is occurring, how do the participants (e.g., students, family members, administrators) perceive and feel about the student and his or her behavior?

Empathy

When we think about the student from others' points of view (e.g., family members, classroom teachers, specific peers), how do we perceive their feelings and reactions? How might we feel or react if we were in their place?

When we think about the student from the student's point of view, how do we perceive his or her feelings and reactions, both when problems are occurring and when they are absent? How might we feel or react if we were in his or her place?

Self-knowledge

How do we handle difficult situations with students, and are our responses productive or nonproductive across different circumstances?

Can we find new ways to more fully engage all students in learning, especially those students who are reluctant, frightened, overwhelmed, or on the social fringes of the school culture?

What are we learning about how others are affected by our reactions when we expect others to follow our directives or when stressful and difficult situations arise?

such as those in Table 8.2 so that understandings emerge that are related to perspective, empathy, and self-knowledge. Moreover, direct observations, if augmented with an ongoing inquiry process, can also address more of the six facets of understanding. Jackson and Leon (1998a) described a process in which one adult shadows another, and continuous dialogue is used to explore the educators' ongoing actions and reactions to the student's behaviors. Videotapes and audiotapes can also be fruitfully employed as part of direct observations to enhance the six types of understanding if an inquiry script that is composed of questions such as those in Table 8.2 is used during viewing.

Assessment Based on Differing Degrees of Concern

Recall from Chapter 7 that interventions can fall into one of three categories based on degree of concern. The first category, enhance practices, is associated with mildly difficult situations. The second category, develop behavior intervention plan, is associated with more severe and/or persistent disruptive circumstances. The third category, develop a comprehensive behavior intervention plan, is associated with especially severe behavioral concerns. The assessment activities used with these three categories will, of course, be different.

At the enhance practices level, assessment activities may be informal and reflective. The need for an intervention may simply arise from the observation that one or more students are sometimes less engaged in the curriculum than the teacher desires or there is a need to channel some of the social membership, excitement, or "clowning" activities into more productive avenues of expression. Monitoring the intervention may require assessment activities that are no more involved than casual dialogues between the teacher and one or more students, coupled with teacher observations within different instructional and social situations. When assessment considerations associated with the enhance practices step are framed in terms of the three purposes for an intervention that were offered in Chapter 7 (i.e., promote growth and learning, enhance the comfort of the student and others, create understanding), the teacher's assessment activities may be directed toward a single facet of one of these purposes. For example, a teacher may informally observe that one of the students is being teased by others. This may suggest the need for an intervention that fosters understanding, and this intervention obviates certain follow-along assessment processes (e.g., look for changes in understanding in other students' casual comments; look for changes in patterns of teasing).

As the degree of concern rises, additional resources may need to be secured and over a longer time period to assess the situation. Functional behavioral assessment activities are required when the degree of concern reaches the point at which a behavior intervention plan is required. Typically, by this point, the dialogue processes should involve the student, general and special education teachers, and the student's parents or guardians. Assessment activities must now include the team members' explanations for and interpretations of the problem behaviors. When framed in relation to the previously identified three purposes for an intervention, assessment activities for developing a behavior intervention plan should take into account all three purposes. For example, the team may assess 1) a student's progress in his or her classes and how this progress can be enhanced; 2) a student's comfort level within different situations, and how stress levels that are associated with the behavior can be prevented or minimized to enhance class participation; and 3) a student's understanding of the expectations within different situations and how these translate into self-management activities.

When the degree of concern reaches the point at which a comprehensive behavior intervention plan is required, a team of individuals must be involved in all assessment activities, and team membership may now include various related services professionals (e.g., psychologist, school counselor). By this point, assessment activities must provide information that addresses all three purposes for an intervention, and they must contribute to the design of plan components that encompass the four areas associated with effective behavioral support (see Chapter 5 for more details):

1. Person-centered planning
2. Relationship development
3. Hypotheses-based intervention
4. Crisis intervention

The assessment issues become especially complex when reintegration is a factor, because educators may not know how the student will respond once he or she is returned to the general education setting. It is important to not give too much weight to behavioral information that was gleaned from the more restrictive setting. For instance, a student who frequently screams for adult attention in a self-contained classroom for students with severe disabilities will not necessarily do so within a general education classroom. Similarly, functional behavioral assessment results from the more restrictive setting must be viewed as tentative and suggestive, because the student's behavior may change when he or she experiences the relatively greater freedom and increased responsibilities of the general education classroom. Of even greater consequence, information on social and learning preferences are often suspect because of limited opportunity in the self-contained setting. Experience indicates that the most essential data during reintegration are those that one gathers about the adults in the two environments: 1) the skills and commitments of the adults within the more restrictive environment and 2) the commitments, expectations, and skills of the adults within the general education environment that represents the student's natural community.

Assessment and Intervention as a Continuous, Cyclical Process

The importance of linking assessment and intervention has been recognized within educational practice for some time. Data-based decision making is one example, in which assessment activities anticipate and help prescribe the design of appropriate interventions (Shapiro, 1996). It is recognized in support-based assessment that there is a reciprocal connection between assessment and intervention. In fact, as implied in the Chapter 7 discussion of revising intervention plans, interventions themselves must be viewed as data when circumstances require new and additional intervention procedures.

There are four especially important implications when assessment and intervention are viewed as being inextricably linked in a continuous cycle. First, because interventions involve making ongoing changes in activity and interpersonal contexts, assessment activities must continuously incorporate these variables into what is examined and measured. Behavioral and ecobehavioral assessment specialists have long acknowledged the need for assessing elements of the social ecology when gathering data about behavior (Greenwood, Carta, Kamps, & Arreaga-Mayer, 1990; Odom,

Peterson, McConnell, & Ostrosky, 1990; Stanger, 1996). Support-based assessment affirms and extends these practices by mandating that educators provide detailed consideration of both constant and evolving contextual variables, as well as participant interpretations of these variables, which can affect how an intervention is conducted or its results. This activity is especially important when considering how to gather and use data about continuing incidences of problem behaviors after a plan has been implemented. Just as during the planning phase (see Chapter 7), these data should consist of descriptions of incidents that are embedded within the ecological and interpersonal contexts in which they occur.

Second, especially given the principles of heuristic decision making, it is essential to measure the integrity of the implementation of the behavior support process (Duchnowski, 2000). As shown in Chapter 10, this can be done by first developing a checklist of the various recommendations, steps, and strategies that are associated with the behavior intervention plan. Then, the educator who is responsible for monitoring the plan's implementation and results examines through reflections, interviews, and/or observations what components of the plan are actually being used by different participants and how frequently they are being used, as well as the participants' impressions about each intervention procedure's utility, ease of use, and effectiveness.

Third, because critical information may appear at any point in an intervention, assessment needs to occur in an ongoing fashion. This process is especially important given the dynamic nature of school environments because unexpected and surprising changes—for better or for worse—can be anticipated throughout the course of an intervention. Continuous assessment not only helps educators keep current with the ongoing effects of their intervention but also helps them monitor the fidelity of intervention implementation, which becomes critical when decisions about plan revisions are considered.

Fourth, especially when degree of concern has been high, the cycles of assessment and intervention should not be viewed as complete until the student is living and learning within the community of his or her peers, with or without additional supports. This means that when students are placed in more restrictive settings—such as self-contained classes, special schools, and residential programs—assessment and intervention should not be terminated until the individuals are successfully reintegrated into a designated natural community for an extended period of time. This means that educators who work within these settings must increasingly view their assessment and intervention responsibilities as extending into neighborhood schools and other natural communities.

Social Validity

As has been noted many times in this book, the goals, the proposed intervention processes, and the resulting outcomes must be authentic and viewed as worthwhile by the student and his or her family, teachers, and friends. In fact, the recipient's acceptance of the processes and outcomes of the support activities should carry as much weight in how decisions are made as the school's judgment of a plan's suitability. This idea is captured in the concept of *social validity*, which Lloyd and Heubusch defined as

> The extent to which the goals of intervention practices, the procedures used to pursue those goals, and the outcomes of our efforts to reach those goals are acceptable to the community of people concerned with individuals who the procedures are intended to help. (1996, p. 8)

The social validity of an intervention is assessed by examining the social significance of the goals, the social appropriateness of the procedures, and the social importance of the outcomes (Wolf, 1978). With respect to the social significance of the
goals, the primary criterion is whether the goals can truly make a difference for the
student. Goals that are based on factors such as the expectations of general education
teachers or the needs of family members may yield more socially valid results than
those based on, for example, lists of skills that are gleaned from a purchased social
skills curriculum (see Lloyd & Heubusch, 1996).

Wolf (1978) indicated that the social appropriateness of the procedures involves
consideration of ethics, cost, and practicality. Horner and colleagues (1990) emphasized that intervention procedures that are grounded in positive behavioral support
should be acceptable given the practice standards set by the larger society. They recommended that social validity be considered not only in the selection of intervention
procedures but also in decisions about their application. For example, positive reinforcement procedures can be delivered in a disrespectful manner, such as giving stickers to a high school student in a general education program for acceptable behavior in
the classroom. Similarly, Meyer and Evans talked about the importance of "the grand-
mother test," or the degree to which a proposed intervention procedure meets "standards that are common for nondisabled persons" (1989, pp. 69–70).

Finally, with respect to outcomes, the basic question is, "Are consumers satisfied
with the results, all of the results, including those that were unplanned?" (Wolf, 1978,
p. 210). In the final analysis, it is the consumers' (students, teachers, family members)
perceptions of well-being that counts. For example, in an intervention designed to
lessen the aggressive acts of a group of young children toward their infant or toddler
siblings, Koegel, Stiebel, and Koegel (1998) employed a simple rating scale to assess
the broader impact of the intervention on the affected parties (i.e., children, parents,
strangers). The rating scale established that child happiness, parent happiness, and
stranger comfort with the family were positively influenced as aggressive acts
decreased.

Social validity poses a number of implications for assessment. First, emphasizing
points made in Chapter 7, data that reflect progress on the plan's short- and long-term
outcomes must become the primary focus of the educators' assessment activities. Of
course, some might argue that measures of problem behavior are equally vital for
assessing student progress. Nonetheless, the use of these data for this purpose should
be tempered by first asking the following question: If measures of short- and long-
term student growth and success are showing improvement, does this not mean that
problem behaviors are becoming less of a concern? If the answer to this question is
"yes," then problem measurement can be deemphasized as a primary measure of student success or failure.

In addition, practitioners should incorporate social validity issues when they are
developing the questions that they will use to guide their assessment and intervention
processes. Questions that are designed to probe social validation concerns may be
especially critical when a student is in a more restrictive setting. Such questions can
steer the team away from primarily focusing on management concerns within the
restrictive setting toward authentic outcomes within natural communities. "Does the
proposed outcome result in this student's gaining access to peers who can provide
good role models?" and similar questions can help shift the team's attention from the
student's disruptive behaviors within the restrictive environment to examining more
authentic, long-term results. Questions that are designed around social validation

concerns can also be applied to considerations of specialized techniques that might be recommended by an educational team. As a final point, Katsiyannis and Maag noted that functional behavioral assessment "entails following a series of procedures to arrive at socially valid interventions" (1998, p. 281). In other words, interventions that are derived from functional behavioral assessment can inherently satisfy some social validity concerns because they are premised on the individual's motivations and needs.

ASSESSMENT FOR CREATING THE INTERVENTION

Chapter 7 indicated that forecasting is a major activity when creating an intervention. Forecasting entails juxtaposing information about desired outcomes and behavioral hypotheses with the intervention options that arise out of the analysis of these issues. A team can then generate projections of the likely effects of different interventions. In substantial measure, forecasting involves contrasting what the student presently participates in, and which problems interfere with that participation, with what the educators want the student to participate in, and how they can attenuate problems that interfere with that participation. Skilled forecasting depends on assessment information that depicts a student's present and/or potential patterns of participation in various academic and social activities, especially within general education classes and related settings. It then depends on information that identifies behavioral hypotheses that connect behavioral problems with likely setting, antecedent, and motivational factors.

Regarding these two broad categories of assessment, more research has been conducted on developing assessment procedures to gather functional behavioral assessment information for support planning. This is unfortunate, because relying too heavily on functional behavioral assessment—in the absence of broader information that is related to current and desired general education involvement and participation—can sometimes result in deficiencies in a behavior intervention plan (see Display 8.1). Yet, functional behavioral assessment does form an essential and well-established basis for much that occurs within positive behavioral support (Bishop & Jubala, 1995), so it is discussed in detail next.

Functional Behavioral Assessment

Some people interchange the terms *functional behavioral assessment* and *functional analysis*, but the two terms have distinguishable meanings in the literature. Functional behavioral assessment involves gathering data by using any number of strategies to generate hypotheses about variables that reliably predict and maintain problem behavior (Horner & Carr, 1997). It enables educators to perceive the purposes for problem behaviors and to better understand the situations in which they occur. Educators within natural settings (e.g., school, home, the community) can readily apply functional behavioral assessment strategies.

Functional analysis is the term used to identify a subset of functional behavioral assessment techniques in which the distinguishing characteristic is experimentally controlled variation. An educator who uses *experimentally controlled variation* systematically presents and withdraws the hypothesized variable(s), then observes the resultant behavioral changes. The time and control requirements that are associated with experimental analysis are often difficult or inadvisable to arrange in natural contexts; therefore, educators often resist using these techniques (Vaughn & Horner, 1997). It

DISPLAY 8.1—RISKS IN USING FUNCTIONAL BEHAVIORAL ASSESSMENT INFORMATION WITHOUT CONSIDERING A BROADER BASE OF ACTIVITY PARTICIPATION INFORMATION

Risk	Description
Myopic outlook	The outcome of the intervention may be conceptualized as simply the absence of problem behavior. Accordingly—and possibly to the detriment of enhanced participation in natural communities—intervention efforts will focus exclusively on either short-term prevention or the simple one-to-one replacement of the problem behavior.
Idiosyncratic causes	Functional analysis may uncover behavioral hypotheses that are only applicable within the settings or activities that the student is presently in, which may fail to represent the full range of settings and activities associated with typical peers. Educators then focus their intervention efforts on a limited range of "causes," never addressing other more important explanations for the behavior that could be hypothesized if activity participation within a broader range of settings was analyzed.
Restricted range of replacement behaviors	The skills taught through the intervention process may be limited to those most directly connected with the hypothesized motivations for the behavior. Hence, the broader range of skills needed for successful general education participation, perhaps with accommodations or modifications, will neither be considered nor taught as part of the intervention.

How important is formulating long-range participation goals for reducing the likelihood of these risk factors?

Consider a student who does not have access to a setting in which eventual participation is a proposed outcome. How could educators gather information about factors that need to be considered before placing the student into the new setting for the first time?

(Based on Jackson [1998, April].)

is, however, probably unnecessary for educators to commit time and energy to these activities because other more economical assessment activities can suffice when planning a school-based intervention. Moreover, the trial-and-error processes that are associated with plan implementation and revision can provide similar data, albeit in a more ambiguous form. For these reasons, functional analysis is not considered further in this discussion. (The interested reader should see Jackson & Leon, 1998a, for an illustration of how to reframe functional analysis to answer a variety of helpful explanation and application questions.)

As indicated in the Chapter 5 discussion of hypothesis-based intervention, the purpose of a functional behavioral assessment is to understand why a person behaves in a particular way under particular conditions. Three activities that are germane to conducting a functional behavioral assessment are 1) reviewing existing records, 2) interviewing informants, and 3) directly observing the behavior in context. Especially powerful analyses are possible when educators triangulate data from all three sources to generate hypotheses about why certain behaviors are present or absent within differing situations and contexts. Ways to collect these three types of data are considered next.

Reviewing Existing Records   Historical data are rarely sufficient in and of themselves to generate useful hypotheses about problem behaviors, but such data can sometimes help clarify puzzling situations. For example, the review and analysis of past school records—including but not limited to office referrals, absences, and health information—may shed light on patterns of behavior over time. Historical records can reveal behavioral concerns that are cyclical, related to ongoing and long-term medication changes, or connected with major life transitions, and such factors can then be taken into account when educators design interventions.

Another type of data that can be useful to review is the student's responses to prior interventions. As noted by Tilly (1999), the effectiveness of any educational intervention for an individual can be determined only through its implementation. Thus, an analysis of what has and has not worked in the past may help to determine what aspects of an intervention would be particularly beneficial in the future.

At the same time, caution is urged in using past records for making intervention decisions. Past interventions may have been implemented without conviction and without any real desire for success, or the reported information may only reflect a small part of the whole story. In fact, to avoid the formation of unfair biases, Jackson and Leon (1998a) recommended that a review of past interventions—indeed a review of historical information in general—should happen only after other kinds of more current information have been collected. Moreover, it may be more fruitful if this review focuses less on what has been tried and has reportedly failed and more on whether there is a history of punishment or of adults attempting to manage the student's behavior through repeatedly introducing and then abandoning point systems and contracts. Such data can provide a rationale for moving in a new direction, as well as speak to long-standing difficulties in the adult–student relationship.

Interviewing Informants   Informant-based assessment techniques, once considered an afterthought when planning an intervention, have been elevated to their rightful place as essential tools for achieving a comprehensive understanding of a problem and for designing a viable support plan. Informant-based strategies refer to assessment procedures that rely on people (informants), typically parents, educators, and/or students, as sources of information about a student and his or her behavioral issues. Such strategies can involve directly interviewing a person, giving a person a questionnaire or survey to complete, or some combination of these procedures. It may be as simple as informally asking two or three questions to tap a student's motivations or as complex as asking a series of questions to understand behavior in a variety of settings and with a variety of individuals. Of course, the student should also serve as an informant in the process, lending his or her own perspective to the concerns that are being raised by others.

Jackson and Leon (1998a) suggested that the individuals selected to be interviewed should 1) know the student well, 2) be involved daily with the student, 3) routinely communicate with the student in the student's primary communication mode and language, and 4) have an investment in the behavior support process. When collecting these data, it should be recognized that they represent perceptions, reflecting the personal emotions and experiences of people who have a relationship with the student over a period of time.

Taylor and Bogdan described an interview as "a conversation between equals, rather than a formal question-and-answer exchange" (1984, p. 77), and this point is worth remembering when conducting interviews with family members and others. Informants are more likely to offer information, ideas, and insights that can contribute to the functional behavioral assessment if there is genuine respect for them. It is also important that the interview be conducted in a manner that is as culturally sensitive as possible (Snell & Brown, 2000) and that the questions are composed and framed in a common language.

Although interview questions and procedures can be designed by a team of educators to meet their own assessment needs, a number of useful interview devices are widely available in the published literature. The Motivation Assessment Scale (MAS; Durand, 1990) is an instrument that can be used to gain information regarding the specific purposes associated with a student's behavior. The MAS has 16 items, which are brief questions such as the following: "Does the behavior occur following a request to perform a difficult task?" (p. 48). Each question is scored using a scale that includes the ratings "always true of the individual," "almost always," "usually," "half the time," "seldom," "almost never," and "never." Total scores are then computed for each of four possible motivations for a behavior, which are "sensory," "escape," "attention," and "tangible." Next, a relative ranking is computed and can be used in combination with data from other sources to generate meaningful hypotheses. For example, a teacher who assesses a preschooler with this scale might find that the child uses hair pulling, and sometimes pushing, to escape unpleasant situations and to secure desirable activities. This information might then be applied to developing an intervention that could focus on teaching the student alternative ways to communicate the need for a break or a desire to engage in a particular activity, teaching adults and peers how to honor these communications, and/or preventing these behavioral concerns by offering the student more opportunities to control the activities in which he takes part.

Brown's (1996) checklist of questions is especially consistent with this book's emphasis on collaborative inquiry. Her list of 40 questions is organized into the following categories: environmental, communication, choice and control, teaching and implementation, and physiological. Questions such as, "Does it [problem behavior] happen in small/open environments?" and "Does it happen when there are unexpected changes in routines/environment?" tap environmental issues. The questions offered in this checklist are especially useful when designing a behavior intervention plan because they can "spur discussion about a diverse range of possible issues affecting this person's life" (Brown, 1996, p. 19).

Another resource, the Information Gathering Tool (Jackson & Leon, 1998a) is especially applicable for designing comprehensive behavior intervention plans. This tool includes a broad range of questions that are aimed at constructing a very thorough understanding of the student. The tool is completed through a dialoguing process in which several individuals (or a full team) expound on the myriad circumstances associated with the behaviors of concern. Jackson and Leon also provided two checklists that can be used to shed light on complex functional relationships between suspected setting antecedents within the home and/or school environments and specific behaviors. Sample questions from the Information Gathering Tool are shown in Table 8.3.

As noted previously, it can also be advantageous to interview the student to learn about his or her reasons for the behavior (Kern et al., 1994). By inviting the student to be a part of the process, this approach has the added benefit of crediting the student with self-understanding. It also provides an opportunity for the adults to express respect for the student's self-identified reasons for the behavior. One example of a student-directed functional behavioral assessment interview form is provided in the handbook by O'Neill and colleagues (1997).

The provided examples are only a few of the many informant-based assessment resources that exist. Other checklists, scales, and questionnaires have been developed to gather information that addresses the student's communicative intent when expressing a behavior (Demchak, 1993; Donnellan, Miranda, Mesaros, & Fassbender, 1984) and descriptions of the conditions under which the behavior is likely or not likely to occur (Dunlap et al., 1993; Kern et al., 1994). Applying these materials can help a teacher or a team generate hypotheses for behaviors so that teaching and prevention interventions can be designed that take into account student motivations and precipitating antecedent conditions.

Clearly, the major advantages of informant-based assessment strategies are that they provide educators with insights into the nature and causes of behavior from those who know the student well and that they can help educators better understand the student through a better understanding of the individuals who have relationships with the student. Moreover, such strategies can be easily tailored to the specific degrees of concern for a particular situation—from simple reflection questions when one is enhancing practice, to short formal interviews (e.g., Brown, 1996) when developing a simple plan, and finally to extended and detailed interviews (e.g., Jackson & Leon, 1998a) when developing a comprehensive plan.

Directly Observing the Behavior in Context   Direct observation refers to the systematic recording of the student's behaviors, the corresponding responses and reactions of others within the environment, and the correlated activities and events that precede and follow the behaviors that are under scrutiny. The records that result from such efforts are most useful when the observations have been conducted over extended time periods and in natural settings. Such observations can be conducted by hand-held computers, but they are most often accomplished by educators using paper-and-pencil recording forms. Generally, an observer tries to be unobtrusive; that is, he or she conducts observations in a way that the student and others go about their typical routines in relatively typical ways.

From the early 1970s to the late 1990s, maintaining a systematic record of the rate of occurrence of one or more operationally defined behaviors was viewed as the primary means for establishing that a program worked. At the beginning of the 21st

Table 8.3.   Sample questions to pose when designing a comprehensive behavior intervention plan

Vision and Current Educational Activities

1. What are the lifestyle plans and long-term expectations for this student?
2. Is the student's current educational plan adequately and reasonably aligned with the vision described in Question 1?
3. Does the student have a network of peers who are supportive of his/her participation in the life of the school, interpersonal needs, and/or learning needs?

Behavior Assessment

4. What are the behavior pattern(s) that prompted the development of this behavior support plan?
5. What explanations for the behavior are offered by the student?
6. What explanations or suggestions for the behavior are offered by peers and friends?
7. Are any of the following conditions/events occurring that might relate to one or more of the behavior pattern(s)?
   - Alertness, arousal, sleep cycles
   - Medical/medication conditions
   - Alcohol/drug-induced states
   - Recent lifestyle changes or traumatic experiences
   - Acute or chronic pain
8. How does this student communicate that he/she would like attention or to show someone an accomplishment? Do challenging behaviors play a role?
9. How does this student communicate that he/she would like a break, would rather be doing something different, or would like to be left alone? Do challenging behaviors play a role?
10. How does this student communicate that he/she needs assistance or that something he/she is doing is not going well? Do challenging behaviors play a role?
11. How does this student communicate that he/she is upset about something, that he/she is experiencing pain, discomfort, or fear? Do challenging behaviors play a role?
12. How does this student communicate that he/she wants something, or wants to do something that may or may not be available? Do challenging behaviors play a role?
13. How does this student communicate a need for affection or intimacy? Do challenging behaviors play a role?
14. Is there evidence that this student is experiencing frustration or deep despair when trying to communicate thoughts, ideas, or simply needs? Do challenging behaviors play a role?
15. Do any of the behaviors seem to occur simply because they feel good or because they generate excitement or consternation in others?

From Jackson, L.B., & Leon, M.Z. (1998a). *Developing a behavior support plan: A manual for teachers and behavior specialists* (2nd ed., Appendix A). Colorado Springs, CO: PEAK Parent Center, Inc.; adapted by permission.

century, however, it is best that one looks at a broader range of change indicators—including the perceptions of educators, family members, and peers—to ascertain how others are experiencing the student's learning and behavioral changes within the activities that are also part of their daily lives. Nevertheless, as a diagnostic process that is part of an overall functional behavioral assessment, direct observations can contribute to the development of a better understanding of the precipitating circumstances that have led a team to consider developing a behavior intervention plan. Such observations are especially useful if, in conjunction with other data sources, they contribute to the construction of a database that

- Provides rich descriptions of the behavioral concerns in relation to their situations of occurrence and nonoccurrence
- Makes evident patterns of incidences across time, especially when there are variations in rate that are linked to particular time periods

- Supports certain predictions about significant motivational or situational factors while ruling out other predictions
- Helps point the way to specific social, activity, or schedule changes (Jackson & Leon, 1998a, p. 11)

As has been stressed throughout this discussion, the usefulness of data gathered through direct observations depends on the way that questions are formed and asked, which then dictates the data needs of the educational team (see Display 8.2).

Traditionally, a first step in conducting systematic observations has been to translate broader conceptualizations of a problem into specific, concrete behaviors; for instance, "aggression" becomes "hits a peer with hand or fist." Such an operational definition undoubtedly facilitates objective measurement; however, it can sometimes result in a behavior being reduced to units that are too small to represent the scope of teachers' and others' concerns. This means that, when translating behaviors into something measurable, care must be taken to ensure that definitions and descriptions are neither too general nor too specific. That is, they must permit measurement but still preserve the wholeness that makes the behavior meaningful to members of the school community and others.

One of the most useful applications of direct observation strategies is to collect data that permit the analysis of behavior patterns in relation to time. The traditional tool for this method is scatter plot assessment (Touchette, MacDonald, & Langer, 1985), and the typical data recording form is an interval recording device that represents the full time period of the individual's day.

By inspecting the daily incidences of one or more behaviors during a 2- to 3-week period, scatter plot assessment yields information on the temporal patterns of the measured behaviors, as well as any major patterns of behavioral covariation. Depending on how the data sheet is designed or on the other records that are being

DISPLAY 8.2—KNOWING WHAT QUESTIONS TO ASK

Stella is in kindergarten and has many strengths. According to her teacher, however, she bothers others during group time and rarely pays attention. Which set of questions would most likely lead to a deeper understanding of the individual and her behavior in context? Why?

SET A
1. How many times did Stella push a peer?
2. What percentage of intervals was Stella paying attention?
3. What were the consequences for Stella's off-task behavior?

SET B
1. In what activities does Stella actively engage on a "good day"?
2. What happens right before and right after Stella disrupts the group?
3. In what situations and activities does Stella successfully interact with her peers?

maintained, scatter plot assessment can also provide information on behavioral incidences in relation to settings, educational activities, or other environmental variables
(e.g., people present). Oliva and Brown (1994) reported an analysis of scatter plot data
that revealed that a particular individual was more likely to exhibit problem behaviors
when his or her personal attendant left for the day. This led to the hypothesis that a
viable intervention tactic would be designating a clearly identified alternative person
to whom the student could turn for help or comfort.

For students, the time period that must be represented is generally the entire
school day across all 5 weekdays. This requires a form such as the one in Figure 8.1,
which is completed for a fourth-grade student named Juan (see the appendix at the end
of the book for the blank version of this form). To fill out the form, one begins by list-
ing in the key up to three behaviors that are of interest. Then, throughout the day, a
designated person records incidences by circling the appropriate number(s) at the end
of each time interval in which any of the behaviors occur. Obviously, someone who is
often with the student through the day (e.g., a classroom aide) should collect the data.

In Figure 8.1, it can be seen that Juan is more likely to shove students right before
certain end-of-class transitions (e.g., physical education [P.E.] to math class, art to
social studies), but much less likely to do so if he is going to a preferred setting (e.g.,
transition from music to lunch). Inspection of these data might result in the educator
seeking additional information about what happens when Juan shoves students. The
educator might learn that shoving students results in Juan's being kept in the setting
to be reprimanded for several minutes, which ensures a late arrival to the next, less
preferred class. On one hand, a hypothesis that might be derived from these facts is
that shoving students serves an escape function for Juan, as he is more likely to engage
in the behavior when he likes the present setting and dislikes the next one. On the
other hand, another hypothesis might be that Juan likes the attention that he receives
from the teacher even though it is a reprimand. In either case, these data provide the
beginning point for a functional behavioral assessment that can direct the educator's
attention to particular intervention procedures.

Another traditional and well-known technique that is often used in functional
behavioral assessment is an A-B-C analysis, in which *A* stands for antecedents, *B*
stands for behaviors, and *C* stands for consequences (Bijou et al., 1968). An A-B-C
analysis focuses on the specific relationships between the behavior patterns that are of
concern to an educator and antecedent and consequent events that co-occur with the
behavior patterns. Collecting such data requires a recording form that includes at least
three columns, one each for describing 1) the antecedents that precede a behavior, 2)
the behavioral episodes themselves, and 3) the consequences that follow the behavior.
(Some especially useful forms have extended the basic A-B-C concept to include
things such as the people present during each incident, the student's reaction to the
consequences, and even the perceived function of the behavior for the student; see
Browder, 1991; Jackson & Leon, 1998a; O'Neill et al., 1997). Typically, the stimulus
for recording data on the form is the occurrence of the challenging behavior, and the
data are often recorded in narrative form. Nevertheless, one can also use the A-B-C
process to record a continuous description of events, which can reveal how a behavior covaries with specific antecedents and consequences. After collecting from 2–3
days to 2–3 weeks of data, an analysis of consistent A-B-C patterns can aid in the
development of hypotheses regarding the ecological circumstances that precipitate
the challenging behavior and the consequences that may maintain it.

Scatter Plot Data Collection Form

Name of student: Juan   Name of observer: K. Donner   Dates: 12/11/00–12/15/00

Each time block contains a rating scale of 1 / 2 / 3. Circled numbers indicate a recorded incident (shoves). The daily schedules are as follows (time blocks in 15-minute intervals from 8:00 to 3:00):

MON
Time	Activity	Incident
8:00–8:15	Spanish	
8:15–9:00	P.E.	circled 1 at 8:45–9:00
9:00–9:30	Math	
9:30–10:15	Reading	
10:15–10:30	Rec.	
10:30–11:00	Social Studies	
11:00–11:30	Science	
11:30–12:00	Music	
12:00–12:45	Lunch-Recess	
12:45–1:45	Writing Lab	
1:45–2:15	Spelling	
2:15–2:30	Rec.	
2:30–3:00	Reading	

TUE
Time	Activity	Incident
8:00–8:45	Reading	circled 1 at 8:45–9:00
9:00–9:30	Writing-Lab	
10:15–10:30	Rec.	circled 1
10:30–11:00	Math	
11:00–11:30	Science	
11:30–12:00	Computers	
12:00–12:45	Lunch-Recess	
12:45–1:15	Art	circled 1 at 12:45–1:00
1:15–1:45	Social Studies	
1:45–2:15	Science	
2:15–2:30	Rec.	
2:30–3:00	Library	

WED
Time	Activity	Incident
8:00–8:15	Spanish	
8:15–9:00	P.E.	
9:00–9:30	Math	
9:30–10:15	Reading	
10:15–10:30	Rec.	circled 1
10:30–11:00	Social Studies	
11:00–11:30	Science	
11:30–12:00	Music	
12:00–12:45	Lunch-Recess	
12:45–1:45	Writing Lab	
1:45–2:15	Spelling	
2:15–2:30	Rec.	
2:30–3:00	Reading	

THU
Time	Activity	Incident
8:00–8:45	Reading	
9:00–9:30	Writing-Lab	
10:15–10:30	Rec.	
10:30–11:00	Math	
11:00–11:30	Science	
11:30–12:00	Computers	
12:00–12:45	Lunch-Recess	
12:45–1:15	Art	circled 1 at 12:45–1:00
1:15–1:45	Social Studies	
1:45–2:15	Science	
2:15–2:30	Rec.	
2:30–3:00	Library	

FRI
Time	Activity	Incident
8:00–8:15	Spanish	
8:15–9:00	P.E.	circled 1 at 8:45–9:00
9:00–9:30	Math	
9:30–10:15	Reading	
10:15–10:30	Rec.	circled 1
10:30–11:00	Social Studies	
11:00–11:30	Science	
11:30–12:00	Music	
12:00–12:45	Lunch-Recess	
12:45–1:45	Writing Lab	
1:45–2:15	Spelling	
2:15–2:30	Rec.	
2:30–3:00	Reading	

KEY
1 = Shoves students

Comments:
Incidents occurred right at end of period

Figure 8.1. An example of a scatter plot recording form. (Key: P.E. = physical education, Rec. = recess.)

180

Figure 8.2 is an example of how an extended A-B-C analysis can be used to examine the circumstances that surround Mark's tantrum behavior. Mark's kindergarten teacher had set up six stations, or centers, in her classroom. She assigned children to a center or allowed them to choose one, depending on the day, the activity, and the student's needs. As shown in the figure, Mark displayed tantrum behavior when he was assigned to the number center. Additional observations confirmed that Mark's tantrums were most likely to occur and be at their worst when he was assigned to the number center. The teacher then used these data, plus other information about Mark, to hypothesize that Mark was attempting to escape from the situation because he was intimidated by the math game at the number center. Building on this information, Mark's teacher expanded the range of activities at the number center to include other activities, such as one that involved science fiction characters that were of interest to Mark.

Two guidelines from Jackson and Leon (1998a) are useful to consider regarding how one collects data for an A-B-C analysis. First, they suggested that observational periods comprise a variety of activities and settings, including periods when the problem behaviors typically occur and periods when they do not occur. Second, they suggested that frequent, intermittent observations conducted for short time periods (e.g., from 20 minutes to 2 hours) over several weeks are more useful than continuous observations conducted all day for 2 or 3 days.

Participation in General Education Classes

Miller, Epp, and McGinnis (1985) recognized the need for comprehensive analyses of settings to determine the degree of match, or fit, between a student's behavior and existing environmental standards and expectations. They indicated that the major implications for data collection are that "assessment of behavior must occur within a student's school setting across time and under a variety of physical, social, and instructional environmental variables; and that the standards must be identified" (p. 61). Over the years, a number of instruments have emerged that focus on assessing and enhancing environmental match. One example is the Ecological Factors Checklist (Jackson & Leon, 1998a), which is a tool for noting the impact of a broad range of ecological factors (e.g., seating arrangement, instructional adaptations) on the student's learning and behavior. Another example is The Instructional Environment Scales–II (TIES-II; Ysseldyke & Christenson, 1994), a system that was designed to assess students' instructional and classroom environment needs. These instruments exemplify the principle that the environment and the student must be considered together throughout the assessment process.

Such instruments can be used in any educational setting to assess what is needed to enhance a student's level of participation. In this discussion, the term *participation* refers to how engaged and involved student is within the social and academic activities that are associated with his or her general education classes or other school-related activities. When coupled with functional behavioral assessment, a thorough examination of general education participation allows the educator to fully characterize the conditions that precipitate the need for an intervention. Because a major goal of positive behavioral support is for all students to successfully participate in their natural communities, the following suggestions and techniques are tailored to assessing a student's levels of participation exclusively within general education classes.

Name of student: Mark

Name of teacher: M. Ariel

Name of observer: D. Robbins

Date: 9/10/01

Behavior to analyze: Tantrums

Time: start/stop		Staff-to-Student ratio	Antecedent	Behavior: positive/negative	Interaction	Consequence	Student reaction
8:30	8:45	2:18	The teacher read a story.	Mark attended to the teacher.	With all students	The teacher allowed Mark to choose a center.	Followed directions
8:45	9:00	1:4	The teacher gave the cue for Mark to choose a center.	Mark chose the sand table and poured sand from one container to another.	With Josh and Jacob	An associate commented on Mark's cooperative play.	Smiled
9:00	9:15	1:3	The teacher assigned Mark to the number center.	Mark had a tantrum.	None	The teacher removed Mark from the center.	Was sullen
9:15	9:30	1:4	The teacher gave Mark the cue to choose another center.	Mark chose the music center and played the toy zither.	With another child who was playing the triangle	Mark produced music.	Was engaged
9:30	9:40	2:18	Mark made the transition to outdoor play.	Mark put on his coat and gloves.	Talked with a peer	Mark went outdoors.	Was positive

Figure 8.2. An example of an expanded A-B-C analysis.

Participation assessment should consider events at three layers within the general education setting:

1. Participation in the interpersonal relationships of the class during academic instruction and at other times, as indicated by class affiliation patterns and friendships
2. Participation within specific classroom activities of varying types, as indicated by engagement levels and completion of class work
3. Participation in the content of the curriculum, as indicated by learning and performance within various content areas

Information that is gathered about a student's class participation at these three layers can then be used to generate ideas for enhancing the student's participation in the academic and social activities of the class. The goal of increased participation can be addressed either through the development and implementation of recommendations for improving the engagement of all students (e.g., using differentiated instruction with all students) or for bolstering the engagement of particular students who are having difficulties (e.g., providing individualized accommodations and modifications).

The ensuing discussion about conducting participation assessments considers three issues. First is a general discussion of informal assessment methods, as educators will usually rely on these to gather their information. Second, details are offered on the concepts and methods of discrepancy analysis, which plays an important role when using various direct observation strategies. Third is an exploration of how such an analysis is conducted when a student is in a self-contained classroom or facility.

Informal Assessment Methods   Class participation can be assessed by examining a student's past records, such as his or her academic portfolio, recent tests in different subject areas, and report cards. As mentioned previously regarding other forms of records, caution must be exercised in how such data are interpreted. For example, records may show that a particular high school student has taken mostly basic math classes, in which he has earned "C"s, and has been an excellent student in various industrial arts classes. It is not uncommon for educators to interpret such records as indicators of the student's essential competencies and interests without further reflection or examination. It is, in fact, possible that this student was advised by a well-meaning counselor to take classes that are not part of college preparation, especially classes in which the student is interested. The student may be earning "C"s in math because he is unchallenged by the content, and his good performance in the industrial arts may mirror what he could be doing in more academically oriented classes if the respective teachers expressed high expectations for him.

Educators can also assess participation levels by using informants (e.g., general educators who have instructed the student over long periods of time) within different subject areas or varying instructional formats. Again, care must be taken to consider the teacher's instructional arrangements and overall expectations for students. A high school teacher who wants all of her students to leave her tenth-grade English class with "more grammatical skills, plus basic vocabulary and spelling skills" sets considerably lower expectations than another teacher who stresses a love of literature and an application of the literature's lessons to one's personal life and society at large.

The student with challenges and his or her peers can also be asked about his or her participation levels. Using relatively open-ended questions, the inquiry process can initially start at a general level (e.g., "Tell me about Ms. Belladonna's class"); then, probe questions can be used to delve deeper into particular concerns (e.g., "So, why is it that you don't like group work?" "Why do you find it hard to talk with Frederica?"). These data can be combined with teacher reports to arrive at a more complete picture of participation problems and promises at the interpersonal, activity, and content layers within the class.

Another way to assess participation in general education is an examination of a student's class schedule. This process can be especially critical for a student in a special education program, as there is a risk that he or she will be spending large blocks of time in settings other than general education classes, including resource rooms or self-contained classes for "life skills." By revisiting the student's IEP goals and objectives in relation to the general education class offerings, schedule analysis can be used to deliberately increase the student's participation in general education (Field, LeRoy, & Rivera, 1994; Giangreco, Cloninger, & Iverson, 1998; Jackson & Leon, 1998a).

Finally, activity participation can be assessed by observing the student in classes, then creating a record of his or her participation, accomplishments, and any learning and participation supports currently in place. Observations should cover a variety of different kinds of learning activities and situations, in which the goal is not to "catch the student at his or her worst" but, rather, to gauge what typical days are like and how they vary in relation to participation. Sometimes, when conducting in-class observations, it is useful to partition an observed classroom activity (or class period) into beginning, middle, and end intervals to see whether the student's participation increases or decreases as an activity progresses. On one hand, a student may be quick to initiate an activity but become bored easily and fail to complete it. On the other hand, it may be difficult to gain a student's attention at the beginning of an activity, but once he or she is engaged, the student completes the activity.

Discrepancy Analysis Procedures   Activity participation assessment often requires discrepancy analysis, in which the student's ongoing activity engagement is contrasted with that of other students within a class. The term *discrepancy* can apply to remediation-based assessment as well as to support-based assessment. In remediation-based assessment, a discrepancy is noted in the student's actions as compared with those of other students who successfully participate in particular classroom routines. Reducing the discrepancy involves first teaching the student the missing skills, or providing compensatory skills, so that the student can successfully meet a given norm or eventually qualify for participation. In support-based assessment, the discrepancy is also noted; however, reducing the discrepancy involves first providing supports so that the student can participate regardless of his or her learning and behavioral difficulties.

One method for collecting data that utilizes discrepancy information is the response discrepancy observation method (Rhode, Jensen, & Reavis, 1995). The observer who uses this method alternately records the behavior(s) of the student and the behavior(s) of his or her peers every 10 seconds. The results yield data to support or refute a discrepancy between the behavior of a student and his or her classroom peers. Such data sometimes identify whether the student needs more support or the teacher needs to enhance classroom instruction or management procedures. For example, within a particular activity, if a particular student was actively engaged 50% or less of the time and his peers were engaged 70% or more of the time, one could conclude that the individual student needs additional assistance or supports to bolster his participation. Conversely, if the student was actively engaged 40% of the time and his peers were engaged about 43% of the time, one might conclude that the teacher needs to reexamine the way directions are given, instructional activities are designed, curriculum materials are selected, or the students are recognized for their accomplishments.

An especially useful device for assessing class participation discrepancies and resulting support needs is a typical person inventory (Browder, 1991; Calculator & Jorgensen, 1991; Filbin, Rogers-Connolly, & Brewer, 1996; Jackson, 1992). A typical person inventory provides a qualitative description of the student's participation in relation to that of other students within the context of the general education classroom routines and activities. Typical person inventories can be created on an as-needed basis by partitioning a piece of paper into three columns. As a class progresses, an observer keeps a running record of the actions and activities of typical students (first column), the actions and activities of the student whose participation levels are being examined (second column), and ideas for supports and accommodations that could fill the gap (third column). As an illustration, consider Daniel, the kindergarten-age student whose vision was presented in Chapter 5 (see Display 5.1). Daniel had been placed in a self-contained room in a center-based program, where he worked on adaptive skills and selected basic academics. During his several months in the special program, Daniel's behavior deteriorated enough that his family decided that perhaps a more inclusive setting would be beneficial. The school district moved Daniel to his home school, which fully included students with "severe needs." When Daniel was first placed in his new general education class, he had substantial difficulty engaging in the lessons and he displayed a number of behavioral problems (e.g., wandering out of the room, acting out when given an instruction). Consequently, he was assigned a full-time paraprofessional on a temporary basis. In the following weeks, educators completed a number of different analyses to enhance Daniel's class participation, reduce problems, and increase learning. One of these was a typical person inventory, and some sample entries for Daniel are shown in Table 8.4.

A number of adaptations like those shown in Table 8.4 became the support plan for Daniel. In conjunction with a new IEP that was more appropriate for the general education setting and curriculum, these adaptations were implemented throughout

Table 8.4.   Excerpts from several typical person inventory samples for Daniel

Activity	Classroom routine	Discrepancy analysis	Proposed adaptations
Opening	The children are sitting in a semicircle, and one is invited to lead the class in reciting the alphabet.	Daniel is sitting with the children but not watching the teacher. When he is invited to lead, he does not get up.	A designated peer could tap Daniel and repeat the teacher's invitation. The same peer could show Daniel how to lead as needed.
Library	The children are looking at books on the shelves. Some are taking books to the checkout desk.	Daniel wanders out of the room and gazes at things in the hallway.	The library assistant could provide brief reminder instructions.
Math center	The teacher gives the class a verbal cue to count with her. The children count from 1 through 20 in unison.	Daniel looks at another student and misses the cue to count, then acts out when reminded.	The teacher could tap Daniel on the shoulder, establish brief eye contact, and give the class a verbal cue to count.

the school day. Within 8–12 weeks, Daniel had made sufficient progress so the full-time paraprofessional's role was faded to part-time support for academics only. Over the next several years, Daniel continued to make remarkable social and academic progress, and no additional behavioral support efforts were needed beyond the simple adaptations made to enhance and maintain his class participation. Daniel is now going into his fifth year of being successful in a fully inclusive education environment. He requires supports for learning and participation, but his behavioral problems have virtually disappeared.

A relatively elaborate Typical Person Inventory Form appears in the appendix. Along with columns for keeping a running record of what the other students are doing (classroom routines), what the particular student is doing if it differs (discrepancy analysis), and what modifications are necessary to close the gap (adaptations), this form adds several other columns. There are, for example, pre-intervention and post-intervention columns for indicating the level of support that is presently required to keep the student actively engaged in the classroom routine. As the pre/post key on the form indicates, a five-point scale reflects the student's level of independent involvement. The support person column is for assessing the use of direct peer or adult supports for ensuring participation. As shown in the support person key on the form, an observer can indicate whether an adult (A) or a peer (P) other than the teacher is supporting the student. An observer can use the related objectives column to generate potential learning objectives that, if included in the student's IEP, can enhance his or her ongoing activity involvement.

Students in Self-Contained Settings   An especially challenging situation can occur when a student is in a more restrictive setting and there are plans to reintegrate him or her into general education. As stressed throughout this book, it is difficult to use knowledge of behaviors and participation levels within self-contained rooms and facilities to predict what will occur in more natural school settings because the conditions of these two settings often differ. Perhaps if the student was previously in general education or is presently in a few, limited general education classes, interviews with these teachers can help establish some participation patterns. Of course, one must bear in mind that these teachers have particular relationships with the student that may or may not be evidenced when a broader reintegration process occurs. Moreover, especially with the passage of time and the student's movement into higher grades, past data are suspect because they may describe learning conditions that are no longer relevant.

The following two-step procedure is useful for analysis and projection. First, a teacher or behavior specialist who knows the student well visits and interviews teachers in the proposed placement environment to collect information on the standards, expectations, and supports of typical classrooms and other school situations. One way to gather these data is to observe a typical day within the proposed class or classes and construct a narrative record of activities, participation expectations, and the natural supports provided by the teacher and others across different instructional formats. Second, a meeting is held in which members of the old and new education teams (especially the teachers) discuss the student's learning and participation expectations in relation to existing classroom supports, then consider other supports that could possibly enhance student participation.

Tables 8.5 and 8.6 demonstrate two interrelated analyses procedures that can be used when planning for reintegration. The content of these tables is taken from a larger plan that was developed for Carlos, a first-grade student who was introduced in

Chapter 5. He was fully included in the classroom and frequently displayed intensive rage (see Table 5.2). Table 8.5 gives examples of a two-step analysis process in which the natural classroom supports associated with specific activities are first examined and

Table 8.5. Natural and added supports by setting

Setting	Natural	Added for Carlos
Arrival	The teacher verbally reminds children of class expectations. The teacher positions herself for giving assistance.	Carlos is greeted at the classroom door by a "greeter." A buddy helps Carlos with his coat. The paraeducator takes Carlos to class.
Literacy	Verbal reminders and instructions are given at the onset of literacy activities. A generally fixed set of activity transitions occurs in unison. Relevant materials are dispersed throughout the room. The teacher gives verbal and visual prompts about whom she is working with at any given point in time. The adults occasionally "correct" and "remind" students of expectations.	Carlos is free to make choices from available options. A picture schedule defines his options. Compliance negotiation occurs, but the natural activities of the class are constantly stressed. Breaks and alternate settings are available for Carlos, and he is encouraged to return to class. Water or juice is available. Carlos uses parallel activities in class (e.g., listens with earphones to stories on audiotape). Ongoing paraeducator support is available.
Large group	If the teacher is reading a story, she reads expressively from front of classroom, with the paraeducator in the background. The children can comment freely as long their comments are related and not boisterous. The teacher uses some redirects.	Seat Carlos next to someone with whom he gets along (i.e., use "seat buddies"). Give Carlos his own spot near the back of the classroom. Allow Carlos to help the teacher. Have the paraeducator in the background (i.e., shadowing). Permit him to have breaks as needed.
Lunch	Clear routines exist for before, during, and after lunch. A large group of students adhere to the routine. The teacher monitors and corrects some line-up behaviors. Several adult monitors are in the lunchroom.	Carlos gets in line when it is time to leave class. The paraeducator stays with or near Carlos. If Carlos wants to walk ahead, let him. Carlos has his own spot in the lunchroom with a lunch buddy. Inform the lunch monitors to offer Carlos support as needed.
Recess	Natural play and conversation occur throughout the area. There are few restrictions on activity choices.	The paraeducator observes from nearby. Carlos goes out the door with a buddy, but Carlos and his buddy do not have to stay together while outside. The buddy helps Carlos line up.

Table 8.6.   Desirable and acceptable behaviors by setting

Setting	Desirable	Acceptable for Carlos
Arrival	Come directly to class. Promptly hang up coat and place lunch in the lunch cart.	Carlos may make a few stops along the way. Carlos hangs up his coat or places his lunch in the lunch cart after a second reminder to do so.
Literacy	Self-select and participate in the learning activities of the other students who are engaged at various centers, with accommodations and modifications. Work with the teacher at her desk during the teacher's "help time."	Carlos self-selects and participates in preferred activities that are literacy related but may not be among the options offered to others (e.g., using the computer). Carlos may take breaks whenever he needs them. Carlos may help the teacher distribute materials. Carlos may watch others rather than participate.
Large group	Do not touch the other children more than they touch each other. Stay in place.	Carlos may touch others as long as the touching is not intrusive. Carlos may listen to the teacher from various places in the room.
Lunch	Line up and stay in one spot. Raise hand to go out for recess after eating, then go to recess.	Carlos may go ahead of the other students to recess when he is done eating.
Recess	Play with others intermittently. Play by self on the playground equipment.	Carlos goes outside, stays on the playground, and adheres to major rules.

detailed, then expanded through the generation of individually tailored additional supports. Table 8.6 shows a parallel two-step process in which the general behavioral expectations for students within these different activities are detailed and modified as necessary so that Carlos can succeed in ways that are different from his classmates but acceptable to the classroom teacher. An Expectations and Supports Form, which integrates these analyses, appears in the appendix at the end of the book.

Of course, for the preceding kinds of analyses to become routine parts of the transition process, the professional roles of teachers working within self-contained settings will often need to be reframed and their specific responsibilities reprioritized. Teachers within more restrictive settings must come to see themselves as agents primarily responsible for assisting a student in successfully reentering his or her natural community. The educator's job must focus less on equipping a student with "social," "self-control," and "good behavior" skills, which may or may not transfer into less controlled environments, and more on analyzing specific student–environment matches and to help receiving environments develop the needed supports for students with challenging behaviors and their teachers to experience success.

ASSESSMENT FOR IMPLEMENTING THE INTERVENTION

The majority of the empirical research studies that address behavioral problems use measurement procedures that focus on the presence or absence of specific behaviors and skills before and after an intervention, and these data are then offered as evidence of the intervention's impact. Using such precise measurement procedures makes sense when developing, confirming, or challenging basic scientific principles of learning and behavior. As mentioned previously, however, using these kinds of measures to assess student growth and change in school is a practice that needs to be revisited. Of course, it is, in part, a social validation issue: What changes need to occur for one to be able to say that a person, his or her peers, and/or the school community are experiencing benefit? Paralleling the research literature, educators were encouraged in the past to treat discrete behavior and skill measures primarily as indicators of such change. There was little consideration for whether such measures were really perceived by families, students, or other educators as authentic evidence of growth or whether the measured skill and behavior changes actually correlated with other more substantial differences in the lives of the students who were subject to interventions. In this book, perceptions of change and participant experiences of meaningful differences in their lives take clear precedence over discrete "skill acquisition" and "behavior reduction" measures when assessing the results of an intervention. The discussion of these issues is organized in relation to the six key activities that are associated with a behavior intervention (identified in Chapter 7). These activities are as follows:

1. Put in place educational and environmental changes
2. Put in place professional development
3. Put in place incident response and crisis procedures
4. Ensure critical communications
5. Ensure on-demand problem solving
6. Evaluate change in the learner and the community

With few exceptions, this section's discussion of assessment in relation to these six activities focuses more on the questions that need to be asked than on specific measurement procedures. Depending on level of concern, these questions can often be addressed using informant-based strategies, embedded within informal conversations, formal interviews, and shared dialogues between team members. Direct observation strategies can also be used, sometimes serving an important confirmatory role by validating or raising questions about what educators and family members report. In addition, the questions that are offered here should be augmented with those offered in Table 8.2 to ensure that the different levels of understanding are addressed throughout the post-intervention assessment process.

Put in Place Educational and Environmental Changes

Increasingly, experts (Duchnowski, 2000; Singer, 2000) are recognizing the need for post-intervention evaluation activities that assess the integrity of intervention implementation, or the degree to which the recommended and proposed intervention procedures are being carried out and how they are being conducted. In fact, in his review of Office of Civil Rights and court decisions related to IDEA '97, Smith (2000) found that one of the concerns raised in cases that are related to behavioral issues is fidelity of intervention implementation.

Based on Chapter 7's differentiation of the various kinds of intervention steps and procedures that should be incorporated in typical interventions, some important questions to ask include the following:

- How are intervention steps and procedures that are not optional (i.e., fixed decisions) being implemented and with what problems and results?
- How are intervention steps and procedures that permit several alternative actions on the part of educators (i.e., fluid decisions) being carried out by different individuals in different settings and with what problems and results?
- Which educators are using intervention steps and procedures that are self-selected and can be applied in different ways depending on situations and needs (i.e., recommendations)? How are these being applied and with what problems and results?
- What unplanned, unexpected, and/or uncalled for intervention steps and procedures are being used and with what results for the student and for others?

Given heuristic decision making, the process of examining intervention fidelity is not fulfilled by simply measuring consistency of follow-through. Rather, it is a process in which the implementation of the various steps and procedures that are required, recommended, and contraindicated by the plan are examined across time, as well as in relation to various educators' other activities, to assist the team in enhancing the effectiveness of their intervention.

Put in Place Professional Development

In many situations, the fidelity of intervention implementation depends on whether the staff's training needs are being met. When a plan is based more on fluid decisions or recommendations than on fixed decisions, ensuring that training has been provided can be the key to the student's success. Moreover, there are critical issues associated with what content the training has actually covered. Some of the important questions include

- Has the training addressed how a plan's success depends more on the student becoming an accepted and participating member of the school community than on implementing behavior control processes?
- Has the training addressed steps for behavior prevention?
- Has the training addressed steps for teaching and encouraging adaptive alternatives for the student to use in place of the challenging behaviors?
- Has the training addressed steps for crisis support?

In most circumstances, it is also important that training processes extend beyond the particulars for addressing behaviors and into issues of instruction. This is especially true when technologies are introduced to enhance learning. For example, if a child with a visual impairment is beginning to use a Braille n' Speak device, is the general education teacher aware of the device's features and capabilities (e.g., a calendar program that can be used for assignments)?

Put in Place Incident Response and Crisis Procedures

It is especially essential to ask probing questions early and often about the use of any crisis response procedures. Some of the questions that need to be addressed include

- Are there potentially important variations in the way the procedures are applied by different adults?

- Are the procedures having the effect of calming things down and returning order to the situation?
- Could more appropriate procedures be used?
- What are some of the different emotional and behavioral reactions students or educators express when the procedures are anticipated, applied, or reflected on after their use?

It cannot be stressed enough that it is inappropriate to expect staff, especially paraprofessionals, to carry out complex crisis support procedures without ongoing, in situ training. It is not uncommon for programs that require crisis support to implement procedures without appropriate training. Then responsibility for a serious judgment error is relegated to the untrained paraprofessional when, in fact, the administrative and teaching personnel who failed to address training needs are truly responsible.

Ensure Critical Communications

Other activities that are pivotal in defining whether a behavior support effort will fail or succeed are those associated with ensuring that critical communications occur among all involved parties. This means that questions such as the following need to be asked:

- Have administrators been informed of the proposed intervention plan and its overall effects on their distribution and use of time, material, and personnel resources? Are there mechanisms for keeping them informed as changes are made in the plan?
- Have the student, participating family members, educators, and peers been informed of their responsibilities under the proposed plan and of the lines of communication for reporting difficulties and engaging in problem solving? Are there mechanisms for keeping them informed as changes are made in the plan?
- Have other members of the school community been informed of elements of the plan that affect them in their school activities and responsibilities? Are there mechanisms for keeping them informed as changes are made in the plan?
- Are there ways to ensure that progress is communicated to all members of the school community, especially to those who have an investment in the plan's success?

The role of families as full partners in any behavior support effort must be recognized when thinking about critical communications. Hence, it is recommended that formal processes be developed to regularly gauge the family's perceptions of and responses to a plan as it unfolds. One promising instrument for gathering this kind of information is a 20-item goodness-of-fit survey developed by Albin and colleagues (1996). This tool can help determine whether a match exists between the support plan and the family's values and lifestyle.

Ensure On-Demand Problem Solving

Heuristic decision making opens the way for using a number of different intervention steps and procedures, depending on circumstances. Hence, it is paramount for educators to have mechanisms for processing the effect of an implemented step or procedure. Some of the questions that need to be addressed include

- Are problem-solving activities (e.g., meetings, informal discussions) occurring as scheduled and/or in a timely manner?
- What kinds of information are being used in problem solving, and how are the data being analyzed during problem-solving activities?
- Are the relevant parties gaining access to all of the information that they need for successful problem solving?
- What kinds of misinformation are influencing problem-solving activities, and who is providing the misinformation? Why is this information being circulated by these individuals?

Ongoing and thoughtfully conducted measurement activities can provide an especially solid base for problem solving as well as for addressing issues related to revising a plan. In thinking about measurement for problem solving, it can be useful to make a distinction between two types of data-collection processes. In the first type, *static measurement*, highly discrete measures are defined in advance and data on these measures are collected regularly, with an emphasis on consistency of definition across the phases of an intervention. In the second type, *dynamic measurement*, measures may evolve in their definitions, measures that proved to be unhelpful are dropped, and new measures are added with the changing conditions and contexts of the intervention. What makes the latter type of measurement appealing for problem solving is that dynamic measurement acknowledges that new and different measures are sometimes needed for different kinds of issues and concerns and that what defines success and failure across time can change the measures that are needed.

Evaluate Change in the Learner and the Community

The effect of the intervention on the student and others is the bottom line when it comes to the value of a specific behavior intervention plan. Questions regarding this issue include

- How has the student progressed in becoming a participating member of the school community?
- What about other members of the school community? Are they seeing positive change? Are they experiencing greater comfort and safety? Are they meeting their other obligations as educators and students? Are they experiencing growth?
- Is the student growing in terms of his or her learning, fewer incidences of problems, and/or better support for problems when they occur?
- If positive changes are not happening in a timely manner, are these findings connected with issues of intervention fidelity, crisis response, training needs, critical communications, or problem solving?

One of the most powerful ways that change can be expressed, and its presence assessed, is by keeping a record of the stories that educators spontaneously tell each other (Jalongo, 1992). When teachers routinely say, "I once again enjoy teaching," or mention, "Elaine is such a different person" (instead of complaining about what Elaine did in class), the team has a sense that something significant has happened in their lives and in the lives of their students. Chapter 10 in particular illustrates the power of the storytelling process as a form of data.

GUIDED INQUIRY REVISITED

This chapter details an array of assessment processes and techniques, all of which are appropriate for use in educational settings. When these processes and techniques are applied in various combinations with each other, educators can have some level of confidence that reasonable and hypothesis-derived interventions are being selected and that intervention results reflect important authentic outcomes. At the same time, one must not be fooled by what could be called the "siren call of objectivity," when the data assume an exaggerated importance and a quality of "rightness" that lulls one into forgetting the human dimension. As discussed previously, it must be understood that behavioral assessment activities are themselves embedded within the cultural and experiential contexts of the specific schools in which they are conducted.

Grasping the latter point is of the utmost importance if one is to enter into assessment activities with a balanced understanding of what such activities can and cannot accomplish in relation to program design and performance. For example, assessment can help explain how often and for what reasons a child pulls his or her classmates' hair, and it can provide some clues for developing prevention steps and promoting adaptive alternatives. Yet, the same information collected in two different schools could evoke entirely different reactions and responses from the respective teams of educators that develop and implement the child's behavior intervention plan.

Consider for a moment two schools: A and B. The education teams in both of these schools may be equally concerned with the child's development. Nonetheless, the educators in School A think that the behavior is extremely disruptive and threatens others' safety and learning. These educators perceive disability as the cause of the behavior and believe that the student should be in a special program with other children who are "the same." They also see educational growth and opportunity as being contingent on the reduction of hair pulling. In contrast, the educators in School B see the behavior as disturbing but point out that students and faculty accept and appreciate the child. These educators believe that the behavior is primarily rooted in situational variables that they themselves control, and that this student represents part of a broader diversity that is accepted and welcomed in their school. Finally, they see the reduction of hair pulling as being contingent on educational growth and opportunity. Now, imagine for a minute how these two different groups of educators would perceive, interpret, and translate the exact same data on the student's hair pulling.

This illustration is intended to communicate two messages. The first is that most data on a child's behavior cannot be interpreted meaningfully when viewed in isolation from the individual and collective understandings that form the school community members' reality models. Put differently, rates of behavior without context and many other forms of "objective data" have considerably less value when they are examined independent of the perceptions and interpretations of those who experience the behavior.

The second message is derived from the first one. If behavioral data are best understood by examining how a particular group of educators interpret them, then one must reconsider what it means to use data responsibly when designing interventions. For instance, these two schools might use the same baseline data to develop entirely different overall programs for this child, which reflect not the child's particular needs but the two school cultures. It is even possible that School B sees no need for a behavioral program outside of what is already being provided educationally, even as School A perceives this child as having "intense programming needs." Finally, say that the educators at School A lack both understanding and skills for implementing an appropriate support plan for this student, yet this is the school that the student attends. This raises issues that are similar to those raised by Albin and colleagues in their discussion of "contextual fit," which is "the congruence or compatibility that exists between specific features and components of a behavioral support plan and a variety of relevant variables relating to individuals and environments" (1996, p. 82). From this perspective (assuming that one has some control over which school a student attends), achieving the best program requires determining whether another school might be better for this student. From a support perspective, School B is clearly favored.

Most educators would not have the luxury of taking this child out of a School A and placing him in a School B, nor should this student have to move around to find a school that will accept him and appropriately support him. The primary point of this comparison is to stress the importance of using guided inquiry, which was introduced in Chapter 6, when working in difficult or reluctant schools. Imagine that a special education teacher who has School B values transfers to School A. For this new teacher to effectively operate in this environment, he or she must be able to navigate the social and political obstacles that are present in the school, and this requires knowing how to choose and use assessment data to best promote the student's support needs and interests.

In the context of this discussion, the guided inquiry concept stresses that understanding and innovation arise when educators work as a team to co-construct their knowledge through exploring questions that address a number of levels of understanding (e.g., explanation, empathy). For this new teacher, this represents a dual-edged sword. On one hand, he or she may know what an appropriate intervention looks like for this student but may also know that the implementation of such an intervention is in doubt given the other players in this situation. On the other hand, innovation can emerge out of a well-conceived guided inquiry process. Hence, change can happen in School A and, ultimately, for the child if the individual (in this case, the special educator) constructs his or her assessment activities and decisions in relation to a larger inquiry process, in which he or she comes to understand—and work effectively with—the attitudes, feelings, and perspectives of the other members of the school community.

As shown in this discussion, guided inquiry represents an important tool for developing appropriate supports. However, the road to success in a school similar to School A will require something more: strategic action. As defined in Chapter 7, strategic action is a process by which a concerned educator develops and implements an intervention that simultaneously takes into account the school culture's short-term realities and the student's long-term, ideal support needs. As the intervention unfolds across time, and as the school community's understanding of the student's support needs becomes more mature, the supports provided to the student shift from being steps and procedures that reflect boundaries set by the school culture to steps and procedures that reflect the student's real support needs.

In sum, approaching these issues from a "goodness-of-fit" perspective (Albin et al., 1996)—achieving a match between a school's culture and a student's support needs—requires an intervention plan that begins to address student's needs but may be compromised by social and political realities. An educator who employs guided inquiry and a strategic action framework uses this discrepancy, which certainly changes over time, as a basis for continuous decision making and eventually matches what the school actually provides for a particular student and the student's assessed behavioral support needs. Upcoming chapters, especially Chapters 10 and 11, reflect this emphasis on both guided inquiry and strategic action when behavior support plans and processes are developed and implemented in schools.

Positive Behavioral Support Practices and Their Applications

Chapter 9

Enhancing Positive
Behavioral Support Practices

with Marjorie Z. Leon

*"I find the great thing in this world is not so much
where we stand, as in what direction we are moving."*
—*Oliver Wendell Holmes*

Recall from Chapter 7 that challenging behaviors can be organized on a continuum that stretches from lack of student engagement and intermittent minor disruptions, to persistent minor disruptions and occasional severe disruptions, to persistent severe disruptions and dangerous behaviors. It was suggested that this continuum provides a basis for partitioning behavioral problems into three overlapping categories, which reflect the degree of concern. These three categories call for different types and levels of resource commitments and intervention activities: 1) enhance practices, 2) develop a behavior intervention plan, and 3) develop a comprehensive behavior intervention plan.

This chapter is concerned with the first activity, enhance practices. It presents ways that educators, especially classroom teachers, can improve their positive behavioral support skills so that they are more understanding of and more proficient in handling those irksome, intermittent, and usually minor behavioral issues that can offset the joys of teaching. As suggested in Chapter 7, these skills are usually associated with planning and support activities such as improving interpersonal relationships with students, reflecting on one's instructional and classroom organization activities, and conducting relatively informal functional behavioral assessments.

As any good teacher knows, orchestrating learning and behavior in a typical classroom or other school setting is more complicated than it looks. Educators must often make spontaneous and unique support decisions in the midst of complex routines, and they must have a clear-sighted sense that such decisions ultimately enhance student learning and preserve community. Chapter 6 showed that dynamic systems such as schools and classrooms require heuristic decision making if educators are to make decisions that are effectively configured, on average, to the conditions that are present when specific behavioral concerns arise. Ecological rationality is the primary guiding principle in heuristic decision making (Gigerenzer & Todd, 1999): Educators use factual knowledge plus their intuition to make immediate and ongoing decisions that match prevailing circumstances, adhere to positive support principles, and honor the overarching learning and discipline goals that define the very purpose for such decisions.

A particular educator's experience and regular practice in making sound heuristic decisions when overall concern about behavior is minimal can provide the foundation for making similar decisions when degree of concern is greater. In other words, learning to think and to act by using principles of positive behavioral support on a day-to-day basis make it possible for the educator to apply these principles in more rigorous and stressful situations, in which the problems are more difficult or seem intractable. This is a critical point. At the beginning of the 21st century, few educators' training has prepared them to routinely utilize positive behavioral support principles in an heuristic fashion for planning their classes or addressing specific behavioral concerns. Traditional classroom and behavior management training has focused on forming structures, such as systems of reinforcers and punishers for contingent responding to "good" and "bad" behaviors. For many educators, the primary and essential reason for developing these external structures is to augment existing interpersonal relationships and instructional processes and thereby ensure compliance with classroom and school expectations. Hence, the very notion that effective instruction and discipline can emerge from positive interpersonal relationships, good teaching practices, and seeking to understand others is a relatively unexplored concept for many educators and researchers.

To understand what constitutes a "support practice," one must recognize that all factors within an educational environment can affect behavior, and any one of these can be viewed as a candidate for a support practice if its application is delineated in relation to support principles. Bishop and Jubala (1995) included variables such as rules, regulations, procedures, curriculum, instructional strategies, materials, staff, and peers in their list of factors to be considered when developing and using positive behavioral support. From this perspective, educators have a wide range of possible strategies for enhancing their support of students.

Four general categories of support practices are considered for the purposes of this chapter:

1.   Affective supports
2.   Schedule and activity supports
3.   Peer supports
4.   Teacher style supports

Consecutive sections define each category, examine its relationship to the six facets of understanding (Wiggins & McTighe, 1998), and describe a small number of related exemplary practices. Following the discussion of these categories is a checklist that educators can use to assess and think about their own growth in the use of these practices. The chapter then concludes with reflections on how positive behavioral support practices relate to the concept of student "voice."

Of course, from an heuristic decision making standpoint, these categories only provide a general framework for thinking about one's practices, and the associated examples only illustrate what is possible within the boundaries of a category. Nevertheless, defining specific categories of support and offering small, finite sets of exemplary practices facilitates the emergence of an evolving discourse on positive behavioral support among educators. At the beginning of the 21st century, most schools lack such a support-oriented discourse. When it does exist, it is often an extension of applied behavior analysis, which is only one of the several contributing theoretical models (see Chapter 2).

AFFECTIVE SUPPORTS

Affective supports are practices that assist a student in experiencing a positive emotional connection with educators, a positive regard of self, and stability when emotional well-being is shaken by internal or external causes. Affective supports help maintain a focus on learning in the classroom because they create a background sense of well-being and safety in a student. With respect to the six facets of understanding, one could consider such questions as

- If part of my problem is that I do not really care for this student, are there some things that I can think about or do to help me like and respect this student more? (application)
- Do students see my acknowledgement of their work as appreciation of their talents or as attempts to manipulate their output? (interpretation, perspective)
- How would my self-esteem be affected if someone reacted in this particular way to my behavior? (self-knowledge)

School counselors have formal training in these kinds of issues, and teachers might want to collaborate with them or secure direct services as necessary. Yet, there is much that teachers can do to offer these kinds of supports. Six examples of affective supports are

1. Neutralizing routines
2. Social interpretation or reframing
3. Relationship transfer
4. Positive unconditional regard
5. Use of literature
6. Positive communication between educators and the family

These supports are discussed in detail next.

Sometimes, a student comes to school or to class agitated or upset due to something that happened at home, on the way to school, or at some earlier point in the day. *Neutralizing routines* are one way to return a student to a relaxed and responsive state so that he or she can resume work (Horner, Day, & Day, 1997). Neutralizing routines are planned opportunities for a student to regain his or her composure through engaging in an activity that is known to help reinstate calm and reorient the student to the task at hand. Neutralizing routines must be individually prescribed: For one student, an effective neutralizing routine might be briefly engaging in a preferred activity before beginning his or her academic work; for another student, it might be sharing the difficult experience with a respected adult or peer before coming to class.

Horner and colleagues (1997) arranged to offset the negative impact of specific previous events on three adolescents by determining a "routine" that could calm each individual and assist him or her in returning to the scheduled activity. One individual, for example, became upset whenever a planned outing was canceled. The calming routine for this person was "(a) to formally reschedule the same event on his calendar for another day and (b) to spend 5 to 10 min reviewing Pat's 'yearbook' (a set of pictures from his past)" (p. 606). Of course, teachers who have nurturing relationships with students can more easily detect the need for a neutralizing routine and help mitigate negative situations before they affect the student. When in doubt, a teacher can use functional behavioral assessment to establish the reason for a student's becoming upset and to identify a potentially effective neutralizing routine.

Social interpretation, or *reframing* (Maag, 1999), helps students to understand the meaning of and clarify their thinking regarding behavior that is directed toward them. For example, on a particular day, a middle-school student may not respond to another student's greetings, and the latter student becomes miffed that his overtures were ignored. Through social interpretation, however, the ignored student comes to understand that the unresponsive student was preoccupied because she had just received bad news regarding her family. As another example, a fourth-grade student becomes upset whenever a particular boy teases her. The teacher may, if observations prove so, tell the girl that teasing is the boy's way of saying that he likes her and is too shy to admit it. If encouraged to translate "You're ugly" into "You're special to me, and I want to get to know you," then this girl can rethink her responses to the boy's teasing. (See Nichols, 2000, for a discussion of functional behavioral assessment in relation to the impact of cognitive and emotional variables on behavior.)

Relationship transfer is using a solid, positive relationship between two people to engender other relationships that can make adapting to a new setting possible for a fearful student. This practice is illustrated in Luiselli's (2000) study of a child who was initially agitated whenever her mother attempted to leave her at her inclusive preschool. A systematic fading procedure was used in which the mother's involvement lessened gradually over time. This resulted in the child's gradual and successful shift in attention from her mother's presence to the class activities and the peers and adults in the classroom.

Positive unconditional regard is the practice of exhibiting ongoing respect and caring for a student regardless of the student's successes and failures. A teacher may first have to examine his or her own feelings about the child, then generate ways to think more positively about the child before he or she can express sincere positive, unconditional regard. Jones and Jones (1998) offered an interesting perspective on positive regard. They depicted developing positive relationships with students as something like establishing a positive relationship bank account. They explained, "Just as a person has to make deposits into a checking account to make a withdrawal, educators need to have positive interactions with students if they want students to respond positively to adult requests for effort or modified behavior" (p. 85). Some students come to school having had limited positive interactions with adults in their lives, so teachers need to make generous deposits in these students' positive relationship bank accounts.

There is an interesting line of research within applied behavior analysis that is examining the concept of *noncontingent reinforcement*, which seems related to the practice of positive unconditional regard. Noncontingent reinforcement means providing positive reinforcement independent of an individual's specific behaviors, and it has been shown to correlate with positive changes in problem behaviors. For example, Derby, Fisher, and Piazza (1996) used noncontingent attention on a continuous schedule for a 12-year-old girl who was hospitalized for severe self-injury and self-restraint. When she received noncontingent reinforcement, the girl's problem behaviors occurred at low levels. In contrast, when she received attention only if self-restraint behaviors were observed, both self-injury and self-restraint occurred at high levels (see also Vollmer, Iwata, Zarcone, Smith, & Mazaleski, 1993).

The *use of literature* can also be a form of affective support. Depending on their own particular life experiences, students may identify with characters in a novel or story and experience a sense of common humanity, a different understanding of their difficulties, or new solutions to their own problems. (For discussions of bibliotherapy, see Lenkowsky, 1987, and Riordan & Wilson, 1989.) Similarly, specific reading selections can be used to model how to behave in certain situations, as is seen in the literature-based curriculum of the Child Development Project (Lewis, Schaps, & Watson, 1996). Anderson's (2000) study used a Shakespeare play to teach social skills to adolescents with learning difficulties. The intervention involved examining and reporting on the social skills of the characters in Shakespeare and how to interpret events and feelings. Whatever the purpose, the use of literature can enable individuals to understand their situations more fully through reading about someone who faces similar circumstances and sometimes overcomes them.

Good relationships between parents and teachers can also help facilitate good relationships between students and teachers. Indeed, home–school partnerships are identified as a critical element in many successful and caring schools (Epstein, 1995). *Positive communication between educators and the family* can thus be viewed as a critical practice for developing and sustaining such relationships. Koegel, Koegel, Kellegrew, and Mullen (1996) described a specific example of how coordination between home and school activities can lead to improved behavior. Some young children were disruptive during circle time at school. Their parents were asked to read them a story the night before the teacher read the same story at circle time. When parents read the story within a positive context (e.g., bedtime routines), the children were more attentive and less disruptive the following day than when the children did not have the story read to them at home.

SCHEDULE AND ACTIVITY SUPPORTS

It has long been recognized that appropriate structure and predictability in routines are signature characteristics of good teaching (Wehby, Symons, & Canale, 1998). Schedule and activity support practices make routines more explicit or provide adaptations and modifications to the activities or curriculum. Questions to consider in terms of the six facets of understanding include

- What occurs on some days and not on others that seems to make it difficult for this student to make transitions from one class to another? (explanation)
- What suggestions might the student's parents have for helping him or her feel at ease and learn in history class? (application)
- How do I feel when I am in a new place and I do not know the expectations of those around me? (empathy)

Schedules and activities can be modified and adjusted in many ways for students who need these kinds of supports to enhance their participation and comfort in routines. Six types are

1. Opportunities for choice and reasonable control
2. Predictable routines and signals
3. Rest and break options
4. Anticipation cues
5. Accommodations and modifications
6. Creative scheduling

The following paragraphs examine these support options.

Giving *opportunities for choice and reasonable control* can be a relatively simple but effective antecedent modification that often prevents problem behaviors from occurring. Bambara and Knoster (1998) recommended that students be given as much control over tasks, materials, and activities as possible. A number of substantiating studies have shown that providing options within academic and work tasks (Parsons, Reid, Reynolds, & Bumgarner, 1990) and within daily routines (Bambara, Koger, Katzer, & Davenport, 1995) can have marked positive effects on activity participation levels, with corresponding reductions in behaviors that interfere with participation.

A second schedule and activity support is providing students with *predictability* within their activities and routines. Not all students, of course, want or need high levels of predictability in their daily routines. For those who do, however, clarifying the daily class schedule, specific activity expectations, and even activity beginning and ending points can often prevent behavioral difficulties from arising or becoming more pronounced. With respect to daily schedules, some students may require a picture schedule to help them anticipate upcoming events and expectations; others may need a written schedule that details changing expectations. For some students, intermittent verbal reminders of a particular day's scheduled events will suffice. Some students may also benefit from video priming. Schreibman, Whalen, and Stahmer (2000) used video priming with three young children to alert them to upcoming events (e.g., excursions to the mall) during which problematic behavior was likely. Viewing a brief videotape that incorporated segments of events to come was sufficient to reduce the children's tantrums. Research has indicated that three conditions need to be met for this kind of priming to be successful: "(a) the priming session should be completed prior to the event, (b) there should be low demands during the session, and (c) the priming session should have potential sources of reinforcement" (Schreibman et al., 2000, p. 9).

A third practice related to schedule and activity support is providing *rest and break options* to students. In practice, it is sometimes helpful for these break options to occur in a separate setting or at least in another part of the classroom. When a student is given the choice to move to another area and spend a few minutes in a relaxing activity or posture, crisis levels associated with a behavioral problem can often be avoided, and the student can be more receptive to learning upon his or her return to work.

The practice of giving students break options as a way to reduce problem behaviors has been extensively researched as a communication issue with students who have special education needs. Lalli, Casey, and Kates (1995), for example, described a study involving three children in an inpatient hospital unit who were either physically abusive toward themselves or would hit or throw objects at others. Each student was given a way to communicate that he or she needed a break from assigned tasks. At first, the students took frequent breaks; however, as the training progressed, more task completion could be required before a break was provided. It is unclear from the study description whether the educational tasks themselves were interesting or boring to the students, nor is it clear what role the isolated setting played in exacerbating the behaviors. Nevertheless, the study did show that giving these students a means to request and secure breaks reduced problem behaviors and helped maintain activity engagement. Similar results were also obtained in a study involving a student who used an augmentative and alternative communication system and was served in a general education class (Jackson et al., 1991). The student's disruptive behaviors were handled by teaching the student to request brief breaks when he became agitated. One incident in this study is particularly noteworthy. The general education teacher was concerned that this student would abuse the break privilege by taking breaks to get out of class. Her fears turned out be unfounded; in fact, as the study progressed, the student requested adding a new symbol to the augmentative communication system: *back-to-work*.

Anticipation cues refer to environmental, interpersonal, or instructional cues that tend to occasion challenging behaviors in specific individuals. When teachers are aware of how particular cues routinely "trigger" certain behaviors, they can use their knowledge of these antecedent–behavior relationships to reduce the problem behaviors. Hypothesis development can play a role here; the teacher can pose questions such as, "If I use a different set of materials, will this student be more interested in the assignment?" to guide hypothesis development.

One approach to working with anticipation cues is for the teacher to remove or alter the cues, or the student's awareness of the cues, to change the way that a student responds. For example, Tustin (1995) showed how an "advance notice" system for activity transitions reduced difficult behaviors that were associated with specific transitions. Yet, although changing the antecedent may sometimes be helpful, a more important response may be for the teacher to reexamine his or her content and methods of instruction to see if improvements are needed. Rolider and Axelrod pointed out that academic tasks that are "too long, boring, presented in a confusing manner, and on which a student has previously made errors" can often trigger inappropriate behaviors (2000, p. 7). Rolider and Axelrod also noted that becoming sensitive and proactively responsive to how such cues affect a student's behavior can have a positive effect on student–teacher rapport.

The literature has noted an important connection between academic difficulties and behavior disruptions (Clarke et al., 1995; Munk & Repp, 1994). It follows that constructing effective *accommodations and modifications* for academic tasks is an essential practice, especially in general education classes that serve highly diverse groups of students. Access to identical learning opportunities, in conjunction with accommodations such as "teachers who slow down instruction when needed, explain concepts and assignments clearly, teach learning strategies, and teach the same material in different ways so that everyone can learn" are features of classrooms that both students with and without learning difficulties value (Klingner & Vaughn, 1999, p. 23). Whenever effective accommodations and modifications can be provided to a student, these should be used in lieu of pulling a student away from the learning activities of others, which can affect the student's access to the curriculum, class and peer group membership, and self-esteem.

Finally, *creative scheduling* is an approach to arranging and rearranging events during the day according to a particular individual's rhythm, pace, and preferences. Brown's (1991) study examined creative scheduling and showed that respecting a person's scheduling preferences in relation to time, content, and sequence favorably affects challenging behaviors. Although this study was conducted in a residential context, the same logic can be applied in schools, especially high schools. For example, high school students can be encouraged to select the types of classes they want, the order in which their classes occur, or both. Although this may seem like an obvious support practice for most students, especially in high school, the stark reality is that many students with disabilities do not control their daily schedules. This is especially true for students with severe disabilities, whose often restricted range of class opportunities would be unimaginable for students without disabilities.

PEER SUPPORTS

Peer supports are practices that are designed to connect students more closely with each other. They often capitalize on the classroom curriculum content and instructional activities to nurture relationship development. When setting up peer supports in terms of the six facets of understanding, the following questions may be asked:

- What is this student's relationship with other members of the class, and which of the student's strengths could be used to expand these relationships? (explanation)
- After a brief removal because of a tantrum, how does this student feel when the other students watch him or her reenter the classroom? (interpretation)
- What am I doing to model acceptance and understanding of differences between students? (self-knowledge)

Using the following six methods can establish enhanced peer connections:

1. Peer buddy arrangements
2. Cooperative learning activities
3. Classwide peer tutoring
4. Base groups
5. Extracurricular activities
6. Peer mediators

Peer buddy arrangements consist of one student assisting another student for behavioral, academic, and/or social purposes. It can be arranged to occur on a regular basis with the same student over a period of time or can occur spontaneously with various students for shorter time frames. As briefly described in Chapter 5, Janney and Snell (1996) reported how peers informally assisted their fellow students with significant support needs in four different schools from kindergarten through third grade. This qualitative study shed light on peers' receptivity and eagerness to assist their fellow students with disabilities, as well as the level of reciprocity involved in some of the interactions. At the secondary level, Hughes and colleagues (1999) showed how opportunities for friendships and social relationships were expanded for students with disabilities and their peer buddies at 11 comprehensive high schools. In this peer buddy program, students without disabilities earned course credit for learning about ways to include students with disabilities in school activities and by spending time each day supporting the students' inclusion. In a review of peer-mediated interventions (which often involve peer buddy arrangements), Gable, Arllen, and Hendrickson (1994) noted that, often, the participating students also reap both social and academic benefits.

Cooperative learning activities, discussed at a theoretical level in Chapter 3, have long been known to provide social as well as academic benefits. Sapon-Shevin, Ayers, and Duncan pointed out two values that are critical to the successful implementation of cooperative learning: "1) Everyone is good at something and can help others, and 2) Everyone is entitled to and can benefit from help and support from others" (1994, p. 50). The authors also pointed out that cooperative learning is most effective when it is multilevel, multimodal, and integrated across subject areas. Kelly (1994) suggested a number of strategies for involving students who may be potentially disruptive within the group processes. These strategies include changing the way that students in the group are evaluated, assigning a student who is likely to be nurturing to a group with a student who is withdrawn, and coaching a student who is a "low achiever" in advance so that he or she can contribute to the group.

Classwide peer tutoring (Greenwood, Delquadri, & Carta, 1988) is an approach in which all students receive and provide tutoring. Typically, students work together on a specific skill for 15–20 minutes, intermittently exchanging roles. A scripted approach is used, whereby the teacher first models and later monitors the tutoring process. Classwide peer tutoring has proven beneficial in reading, spelling, and mathematics with many different kinds of learners (DuPaul, Ervin, Hook, & McGoey, 1998; Fuchs, Fuchs, Mathes, & Simmons, 1997; Greenwood, Delquadri, & Hall, 1989). Fuchs and colleagues (1997) examined the use of classwide peer tutoring model with students who were "low achievers" (some with and some without identified disabilities) and students who were average achievers regarding reading comprehension. The authors found that, given three 35-minute sessions per week, the students involved in classwide peer tutoring outperformed their counterparts in classes that did not use this model.

Base groups can also foster a sense of community among a group of students. Jones and Jones (1998) suggested that base groups, each consisting of four students, should meet several times during the week for 5–15 minutes to check on everyone's understanding of their work and their progress. If a student is absent, a member of the group takes notes for or relays important information to him or her. If someone is struggling, a member of the group may try to explain the material before seeking teacher assistance. In any event, each student knows that three classmates will be in regular contact with him or her and will offer assistance when learning becomes difficult.

Extracurricular activities provide yet another opportunity for peer support. A student who struggles in several subjects might be, for example, an avid and contributing member of the school's drama club. In the club, this student has an opportunity to excel, be seen as successful by peers, and engage in joint activities that can lead to valued friendships. Such friendships can, in turn, lead to assistance and support with academics.

The final practice that enhances peer support is the use of *peer mediators.* Many schools have adopted peer mediator programs to resolve student–student conflicts (Bodine & Crawford, 1998). Peer mediators use negotiation, mediation, and consensus decision-making processes and skills to resolve interpeer conflicts. Some common situations that they may help diffuse are put-downs and teasing, playground conflicts, and turn-taking and possession conflicts. Peer mediators often prevent crisis situations by addressing a conflict before it becomes more serious. Peer mediator programs that are at a schoolwide level can be especially effective, and Chapter 12 offers more details on these programs.

TEACHER STYLE SUPPORTS

Teacher style supports are practices that define how teachers interact with students on matters in which teachers have primary jurisdiction, such as discipline and instruction. Questions for implementing teacher style supports that are related to the six facets of understanding include

- What are some ways that I use to monitor student problems, and how effective are these for conflict resolution? (application)
- How do students feel about my discipline style given their own needs for self-expression and autonomy? (interpretation)
- How would I feel if I was told what I just said to these two arguing students? (empathy)

The teacher style practices described next are

1. Rapport building
2. Debriefing
3. Behavioral momentum
4. Embedding instructions
5. Self-monitoring
6. Stepping back

Rapport building is useful for teachers who are searching for new ways to develop more effective instructional relationships with students (Carr et al., 1994). Rapport building, which can also be viewed as an affective support practice, involves verbally and nonverbally communicating interest in a student and in his or her life situations. According to Carr and colleagues, rapport building entails a teacher's becoming associated with the activities that a specific student values and prefers. In practice, when a student can count on personally rewarding social events and activities occurring within a particular teacher's class, the student will increasingly value that teacher. Accordingly, the student is more likely to respect and listen to that teacher, especially in comparison with a teacher who has not connected with the student in this way.

Debriefing involves the student's reflecting on his or her own behavior with the teacher. Debriefing refers to short, planned interactions between a student and teacher that have traditionally followed the occurrence of challenging behavior, but can also occur after positive behavior (Sugai & Colvin, 1997). Typically, a debriefing interaction lasts 3–5 minutes. It usually involves reviewing the details of a behavioral incident, focusing on precipitating circumstances, consideration of more acceptable responses, and preparation for returning to the classroom. The language that an adult uses in a debriefing session is an important consideration. For example, after a disruptive incident, a teacher could ask a student, "What did you just do to Sean?" This question will probably evoke an entirely different student response than the potentially more appropriate, "What just happened?" The latter question is more likely to result in a recapitulation of events that can actually assist the student in thinking about his or her behaviors in relation to his or her own needs, feelings, and motivations.

Behavioral momentum is a practice that can be used to increase compliance to teacher directives. It involves positioning a usually resisted request after a series of requests that have a high probability of compliance (Maag, 1999; Rhode, Jenson, &

Reavis, 1995). High probability requests are those that the student has followed many times in the past and is likely to follow in the future. By first letting the student comply with a series of preferred requests, momentum is gained for compliance when a frequently resisted request is then made. For example, after coming in from recess, a preschool-age student is asked to describe what she did on the jungle gym, helped with taking off her coat, asked if she would like some water, and then instructed to come to circle time. A related strategy, "joining the child" has been described by Maag (1999). Instead of standing back and repeatedly demanding compliance, the teacher assists the student with the expected task, possibly even leading and doing much of the task for the student. As Maag suggested, such a strategy can be a prerequisite to the eventual development of the needed trust and respect that facilitates healthy forms of student compliance.

Embedding instructions is another practice that takes various forms and can be used in different ways. Similar to behavioral momentum, it is a technique that is designed to improve a student's willingness to respect and adhere to teacher directives. In its most typical form, a teacher's directive is replaced at various points within natural classroom activities with either instructional choices (e.g., "Which would you rather do, A or B?") or conditional choices (e.g., "When you are ready, please do A") (see Bambara et al., 1995). Research findings indicate that many individuals who resist directives are more likely to be responsive when they are given latitude about what to do and/or when to start it (Bambara et al., 1995) (see Display 9.1).

Two variations of this practice are especially noteworthy. First, in a study involving four preschool-age children whose teacher identified as being especially disruptive, Blair, Umbreit, and Bos (1999) used hypothesis-based intervention processes to identify individualized preferred activities and instructional parameters that were associated with lower rates of problem behaviors. By incorporating (embedding) these preferred experiences into the existing curricula, problem behaviors were "reduced

DISPLAY 9.1—STAYING IN TOUCH

Andre, a third-grade student, sometimes became agitated and would emotionally "shut down" just before striking out at certain peers. Andre's teacher wanted to help him calm down and communicate during such times. The teacher decided to offer Andre two types of help during these difficult times. She provided him with two cards; one said, "Stay by my side" and the other said, "Come back in two minutes." Either way, the teacher stayed connected with Andre, demonstrating a sincere interest in his feelings and needs, and thereby assisting him when behavior escalation was likely.

In order for such a scenario to be effective, what type of relationship must already be present between the teacher and the student?

How does one purposefully develop such a relationship?

dramatically" (p. 162). Second, Maag (1999) described a strategy in which students are instructed "to do what they are already doing while interspersing the request for a desired behavior" (p. 11). Maag offered the following example of an embedded instruction: "Mary, as you shuffle your papers, open your math book to page eighteen while you are talking to Susie" (p. 11). In this situation, the desired behavior (opening the math book) is indicated in a directive that acknowledges and even humorously accepts the student's present activity, regardless of its desirability or appropriateness.

Especially when used in conjunction with behavioral momentum, embedding can, over extended time periods, improve situations in which a student is especially unwilling to follow teacher directives. Carefully distributing a variety of choice options and high probability directives within and across the school day is an important, if not necessary, first step for a student who has compliance problems.

Self-monitoring is a method in which a student records his or her own behavior and compares it with a standard or goal. Broden and colleagues (1971) were among the first researchers to show the benefits of self-recording in classrooms for increasing study behavior and reducing calling out in class. Although a teacher apparently relinquishes control by encouraging self-monitoring, the greater benefit is that the student exerts control of his or her behavior. This transfer of control can lead to improved behavior across many situations, even when the teacher is not present. Self-control and self-monitoring are viewed as important constructs within theories of cognitive behavior modification, which were discussed more fully in Chapter 2.

Stepping back occurs when a teacher steps back from a frustrating situation to reframe it and see it in a different light. For instance, if a student is not following a classroom rule, a teacher's first inclination may be to correct the student. If it is a relatively minor infraction and of no real consequence to the other children's learning, however, then sometimes it is best to simply ignore the infraction. Townsend (2000) asked teachers to use the "So what?" test to distinguish between arbitrary and meaningful expectations. She gave the example of a student sitting on his knees while working. Although this posture may violate an in-seat rule, the child is certainly engaged in academic work. Therefore, so what if he is sitting on his knees? This attitude helps educators put into perspective what really matters in a classroom. Humor can also be incorporated into the stepping back practice to help defuse conflict situations, even as it helps maintain a positive classroom atmosphere.

SELF-ASSESSMENT OF SUPPORT PRACTICES

The preceding four sections identified a number of practices that reflect principles of positive behavioral support. The checklist in Figure 9.1 is offered to assist educators in actively thinking about and learning new support practices. The checklist's measurement scale was inspired by a common medical school adage: "One first learns about it, then one does it, and finally one teaches others to do it." The blank version of this checklist is provided in the appendix.

As indicated previously, support processes cannot be easily broken down into finite sets of strategies or procedures. Numerous interactions within a school day require varied responses that must be construed "in the moment." Walker, Colvin, and Ramsey (1995) recommended the use of "*opportunistic teaching*" as a means of developing socially competent performance. Teachers best provide support by being alert to the teachable moments that occur throughout the school day, first offering what is needed to facilitate student participation or communication and then

A Checklist for Self-Assessment of Enhanced Practices

Type of support	Needs more information	Needs practice and reflection	Uses technique and can share with others
Affective supports Neutralizing routines		X	
Social interpretation or reframing			X
Relationship transfer		X	
Positive unconditional regard		X	
Use of literature	X		
Positive communication between school and home		X	
Schedule and activity supports Choice making			X
Predictable routines and signals		X	
Rest and break options			X
Anticipation cues	X		
Accommodation and modification		X	
Creative scheduling	X		
Peer supports Peer buddy		X	
Cooperative learning		X	
Classwide peer tutoring			X
Base group	X		
Extracurricular activities		X	
Peer mediators			X
Teacher style supports Rapport building		X	
Debriefing	X		
Behavioral momentum		X	
Embedding instructions	X		
Self-monitoring	X		
Stepping back		X	

Figure 9.1. A checklist for self-assessment of enhanced practices.

reflecting on the effects of these actions. A simple test that an educator can use when considering the usefulness of a possible new support practice is, "Would this strategy be something that might help me in my own life during a difficult situation?"

It is also important to bear in mind that change in and of itself is the prevailing constant in human social interaction. Therefore, a key to effective support is being in a state of readiness to think quickly and respond with spontaneity to students as new situations and circumstances arise and as old behaviors are reconfigured by the student into new patterns (see Display 9.2).

DISPLAY 9.2—THE SPONTANEOUS USE OF SUPPORT PRACTICES

Cody, a student in middle school who loves adult attention, often gets into trouble for minor property damage and acting-out behaviors. One day, the special education teacher who helps arrange his general education supports happened to walk by him as he was returning from the restroom. Cody looked at her, grinned, and reached out as if he were going to pull the fire alarm. Then he challenged the teacher by saying, "What can you do to stop me?" In a normal, sincere tone of voice, the teacher responded, "Nothing, but I will be here to support you as you go through the school's consequences." Cody put down his hand and continued walking down the hallway.

What might have happened if the teacher raised her voice and challenged Cody?

What might have happened if the teacher pretended to ignore Cody?

Was there any guarantee that this particular spontaneous verbal strategy would work for this particular incident?

Regardless of whether this strategy works, what is the message that it communicates to Cody, and how does it differ from the message that is communicated by other adult reactions (e.g., confrontation, ignoring the behavior)?

SUPPORT PRACTICES AND THE "VOICE" OF STUDENTS

Kunc and Van der Klift (1995a) confront the viewer of *A Credo for Support* with an unsettling contrast between the way that educators often think about challenging behavior and the experiences of the individuals who are the recipients of behavior change interventions:

Be still and listen.

What you define as inappropriate may be my attempt to communicate with you in the only way I can.

Do not try and change me, you have no right.

Help me learn what I want to know.

Do not hide your uncertainty behind "professional" distance.

Be a person who listens and does not take my struggle away from me by trying to make it all better.

These lines are powerful, and they should encourage all of us in the education field to rethink what being a "change agent" involves. One lesson that can be drawn from these lines is that effectively enhancing growth and change in others requires transforming ourselves, especially how we think about and react to perplexing behaviors that we wish to eradicate. A quick review of this chapter's discussions about positive behavioral support practices affirms this point. The discussion has emphasized changing ourselves so that we as educators can become more understanding of students who have behaviors that challenge our view of what is "appropriate," our systems of rules, and our ways of thinking about right and wrong.

Yet, another lesson can be drawn from these poetic lines, that of respectively listening to the voices of those whom we wish to change. As described by Baker (1999), the concept of *voice* has a long history in Western society. In the 17th century, *voice* primarily referred to revelations from God that could only be received by identified emissaries, such as priests. In the mid-18th century, in the works of Rousseau and others, the meaning of *voice* began to shift so that all people could experience it within their own consciences. Voice expressed directly by the people began to replace voice expressed through the select few.

At the beginning of the 21st century, voice continues to express ideals of democracy, "universally understood" as that which enables "silenced Others to speak" (Baker, 1999, p. 366). Clearly, the missing voice in behavioral intervention research and practice is that of the student. As educators who are responsible for these students' growth and well-being, we can no longer afford to continue inventing strategies and intervention methods that rest on the increasingly tenuous foundation of immediate relief rather than on the growth of the student and the evolution of the broader community.

The key point in this closing discussion is that enhancing our practices is not so much about equipping ourselves with a new set of tools and techniques. Rather, it is about learning to listen to the messages conveyed by others' behavior, reflecting on our own practices using the six facets of understanding from Wiggins and McTighe (1998), and then learning to respond in continuously new and unique ways. The responses that are developed through this inquiry process should honor the dignity of each student while educating all students within natural school communities. In Chapters 10 and 11, which deal with more difficult behavioral situations, this key point remains a guiding force for conceptualizing intervention planning and implementation processes.

Chapter 10

Developing and Implementing Solution-Focused Behavioral Support Plans

with Ginny Helwick, Marjorie Z. Leon,
Shanda Harrell Schlagenhauf, and Sunhi Bak

*"The way one defines a problem will determine in
substantial measure the strategies that can be used to solve it."*
—*Nicholas Hobbs*

Chapter 9 examined ways in which educators can enhance their positive behavioral support practices so that problems are less likely to arise or are channeled into the classroom's learning activities. As described in Chapter 7, however, some behavior can be so disruptive that simply enhancing one's practices is insufficient. Instead, formal planning is required. Typically, such planning is instigated in response to an acute behavioral problem, concerns for safety, or the persistence of the behavior over time. In any event, the reflective inquiry processes that are used to enhance practices can also be used to plan and implement more formal behavior intervention plans. Yet, a planning format that guides these processes is needed.

This chapter begins with a critical examination of the traditional behavior intervention planning and implementation practices that are presently used in formal plan development. These practices are grounded in the way that many teachers and other educators frame and understand their roles and discipline needs, as well as in their interpretations of applied behavior analysis. It can be argued that these traditional practices are seriously wanting relative to what positive behavioral support interventions need to accomplish. Next, the chapter proposes a different planning and implementation format that is inspired by solution-focused concepts, grounded in theories of discourse and collaborative processes for the construction of shared knowledge, and structured as an ongoing guided inquiry activity. The discussion of the proposed format starts with a rationale for the format. This is followed by a discussion of the format's major elements, how the format is used during planning and implementation, and how it is applied to a student with challenging behaviors. Finally, in light of the format's radical departure from traditional planning formats, a series of questions that readers are likely to pose are presented and explored.

As this chapter critically examines, then departs from, certain planning and implementation practices that have guided behavioral intervention activities since the 1970s, the reader should consider the following caveat. Although applied behavior analysis has driven many of the planning practices that are criticized here, the problems that are identified only compel us to look for new ways to plan and conduct behavioral interventions. They do not present a case for discarding the many theoretical and practical contributions of applied behavior analysis to the education profession.

TRADITIONAL PLANNING AND INTERVENTION PRACTICES

As described in Chapters 2 and 5, best practices in applied behavior analysis have undergone an important evolution. Traditional approaches focus on gathering baseline data, then selecting interventions "generally based on the experiences of the interventionist"; contemporary approaches focus on assessing the hypothetical functions of behavior, then selecting interventions based on these functions (Repp, 1999, p. 240; see especially Scott & Nelson, 1999b). Despite contemporary views on best practices, however, hypothesis-based intervention remains more the exception than the rule in the practices of educators at the turn of the 21st century (Scott & Nelson, 1999a; Singer, 2000; Smith, 2000). Hence, any discussion of current practices in schools must consider both traditional and contemporary approaches to behavior intervention planning and implementation.

An Aggregation of Present Practices

To instruct effectively, teachers expect a certain amount of order in their classrooms. Although teachers' tolerance levels differ, all teachers can reach a point at which they feel that their teaching is less effective because of too many classroom disruptions. In some cases, a student who seems to have difficulty participating appropriately in class begins to affect the others' learning opportunities. Perhaps a teacher feels that he or she has to spend too much time refocusing the class after disruptions occur.

Teachers often respond to these concerns by relying on an existing behavior management structure. This structure may include glances and verbalizations that are intended to remind or warn a student, talking with the student, in-class isolation from peers, and/or briefly removing the student from the classroom. Many times, these procedures are framed within some form of point system, wherein all of the students are rewarded for their work and efforts but also experience negative consequences when the teacher believes that they are needed. Of course, teachers vary greatly in the degree to which they use negative consequences and for what behaviors they use them, even when their classroom management system is part of a schoolwide system.

As a problem becomes more difficult, the teacher may experience a downward spiral, in which the behavior remains a problem and the teacher feels less in control and more frustrated with the direction of learning in the class. The exasperated teacher may, at this point, begin doing more of the same but doing it harder: reprimands become louder, punishment becomes more severe and intense, and the teacher may even impose a punishment on the entire class. By this point, the classroom atmosphere may have declined so precipitously that neither the student who is the center of the problem nor the other students are happy. By now, if not before, the ultimate goal of the academics is being compromised. In addition, other students may perceive that the negative attention could just as easily be shifted toward them and that their weaknesses could become the focus of the teacher's wrath. They may personalize the punishment as if it were given to them as well. Such events negatively influence the teacher's relationship with his or her students.

In any case, the classroom teacher is now concerned with eliminating the problem because it is affecting learning and the classroom atmosphere. The next most likely response is the development of a behavior intervention plan. Such a plan may be developed by the classroom teacher or by one or more other individuals if the teacher feels the need to consult with specialists. They may form a team, which could include a special educator, a behavior specialist, a psychologist, a parent, and possibly an administrator. If a team is going to prepare the plan, then the general education teacher might be the person who coordinates the plan's development. Alternately, a specialist who is the student's service coordinator might handle the plan design, especially if the student receives special education services. Depending on the school's policies and how the child is being perceived, this process may be informal; it may occur as part of the child study team's responsibilities; or, if the student has an IEP, it may occur as part of the IEP team's duties.

Such a plan may consist of a number of different elements and processes, but its creation and implementation will typically reflect the following six steps. First, the teacher or team defines more precisely the behaviors that are considered problematic. This exercise may first generate an unwieldy list of problem behaviors, which can then be refined into behavior clusters that characterize and differentiate different kinds of episodes. For example, the teacher's list might include acting silly, kicking, yelling, and running in the hallway. Further reflection, however, may show that acting silly tends to occur alone; kicking and yelling tend to occur together and follow an episode of silliness if a peer expresses disapproval; and running in the hallway is independent of yelling, kicking, and silliness. At this point, the teacher or team might reconstruct the list to treat behavior clusters as single units and establish priorities. However, a common practice is to simply treat each behavior as an independent unit and give all behaviors equal weight, which results in the delineation of a generic slate of "problem behaviors" that the intervention is to address. Regardless of whether the teacher or team works from a prioritized set of behavior clusters or views all behaviors as "separate but equal," the remainder of the program development process will now revolve around these identified problems.

Second, the teacher or team is likely to collect a baseline of the "targeted" behavioral concerns. Some teachers and teams use functional behavioral assessment procedures at this point to identify relevant settings, antecedents, communicative intents, and motivational factors. This process often emphasizes "diagnosing" the variables that seem to provoke or reinforce the different forms of problem behavior. Nonetheless, the more pervasive school practice is to simply collect frequency data on the behaviors so that the problem's seriousness is amply documented and upcoming efforts to eliminate the behaviors can be assessed.

Third, once baseline data are collected, the teacher or team is likely to turn their attention toward delineating replacement behaviors and skills. Some teachers or teams use functional behavioral assessment information to identify replacement behaviors that can help the student meet needs that are directly connected with the problem behavior (e.g., asking a peer for help in class instead of acting out). In many cases, however, the identified positive behaviors will simply be the mirror opposite of the problem behaviors. To illustrate, the positive behavior for a student who is off-task becomes "being on-task," and the positive behavior for the student who yells in class becomes "working quietly."

Fourth, the teacher or team next considers developing discrete instructional procedures to increase positive behaviors (e.g., shaping, using a reinforcement system), as well as procedures to reduce problem behaviors (e.g., interrupt and redirect, response cost). If the teacher or team completed a functional behavioral assessment, they may attempt to alter the behavior's antecedents and/or consequences to prevent or resolve behavioral problems. There may also be efforts to change certain communication patterns, including communication with the student in situations in which the problem behavior is likely or is in progress. The latter procedures provide a direct way to discourage the problem behavior and teach the student the desired replacement behavior. Often, however, both the instructional procedures and the behavior reduction procedures are simply extensions of an existing behavior management structure. In terms of positive behaviors, likely extensions include the following:

- Individualized reinforcement (e.g., computer time, special time with teacher)
- More teacher-selected choices for the student (e.g., "Sarah, what do you want to do now? Would you rather complete your science project or do your math homework?)
- Direct instruction in one-to-one or small group formats for fostering social skills or anger control skills
- Scripted procedures for reminding the student about his or her responsibilities (e.g., "Johnny, you have a choice about whether to do your work, but you know what happens if you don't")

A common procedure for behavior reduction is developing a hierarchy of negative interventions that are intended to discourage the behavior. These could include ignoring the behavior, specific verbal reprimands, response costs (e.g., loss of recess time, loss of points toward a prize), and one or more of a number of different time-out or removal options to be used when the behavior reaches the crisis point.

Fifth, the teacher or team formalizes and implements the foregoing four steps as the formal behavior intervention plan. The formal plan is typically a set of specific prescriptions that, because of their apparent and direct association with the targeted behaviors, are viewed as the key to the student's successful adaptation. The goal of the implementation process is the student's adherence to preexisting boundaries of what constitutes appropriate behavior in the adults' view and the acquisition of positive skills that help return the situation to its original equilibrium. Accordingly, measurement focuses on the upward and downward movement of the behaviors that are described in the plan. This process, of course, often places the onus of responsibility for change squarely on the student.

Sixth, if success is not forthcoming, the teacher or team might try to revise specific components of the plan. However, because the plan's prescriptions seemed so logically connected with the descriptions of the behavior, it is just as likely that the plan will simply be implemented with greater intensity or that the teacher or team will move rapidly toward some form of removal of the student from the general education environment.

Limitations

Given what typically occurs in schools, there are seven pitfalls that planners encounter when using the previously described format to formulate and implement behavior intervention plans. The first pitfall is that, as a consequence of the format's first step, the entire planning process hinges on and is driven by "the problem behavior." This single event has major repercussions for the remainder of the planning process and, ultimately, for what happens to the student. Recall from Chapter 7 that a cardinal rule in intervention design is to start with goals that define authentic success and to avoid defining the end state as simply the absence of the problem. Although later steps in the six-step format do encourage delineating alternative skills and replacement behaviors, this first step establishes a mind-set that makes the planners prone to define the solution they seek as relief from the problem. Of equal consequence, this process potentially derails from the outset any point of view that the student's behavior is not a problem but, rather, is a potentially understandable reaction to a larger systems issue. As planning begins with the presumption that the problem resides in the repertoire—or even the character—of the student, the process does not readily lend itself to examining broader instructional setting, teaching, or learning issues that might be complexly associated with the student's behaviors.

The second pitfall relates to a tendency described by Maag (1999) for behavioral interventions to be linear. That is, whatever was being done in the past is proposed for the future, but with greater rigor and force. This means that there is considerable risk that the solutions selected in the planning process will be very much like the ineffectual solutions that the educators were already using, but they will now be applied with greater intensity, formality, and consistency and be sanctioned by other adults. This is because, with the exception of functional behavioral assessment, there are no real mechanisms inherent within the planning format to ensure that solutions will not simply be the behavior management steps that are already in progress. This is an especially important concern when the planners have little background and training in positive behavioral support.

The third pitfall is an extension of the second. Because the format tends to channel already familiar intervention strategies into the formal plan, this inhibits the generation of new and innovative solutions to the concerns at hand. As described in Chapter 6, a key to working within complex, dynamic systems is to be able to generate novel solutions as problems emerge. Of course, a typical recourse to this pitfall is for the school to bring in an "expert." Along with other problems that the expert model presents (see Chapter 6), the expert may offer prescriptive but alien solutions that are at risk for not being carried out or being carried out with significant lack of fidelity (see Smith, 2000).

The fourth pitfall is that the six-step format leaves wide open the possibility that a plan constructed by the adults will solely address their own needs within the educational environment and not the real needs of the student. In fact, when students are brought into planning sessions, they may simply be informed about their problem, told what they should be doing instead, and their advice is sought largely on method (e.g., "How many points should we give you for . . ."). The simple truth is that students who are brought into planning sessions under this model are often subtly and directly pressured to concede to the will of the adults, which then sabotages even the possibility of meaningful student–teacher collaboration. This event is made probable by the first step in planning, in which the problem is centered on the student from the outset.

The fifth pitfall is a product of the range of issues that are addressed and not addressed by the format, in combination with the narrow focus on the student as problem. Recall from Chapter 7 that effective behavioral interventions express the quality of richness. That is, the strategies and procedures that constitute the plan's recommendations and decisions branch across a variety of programming areas (e.g., instructional design, social competence, class membership, modeling after peers who represent good models). Such branching can only be facilitated if there is some form of inquiry scaffold that is inherent to the planning process that ensures consideration of different programming areas. The previously described six-step format contains no such scaffold, and the problem-focused nature of the planning process reduces the likelihood that such a scaffold will spontaneously emerge as planning proceeds. This pitfall is especially insidious because situations involving human behavior in complex and changing contexts reflect intransparence. Recall from Chapter 6 that intransparence means there are critical chains of cause and effect within dynamic social and activity environments that are often hidden from the intervention decision makers and that "what we really want to see may not be visible" (Dörner, 1996, p. 40).

The sixth pitfall is also a product of the format's limited range of addressed issues and its problem orientation. A team of educators and family members is likely to already have a wealth of ideas that could enrich a plan with potential solutions to the behavioral concerns, especially given the property of intransparence. Because of the restricted range of issues and solutions that are addressed within the six-step format, however, this wealth of ideas often remains untapped as intervention planning unfolds.

The seventh pitfall is also a product of the format's orientation toward the student as the problem. Because the team equates problem resolution with the elimination or replacement of the student's behavior, evaluative measures of program success or failure largely focus on counts of student behavior. There is little or no consideration of adult behavior or any other aspects of the ecology that may be contributing to the problem.

It is true that an observant and sophisticated team could watch for these pitfalls and seek ways to navigate around them as they surface during planning and intervention. For example, if the team uses functional behavioral assessment, there is a reasonable chance that the resulting intervention plan will contain certain types of innovations that are tailored to particular student needs. Other teams may seek assistance from instructional guides or from the research literature. Nevertheless, there is little in the six-step format itself to prevent some of these seven problems from occurring, and the format makes some configurations of these problems very likely to occur. Furthermore, because of the history of behavior management in public education, one can almost invariably guarantee that some or most of these problems *will* occur.

Having a potentially resolvable situation go wrong is tragic for educators and students. Educators experience frustration, wonder why they cannot get these "researched-based" procedures to work, and are likely to shift blame onto the students. Students experience a sense of being manipulated and unfairly treated. Given a prolonged history of such experiences, some students become "designated problems" for some proportion of their school careers. They may adopt a behavior disorders lifestyle (Durrant, 1995), meshing together expectations of wrongdoing that have been communicated by adults, perceptions of themselves as being difficult and unworthy, and disrespectful attitudes of their peers. As a result, their behavior patterns preserve the very qualities that the education team was working so hard to discourage. Worse, some proportion of students will be wrongfully labeled as having an emotional or a behavioral disorder, and their families may be encouraged, sometimes inappropriately, to seek medical attention; some will be sent to self-contained classes or facilities for a significant proportion of their educational careers; and some will eventually be removed from public education, either by choice or through repeated violations of discipline policies.

A DIFFERENT PARADIGM: SOLUTION-FOCUSED BEHAVIORAL SUPPORT

When a teacher or team is faced with persistent behavioral concerns, solution-focused behavioral support represents a new direction in thinking about a student's challenges and how to resolve them. In the process, a group of concerned people sit down together with a set of possible questions to facilitate more holistic thinking about the student, the instructional situation, and the context of the school and class, as well as about the perceptions, language, and thinking that educators use when conceptualizing the problem. Solution-focused planning is distinguished from traditional planning in two ways. First, the team begins "with the end in mind" (Covey, 1989, p. 97); that is, they plan backward from the vision to "an educational approach that is most likely to achieve that vision" (Gardner, 1999, p. 116; see also Wiggins & McTighe, 1998). Second, the team uses a scaffold consisting of a series of focus questions that enhance divergent thinking about the support process.

Solution-focused behavioral support has roots in three fundamental concepts: 1) solution-focused therapy models, 2) collaborative planning, and 3) guided inquiry. These concepts are further described in the upcoming subsection. Other discussions that follow give an overview of solution-focused planning and describe the components of a solution-focused behavior intervention plan.

Three Fundamental Concepts of Solution-Focused Behavioral Support

Solution-focused therapy models owe much to the work of Erikson, a psychiatrist who was "dyslexic, tone deaf, colorblind" and "suffered polio in late adolescence and again in his fifties" (Durrant, 1995, p. 15). Much of Erikson's work came about as a consequence of his efforts to assist others and himself in finding solutions to life's difficulties. Erikson developed the view that limitations are largely mental constructs that can be replaced with other quite different mental constructs and that reconstructing one's view of a situation can help resolve issues and concerns. He also developed a profound appreciation for people's life experiences and how they can be used to effect change, even when one's life experiences result in solutions that may run counter to those offered by a therapist.

Solution-focused therapy, sometimes called "brief" or "constructive" therapy (Durrant, 1995; Hoyt, 1994; Metcalf, 1995), has several fundamental principles (see Display 10.1). Central among these principles is that problems are solved not by focusing on problems but by reframing them to think in terms of the solution space and the alternatives for practice that exist in that space. As applied in schools (Durrant, 1995; Metcalf, 1995), especially with students who have behavioral difficulties (Ross & Schuster, 1996), the solution-focused approach is typically conducted by

DISPLAY 10.1—AN OVERVIEW OF SELECTED PRINCIPLES OF SOLUTION-FOCUSED THERAPY AS APPLIED TO EDUCATION

People construct their individual knowledge of situations and use this knowledge for making sense of experience.
Educators create reality models of their understanding, beliefs, and values about situations. Sometimes, these are so strong that they interfere with the educator's ability to perceive a situation differently and move into new ways of thinking about it.

Problems and how people understand problems are not dependent on pathology.
A student may live in an impoverished neighborhood, have a father who is addicted to drugs, or have symptoms of depression. As there is little that educators can directly do to affect these situations, explanations that are based on sociological factors, fixed characteristics, psychological traits, and categorical disorders are less likely to help with solution creation; they may in fact immobilize the team. Because educators bear the responsibility for meeting the educational needs of students regardless of the students' life situations and conditions, they should focus their attention on things that they can control to alleviate concerns.

People have usually tried to resolve a problem but not successfully.
Frequently, there have been ongoing attempts by a teacher or other educators to solve the concerns associated with a student's behavior. These attempts may have been focused on the problem. The teacher or team may now feel "stuck" on the problem, which interferes with finding alternative solutions.

Problems may often persist because what people are doing about them is maintaining them.
Whatever the original "causes," the way that educators and others try to alleviate a problem may inadvertently prolong the problem. Perseverating on the problem or addressing the wrong facets of the situation may be factors.

People have extensive resources within them.
Educators often have the means within them to solve a problem, but they will not always know which of their ideas or practices are relevant, and some of their strengths and capabilities that have a bearing on a problem will not be known to them.

A problem can be reframed so that it can be viewed in a more helpful manner.
By changing the language used about a problem and thinking about solutions instead of problems, new understandings can emerge, and alternative ways to achieve a positive outcome can be realized. Trying something that is quite different from existing practices might be required.

One does not have to know or be able to exactly define a problem to be able to solve it.
Solutions can be developed that alleviate a problem without educators ever knowing precisely what the problem is. Effective solutions can also emerge when educators disagree on a problem's definition; this can happen without reaching agreement on problem definition.

(From *CREATIVE STRATEGIES FOR SCHOOL PROBLEMS: Solutions for psychologists and teachers* [pp. 11–14] by Michael Durrant. Copyright © 1995 by Michael Durrant. Used by permission of W.W. Norton & Company, Inc.)

counselors as a one-to-one therapy. The concept of solution-focused behavioral support may seem at odds with this because it is designed for teams of educators who are thinking about a student, with or without the student being present. Nonetheless, the therapeutic and the behavioral support versions of solution-focused thinking are more similar than they initially appear. Just as therapy assists a student to reframe his or her problems so that solutions are more forthcoming, solution-focused behavioral support assists a team to reframe its problems with a student so that solutions are more forthcoming. In other words, the behavioral issues are themselves framed as concerns for the teachers who have responsibility for educating the student, not as problems that characterize the student. This, of course, does not mean that some students do not have problems or deep-seated emotional issues; it only means that, within the solution-focused approach, the educators' responsibilities are to solve their problems with the child so that they can continue to meet his or her educational needs.

Collaborative planning is increasingly being recognized as an excellent approach for addressing behavioral concerns (e.g., Lohrmann-O'Rourke, Knoster, & Llewellyn, 1999). Previous chapters (especially Chapter 6) present the reasoning for this, and the following presents this approach's central values:

- A pool of useful knowledge can be created when all people with an investment in the plan have an opportunity to contribute their sometimes unique and sometimes shared experience-derived knowledge about the student.
- Common understandings can emerge about a problem, leading to greater agreement on which decisions get implemented and what success should look like.
- People are often more willing to implement practices if they have had a voice in the design of the practices.

When collaborative planning is integrated with the solution-focused approach, one issue that emerges is how to develop a common language that is solution- and future-oriented, as opposed to problem- and past-oriented. As indicated throughout this book, many educators, special educators, and therapists have been trained to think in terms of deficits and to act in terms of remediation, rather than to think in terms of strengths and to act in terms of accommodations and modifications (see Display 10.2).

Collaboration forms a necessary but insufficient basis for the creation of an adequate and innovative behavior intervention plan. What needs to emerge out of the

DISPLAY 10.2—SOLUTION-BASED VOCABULARY

Many of the words that are used by professionals and parents alike express how deeply education's thinking is embedded within the language of problems. For solution-focused thinking to take root and begin to blossom, it is essential to transform the language that educators use when planning within solution-based meetings. Here are five examples from Hoyt (1994, p. 4) and five examples from Metcalf (1995, p. 39):

Problem-based	Solution-based
Fix	Empower (Hoyt)
Expert	Partner (Hoyt)
Cure	Growth (Hoyt)
Manipulate	Collaborate (Hoyt)
Defects	Assets (Hoyt)
Rebellious	Developing his or her own way (Metcalf)
Co-dependent	People are important to him or her (Metcalf)
Oppositional	Argues a point often (Metcalf)
Shy	Takes a little time to know people (Metcalf)
Isolating	Likes being by himself or herself (Metcalf)

Why is the language that one uses important when it comes to describing students who are in conflict with our systems?

collaborative process are the necessary understandings—combined with an ability and disposition to act informedly, responsibly, and maturely on these understandings—so that a student's behavioral concerns are appropriately addressed. This is made possible within the collaborative process by activities of inquiry, or "a willingness to wonder, to ask questions, and to seek to understand" present situations and their connection with future situations (Wells, 1999, p. 121).

Guided inquiry represents the third concept that underwrites solution-focused behavioral support. As detailed in Chapter 6, guided inquiry involves a team of educators and family members using a series of carefully framed questions as a scaffold to assist their examination of the student's behavioral concerns in relation to their own teaching, interpersonal, and discipline practices. As shown in Chapter 6, one of the benefits of using guided inquiry is that, with properly designed probe questions, the process stimulates discussion of existing practices across a variety of areas that may affect behavior while simultaneously optimizing innovation in these areas (Helwick & Jackson, 1999). Put differently, the value of guided inquiry is that it captures the team members' existing wisdom but then stretches it toward new solutions. The unification of collaboration and inquiry creates what Wells called a community of inquiry, which is "rooted in the understandings gained in the past as they are embodied in the culture's practices and artifacts and, at the same time, situated in the specific present of particular classrooms and oriented to the construction of new understandings" (1999, p. 121).

Overview of Solution-Focused Planning

Solution-focused behavioral support planning, pioneered by Jackson and Leon (1996b), resembles the collaborative inquiry process described by Lohrmann-O'Rourke and colleagues (1999): A facilitator uses sets of carefully composed questions to guide the team through a discussion of issues and potential support strategies; then, the recorded outcome of this dialogue is used to construct a behavior intervention plan for the student (see also Daniels, 1998). Solution-focused behavioral support planning differs in that it is solution-oriented rather than problem-oriented, it offers a richer process of inquiry, and it is deliberately geared toward creating a blend of familiar and innovative practices.

The goals of a solution-focused behavioral support intervention are as follows:

- A student who is more immersed, ready to learn, and comfortable
- A group of adults, now more at ease with the student, who are using a variety of instructional techniques and procedures for enhancing student participation and learning
- An in-place safety net for the stress and behavioral problems that precipitated plan development

These outcomes are not dissimilar to those that would be desired using the six-step format that was described previously in this chapter; however, the means and tools that are used to achieve these outcomes are quite different.

Components of a Solution-Focused Behavior Intervention Plan

Clearly, the way that the questions are framed and organized makes or breaks the guided inquiry process. In solution-focused behavioral support, the objective is the creation and implementation of an intervention plan for a student; therefore, the questions that drive the inquiry process are organized in relation to the four components that comprise a solution-focused plan. These four components are defined and described next.

Component 1: Reasonable and Feasible Outcomes for the Student   The team conceptualizes what could be happening on a typical day in the near future (e.g., in several weeks) that reflects both achievable progress for the student and greater comfort for the classroom teacher and others. It is essential that the team generates positive outcomes that are practicable; planning for even greater growth can and should occur later, as the student and the team experience success with their first efforts. Sometimes, it is helpful to go through the student's day, projecting at each point in the student's schedule reasonable expectations relative to what is occurring at the present time.

Component 2: Changes that Promote Growth, Learning, and Future Success   To begin to achieve the foregoing outcomes, the team next brainstorms ways to enhance the learning opportunities that are provided for the student. The team members also explore additional activities that could, if offered, promote success and personal responsibility in the student's school life. This discussion often uncovers what already works and encourages the team to capitalize on these areas to enhance class participation, a sense of competence, and greater independence. This step focuses on what adults can do to improve their practices as teachers and as socialization agents.

Component 3: Changes that Reduce and Prevent Stress and Enhance Comfort   At this point, the team considers which events are associated with the student's being upset or tendency to exhibit a behavioral concern, as well as which proven and new ecological adjustments in the student's physical, activity, or interpersonal contexts could help prevent or attenuate stressful situations. Because the goal is prevention, the discussion may focus on how to help the student more appropriately meet his or her real and pressing needs. This step is essential even when the student's behavior seems less stress induced and more related to creating diversions or receiving attention (e.g., acting out). When student stress and comfort are addressed during planning, a connection could be discovered between how the student feels in class or in school and the behavior that initially seemed unrelated to these issues.

Component 4: Ways to Address Stressful Situations and Problems When They Arise   Finally, the team considers which behaviors are really of concern in the classroom or in the school, and they develop guidelines for responding to these behaviors when they arise. This step is last in the sequence because experience shows that the other steps, which focus on positive solutions, often reduce the need for the more restrictive procedures. This is also the only point in the entire planning process in which problem behaviors might be defined if the team feels that doing so would be helpful.

For each of these four components, there are between three and ten focus questions that the team members use to guide their discussion and the development of each component of the intervention plan. Table 10.1 provides a brief synopsis of component definitions and examples of specific focus questions to guide the inquiry process. (All of the focus questions are listed in the Solution-Focused Behavior Intervention Planning Form, which appears in the appendix at the end of this book and is discussed under this chapter's "Creating the Plan" heading.)

The format for planning and implementing a solution-focused behavioral support plan has two phases, which represent an abridged version of the protocol described in Chapter 7. The first phase is plan development and initiation, and the second phase is plan implementation and revision. These phases are detailed in the next two sections.

DEVELOPING AND INITIATING A SOLUTION-FOCUSED PLAN

The objective of this section is to prepare the reader to facilitate the creation of a solution-focused, behavior intervention plan for a student with difficult learning and behavioral challenges. As noted previously, compared with traditional planning, there are major differences in the means and tools that are used to design and construct a solution-focused plan. There are three features of solution-focused planning that will be unfamiliar to most educators. First, as suggested in the rationale for using solution-based plans, planning focuses on creating a solution space, with little or no consideration of the problems that anticipated the plan's creation. This means that team members who may typically spend a significant amount of time defining problems

Table 10.1.   Components of a solution-focused behavioral support plan and example focus questions for each component

---

Component 1: Reasonable and feasible outcomes for the student

(What an "okay" or "better than average" day should look like)

- What does a good day look like now? Is this a reasonable outcome for the near future?
- What learning and activity participation patterns would be happening if progress is occurring?

Component 2: Changes that promote growth, learning, and future success

(Enhanced and authentic learning activities)

(Activities and experiences that promote success and self-responsibility)

- Can we create new roles or responsibilities for the students to encourage greater autonomy?
- Are there some ways that we can help the student more effectively participate in classroom activities?
- What responses can we encourage that honor the student's attention, affiliation, or power needs?
- In what activities is the student successful now? Can access to these be increased?

Component 3: Changes that reduce and prevent stress and enhance comfort

(Ecological adjustments that can be made in the physical, activity, or interpersonal contexts that help prevent the behaviors that are of concern to others from happening)

- Are there things that reliably upset the student? Do we know why?
- Are there things that we do now that reduce or alleviate stress, fear, or uncertainty?
- Are there other activity, material, or outcome adaptations that may reduce stress by clarifying expectations or ensuring success? Are there peers who could help?
- Are there safety or predictability signals that we can use when the student is agitated?

Component 4: Ways to handle stressful situations and problems when they arise

(How stressful situations and incidences of problems should be handled when they arise)

- What behavior patterns are of particular concern to the school community?
- At what times of day and in what specific activities do we have these concerns?
- What can we do when the situation is out of control? Who can we recruit to help us?
- How can we promote understanding and acceptance from the other students?

---

must now pull their attention away from the problem and turn to the solutions they would like to see.

Second, most teachers and behavior specialists partition data collection and plan creation into distinct phases. This does not occur in solution-focused planning. Rather, the processes of gathering and using information to create the intervention plan are intermingled, and they may occur in different patterns and at various times.

Third, as previously indicated, the process of generating the plan's operational decisions emerges out of a team inquiry process that is defined by a set of questions. Most teachers and behavior specialists are used to a very different process, in which operational decisions emerge out of data-driven assertions about what the student now does and what he or she needs to be doing instead.

Within the plan development and initiation phase, the major activities are 1) understanding precipitating circumstances, 2) creating the plan, and 3) formalizing the plan. These processes are described next, and then a brief illustration of the outcome is offered.

Understanding Precipitating Circumstances

In many situations, the classroom teacher's concerns establish the need for a more formal behavior intervention plan. Sometimes, a special educator who works closely with one or more concerned classroom teachers will suggest the need for a plan. Optimally, the person who initiates the plan has already developed some understanding of the problem behavior's precipitating circumstances. This understanding may have come about from his or her efforts to resolve the issues without a formal plan, perhaps through reflection on teaching and management practices and thinking about the motivational issues from the student's point of view (see Chapter 9). The initiating educator may even have already conducted a functional behavioral assessment, using tools such as those discussed in Chapters 7 and 8.

In planning for the meeting, the educator should prepare to field questions that show evidence of a thorough knowledge of the student's day, such as

- The student's responses and general behavior in different settings and activities and with different people
- Times when the student is successful, happy, engaged, and ready to learn and when he or she is not
- Other students' feelings and perceptions about the student
- The student's friends, as well as who avoids the student and why
- The conditions under which concerns are likely to arise and why this seems to be the case
- Prominent good day/bad day patterns and why these might occur
- The ways that various adults presently handle problems and why, as well as with what results
- The student's feelings about the social and academic activities in which he or she is involved, with and without peers

The usefulness of this working knowledge depends on the teacher's ability to share it with others as narrative descriptions, apply the six facets of understanding to the information as it is discussed, and forecast the possible impact of various solutions that are proposed in the team meeting.

Creating the Plan

The solution-focused behavior intervention plan is collaboratively created during a formal meeting that is led by a facilitator and attended by people who have a vested interest in the student's success (e.g., teachers, parents, the student). A continuing dialogue among the meeting participants is generated by the use of focus questions that are associated with the four components of a solution-focused behavioral support plan. A rough draft of the formal behavior intervention plan is derived by the facilitator's recording proposed behavioral support goals, recommendations, and decisions as they arise in the group's discussion.

The Facilitator   The facilitator could be the classroom teacher, a special educator, or another person who is familiar with the principles of positive behavioral support (see Chapter 4) and solution-focused planning processes and materials. Typically, it is the facilitator who calls the meeting, asks the focus questions, prompts continued movement through the planning process, manages time, creates the public record of the participants' responses, and formalizes the plan when the meeting is over (see Display 10.3).

The Recording Form   The facilitator uses a specific form to record what the team would like to include regarding each of the four plan components. The Solution-Focused Behavior Intervention Planning Form is reproduced in the appen-

DISPLAY 10.3—SEVEN SKILLS OF A GOOD FACILITATOR

1. A good facilitator knows the plan development process, either because he or she has developed such plans before or—if still learning—has become familiar with the materials and the protocol before the meeting.
2. A good facilitator is flexible, avoiding rigid agendas and using momentary cues to guide the flow of conversation.
3. A good facilitator knows how to respectfully probe to find out the basis for various remarks or suggestions, the different participants' orientation regarding concerns for the student, and the participants' familiarity with a support (as opposed to a management) perspective on behavior.
4. A good facilitator uses people's similar ideas to create consensus and investment and people's different ideas to create additional discussion and reflection.
5. A good facilitator strives to engage all participants at their own comfort level; he or she also knows how to acknowledge the particular roles of the various participants (e.g., checks for the principal's reaction when a new proposal involves other building staff).
6. A good facilitator recognizes that one measure of success is when a team's perspective begins to shift from management to support. Helping a team make this shift requires having a firm grasp on the team's present perspective and knowing how far the team members can be pushed to shift their perspective without losing ground.
7. A good facilitator moves fluidly among the six facets of understanding (explanation, interpretation, application, perspective, empathy, and self-knowledge) to try to comprehend what team members are saying and thinking.

What are some additional skills or characteristics of a good facilitator?

dix at the end of this book. It begins with a cover page and has a separate sheet for each plan component. Each sheet includes the focus questions for that component as well as space for recording the related support decisions, recommendations, and other information. The decisions and recommendations of the participants can be recorded in the form of abbreviated statements or short phrases if they are potentially helpful in plan formalization. Comments and narrative from the discussion can also be recorded directly onto this form.

Note that each sheet for the four plan components lists a time at the bottom of the page. If the meeting cannot exceed an hour, then the facilitator can limit the discussions on each component to these recommended times. (When time limits are not set, meetings typically last from 1 to 2 hours.)

The Meeting Process   At the start of the meeting, the facilitator briefly describes the meeting's purpose and encourages introductions as needed. Then, the facilitator gives all participants a copy of the Solution-Focused Behavior Intervention Planning Form so that they will have access to the four planning components and their respective questions. The facilitator then reviews with the participants the four components, the brainstorming process, and the anticipated outcomes of the meeting. If applicable, the meeting's time limit is announced. Then, the facilitator asks the group members to read the focus questions for all four components and to select a subset of the most pertinent questions from each component for the ensuing discussion.

The facilitator then reads the selected questions aloud. This typically results in an exchange of goals, strategies, practices, recommendations, commentary, and stories that sometimes directly addresses a question, sometimes indirectly addresses a question, and sometimes provides information for other questions or even other plan components. As focus questions are asked and discussed, the facilitator is constantly summarizing and operationalizing team members' comments, as well as checking for understanding, requesting additional information, reiterating major points, orchestrating movement among the components, and contributing his or her own ideas. The facilitator is also recording the ideas and suggestions on his or her copy of the form, which then becomes the primary record of the meeting results.

It can also be useful to create a more visible record of the meeting's progress. This can be accomplished by having a second person record the decisions that are made for each component on a large chart, such as the Solutions Organizer that is shown in the appendix at the end of this book. Using equipment that is available in most copy centers, this chart is enlarged so that all participants can view it at once. The chart is taped to a wall or another surface at the beginning of the meeting, and it is filled out by the second person as the discussion proceeds. Participants may then use the chart's notes to expand and check on the notes that they are taking throughout and after the meeting.

Although the participants should be given some latitude to shift among the four plan components in their dialogue, the facilitator is constantly bringing the team back to the component at hand when the conversation wanders too far. It is especially important that the first three components be addressed before the last component (handling stressful situations and problems). Experience suggests that better and more appropriate problem-handling procedures emerge after the team has thought of the other more positive ways that they can support a student.

Because the team dialogue tends to wander across components, one concern that sometimes arises is whether a particular suggestion or idea "belongs" with one component or another. General rules for determining this follow:

- If the idea states a student outcome (i.e., a goal statement), it belongs with Component 1 (reasonable and feasible outcomes for the student), but if it states an action or a procedure to be implemented by adults or peers, it belongs in one of the other components.
- If the idea is a direct answer to a particular focus question, it belongs with the component that question accompanies.
- If the idea relates to enhancing learning, it generally belongs with Component 2 (changes that promote growth, learning, and future success).
- If the idea relates to prevention, it generally belongs with Component 3 (changes that reduce and prevent stress and enhance comfort).

- If the idea relates to handling concerns when they are arise, it belongs with Component 4 (ways to handle stressful situations and problems when they arise).

Nevertheless, it is not absolutely critical that suggestions or ideas be recorded precisely under the "correct" component. Ideas related to Components 2 and 3 often overlap, but this confusion does not seriously affect program implementation.

Finally, during the meeting, the facilitator must closely monitor the participants' language to help them stay solution oriented and to prevent them from lapsing into unproductive discussions of the problem behaviors. In addition, the facilitator works to ensure that the team's decisions honor, or at least approximate, the principles of positive behavioral support and include new, innovative practices.

Formalizing the Plan

After the planning meeting, the facilitator examines his or her notes to reflect on the team's proposed outcomes, decisions, and recommendations. He or she then uses this information to prepare a formal solution-focused behavioral support plan. The facilitator's final plan is typically a series of abbreviated statements that encapsulate the goals, strategies, steps, and procedures that represent the team's recommendations and action decisions, organized by component. The plan can also include narrative statements that capture important points made during the meeting. Because the plan is a synthesis of the full discussion, specific statements would not be expected to correspond exactly with specific focus questions. A form may be helpful for creating a quick summary of the plan's content. The Plan Summary that appears in the appendix at the end of this book serves as an example, although educators are encouraged to develop their own recording forms.

Some districts may require that a plan's relevant content be transcribed to a standard district form. Such forms are typically problem focused and often of questionable value as working documents. As one might suspect, they are quite problematic as vehicles for communicating solution-focused information to those who need it. Hence, although a district document may be viewed as the plan's official record, the formalized solution-focused behavior intervention plan should be the day-to-day record of the agreed-upon goals, steps, and strategies.

Goals, Decisions, and Recommendations: A Brief Example

To illustrate a final plan's goals, decisions, and recommendations, consider the case of Tyler, a sixth-grade student who spent the better part of his school day in general education classes. Many of his behavioral problems occurred in science class. The precipitating circumstance that was of most concern to Tyler's teachers was that he often had a tantrum while he was being removed from class for being disruptive or inappropriate.

A closer look at Tyler's situation revealed other precipitating circumstances that were actually more important for plan development. These included near-zero levels of participation in class activities. Essentially, he spent his time either playing with his toys (nondistracting behavior) or trying to get the other students to interact with him through being the class clown or acting out (distracting behavior). These problems were exacerbated by the fact that Tyler was not really expected to participate in class;

the accommodations and modifications that were provided to make possible his meaningful participation were few and far between.

The successful plan that was developed for Tyler consisted of a wide variety of goals, decisions, and recommendations. A few of these from each of the four plan components are presented next to illustrate the results of a solution-focused planning process.

With respect to reasonable and feasible outcomes (Component 1), the team agreed that one or several of the support process goals should be *increased partial participation in the class activities.* The team agreed that progress was occurring for Tyler—and, thus, the support plan was working—if the following two patterns emerged in Tyler's daily class participation: *an increase in doing part of what the other students are doing for each activity of the class* and *an increase in attending to the teacher or the other students even if not actively engaged in the specific activity.* The team recognized these as, at best, short-term goals that should be more demanding for Tyler as more and better supports are put into place.

With respect to changes that promote growth, learning, and future success (Component 2), one of the team's many decisions was to create for several science lessons a "setup" activity in which Tyler would engage. This activity was always something related to the science curriculum, such as answering a question about a required reading. In addition, the general education teacher would always give the directive to respond as part of the regular instruction, Tyler would initially be prompted in advance if it was his turn to be called on by the teacher, and Tyler would initially be given credit for answers that were only partially correct. (Note that this strategy provided a beginning point for the teachers, who were still learning how to adapt the curriculum for Tyler, and it also helped Tyler conform to the expectations and activities for the rest of the class.)

With respect to changes that reduce and prevent stress and enhance comfort (Component 3), one of the team's recommendations was to provide Tyler with a peer buddy whenever possible, as working with a peer seemed to enhance Tyler's comfort in the class. In addition, the team decided that Tyler should not be removed from the class, even when he was not appropriately engaged, as long as he was not distracting the other students. Tyler enjoyed being in science class and his tantrums usually occurred during removal from the class, so tantrums could be avoided by not removing him for minor "problem" behaviors.

Finally, with respect to handling stressful situations when they arise (Component 4), one accomplishment in plan development was redefining what constituted a behavior that necessitated removal. In the past, Tyler was often removed from science class simply because he did not seem to be "getting anything" out of the class that day, and removal often lasted for the remainder of the class period. In the newly created solution-focused plan, the use of removal was limited to only those behaviors that disrupted learning in others. Moreover, a removal could only last for a short time period, and it occurred in the hall or principal's office. The team accepted the aforementioned changes after the facilitator led a discussion that contrasted Tyler's possible interpretations of his behavior with the adults' interpretations. Table 10.2 illustrates this analysis.

IMPLEMENTING AND REVISING A SOLUTION-FOCUSED PLAN

In many situations, the classroom teacher will likely oversee the implementation, evaluation, and revision of the student's behavior intervention plan, very possibly with the

Table 10.2.   Perceptions of Tyler's clowning and disruptions in class

From the teacher's point of view	From Tyler's point of view
There are attention and control issues; he's always noncompliant.	Nobody notices me unless I act up, then they manipulate me.
He isn't learning anything; he may not belong in here.	What am I supposed to be doing? I'm bored!
You've always got to keep an eye on him.	Well, I guess I am supposed to act out now.
"Act up, and you're out!"	I never do anything right.
You can't trust him.	They don't like me or trust me!

assistance of a special educator. As described in Chapter 7, the six areas that must be addressed are 1) educational and environmental changes, 2) critical communications, 3) problem solving, 4) professional development, 5) incident response and crisis procedures, and 6) evaluating learner and community changes. For brevity's sake, the discussion of these is collapsed into two subsections.

Educational and Environmental Changes, Critical Communications, and Problem Solving

Component 2 (changes that promote growth, learning, and future success) and Component 3 (changes that reduce and prevent stress and enhance comfort) provide the basis for educational and environmental changes. It may take several weeks to fully implement some of the necessary changes, especially changes related to Component 2. This is because these changes often involve the teacher's reflecting on his or her practice in relation to the plan's specifications, then making the needed changes in his or her daily instruction. For example, if a plan calls for deliberate efforts to increase a student's involvement in a variety of classroom activities, a teacher may need to develop and implement sometimes very different learning activities and grouping practices in the class to enhance that involvement. A teacher will often need to undertake a period of trial and error learning to figure out what is possible, what works, and so on. Lesson and activity accommodations may also be required, and these often cannot be designed and implemented immediately.

Because natural trial-and-error processes are to be expected and permitted if a complex plan is to succeed, plan revision activities may often be ongoing during the early stages of implementation. This requires formal and informal communications and on-the-spot problem solving to be occurring frequently and routinely among the classroom teacher, other educators, family members, and the student. In fact, it is a good idea to intentionally use a working document of the plan that is tentatively revised by penciling in changes, then is formalized after 3 weeks or a month.

Professional Development, Incident Response and Crisis Procedures, and Evaluating Learner and Community Changes

Professional development needs will usually be defined by specifications within Component 2 (changes that promote growth, learning, and future success), Component 3 (changes that reduce and prevent stress and enhance comfort), and Component 4 (ways to handle stressful situations and problems when they arise). A commonly encountered training need arises when plan development activities uncover instructional or discipline practices that are unsuitable, ineffective, and/or provocative in their effects in the student. For instance, during plan development, it may be discovered that various restraint procedures that were used in the past should be dropped, revised, or replaced. Hence, the task becomes one of retraining individuals who were using the problematic procedures to act in the manner that was agreed on during plan development. Meeting such a training need usually takes time because it is more effective to provide training on an ongoing, as-needed basis rather than in a single in-service training.

Incident response and crisis procedures are drawn from Component 4 (ways to handle stressful situations and problems when they arise). These activities require especially careful monitoring procedures. They are needed to ascertain whether the implemented procedures are actually limiting the disruptions and to ensure that they are not backfiring by creating unnecessary frustration, anger, and/or disappointment in either the educators or the student. Also, it is very important to ensure that these parts of the plan are not being implemented in the absence of the implementation of the other support activities, those spelled out in Components 2 and 3.

With respect to evaluating change in the learner and the community, measuring the student's behaviors rarely provides especially useful information. The occurrence or nonoccurrence of behaviors is often directly associated with two other areas in which measurement is possible and can be much more valuable: progress toward the plan's goals (Component 1) and plan implementation activities (Components 2, 3, and 4). Experience suggests that both rating scales and qualitative descriptions of change can be useful in the assessment of how a student is responding to newly developed instructional activities (Component 2), stress and distress reducers (Component 3), and discipline guidelines (Component 4). Sometimes revisiting the functions of a student's behavior via functional behavioral assessment can be useful. For example, one student's challenging behavior shifted from being a way to escape a situation to being a way to secure attention from others. This was interpreted as a positive change for this student, but it required the team to rethink how it was going to address the student's newly evolving attention and affiliation needs.

The Implementation Checklist that is provided in the appendix at the end of this book can be used to assess student growth in relation to the plan's goals (Component 1), and the degree of implementation that is occurring for each of the plan's recommendations and decisions (Components 2, 3, and 4). A teacher records the various goals, decisions, and recommendations on the checklist. Then, the teacher either reflects on his or her own practice or dialogues with others to determine progress toward goals and to examine the integrity of the plan's implementation. The optimal way to gather these data is to complete this form several weeks into the intervention, and then to do so intermittently for the remainder of the school year.

An important distinction needs to be made between evaluating solution-focused plan implementation processes and traditional processes of assessing intervention fidelity. Solution-focused plans often delineate broad expectations for teacher practices, and some number of items will simply be recommendations. Hence, the goal for assessing intervention fidelity from a solution-focused perspective is not to establish that "everything possible is being done." Rather, it is to ascertain which procedures are being used, where they are being used, and how they are being used, and then to consider this information in relation to whether team members believe that the plan is working. When using the Implementation Checklist as a way to make these determinations, there are two broad questions that are answered: 1) What parts of the plan are being used, and do they appear to be working? and 2) What parts of the plan are not being routinely implemented, and do we need to revisit these issues? In other words, in solution-focused planning, the goal of assessing implementation is formative in nature, permitting the team members to reflect on their actions and on what changes in the plan they might consider necessary.

AN ILLUSTRATION OF SOLUTION-FOCUSED PLANNING

At the time his plan was developed, Steve was an 8-year-old student finishing third grade. He spent most of his day in general education classes. Academically, he was doing grade-level work with supports in science and social studies. In reading, he was doing the same activities as the other students but at a significantly lower grade level. Likewise, performance was significantly below grade level in math. In fact, during third grade, pull-out services were used to try to improve his math skills.

Socially, his behavior with peers was described as "immature." He primarily approached and engaged peers by grabbing and striking at them, as well as misusing their class materials and recreation equipment. As one observer said, "He was always trying to play with the other students, but he didn't know how, and neither did they."

Precipitating Conditions

The compelling stimulus for developing a plan for Steve was his almost continuous aggressive behaviors in class, which consisted of grabbing and hitting, as well as biting, kicking, and scratching peers. These behaviors were a serious concern throughout his second-grade year; by third grade, these behaviors were perceived as being part of Steve's character (e.g., "That's just Steve!"). One of his more unusual behaviors was to cover his arms with dots, then leap from desks like a leopard to bite the other students.

During most of the third-grade year, Steve had a variety of behavior management programs, which consisted of various combinations of rewards and punishers, such as stickers, earned computer time, recess removal, time-out, and removal to the special education room. None of these programs proved effective for Steve. In fact, during third grade, Steve received 41 "tickets," which represent a measure of serious conduct violations in this school.

At the end of third grade, the special educator began to reframe Steve's behavior, and a different picture emerged about the precipitating conditions. It became clear that Steve never felt like he was a member of the class, nor did he feel accepted or respected by either the classroom teacher or by peers. It seemed that Steve's own perception of his situation was that he was not expected to perform like a third-grade student but was expected to behave inappropriately. Hence, much of Steve's behavior appeared due to the absence of positive expectations, a dearth of learning accommodations and modifications for supporting those expectations, and few interpersonal relationships that could sustain the positive behaviors that were expected of other students.

Plan Development

At the end of third grade, the special educator decided that a solution-focused behavior plan might be more effective for Steve in the upcoming school year. As the plan development facilitator, she called together a group of individuals who had an investment in Steve's growth: the general education teacher, Steve's father, a paraprofessional, and the student himself. The meeting, which lasted approximately 2 hours, followed the sequence of steps outlined previously in this chapter. The special educator performed her facilitator role as expected. For example, although most participants had no difficulty keeping their attention on specific focus questions, the general education teacher repeatedly tried to shift the team's discussion back to Steve's problems. The special educator responded to this by saying, "I know this is a concern, and we will talk about how to work with this concern later in the meeting, but for now we need to talk about the answers to these focus questions."

As a consequence of solution-focused planning and the team's growing awareness of Steve's belonging and membership issues, the planning largely focused on how to enhance Steve's participation in, positive feelings about, and acceptance within his general education class. The plan that was developed is depicted in the appendix at the end of this chapter. This chapter appendix also shows the specific questions that were addressed by the team within each of the four solution-focused planning components during initial plan creation. As would be expected, for the most part, there is no direct match between specific focus questions and specific goals, recommendations, or decisions; the latter represent a synthesis of the group's full discussion.

Brief Synopsis of Implementation Results

The team could have used quantitative measures of Steve's behavior to assess his progress. Steve received only 4 tickets during fourth grade, compared with the 41 tickets he received in third grade. The team also could have used the number of times that Steve was removed from class as a measure, which would have shown a very significant difference if compared with his previous school years. Behaving as a leopard ceased to be an issue after the first 3 weeks of plan implementation.

The real measures of success, however, were the verbal reports from educators, which were often spontaneous and informal. These reports noted the complex changes in Steve's participation and membership, which began occurring in fourth grade, evolved throughout that school year, and spilled over into his fifth-grade year. For instance, within a couple of months of his plan implementation, at which point Steve was fully included, an observer could spend a class period with Steve and not pick him out as a child with behavioral issues. His behavior had assumed the same qualities as that of the other students within his class. By then, his classmates were treating him as they would treat any other student, including telling him "Stop it" if he was annoying or disturbing them. He was now participating more fully in class activities, including discussion groups, oral reports, cooperative group work, test taking, and independent seat work.

It is important to understand that Steve's progress did not come about because a team created steps, procedures, and consequences for dealing with behavior. In fact, the steps for managing stressful situations and problems when they arise (Component 4) almost never needed to be implemented. Rather, the behavioral problems began to abate because of Steve's social, academic, and class membership progress. Of course, this is the objective of solution-focused planning. As illustrated with Steve, the team learned new ways to help him become the "regular student" that he always was and to reframe their understanding of him so that his problem behaviors were seen from a more balanced perspective.

During fourth grade, the special educator often met with team members to talk informally about Steve. In addition, there was one formal meeting mid-year to adjust the plan to better support Steve's changing needs. A critical part of formal assessment was the educators' evaluation of plan implementation. As previously noted, one of the ways this can be accomplished is to create a checklist that identifies the decisions and recommendations that the team agreed on. The special educator created a checklist similar to the Implementation Checklist in the appendix at the end of this book, and she met with the classroom teacher to dialogue about Steve's plan. Figure 10.1 is a filled-out version of a portion of this checklist. Note that the numbers on this checklist do not indicate frequency of use for particular procedures. For example, the component procedure *removal from class to hallway* was used consistently and was viewed as effective; however, as previously noted, Component 4 procedures seldom needed to be used with Steve.

During Steve's fifth-grade year, the intervention plan continued to exist as a reference document, and many of its support components were naturally being carried out in Steve's classes. Yet, no formal behavior intervention planning was actually needed at any time during this year. In contrast to his 41 tickets in third grade and his 4 tickets in fourth grade, Steve received only 2 tickets during his fifth-grade year.

Of course, unknown events in Steve's life might have contributed to the changes that were apparent when second and third grades are compared with fourth and fifth grades. Steve may have matured somewhat, or there may have been unaccounted-for style differences between his general education teachers during this period of time. Nevertheless, the special educator and her team were sufficiently impressed with the dramatic, positive differences in Steve's behavior, with the way that these differences were contingent on plan implementation, and with the associations between Steve's changes and the team's own changes in practice to credit the solution-focused process for Steve's progress.

CRITICAL RESPONSES TO SOME PRESSING QUESTIONS

For many practitioners, solution-focused planning will represent a very new and different process. Hence, it is appropriate to end this chapter with an examination of six critical questions that readers may want explored. When considering the answers to these questions, it is useful to bear in mind the following quote from Matusov, "I know that I am wrong but I do not know where exactly I am wrong, to what degree, or why. I hope people who disagree will help me clarify these questions" (1996, p. 25). The authors of this chapter honor this sentiment. It is our hope that the planning procedures that were offered in this chapter will lead to debate and dialogue and that our work will be advanced, reframed, and revised by others in the field.

Are solution-focused and problem-oriented planning really that different? An observer might comment that the distinction between initially approaching a behavioral difficulty from a "positive" (solution-focused) as opposed to a "negative" (problem-oriented) approach seems academic. Both approaches seek solutions to problems but in different ways. Moreover, traditional planning procedures (i.e., the six-step format) do consider, along with the negative behaviors, what replacement behaviors the student needs to learn. In addition, planning procedures exist that are based on the problem-oriented model and do incorporate solution-oriented activities such as person-centered planning (e.g., Meyer & Evans, 1989).

Behavior plan item	Implementation rating 0 = Not at all 1 = Occasionally 2 = Consistently	Contribution rating 0 = Not at all 1 = Helpful 2 = Very helpful	Comments
Help teachers and others instill a sense of pride and value	2	2	
Encourage participation in classroom activities	2	2	
Give warnings prior to transition	1	1	
Have familiar adults or peers handle problems, especially peers	1	2	
Provide more frequent access to drinks	2	1	
Use discreet redirects instead of correction in front of the class and friends	2	2	
Remove student to the hallway	2	2	
Remove student to the special education classroom	0	0	

Figure 10.1. A portion of Steve's filled-out Implementation Checklist.

One way to answer this question is to draw a parallel using a study related to a different topic. Helff and Glidden (1998) examined the attitudes of professionals toward families of children with developmental disabilities by looking at selected family-related research literature from the 1970s, 1980s, and 1990s. The purpose of the research was to determine whether professional perceptions of families had become "more positive" or simply "less negative" (p. 457). Their findings were that "when change occurred, it was in the direction of the negativity of articles declining over time; there was not, however, a significant concomitant increase in perceived positivity" (p. 460). This precisely captures the distinction between being positive from a problem-oriented perspective versus being positive from a solution-focused perspective. When one tries to be positive from a problem-oriented perspective, one is at risk for being simply less negative; in contrast, a solution-focused approach requires letting go of the problem, which provides a base for a more positive outlook.

What is the relationship between the focus questions in solution-focused planning and the six facets of understanding (Wiggins & McTighe, 1998)? Helwick and Jackson (2000) found that the focus questions associated within solution-focused planning incorporated all of the six facets of understanding in a variety of ways. Yet, they also found that the particular understanding (e.g., explanation, interpretation) that was addressed by a particular focus question depended on the context set by the team dialogue. For example, if a team was examining the focus question, "Does a student need more breaks or opportunities to rest or more access to food or drink?" the flow of the dialogue might lead to considering this issue from an explanation point of view, an empathy point of view, or an application point of view. To illustrate further, an explanation point of view might include a discussion of a functional behavioral assessment that was completed by the special educator. An empathy point of view might involve a paraprofessional reflecting on how often it seems the child needs to get up and move around, and how the child feels when this need arises. Finally, from a application point of view, the classroom teacher might find him- or herself reflecting on whether break options and more activity changes could be helpful for all students, and he or she may ask the team to consider how these changes could be a part of typical classroom routines.

Is a functional behavioral assessment required before a solution-focused planning meeting? Sugai, Horner, and Sprague posited that a "tremendous amount of preventive work and interventions for simple behavioral problems can be accomplished without the time and expense" that is required by functional behavioral assessment (1999, p. 253). This translates into a need for innovative planning formats that can be used for interventions that do not require sophisticated and extensive functional behavioral assessment activities. The authors then suggested that there is also a need for simple and efficient formats for positive behavioral support planning that incorporate functional behavioral assessment: "The technology must be available to and usable by a range of individuals . . . who have basic behavioral competencies." It must include "forms, formats and implementation scripts" that can enable persons to perform functional behavioral assessment "without excessive preparation and implementation time and effort" (p. 255).

Solution-focused planning takes the middle ground regarding these two positions. On the one hand, although highly formal functional behavioral assessments certainly are not discouraged, the planning process can proceed without them being conducted prior to the meeting. On the other hand, consistent with informant-based assessment strategies, there are specific questions for the team to consider that address the functional bases of behavioral concerns. For example, in Component 2, the team could select the question, "What responses can we encourage [in the student] to honor the student's attention, affiliation, or power needs?" Perhaps the team would select this question from Component 3: "Do certain things reliably upset the student? Do we know why?" In this way, functional behavioral assessment is built into the planning process at a level that is appropriate for many students who require a formal plan.

Can an individual educator develop a plan without a team? The guided inquiry process is more likely to result in goals, decisions, and recommendations that are innovative and will be carried out by other team members if it is conducted in a collaborative fashion. Nevertheless, just as problem-oriented plans are often developed by a single teacher, solution-focused plans can also be developed and implemented by one teacher. Seeking the opinions of others is recommended while the teacher develops the plan, as well as updating other people who work with the student. The same format is used whether one develops a plan alone or as part of a team.

Can solution-focused planning be used in more restrictive environments? This question is commonly asked at workshops and presentations because many special educators still work in environments in which access to general education is minimal (e.g., self-contained classrooms). The answer to this question is similar to the answer to the previous question: We always encourage people to use these procedures instead of problem-oriented procedures because they promote a more positive perspective of the student, adult concerns, and what educators can do to resolve concerns. At the same time, the procedures were designed to help prevent a student's removal from the general education setting. Hence, our research has and will continue to focus on plan development in general education. It is certainly our hope that solution-focused planning can prevent the removal of increasingly larger numbers of students in the future.

What happens when team members perseverate on the problem? One of the facilitator's responsibilities is to keep the team focused on creating goals and solutions that do not depend on reiterating the problem. Sometimes, team members can monitor one another by reminding each other of the student's goals or redirecting each other back to the focus question that was under discussion prior to someone's bringing up the problem.

Nevertheless, there are situations in which either the majority of team members or one especially influential person keeps reiterating the problem, and the necessary progress within the early components of solution-focused planning simply does not occur. This can be a good indicator that a more intensive level of behavior intervention may be required. As shown in Chapter 11, although the problem assumes a relatively prominent role in more intense planning, there is no reason that solution-oriented thinking cannot provide the overall framework.

Appendix

Solution-Focused Behavior Intervention Planning Form
for

Steve
(Name of student)

**Overview of the components of a
solution-focused behavior intervention plan**

Reasonable and feasible outcomes for the student
(What an "okay" or "better-than-average" day should look like)

Changes that promote growth, learning, and future success
(Enhanced and authentic learning activities)
(Activities and experiences that promote success and self-responsibility)

Changes that reduce and prevent stress and enhance comfort
*(Ecological adjustments that can be made in the physical, activity, or interpersonal
contexts that help prevent the behaviors that are of concern to others from happening)*

Ways to handle stressful situations and problems when they arise
(How stressful situations and incidences of problems should be handled when they arise)

Facilitator: A. Simms   Date of plan: 9/10/01

Plan development participants:

R. Chang

M. Arnold

J. Rodriguez

Component 1
Reasonable and feasible outcomes for the student

Focus Questions

• What does a good day look like now?
Is this a reasonable outcome for the near future?

• What learning and activity participation patterns
would be happening if progress is occurring?

• What minimum changes are necessary for us to
feel that the plan is working in several weeks?

Goals, decisions, and/or recommendations

Steve's behavior is generally more appropriate when he is feeling good about himself and is proud of his accomplishments as well as when he feels at ease with the people around him. Presently, he comes to group time, lines up, doesn't argue, and follows teachers' direct instructions if the instructions are clearly structured. We want to see these patterns continue.

Some changes that we would like to see that we think are reasonable

Doing more of that which is expected of his other classmates during class activities (e.g., copying an overhead, raising his hand and answering questions, making comments that are appropriate to the topic under discussion in class)

Being able to verbalize whether his behavior is meeting class expectations when asked to do so (i.e., recognizing what is an appropriate way of responding in class)

Showing more consistent patterns of behavior than presently exist (i.e., fewer of the ups and downs, in which one minute he is fine and the next minute he is disrupting the class); at present, Steve is able to bring himself back "up"

Responding as required to all adults who give him directives, especially on the playground

Time = 10 minutes

242

Component 2
Changes that promote growth, learning, and future success

Focus Questions

• Can we create new roles or responsibilities for
the student to encourage greater autonomy?

• Are there some ways we can help the student
more effectively communicate basic needs?

• Do some of the activities or strategies that we are using
with this student devalue or degrade him or her?

• What responses can we encourage that honor the student's
attention, affiliation, or power needs?

Goals, decisions, and/or recommendations

Steve needs to be expected to do the same things as his classmates. We
should set high expectations for him and not lower the bar because of our view
of his "handicap."

Steve is becoming more verbal, and he needs more frequent encouragement
to communicate and participate in activities with his classmates. In the past,
he was often not required to respond within an activity, so he may have
inadvertently felt left out.

Steve loves to help the teacher and to help others. Some ways that we can
promote this are having him clean up with the teacher, be the line leader,
turn off the classroom lights, and help as other needs arise in the class. Some
leadership roles include being the team captain for his cooperative group and
being the classroom helper. (These activities should be balanced to ensure that
other students get to do them as well.)

Steve has a strong need to feel in control of things; hence, we should find ways
to give him appropriate control over what happens to him. One way to do this is
to give Steve several alternatives to choose from whenever such choices are
possible. For example, for math warm-up activities, he can be asked if he would
rather do them with the group or by himself. We believe that, given a choice, he
will choose the group most of the time, but he will value the control that he
experiences by being offered the choice.

Time = 20 minutes

Component 3
Changes that reduce and prevent stress and enhance comfort

Focus Questions

• Are there things that reliably upset the student? Do we know why?

• Are there things that we now do that reduce or alleviate
stress, fear, or uncertainty?

• Does the student need more breaks or opportunities
to rest or more access to food or drink?

• Are there safety or predictability signals that we can use when
the student is agitated?

• Are there reasonable schedule adaptations that can help with transitions?

Goals, decisions, and/or recommendations

Steve is more comfortable if he feels that he is a part of his peer group, and peers will be at ease with him if they know him better. Therefore, Steve should participate in meetings with selected peers once per week at lunch. The topic of each meeting varies, but sometimes it can be about Steve. This will also help with teaching the other students that they need to expect the same behaviors of Steve that they expect of any other student.

Steve should be forewarned that a transition is coming and told what he needs to do when it happens.

On the playground, Steve is more likely to respond to directives and expectations from people with whom he has a relationship. His discomfort in demand situations on the playground, as well as his acting out, can be reduced by ensuring that there is a familiar peer or adult nearby who can facilitate when Steve is told to do something.

Steve needs drinks and breaks more frequently than most students. When he darts his eyes around and his body goes limp, this is a sign that he needs a drink or a break. In fact a juice break should be used whenever the teacher judges that Steve is starting to have difficulty staying engaged and meeting the expectations of the moment.

Use discreet redirects so that Steve does not feel embarrassed in front of his classmates.

Nibbling healthy snacks (e.g., cranberries, raisins) throughout the day helps prevent Steve from putting objects (e.g., other students' erasers) in his mouth.

If directives are firm and structured, Steve is more likely to follow them. Adults will use the following sequence: 1) Give the directive, and expect him to follow it; 2) give a firmer demand if necessary, identifying the consequence that is used with all students for not following instructions; and 3) enforce the consequence. (Note: The structure and the presence of a mature expectation are important here, not the consequence.)

Time = 20 minutes

Ways to handle stressful situations and problems when they arise

Focus Questions

• What behavior patterns are of particular concern to the school community?

• In what settings do we have these concerns?

• At what times of day and in what specific activities do we have these concerns?

• What can we do when the situation is out of control?
Who can we recruit to help us?

• If temporarily removed,
what will the student be expected to do?

• How can we promote understanding and acceptance from the other students?

Goals decisions, and recommendations

When Steve is out of control and disrupting the learning of others, it may be necessary to remove him from the classroom and to the hallway for a brief period. Once Steve is calm, discuss his behavior with him to help him know what is appropriate.

When difficulties happen, people who can be called on for assistance include the special educator and the counselor. If difficulties are just starting, classmates can be called on, because Steve will often respond to them when he will not respond to an adult.

For disruptions that are too severe to send Steve to the hallway, send him to the special education room until he is calm.

Time = 10 minutes

Chapter 11

Developing and Implementing Long-Term, Comprehensive Behavioral Support Plans

*"Nothing so needs reforming
as other people's habits."*
—Mark Twain

Chapter 10 proposed that problem-oriented planning can be inadequate when it is applied to students who have persistent conflicts within their school or classroom communities. If such practices are inadequate in relation to these conflicts, it is difficult to imagine how they could offer sufficient guidance for extreme and enduring problems that necessitate comprehensive support efforts. Consider, for example, the traditional six-step problem-oriented planning format described at the beginning of Chapter 10 and how it interfaces with the four critical support processes detailed in Chapter 5. The six-step format incorporates hypothesis-based intervention and recognizes that crises need responses. Yet, the latter may be treated as behaviors to replace, suppress, or extinguish rather than as behaviors that require working through, resolving, or supporting. More important, however, certain positive behavioral support processes—lifestyle planning and vision setting, as well as relationship development—are not explicitly addressed by this format. Moreover, this approach seldom considers the larger systems issues that can facilitate or impede the student's access to the valued activities and relationships that can make long-term success possible (Carr, 1997). Perhaps it is not surprising that, as lamented by Turnbull and Turnbull, Carr and colleagues (1999) found that lifestyle change was a "stated intervention goal" in only about 10% of positive behavioral support studies between 1985 and 1996, and it was measured in less than 3% of these studies (Turnbull & Turnbull, 2000, p. 190).

Students who are viewed as having extreme behavioral expressions—that is, acute disruptiveness, safety concerns, emotional vehemence, or even bizarre behaviors or mannerisms—are especially at risk for self-contained placement or long-term removal to alternative, more restrictive settings. As this book has emphasized, the latter practice is seldom in the best interest of students, even so-called typical students.

Typical students also must grow to maturity within a society in which there is substantial behavioral diversity, including the diversity associated with terms such as *mental illness*, *emotional difficulties*, and *severe disabilities* (see Display 11.1).

Some educators, when asked about their views on supporting students who have been labeled as having a behavioral disorder in general education, fear that these students are dangerous and that their behaviors are best treated in settings in which the necessary expertise for addressing these concerns resides. Especially because these

DISPLAY 11.1—THE INCIDENT IN THE SCHOOL BATHROOM

Angela, a fully included fifth-grade student who was known for her difficult behaviors within a variety of situations, had a toileting accident during class. When she was taken to the bathroom for assistance with changing her clothes, Angela squirmed and yelled, resisting the paraprofessional's efforts. Within seconds, there was fecal matter on walls and surfaces in the restroom, and the paraprofessional called for assistance. A very irritated school psychologist soon joined the fray. Along with verbally expressing her displeasure at having to engage in the cleaning activity, she also expressed verbally and nonverbally her view that "this child" did not belong in this school but, rather, needed to be in a special program for "such students."

Outside of the bathroom stood another figure, Maya, a student who was Angela's age. Various adults tried to usher Maya away from the scene, muttering under their breath comments such as, "Just what we needed—a student to go back and tell her classmates the wild things going on with this child in the bathroom!" Nevertheless, Maya stood her ground, looking thoughtful and pensive. She spoke softly to an adult observer who stood nearby and who did not try to send her away. Here is the essence of that conversation:

"There's a boy in my neighborhood who has behaviors, and all the adults tell me to stay away from him. But I know how to talk with him, and he listens to me, and we are friends . . . (pause, period of quiet). My aunt has to come clean the house for my mom. My mom can't clean it, so my aunt comes once a week and cleans it for her. . ." The adult observer asked, "Does your mom have a disability?" "Yes," Maya replied, "She has a physical problem and she cannot walk."

Which of the six facets of understanding does Maya demonstrate regarding Angela?

What role does experience probably play in Maya's construction of this understanding?

If Maya were to tell a classmate what happened, what would be the likely tone and intent of her message?

issues are frequently expressed when the topic of reintegration is considered, perhaps the first question that needs to be asked is, "Are there research-based reasons to believe that the processes used in schools for identifying and placing students with emotional and behavioral difficulties intentionally partial out students who are dangerous relative to those remaining in the general population?"

There is every reason to doubt that this is happening. As presented in Chapter 1, special education does not serve as a vehicle for the protective removal and treatment of carefully screened "dangerous" students; rather, it is often used for the removal of *any* student who is viewed as disruptive, including the preemptive removal of students with labels such as *multiple disabilities*. Moreover, within the general population of students, there are certainly students with varying degrees of meanness, anger, prejudice, malice, and other human emotions that are associated with endangering the rights and well-being of others. Conversely, it is simply an unfortunate stereotype when students with labels such as *emotional/behavioral disorders* are broadly perceived as having any highly uniform trait, including the trait of being "dangerous." It is also highly probable that many truly dangerous individuals are never identified as such during their school careers simply because their exemplary classroom and school conduct does not reveal deep-seated psychological issues that will, at some other place and time, pose a threat to others. Finally, there is the question of causality: If the causes for perceived dangerous behaviors are linked to events and practices within schools, then it is possible that the broader purposes of education can best be served not through removal but through understanding and changing these conditions.

Raising the foregoing concern is important because this chapter proposes steps and procedures for reintegrating, maintaining, and supporting individuals who have been identified by their school systems as having especially difficult or intractable problems and are likely to have long-standing labels such as "emotionally/behaviorally disordered." Experts (e.g., Walker et al., 1996) have often lamented that general education seems to fail with these students, noting that this failure may be due to poor teaching practices, intolerance for behavioral diversity, and the absence of commitment to and training for addressing chronic behavioral concerns. Yet, perhaps this list should also include a reliance on problem-oriented behavior intervention planning, the translation of perceptions and superstitions about mental health and emotional disability into educational policy and practice, and the pervasive removal of students to alternative "treatment" settings without adequate attempts to resolve issues within natural school communities. Many students can succeed in general education when instruction incorporates the processes described in Chapter 3, when intervention plans incorporate the critical support processes described in Chapter 5, and when planning adheres to the protocol shown in Chapter 7. This chapter is designed to show how these support processes can be developed and implemented for more difficult behavioral problems.

The discussion in this chapter begins with an example of the full process of planning, initiating, implementing, and revising a support-oriented comprehensive intervention. A high school student, Brian, is used to illustrate the development and evaluation of such support plans. This is followed by a section that offers a detailed explanation of steps and procedures for planning crisis prevention and support when a student exhibits serious escalating behaviors. An elementary student, Shanda, is used to exemplify the creation of support plans for such problems. The chapter ends with a consideration of issues that are related to schools' capacity to effectively use positive behavioral support practices.

AN ILLUSTRATION OF THE FULL PROCESS

As previously noted, the decision protocol that was developed in Chapter 7 can be condensed or abbreviated according to need but all of its activities might be needed when the degree of concern is high. As Chapter 11 focuses on situations in which there is a high degree of concern, all of the activities that were identified in the decision protocol are considered in the following illustration. The reader may wish to consult Figure 7.6 in Chapter 7 when examining this vignette.

Precipitating Conditions

Brian was a 15-year-old tenth-grade student who was served in a large urban high school. He had a long history of both chronic and acute behavioral problems, including disruptive and acting-out behaviors in classes and in other school settings, aggression toward others, not adhering to class expectations and routines, not following adult directives, and running away to inappropriate places in the school and off school grounds. At the time that Brian's behavioral support plan was developed—just before the Christmas holiday—Brian had stopped attending all of his general education classes except physical education, and the adults' degree of concern about his behavioral problems was very high. Brian was spending all of his time either in unauthorized areas of the school building or in a self-contained special education classroom. Brian's family requested a full inclusion placement, which was consistent with the goals of the special educator. Hence, support plan development was framed as a process of reintegrating Brian back into general education classes.

Plan the Intervention

As shown in Chapter 7, planning the intervention consists of four subprocesses: gather information, formulate outcomes, delineate hypotheses, and generate forecasts. These are described next for Brian.

Gather Information   An outside consultant conducted comprehensive interviews with members of Brian's educational team, and the consultant worked closely with the special educator. Other primary team members included Brian's parents, certain general education teachers, a vice principal, a psychologist, and a speech-language pathologist. Some of the interviews were conducted with groups of two to three people, and some were conducted with individual educators. For these interviews, the consultant used the Information Gathering Tool (Jackson & Leon, 1998a). This instrument yielded information that could be used for

- Lifestyle and vision planning
- Analyzing behavioral concerns and forming hypotheses
- Generating forecasts and solutions for enhanced participation and membership in classes and in the school community; for honoring the student's autonomy and relationship needs; and for developing problem prevention, adaptive alternatives, and crisis support (see Chapter 8 for more details)

In addition, the team used typical person inventories for Brian's general education classes, the MAS (see Chapter 8) to assess specific behavioral concerns within particular contexts, and Jackson's (1996) communication assessment to identify pragmatic communication needs that, if addressed, would improve Brian's overall ability to interact effectively with others. The team also coupled the high school's schedule of classes with informal information about different teachers and their styles to plan the general education classes that Brian would take once the plan was set in motion.

The team conducted some observations of Brian's behaviors in the building, but these observations were viewed as having little relevance for planning. As previously mentioned, Brian was not attending his general education classes. The special education teacher believed that measures of behavioral incidences in the self-contained setting were of no value as indicators of what Brian would do in general education.

Formulate Outcomes   The team systematically directed planning toward expeditiously reintegrating Brian into general education classes, facilitating his participation and membership in his classes for academic and social success, and enhancing his sense of self-control and autonomy. To ensure that they focused on success in general education, the team members developed a vision that included outcomes such as *be among peers in their routine social experiences* and *actively participate in the activities that occur in inclusive settings*. Then, the team developed a variety of placement and support activities, such as *add new general education classes based on interests* and *implement a formal peer helper process*, that were specifically referenced to the vision's positive outcomes. Moreover, Brian's IEP goals and objectives were directly referenced to the realization of Brian's vision. For example, one IEP objective promoted the activity of Brian visiting different classes within the school, reflecting on his experiences with the special educator, then communicating his feelings about classes that he wanted to take. Along with providing opportunities for developing communication skills, this objective also addressed the student's unique contribution to the vision statement: *Controlling my own activities and time and doing what I want to do.*

Brian had a long history of conflicts and difficulties with the school system, so the resolution of these difficulties had to be viewed as a long-term process. Hence, it was also important to include in the plan short-term expectations that represented movement toward the vision but were reasonable for Brian and could give the school staff a sense of success. Thus, for example, it was agreed that after several months Brian would reach the following goal: *following his class schedule each day and going to his classes, even if he doesn't stay for the full period in them.*

Needless to say, Brian's challenging behaviors were carefully analyzed to facilitate developing short-term prevention steps, adaptive alternatives, and crisis-response procedures (see the next section). However, preventing, altering, and managing these behaviors were not viewed as the ultimate outcomes of the support processes. Such behavior changes, although desirable in their own right, needed to be viewed as means to the ends that are defined by the vision, not as ends in and of themselves.

Delineate Hypotheses   To generate hypotheses that could guide the design of setting and antecedent supports and identify adaptive alternatives for Brian's problem behaviors, underlying patterns of behavior had to be distilled from Brian's myriad individual behaviors (e.g., not following class or building routines, disrupting class, running away). A start-up list of nearly a dozen behavioral topographies evolved over 2 weeks of intermittent discussions into five discrete patterns. These patterns were distinguished from each other to some extent by topographical features, but they were especially distinguished by their meaning to the adults and the functions that they served for Brian. Ranked in order of the degree of concern, the team identified the following behavior patterns for Brian:

1. Resisting change (i.e., not complying to a change in an activity)
2. Taking off (i.e., running away from an activity or a request)
3. Grabbing (i.e., forcefully grasping or striking others, sometimes hurting them)
4. Acting as the class clown (i.e., acting out in ways that disrupt the class)
5. Creating dangerous situations (i.e., going to potentially dangerous places, such as construction sites near the school)

The team then linked each of these five patterns with three to seven specific hypotheses. These hypotheses identified external and motivational conditions for both the presence and absence of each of the five behavioral patterns. For example, Brian was most likely to act as the class clown when his behavior during an activity indicated boredom (e.g., looking around, putting down his materials). Brian was less likely to act as the class clown if he was given ways to get attention from others while engaging in long-duration tasks (e.g., securing peer assistance and recognition). Although class clown behavior was maintained by adult and peer attention once it occurred, it was also exacerbated when adults try to control it through "planned ignoring." As another example, because Brian was interested in construction work, behaviors that created dangerous situations were most likely if there was ongoing construction in the school building. They were less likely if an adult anticipated Brian's movement toward a construction site and redirected Brian to another activity.

Generate Forecasts   Behavioral hypotheses that are crafted with care and precision clarify how to generate forecasts for planning student growth, for delineating skill alternatives, and for preventing problem behaviors from occurring. Knowing that planned ignoring will likely exacerbate class clown behavior and the behavior that creates dangerous situations can be effectively preempted by meeting Brian en route and positively redirecting him provides the basis for crisis prevention.

At the same, it is critical that forecasting starts with the plan's formulated outcomes and that behavioral hypotheses are then considered in relation to these outcomes. For example, Brian's vision focused on increasing his relationships with peers in typical school situations and on partial participation in classroom activities. Brian's team forecasted that resisting change, running, and acting as the class clown—known from the hypotheses to be complexly related to social affiliation, task competency, and personal recognition factors—would decrease with increased positive peer attention, a greater sense of self-efficacy in academic activities, and recognition for his accomplishments in classes. Hence, to foster long-term success, the team had to focus on enhanced class membership, accommodated/modified activity participation, and positive regard from general education teachers and peers for Brian's contributions in his classes. From this perspective, the team had to create strategies for reintegrating Brian into his classes (see Display 11.2) and find ways to increase his sense of social acceptance and competency within the academic activities in which other students engaged.

Initiate the Intervention

Chapter 7 showed how initiating an intervention can be partitioned into two subprocesses: construct the plan and recruit resources. These are described next for Brian.

Construct the Plan   Recall from Chapter 7 that a support plan prescribes and directs the activities of the individuals who are involved in plan implementation. This is done by delineating 1) outcomes and goals and 2) decision guidelines that can be fixed (specific actions that must be carried out when particular situations arise), fluid (alternative actions that can be chosen depending on the circumstances), or recommended (general actions that can be used at the discretion of specific plan participants in and across various contexts). A comprehensive plan will not neglect the challenging behaviors and their respective hypotheses when creating these decision guidelines

DISPLAY 11.2—PLANNING FOR REINTEGRATION

Chapter 8 discussed and illustrated analyses procedures for planning a student's classroom support needs and behavioral expectations. For Brian, it was also necessary to prescribe a specific, stepwise procedure for systematically defining classroom support needs and ensuring their successful implementation. The team agreed the following elements were necessary for each class that Brian chose to take:

1. Preentry special educator–general educator meetings to ascertain expectations, the weekly flow of activities, different teaching styles and their prevalence, and how specific IEP objectives could be addressed
2. Preentry completion of typical person inventories that focused on activity/curriculum expectations and levels of acceptable variability in student conduct and behavior
3. Purposeful introduction to the class on Brian's first day of reintegration, with a variety of nonintrusive supports already in place to engage him in class activities and relationships (e.g., having peers greet him and welcome him to class each day, giving Brian special jobs in the classroom)
4. Natural peer supports, which the class designed in brainstorming discussions, for the anticipated problem behaviors (e.g., what peers can do when Brian acts as the class clown)
5. Completion of additional typical person inventories to adjust Brian's participation expectations and supports
6. Ongoing and in-depth analysis of the curriculum content and activities within the various general education classes to generate future IEP goals and objectives that are increasingly based on the general education curriculum and decreasingly based on class access, participation, and communication

Why was it important for the team to establish class and teacher tolerances for variations in behavior and conduct (Step 2)?

Why might it sometimes be necessary to address the details of curriculum content last instead of first in the reintegration process (Step 6)?

and recommendations; however, as noted in Chapter 7, a support plan should focus first on strategic actions that lead to outcomes that are desirable for the student and others. This requires understanding behavioral problems in the context of the outcomes and not vice versa.

There are many ways that proposed outcomes and behavioral assessment information can be translated into goals and decision guidelines within a formal plan. For Brian, the team used the planning format described by Jackson and Leon (1998a). In this format, Brian's proposed goals and support decisions were related to eight design elements: 1) lifestyle plan/vision, 2) behavior patterns and their hypotheses, 3) short-term expectations, 4) long-term prevention, 5) short-term prevention, 6) adaptive alternatives, 7) responding to challenging behavior, and 8) responsibility and accountability. Brief definitions of these design elements, as well as examples of how they were addressed by Brian's team, are shown in the appendix at the end of this chapter. (See Jackson and Leon [1998a] for additional details about how these design elements are defined and how assessment information is translated into action steps.)

An important issue in the construction of support plans is whether commonly employed artificial contingency management systems (e.g., point and token systems, levels systems) should be used in support planning (Henley, 1997; Kazdin & Bootzin, 1972). Certainly, if a participating general education teacher uses some form of token or point system with all other students, the student with behavioral challenges should be part of this same system, with adaptations to the system as necessary. Yet, questions can be raised about the widespread, unexamined reliance on contingency management procedures in schools, especially when the only person in the general education class who is under such a system is the student with a special education label.

Jackson and Leon (1998a) argued that teams might use contingency management procedures for short-term measures but that they should not be mistakenly viewed as primary contributors to long-term growth and behavior change. Experience in schools has generally confirmed this point of view: Contingency management reinforcement systems are sometimes overrated relative to what they can accomplish in terms of authentic behavior change, especially when preexisting activities and relationships within general education classes and schools are thoughtfully used. In behavior support planning, such artificial systems should be used prudently and only to augment existing systems for a student, mainly when the natural processes of acknowledgement and reward seem to require an additional, short-term boost. For Brian, although a token system was initially designed, it was determined in the end that this type of system was unnecessary (see Display 11.3).

Recruit Resources   Resource recruitment for the support process can involve both material and personnel resources. For Brian, the speech-language pathologist was an important source for material resources because she assisted in designing and preparing the communication processes that Brian would need to most efficiently communicate his activity choices in his classes. The major personnel resource needs that were associated with Brian's plan included general education classroom teachers who were willing to work with him, a capable special educator who had the school's permission to create an inclusive program, and a paraprofessional who could serve as a classroom aide but could also work individually with Brian when the demand arose. These personnel resource needs are discussed next.

First, Brian's high school was similar to other American schools, in which general educators often have to be recruited to include special education students in their

DISPLAY 11.3—THE TOKEN SYSTEM

An incident occurred during the construction of Brian's support plan that made clear the distinction between behavioral support planning and traditional behavior management. A behavior specialist recommended that a token reinforcement system be put in place for behavior control and instruction. The special educator believed that this tactic was unwise for two reasons. First, Brian had been on many such systems over the years, and they sometimes proved initially helpful but then quickly lost power. Second, adding a superimposed reinforcement structure to the plan seemed contraindicated. Natural peer and activity supports offered sufficient positive feedback, recognition, and rewards to ensure that the anticipated behavior change and growth processes would occur. The behavior specialist, however, strongly believed in this tactic and continued to advocate for its adaptation. In the interest of consensus, it was agreed that a token system would be developed as a short-term step to help increase schedule adherence and decrease problem behaviors, especially during the fourth-period block. The system was viewed as a backup to be enacted only if the support plan appeared to falter early in the implementation process. As it turned out, the token system never needed to be used.

What guidelines might a team use to decide whether a tailor-made contingency management system is really needed in the behavior support process?

classes. For Brian, this meant that the special educator needed to identify and recruit willing general education teachers, a process that sometimes compromised the selection of classes but also provided access to some excellent teachers.

Second, the special educator had been trained in a teacher preparation program that focused on inclusive services, and she had the personal desire to find ways to include her students in general education classes throughout the day. Fortunately, the school district was open to inclusive practices. In addition, the school itself was willing to let her initiate the process of moving her students from a self-contained program to an inclusive program. This was an essential first step, because the special educator could not be available for Brian or any other student if she herself was self-contained.

Third, the team found a paraprofessional who was excellent in the dual roles of Brian's classroom aide and Brian's individual assistant. The team, of course, faced many now-familiar problems in the use of "one-to-one aides," such as the risk of the student's developing a dependent relationship with the helping adult (see Giangreco, Edelman, Luiselli, & MacFarland, 1997). These problems were viewed as inevitable in the short run, but the team envisioned a future in which Brian's need for assistance could be reduced through better prepared general educators, better material accommodations, arrangements for regular peer supports, and Brian's improved understanding of the academic and social expectations in his classes.

Implement the Intervention

The implementation of an intervention, as shown in Chapter 7, has six major sub-processes: put in place educational and environmental changes, put in place professional development, put in place incident response and crisis procedures, ensure critical communications, ensure on-demand problem solving, and evaluate change in the learner and the community. These are described next for Brian.

Put in Place Educational and Environmental Changes   Given that Brian's vision statement and the activities associated with long-term prevention were closely associated with reintegration into general education, many of Brian's IEP goals and objectives addressed success in his general education classes. Hence, many implementation activities sought to help Brian, his teachers, and his classmates experience success, with *success* defined in relation to the specific expectations of Brian's classes.

In relation to this issue, one of Brian's IEP objectives is especially telling: *Using checklists configured to each general education class, Brian will show improvement in his adherence to class expectations.* To put in place this objective, the special educator met with each of Brian's general education teachers and, using each teacher's class syllabus as a guide, generated a list of class expectations that could serve as indices for assessing Brian's performance. An important point about the list was that the expectations identified for each class were identical to those for all other students in the class. This encouraged participation from the general education teachers and helped with Brian's experience of class membership. Figure 11.1 is a data sheet that shows the kinds of class expectations to which Brian was held, as well as the scale that was used to assess his daily performance.

Creating and using this data sheet had an unanticipated bonus: When there was a record of improvements based on their own standards of conduct, it seemed to help reduce the tendency of some teachers to talk privately among themselves about their misgivings in having Brian in their classes. This, in turn, appeared to enhance the special educator's ability to place Brian, as well as some of her other students, in general education classes.

Put in Place Professional Development   Formal training for the crisis intervention procedures was provided for the special educator, the vice principal, the paraprofessional, and certain general education teachers. Yet, many of the steps and procedures that were associated with the plan could not be usefully communicated through a formal training process. Hence, much of the responsibility for training fell to the special educator as she carried out her daily activities. She had to create ways to

- Quickly communicate expectations to educators on an individual basis
- Present the most important information first
- Regularly observe and meet with these same individuals and to communicate additional information as they mastered initial information to ensure procedural implementation

One of the ways that the special educator initially communicated critical information was by creating a simple fact sheet for each general education teacher. This fact sheet was individually tailored for each classroom teacher based on the special educator's knowledge of their curricula content and teaching styles. The sheet, which was adapted from Jackson and Leon (1998a), is illustrated in Figure 11.2.

General Classroom Performance Checklist

Name of student: _____   Week of: _____

P.E. expectations	Monday	Tuesday	Wednesday	Thursday	Friday
Regular attendance					
Dresses out					
Participates					
Cooperates					
Demonstrates good sportsmanship					
Critical skills expectations	**Monday**	**Tuesday**	**Wednesday**	**Thursday**	**Friday**
Attends class regularly and on time					
Puts forth a conscientious effort each day					
Follows the attendance/class management policy					
Demonstrates good work habits					
Participates in all class activities					
Completes assignments					
Saves work papers and handouts					
Has respect for others and property					
Health expectations	**Monday**	**Tuesday**	**Wednesday**	**Thursday**	**Friday**
Regular attendance					
Prompt					
Cooperation (peers and teachers)					
Prepared for learning					
Receptive to learning					
Meets deadlines					

Figure 11.1. A data sheet used to assess performance in relation to class expectations. (Key: 0 = Behavior is worse than expectations, 1 = Behavior approaches expectations, 2 = Behavior meets or exceeds expectations.)

Program Synopsis

Name of student: Brian   Date: 3/30/99

Name of classroom teacher: Ms. Eldridge

Class and period: Health/Fourth period

Primary support people: Mr. Hawkins, Ms. Sanchez

Educational program at a glance	Positive student profile
1. During class discussions, Brian will contribute by answering one or more simple questions, listening to other students talk, and staying with the group for at least 15–20 minutes.	Brian enjoys being around his peers and interacting with them. Brian can follow simple directions.
2. When given responsibility for leading an activity among his peers, Brian will carry out the specific responsibilities given to him with models and prompts.	Brian can model behaviors or tasks that are modeled by others. Brian will communicate his wants and needs by signed, verbal, and gestural cues.
3. Brian will stay in class for at least 20 minutes every day.	Brian should give the teacher his communication board; if he does not, ask for it.
4. Brian will participate in at least one class project.	

Management Needs: Options

1. Try to listen.
2. Avoid power struggles.
3. When disruptions reach the concern level, CALL FOR HELP!
4. Give Brian alternative responsibilities.
5. Redirect Brian.
6. Model or provide more direct prompts.
7. Back off and come back later.
8. Avoid using criticism as a correction process.

Figure 11.2. A form used to communicate critical information to classroom teachers. (From Jackson, L.B., & Leon, M.Z. [1998a]. *Developing a behavior support plan: A manual for teachers and behavior specialists* [2nd ed., Appendix K, p. 2]. Colorado Springs, CO: PEAK Parent Center, Inc.; adapted by permission.)

It is important to keep in mind that just as Brian was expected to change slowly as he became aware of and comfortable with his community's changing expectations, educators also needed time to grow and adapt to changing expectations. Hence, plan implementation was viewed as an ongoing process that was coupled with student change. Both teachers and the student were given room to make mistakes and to grow as the behavior support process unfolded.

Put in Place Incident Response and Crisis Procedures   Incident response procedures for each of the five behavior patterns and emergency procedures for addressing crises were put in place as described in the foregoing section on professional development. Staff training for handling crises, including the use of protective removal strategies, was completed within the first month of the implementation process. Two-way radio devices were also provided so that team members, particularly the paraprofessional and the special educator, could be contacted easily.

The team correctly anticipated that emergency procedures (e.g., protective removal) for handling crises would rarely be needed if the other components of the support plan were in place. Nevertheless, the team viewed emergency procedures and quick response capabilities as insurance, which helped ease the administration's concerns that Brian's reintegration might pose a problem to the learning and comfort of the other students.

Ensure Critical Communications   Data sheets such as the General Classroom Performance Checklist (Figure 11.1) and the Program Synopsis (Figure 11.2) also helped with critical communications. In addition, the special educator prepared quarterly reports on program implementation and Brian's progress. She prepared these reports for Brian's parents and for the school administration. Although these reports helped reassure the parents and the administrators, they were less important to the plan implementers. The plan implementers relied more on frequent, informal verbal communications to assess ongoing progress and identify problems.

Ensure On-Demand Problem Solving   Although the outside consultant could have been called in, successful problem solving really counted on the availability of the special educator to meet as needed with other adults and on her commitment to the program's overall goals: Brian's attending and remaining in classes; learning the same content that was expected of other students; and engaging in fewer, more manageable problem behaviors. Her availability, in turn, depended on a program in which inclusion generally occurred for all students. Likewise, her commitment to these activities depended on her competencies as an inclusion facilitator with significant service coordination and problem-solving responsibilities (Jackson, Ryndak, Keefe, & Kozleski, 2000; Jackson, Ryndak, Keefe, McCaleb, et al., 2000).

Evaluate Change in the Learner and the Community   During the 1½ years in which the program was in place, problems certainly arose and had to be resolved, especially how to enhance Brian's academic learning and communicate his progress to his family and concerned administrators. Yet, there was notable progress both in Brian's becoming a successful general education student and in his behaviors. This section addresses how such changes were evaluated.

True baseline data do not exist for two primary reasons. First, although many accounts of Brian's behavior were available in his records and from those who worked with him, appropriate and useful descriptions of the behavior patterns within relevant classroom contexts did not exist prior to the support plan's development. Hence, any measures (e.g., frequency counts) of behaviors prior to program implementation were not useful. Second, the team felt that it would be inappropriate to implement a formal baseline data collection period once the plan had been developed. Nevertheless, bear in mind that, early in the fall of his tenth-grade year, Brian had stopped attending all classes except physical education. Moreover, many adults and students in the school perceived Brian as being extremely noncompliant, difficult to deal with, and sometimes dangerous. Hence, Brian's team would have viewed as evidence of success any data that showed enduring patterns of class attendance and appropriate performance, as well as data that showed persistently low rates of problem behaviors. The data shown in Figures 11.3, 11.4, 11.5, and 11.6, which were drawn from a larger volume of data that the special educator analyzed in her final presentation to the team, give some indication of how far Brian had come in less than 2 years. All of these data are from the final quarter in which the program was in place. Figure 11.3 shows transitions between classes, Figure 11.4 shows the average amount of time he was spending in his classes, Figure 11.5 shows his performance in relation to classroom teacher expectations, and Figure 11.6 gives an indication of how often problem behaviors were occurring for four of the five behavior patterns. (The fifth behavior pattern, "dangerous situations," was correlated with "taking off"; hence, no incidences of tak-

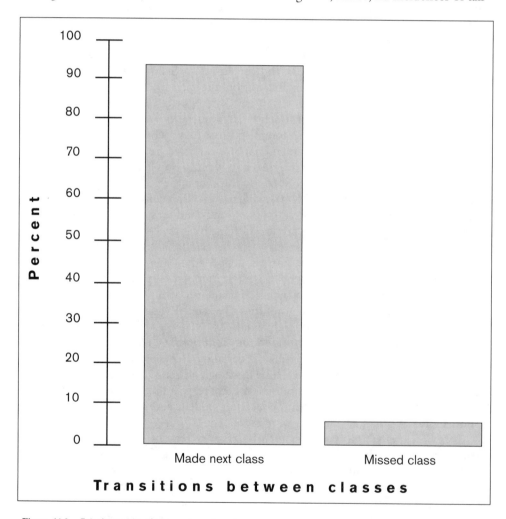

Figure 11.3.   Brian's transitions between classes in spring.

ing off equates to no incidences of dangerous situations.) Taken together, these data speak to a very different Brian, a fact that was attested to in frequent comments by the vice principal and other school personnel in the final meeting during Brian's eleventh-grade school year.

Revise the Intervention

As described in Chapter 7, people who are developing solutions for complex problems are often operating with a mental model that is incomplete or wrong (Dörner, 1996). The quality of richness ensures robustness. Thus, when richness is characteristic of a support plan, it can contribute to the plan's capability for success in spite of the mis-information and misperceptions that can influence its development. In part, this is because the richness helps regulate the balance between stability and innovation when plan revisions are needed. The existence of multiple and varied components provides a buffer that helps mitigate the twin dilemmas of implementing drastic decisions that throw out the good with the bad and oversteering the course of the change process.

Brian's plan was clearly rich. The appendix at the end of this chapter shows that his plan contained numerous separate, distinct steps and procedures for addressing both his long-term and short-term needs with respect to education and behavior. Hence, any needed revisions to the plan were invariably simple adjustments in, rather

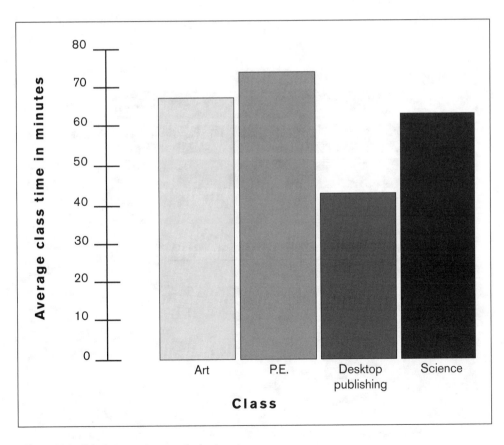

Figure 11.4. Brian's average time spent in class in spring.

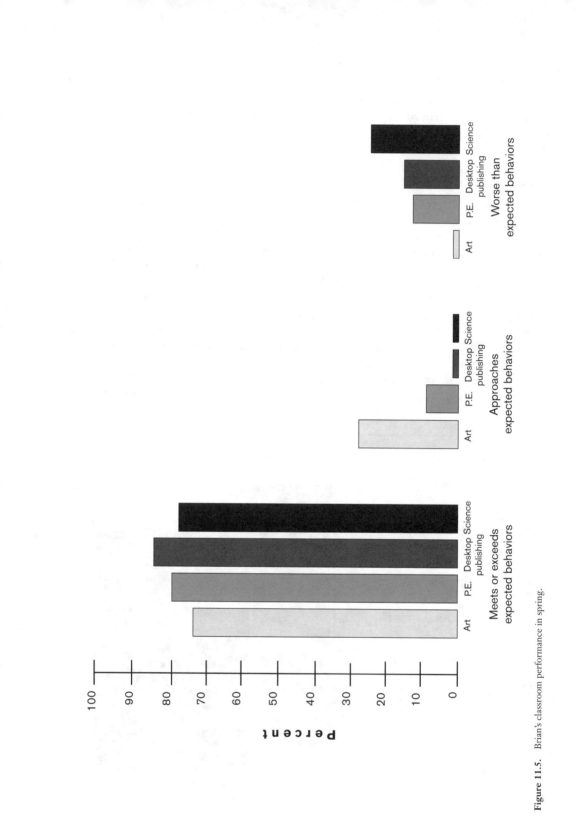

Figure 11.5. Brian's classroom performance in spring.

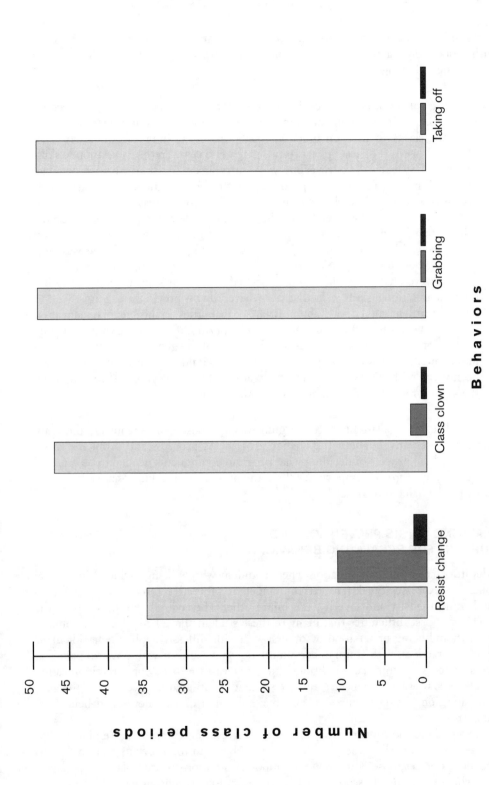

Figure 11.6. Brian's challenging behaviors in spring. (Key: ▦ Nothing happened, ▨ Under control, ▪ Emergency situation.)

than significant departures from, the plan components that were originally proposed during plan construction. Some examples of revisions to the plan that were made include the following:

- The original set of personal options—educational activities in which Brian could engage outside of the general education class when he communicated a need to leave the class—focused on functional skills that were drawn from earlier IEP-identified needs. For example, two of his ten choices were learning money skills and recycling cans. Two revisions were introduced to Brian's list of personal options. The first revision was prompted by the team's noticing that it had inadvertently forgotten to include "return to class" as one of Brian's personal option choices. This revision was made early in program implementation, when it became evident that Brian wanted this option. The second revision was more significant, and it showed how the team was beginning to change its views of what was educationally best for Brian. Near the end of the school year, the offered personal options were changed to be those associated with Brian's academic work rather than the functional skills tasks that were driven by his previous programs.
- As the team learned more about Brian's capabilities in his general education classes, it began to shift Brian's accommodation/modification activities to incorporate not only the class activities but also more of the general education curriculum content. This was an important shift, but it could only occur after Brian had been included for a few weeks and the team could see his potential for acquiring the same (or similar) information as the other students.

In all cases, consistent with the guidelines proposed in Chapter 7, the team thought conservatively about the change process. As progress and problems arose, they treated the process of deciding what program components needed to be retained as equal to, or of greater importance than, the process of deciding what components needed to be deleted or revised.

PLANNING CRISIS PREVENTION AND SUPPORT FOR ESCALATING BEHAVIORS

Educators face a difficult situation when a student who is being included in general education expresses quick and extreme anger or protective responses that, as they escalate in intensity and severity, can injure others. Behavioral extremes can be the products of past difficulties that many of these students have had with communicating with and being understood by others; with thoughtlessly applied behavior management practices; with abuse in certain relationships; and/or with physical pain that is associated with internal conditions. Nevertheless, the behaviors are significantly problematic to warrant concern, and the student's continued involvement in the general education setting requires an effective and often quickly developed behavioral support process.

Sometimes the concern is simply time: The team needs time to assemble a comprehensive plan, such as the plan described for Brian in the previous section. In this situation, one response is to create a temporary solution-focused plan (see Chapter 10), which gives the classroom teacher strategies for prevention while also offering short-term steps for handling problems in a safe and expedient manner. In other situations, however, especially when serious injury to others is a definite risk, some form of short-term removal may be needed to give the team time for planning reentry and successful support.

In at least some situations, the sheer complexity of the behavior patterns, coupled with their potential for harm, requires planning and analysis activities that go beyond what has been described so far in this chapter and in previous chapters. The planning and analysis activities described next use the same tools and concepts that were used with Brian, but they are reconfigured in relation to especially complex patterns of behavioral expression and escalation. These planning and analysis activities are called *Escalation Support Planning* (Jackson et al., 1998). These procedures are illustrated for a fourth-grade student named Shanda.

Shanda frequently lashed out at and scratched adults (and occasionally peers), and she usually screamed intensely while engaging in these behaviors. Sometimes more than once per day, the lashing out and screaming would escalate into an extreme tantrum that included thrashing, crying, kicking, lying on the floor, and going to inappropriate places in the school (e.g., other children's classrooms). For Shanda, each tantrum often lasted for a half-hour or longer.

At various times, educational services were provided for Shanda at home because of her recurring medical complications. Shanda experienced frequent infections and hospitalizations, and she was often absent from school for prolonged periods of time. Nevertheless, Shanda received substantial proportions of her educational services in age-appropriate general education classes, without any pull-out services or special classes. Although important in its own right, the way that Shanda's inclusive education was implemented is not the topic of this discussion. Instead, the focus is on the analysis of her escalating behaviors and how this analysis was translated into a behavioral support plan. This support plan helped make inclusive education both feasible and fruitful for Shanda and others within her educational environment.

Overview of Escalation Support Planning

Creating an escalation support plan requires blending educational placement decisions and vision development with planning for prevention, replacement skill instruction, and crisis support that addresses all of the behaviors within a student's escalation sequence. Planning and analysis activities that can yield an effective escalation support plan focus mainly on constructing, then repeatedly revising, a flowchart that 1) documents the general education placement and vision and 2) interprets behavioral hypotheses that address setting, antecedent, consequent, and motivational factors into action steps for the classroom teacher and others. (The flowchart should, of course, augment and summarize information that is also covered in more detail in a formal plan document). Flowchart configurations will differ according to specific concerns; Figure 11.7 illustrates a configuration that was fitted to behavioral concerns for Shanda. As this diagram illustrates, an inclusive placement is planned, and elements of the student's vision are delineated. Then, using a battery of behavioral assessment activities, the behaviors are identified and organized in relation to how they flow out of each other in the escalation sequence. Prevention strategies and adaptive alternatives are then formulated for each and every behavior in the sequence, and crisis support procedures are designed where such steps are needed. When constructing a flowchart, it is best to use a large piece of easel paper and a thick pencil to draw the chart and to sequence, fill in, erase, and rearrange information in and around the boxes. A more refined flowchart can then be prepared later from this work in progress, which will encompass all of the final recommendations.

The escalation support planning process has six steps (see Figure 11.8). In the first step, lay the foundation, the education team projects a successful inclusive placement as a primary goal and develops a vision for the student's successful adaptation to that setting. In the second step, analyze patterns, the team constructs an escalation support planning flowchart (see Figure 11.7). In the third step, analyze functions, the team uses functional behavioral assessment to determine the ways that the different behaviors meet the student's specific needs. In the fourth step, create prevention strategies, the team members use the functional behavioral assessment information to specify how each of the identified behaviors can be anticipated and prevented through environmental alterations, and they incorporate these ideas into the flowchart. In the fifth step, generate replacement skills, the education team develops adaptive alternatives that the student could use to successfully meet the needs that were originally fulfilled by the problem behaviors, and the team also incorporates these into the flowchart. In the sixth step, develop crisis support procedures, the team creates procedures for handling the especially serious problem behaviors and documents these procedures in the flowchart.

The Six-Step Planning Process

The following six subsections provide details for the escalation support planning process. A single individual who knows the student well could complete the planning and analysis activities that are incorporated within this six-step process. Yet, it is often better to use a facilitator who guides an education team through the behavioral analysis activities and subsequent plan construction. The person who is responsible for the plan, especially if this person is a facilitator, should be skilled in team leadership and positive behavioral support planning. He or she should also have a solid foundation in the application of this book's values, concepts, and processes, especially as described in Chapters 4, 5, 7, and 8 and in the beginning of Chapter 11.

Step 1: Lay the Foundation   A student's serious escalating behaviors may appear so dysfunctional at the start of a comprehensive intervention that it is hard for teachers and administrators to imagine how the student will participate in their school and in their classes as a positive change process unfolds. The team's fears are understandable in the absence of something positive to look forward to, and this can threaten a student's general education placement from the start, even given comprehensive assessments and supports that are developed by a highly experienced group of practitioners. Vision planning can help. It assists the team in envisioning a student's long-term progress as desired by the school community.

Shanda's situation provides an illustration of the foregoing dilemma. She had spent much of her previous school career in self-contained classes and she lacked even the most rudimentary social and academic skills that are associated with functioning in a typical class with peers. Typical person inventories conducted for Shanda in the general education class, for example, showed wide discrepancies between other students' actions during lessons, transitions, and free time and Shanda's actions in these same activities. When the other students sat at their desks and listened to the teacher present new information as part of a science lesson, Shanda usually walked around the room and tried to engage other students in social interaction, or she left the room and looked for something to do in the hallway or in another classroom. Although

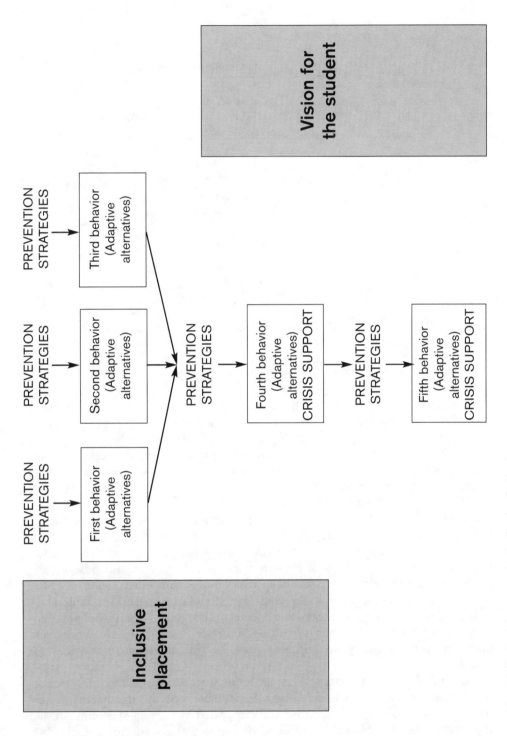

Figure 11.7. Escalation support planning flowchart for Shanda.

267

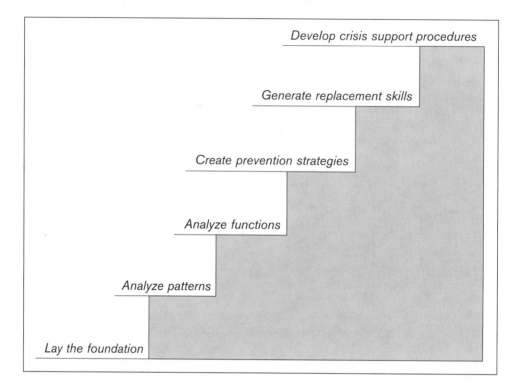

Figure 11.8.   The six steps for designing an escalation support plan.

many adults mistakenly viewed such behaviors as a product of Shanda's "disability," they largely reflected factors such as a lack of experience engaging in age-appropriate learning activities with supports; the absence of a sense of class membership; adult and peer expectations that she would invariably behave in inappropriate ways; and a history in self-contained settings, where inappropriate forms of social interaction could often be the norm rather than the exception.

Although placement in her neighborhood school needed to occur first, the education team also had to form a clear vision of the changes that would allow Shanda to become a better functioning, productive member of the school community. Therefore, they developed a vision for Shanda that projected her as a student who followed and was part of the typical class routines given activity accommodations and modifications, had positive and satisfying relationships with other members of her class, and had a sense that she was in control of school experiences (see Table 11.1). In large measure, this vision became the document that guided educational programming—much more so than the verbalized and documented concerns, needs, and problems that pervasively accompanied previous IEP development activities for Shanda.

Step 2: Analyze Patterns   When analyzing what is suspected to be an escalating sequence, it is necessary to delineate behavioral concerns in ways that match how the student's behaviors are understood and recognized by the school community and then to document how the behaviors relate to or are potentially affected by each other. Such analysis requires carefully specifying the more pervasive patterns and examining their co-occurrence probabilities through scatter plot analysis, intermittent systematic

Table 11.1.   Creating a vision for Shanda

Develop an authentic vision	Part of the vision developed for Shanda
Engage in the activities of the other students, with accommodations and modifications (participation)	Increasingly participate in appropriate ways in class activities with supports
Be part of peer social groups (membership)	Experience a variety of natural peer relationships in her school day, which extend to her neighborhood
Be able to do things that the student enjoys within appropriate contexts (autonomy)	Defer her wants to more appropriate times when they do not interfere with class participation

observations, and/or interviews with people who know the student well. The purpose of gathering data is to determine the degree to which certain behaviors occasion other behaviors and the frequency of co-occurrence patterns.

Figure 11.9 illustrates three of the many possible patterns. In Pattern A, three behaviors can occur at any time, but only one sometimes occasions the two other sequentially connected behaviors. In Pattern B, two behaviors can occur at any time, and one can escalate into a second behavior, which then may branch into one of two other behaviors. In Pattern C, three distinct behaviors can occur at any time—and two of them can sometimes occur simultaneously—but these three behaviors have little or no sequential relationship with each other.

If an escalating, sequential pattern is present, then a flowchart draft is constructed that characterizes the specific relationships among the behaviors. As previously mentioned, this flowchart serves as a worksheet for the remaining steps in the analysis, so it should be written in an erasable medium and on a surface that gives ample space for adding notations and revisions as the analysis unfolds. Figure 11.10 is a simplified version of this flowchart for Shanda. As indicated in this diagram, the behaviors that potentially start the chain can be grouped as follows:

- Dependency on adults (i.e., a tendency to overassociate with a support provider—often a paraprofessional—so that Shanda drops classroom expectations to socialize with this person and/or demands that this person perform requested actions)
- Behaviors that express "I want" (i.e., spontaneously and suddenly expressing a desire for an object, person, or activity that is not an option given current expectations for Shanda and the rest of the class)
- Socializing at the wrong time (i.e., socializing during instruction by moving about the classroom and attempting to engage peers in social interaction)
- Behaviors, usually in combination, that represent a mild tantrum (i.e., not following an adult directive, pinching, biting, screaming, throwing objects)
- Behaviors that represent a major tantrum (i.e., the same behaviors that represent a mild tantrum but more pronounced and with a duration of about a half-hour)

Shanda's escalation sequence typically followed this pattern, especially before her support program was implemented: One of the three behaviors at the top of the flowchart occurred, often escalating into a mild tantrum, which then frequently progressed to a major tantrum.

Step 3: Analyze Functions   Once the team has identified the student's behaviors and their patterns of occurrence, the next step is to analyze each behavior pattern separately with respect to setting, antecedent, consequent, and motivational factors.

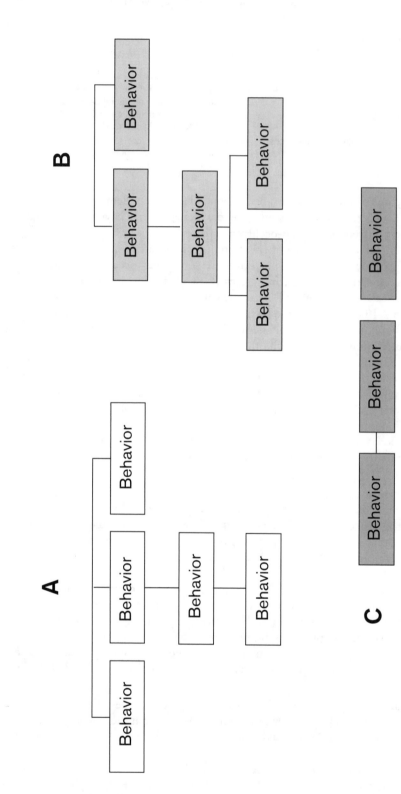

Figure 11.9. The three different behavior association patterns.

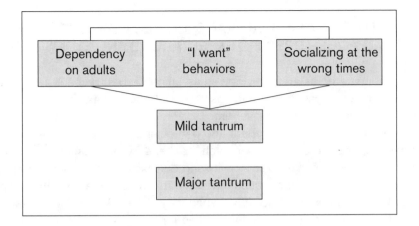

Figure 11.10. Shanda's behavior patterns.

Using techniques described in Chapters 6, 7, and 8 (see also Jackson & Leon, 1998a; Repp & Horner, 1999), the team develops a series of hypotheses that delineates the conditions in which each behavior is both likely and unlikely to occur. Table 11.2 gives abbreviated examples of some of the hypotheses that were developed for Shanda in relation to her five behaviors.

Step 4: Create Prevention Strategies   When behavioral hypotheses are coupled with information on specific times, classroom activities, and participation levels, they can guide the team in generating ecological and interpersonal supports that can mitigate many problem behaviors and enhance student engagement. It is, of course, essential that this analysis be accomplished on a situation-by-situation basis for the entire school day, as conditions and appropriate supports will vary across school settings and activities (see Display 11.4). As previously mentioned, the team should generate prevention strategies for each behavior pattern and then record these strategies on the student's flowchart above the behavior pattern that they help prevent.

Table 11.2. Examples of hypotheses for Shanda

In general	For Shanda
First behavior	**Dependency on adults**
Presence hypothesis	More likely when adults hover
Absence hypothesis	Less likely when she knows what to do in an activity
Second behavior	**"I want" behaviors**
Presence hypothesis	More likely when she is losing interest in an activity
Absence hypothesis	Less likely when toys are out of sight
Third behavior	**Socializing at the wrong times**
Presence hypothesis	More likely during independent seat work
Absence hypothesis	Less likely when she is engaged or in small group work
Fourth behavior	**Mild tantrum**
Presence hypothesis	More likely when the other three behaviors do not achieve the desired results
Absence hypothesis	Less likely when she is distracted by a class transition
Fifth behavior	**Major tantrum**
Presence hypothesis	More likely when a mild tantrum is ineffective
Absence hypothesis	Less likely when she is distracted during a minor tantrum

DISPLAY 11.4—NATURAL SOURCES OF PREVENTION: TEACHER-SPECIFIC EXPECTATIONS AND SUPPORTS

Prevention strategies are often viewed as being derived primarily from functional behavioral assessment findings. Although these data are useful, many preventive supports emerge over time, and they are unique properties of the relationships between the student and particular general education teachers. These supports are embedded in each teacher's expectations for the student and in his or her individualized activity and discipline management styles. Here are some examples of the tactics that three teachers came up with during Shanda's second year of inclusion, when they were asked to identify their expectations for Shanda and what worked for them to help her be a part of the class.

Teacher	Expectations	Effective ways to prevent problems
Homeroom/ academic	Partially participate in class by emulating what other students are doing	Give Shanda the same materials as all other students
	Know where resources are and get them as needed	Allow Shanda to get up and stretch her legs
	Increase verbalizations in response to questions	Have the special educator in class even when Shanda is absent so that class membership becomes clear to Shanda
Music	Remain seated Participate with modeling	Have the student near Shanda encourage participation
		Talk firmly to Shanda when her behavior is outside the rule boundaries
P.E.	Listen or look around when instruction or fun is in progress	Have the teacher invite Shanda to join if she will not join
	Come in with peers without having to be forced to do so	Respond to any of Shanda's initiations by looking at her and acknowledging her initiations

Behavioral problems may begin occurring again after a period in which the program seemed to be working if the use of preventive supports has fallen off. Elaborate on how each of the following factors may explain a diminishing use of natural prevention tactics:

- *General and special educators are confused about their roles*
- *A general educator does not recognize the powerful influence that he or she exerts over the student's behavior*
- *Special educators have assumed too much ownership of the situation and/or general educators have relinquished ownership of the situation*

Figure 11.11 shows some of the prevention strategies that the education team generated for Shanda's five behavior patterns. For example, one of several ways to prevent "I want" behaviors from becoming problems was to discover curriculum- and class-appropriate activities that Shanda enjoyed, then make these activities more accessible and readily available to Shanda. This, of course, required prolonged exposure to the general education curriculum so that Shanda could discover which activities she enjoyed that were part of the curriculum. Activities that Shanda liked were made into parallel activities. The team defined a *parallel activity* as a curriculum-appropriate activity that Shanda enjoyed and 1) in which she could be redirected to engage when she appeared to lose interest in the present class activity or 2) to which she could be given access at any time. For example, during a geology unit, the team discovered that Shanda really enjoyed the study of rocks. The science teacher set up a geology table, complete with numerous rock samples, in the back of the classroom. The table was for all of the students, and Shanda had ready access to it through either redirection or a direct request. It is important to be aware that, although engagement in a parallel activity was an acceptable alternative to the escalation pattern that routinely followed thwarted "I want" behaviors, the long-range desired alternative was *always* engagement in the general classroom activity. Hence, Shanda was continuously expected to at least partially participate with the other students in their activities throughout the day, and she was intermittently encouraged to rejoin her classmates whenever she shifted to a parallel activity.

Clearly, the effectiveness of the prevention efforts depends on having varied and different supports for each behavior, and these supports must be linked directly to the behavioral hypotheses and/or to the typical activities and routines of the class. The presence of numerous functionally relevant options, plus the cumulative effect of having all behaviors in the chain addressed, can offer assurance to the classroom teacher that safety and order will be the rule rather than the exception.

Step 5: Generate Replacement Skills   One property of hypothesis-based intervention that makes it so appealing is that it treats all behaviors as forms of adaptation in relation to real human needs. This suggests that reducing problem behaviors often requires equipping students with skills for meeting their needs in ways that the school community considers appropriate. An escalation support plan builds on this premise by encouraging the team to develop adaptive alternatives for all behaviors in the escalation chain by using functional behavioral assessment information. As with prevention strategies, when this information is coupled with data on times, activities, and participation, it helps the team delineate skills that the student can use to meet his or her needs.

The flowchart should visually emphasize the importance of the adaptive alternatives. For example, problem behaviors in the boxes can be erased, then rewritten in smaller print and parentheses, and the adaptive alternatives can then be recorded in

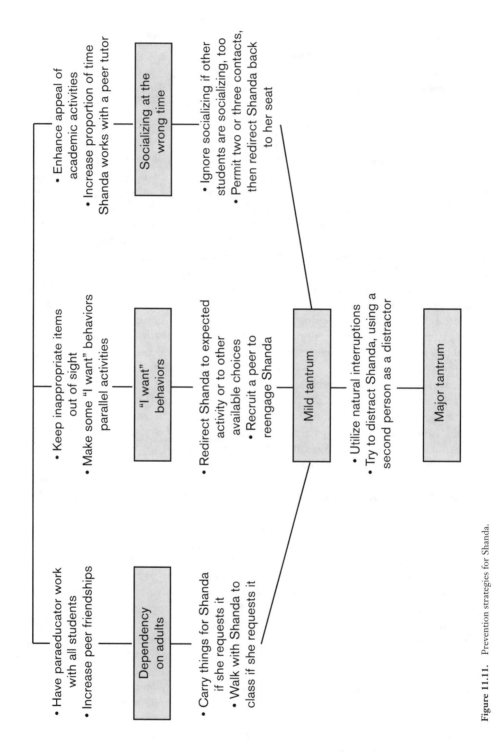

Figure 11.11. Prevention strategies for Shanda.

- Enhance appeal of academic activities
- Increase proportion of time Shanda works with a peer tutor

Socializing at the wrong time

- Ignore socializing if other students are socializing, too
- Permit two or three contacts, then redirect Shanda back to her seat

- Keep inappropriate items out of sight
- Make some "I want" behaviors parallel activities

"I want" behaviors

- Redirect Shanda to expected activity or to other available choices
- Recruit a peer to reengage Shanda

Mild tantrum

- Utilize natural interruptions
- Try to distract Shanda, using a second person as a distractor

Major tantrum

- Have paraeducator work with all students
- Increase peer friendships

Dependency on adults

- Carry things for Shanda if she requests it
- Walk with Shanda to class if she requests it

274

larger print and perhaps with a different colored marker. Figure 11.12 shows some of the adaptive alternatives that the team generated for Shanda's flowchart. Dependency on adults' behaviors, for example, could be reduced when Shanda knew by experience the alternative behaviors that were expected of her in different situations throughout the school day. Socializing at the wrong time could become less of an issue if Shanda was provided with activity- and context-specific communication skills that met attention and affiliation needs without interfering with other students' learning.

The absence of adaptive alternatives for a major tantrum requires comment. First, note that Shanda does have the option to express anger more adaptively at the mild tantrum point. Although baseline information indicated that this replacement behavior was rare, it did occur, especially if an event distracted Shanda from the original reason for anger. Second, once Shanda was engaged in a major tantrum, the team questioned whether she could control her actions. Thus, they doubted that teaching Shanda an alternative behavior would be fruitful.

Step 6: Develop Crisis Support Procedures   In this final step, the team addresses procedures for handling serious problems when they arise or are in progress. By this point in the planning and analysis process, the team will likely see that previous accomplishments mitigate many and sometimes most behavior patterns in the chain. At the same time, the team members also have a clearer perspective on which behavior patterns require more attention to ensure safety and security for all of the students and adults.

As with the other steps in escalation support planning, crisis support procedures can be directly recorded on the flowchart. The specific crisis support procedures are recorded in the boxes of their respective behavior patterns, perhaps with another colored marker. As shown in Figure 11.13, crisis support procedures were not required for the first three behaviors in the chain, but they were required for Shanda's mild and major tantrums. In the case of mild tantrums, the general education teacher could decide that Shanda needed to leave the room until Shanda calmed down; in the case of major tantrums, district-approved procedures for removal and protective restraint could be used. Yet, the team was delighted to discover during the first year of plan implementation that if the adult with whom Shanda was angry with was to "trade off" with another adult while Shanda was still in the early (mild) stages of the tantrum, Shanda's anger tended to dissipate. As the classroom paraprofessional and the special educator were almost always the targets of Shanda's anger, trading off generally meant having someone else available to assume this person's instructional responsibilities until Shanda calmed down.

BEHAVIORAL SUPPORT, REINTEGRATION, AND SCHOOL CAPACITY

This chapter has illustrated steps and procedures for planning and implementing support plans for students with serious behavioral challenges. The discussion has focused on students for whom the goal of the support process is their success in general education while ensuring reasonable levels of safety and comfort for others. It is essential to realize that these steps and procedures are only successful if behavioral concerns are viewed as being embedded in the relationship between the student and his or her environment. This does not mean that some students do not have real emotional and behavioral issues. However, it does mean that both understanding problems and seeking solutions should center on the ecological and interpersonal conditions of the student's school community, not on behavioral remediation within isolated settings. This

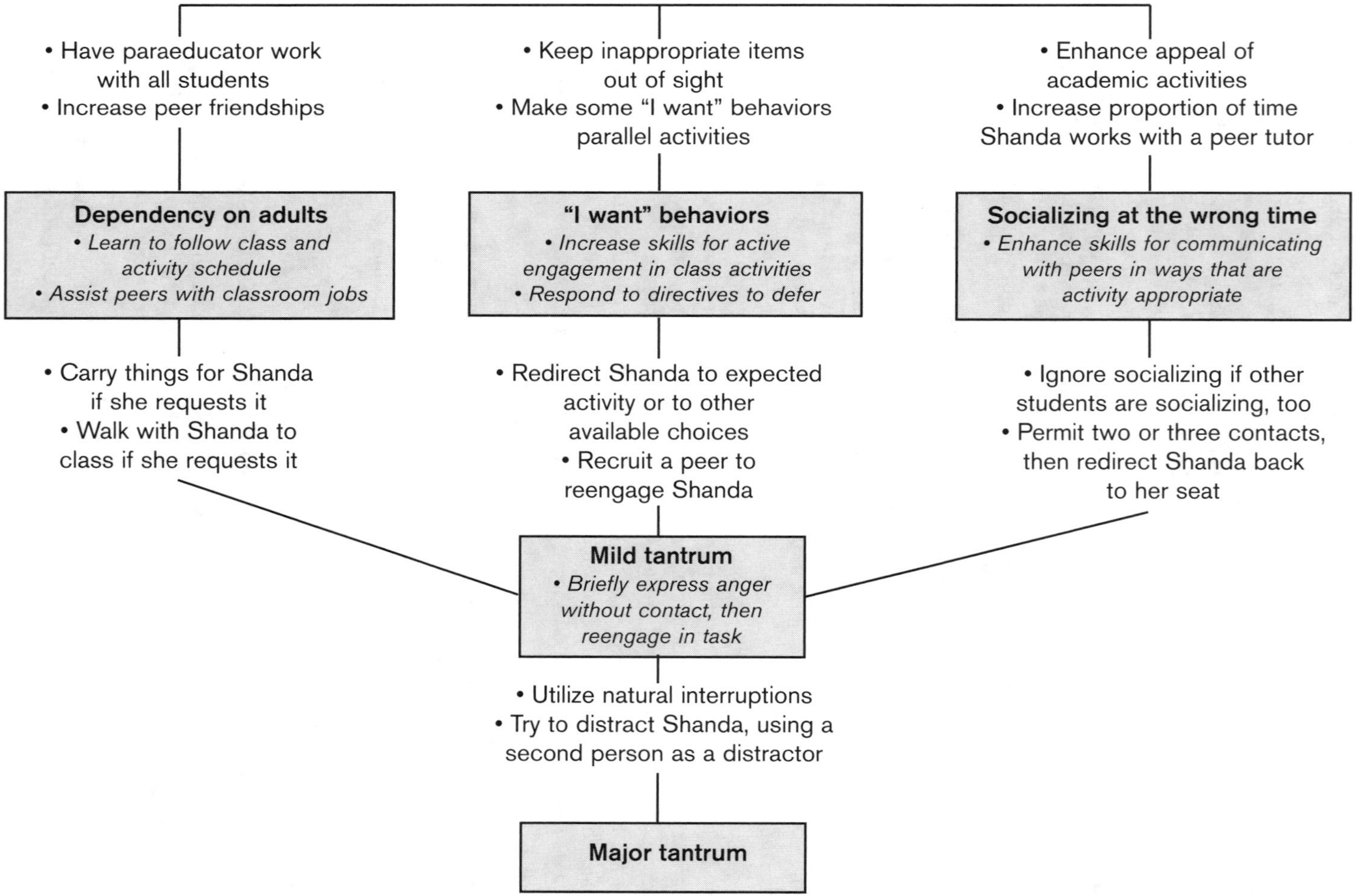

Figure 11.12. Adaptive alternatives for Shanda.

Dependency on adults
Learn to follow class and activity schedule
Assist peers with classroom jobs

- Carry things for Shanda if she requests it
- Walk with Shanda to class if she requests it

"I want" behaviors
Increase skills for active engagement in class activities
Respond to directives to defer

- Redirect Shanda to expected activity or to other available choices
- Recruit a peer to reengage Shanda

Socializing at the wrong time
Enhance skills for communicating with peers in ways that are activity appropriate

- Ignore socializing if other students are socializing, too
- Permit two or three contacts, then redirect Shanda back to her seat

Mild tantrum
Briefly express anger without contact, then reengage in task

- Utilize natural interruptions
- Try to distract Shanda, using a second person as a distractor

Major tantrum

- Have paraeducator work with all students
- Increase peer friendships

- Keep inappropriate items out of sight
- Make some "I want" behaviors parallel activities

- Enhance appeal of academic activities
- Increase proportion of time Shanda works with a peer tutor

276

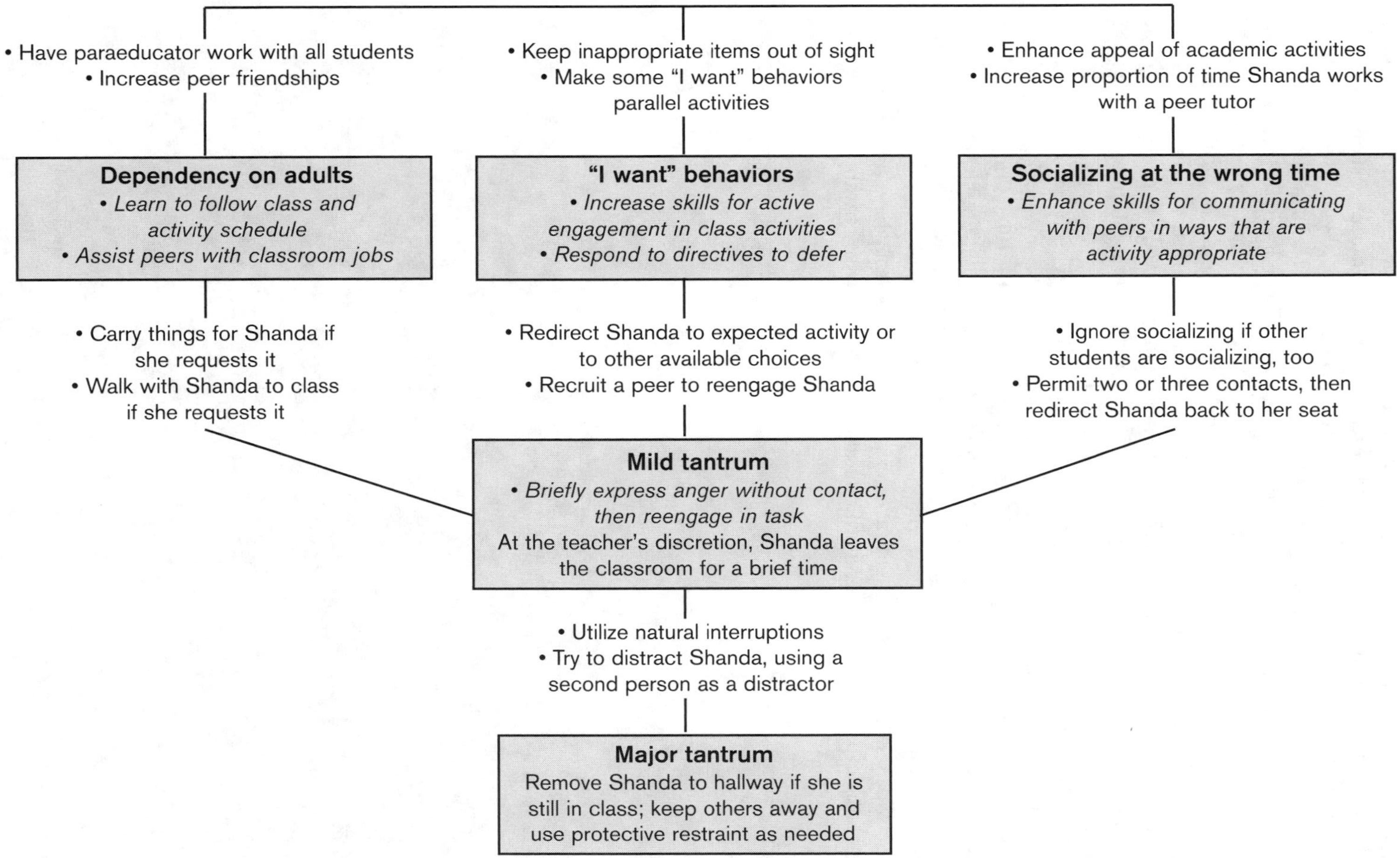

- Have paraeducator work with all students
- Increase peer friendships

- Enhance appeal of academic activities
- Increase proportion of time Shanda works with a peer tutor

- Keep inappropriate items out of sight
- Make some "I want" behaviors parallel activities

Dependency on adults
- *Learn to follow class and activity schedule*
- *Assist peers with classroom jobs*

"I want" behaviors
- *Increase skills for active engagement in class activities*
- *Respond to directives to defer*

Socializing at the wrong time
- *Enhance skills for communicating with peers in ways that are activity appropriate*

- Carry things for Shanda if she requests it
- Walk with Shanda to class if she requests it

- Redirect Shanda to expected activity or to other available choices
- Recruit a peer to reengage Shanda

- Ignore socializing if other students are socializing, too
- Permit two or three contacts, then redirect Shanda back to her seat

Mild tantrum
- *Briefly express anger without contact, then reengage in task*
At the teacher's discretion, Shanda leaves the classroom for a brief time

- Utilize natural interruptions
- Try to distract Shanda, using a second person as a distractor

Major tantrum
Remove Shanda to hallway if she is still in class; keep others away and use protective restraint as needed

Figure 11.13. Crisis support for Shanda.

277

also does not mean that students cannot be held accountable for their behaviors. However, it does mean that schools and teachers must also accept responsibility for their social and discipline climates, and they must consider the degree to which behavioral problems are partly of their own creation (Furlong & Morrison, 2000).

A dilemma that remains largely unaddressed in public education is how to successfully reintegrate students with serious behavioral concerns into general education following prolonged placement in self-contained classes, schools, or residential facilities. This chapter and previous chapters have offered ways to fruitfully explore this transition. Nevertheless, the situation in which both general and special education personnel are truly committed to reintegration as part of the solution to a behavioral problem is still a relatively rare event in public education.

School communities that effectively educate students with behavioral concerns within general education classrooms, truly use removal as a last resort, and regularly undertake reintegration have something in common: a critical mass of teachers and administrators who value acceptance and understanding, exhibit high levels of collaboration, are skilled at using natural supports, and demonstrate flexibility in addressing individual student challenges. At the beginning of the 21st century, a number of schoolwide models are emerging that offer promise because they have the potential to stretch the capacity of schools regarding these skills and values. This topic is explored in Chapter 12.

Appendix

Elements of a Comprehensive Plan
and Example Components from Brian's Plan

Vision

A vision is a set of broad, positive outcomes that addresses age-appropriate activity participation, social membership, and personal autonomy. Vision statements designate what the student could be experiencing in the natural community at a future point if the support processes and instructional activities specified in the plan are in place and working. The vision charts the course by defining what broad outcomes the team seeks; these are then translated into more immediate expectations in the short-term expectations section of the plan and into action statements in the long-term prevention section of the plan.

For Brian, there were seven major vision statements, which included the following:

- Be among peers in their routine social experiences (membership).
- Actively participate in the activities that occur in inclusive settings (activity participation).
- Control his own activities and time and do what he wants to do (autonomy/self-control).

Behavior Patterns and Explanatory Hypotheses

Specific, discrete behaviors are organized into patterns in relation to how they co-occur, what they mean to the adults and peers of the community, and how they seem to fulfill the student's needs. For each identified pattern, as many hypotheses as needed are generated to fully represent the community's understanding of the behaviors and their functions for the student. The behavior patterns and their respective hypotheses then provide the basis for generating the decisions and recommendations associated with the short-term prevention and the adaptive alternatives sections of the plan. Behavior pattern information also helps in crisis planning within the "responding to challenging behavior" section of the plan.

For Brian, behavior patterns included:

Resisting Change: Not following (or returning to) a scheduled or instructed activity, which may be accompanied by behaviors such as suddenly sitting on the floor, false crying, and holding his head. *Abridged, selected hypotheses:* Most likely to occur when he is enjoying an activity that must come to an end for a scheduled change to occur, the upcoming activity is hard, or he does not know what is coming up next; least likely to occur if he knows what is coming next and he has reason to positively anticipate it.

This plan appears in an abbreviated form in the interest of space. The presented components simply illustrate element construction and plan composition.

Taking Off: Running away from an activity or request, which may include pushing things out of his way. *Abridged, selected hypotheses:* Most likely to occur when he is bored with an activity or is asked to do an activity that he does not like doing; least likely to occur if he is engaged in an activity that he enjoys or he is receiving positive attention for activity participation regardless of whether he likes it.

Grabbing: Reaching out and forcefully grasping others and other forms of brief striking out (kicking and pulling hair). *Abridged, selected hypotheses:* Most likely to occur in situations in which he senses a threat to his space or to his freedom to move about or when he is trying to communicate and is not being understood; least likely to occur when he is independently engaged in an activity that he knows how to do and no adults are "hanging over him."

Class Clowning: Disrupting a class or activity by giggling, making obscene gestures, standing in the middle of the room, or walking around the classroom. *Abridged, selected hypotheses:* Most likely to occur when an activity has been in progress for awhile and he is getting bored; least likely to occur if Brian has other responses that he can use during difficult or extended activities to experience positive regard and attention (e.g., calling on a peer).

Dangerous Situations: Going to a potentially dangerous place, such as a construction site in the school or off the school grounds, then trying to participate in the workers' activities (when it occurs, it occurs in conjunction with "taking off"). *Abridged, selected hypotheses:* Most likely to occur if he knows the whereabouts of a construction project; least likely to occur if his movement toward a site is anticipated and he encounters an adult along the way who redirects him to another activity that can be done together.

Short-Term Expectations

Short-term expectations are patterns of peer affiliation, social interaction, curricular engagement, and classroom/school life participation that can be reasonably expected to occur fairly regularly once the plan has been in place for several weeks or months. These could be created by having the team envision what a good day has looked like in the past, then using this portrait to generate descriptors of short-term expectations.

There were six short-term expectations for Brian, including these four:

- Follow his class schedule and going to his classes, even if he does not stay for the full class periods.
- Use gestures, signs, speech, or his picture communication system more regularly to indicate a need for an activity change in place of taking off or grabbing others.
- Become less likely to resist change during class transitions.
- When he chooses to leave a general education class before it is over, he elects to do one or more of a number of alternative activities within the school that relate to his educational growth.

Long-Term Prevention

Long-term prevention consists of planned, regular, and supported access to age- and peer-appropriate experiences, such as 1) valued activities, which are typical school activities, including activities that are enjoyed by peers and adults and/or by the student; 2) valued relationships, which are relationships with typical peers and key adults, including relationships with potential for providing support, friendship, and status for the student; and 3) opportunities for choice and control, which should honor the student's basic physiological, safety, and affiliation needs and must incorporate necessary communication supports (e.g., peer relationships, augmentative and alternative communication devices). As the student becomes invested in these activities and life experiences, the probability increases that the student will engage in more acceptable behaviors and be accepted by others.

For Brian, there were four major long-term prevention steps, which included these three:

- Add new general education classes to Brian's schedule based on interests and needs, focusing especially on the problem class periods (third and fourth). Options include science explorations, construction systems, drama, pottery, and business classes.
- Implement a formal peer-helper process for certain periods of the day. (Periods are to be determined once his schedule is firm, he has been in his classes for several days, and patterns of participation and engagement are beginning to emerge.)
- Provide unscheduled independent activities—usually related to his IEP—that Brian can do whenever he reaches his tolerance point in general education classes. (These "personal options" can be used to promote good choice making and autonomous action and learning, but they do not replace the team's primary focus on general education participation and membership.)

Short-Term Prevention

Short-term prevention consists of a list of recommended, fixed, and/or fluid strategies, steps, and procedures that can be used within the school community to support curriculum and activity participation, prevent problems from occurring in the first place, and/or curtail problem acceleration when behaviors start to occur. Often derived from the behavioral hypotheses, the generation of these strategies, steps, and procedures typically requires the team to reflect on the antecedent and consequent events that are associated with the occurrence and nonoccurrence of each and every behavior pattern, then to generate specific action steps that teachers and students can take to avert and ameliorate these patterns. The list can include 1) accommodations and modifications that are associated with the general education curriculum or specific classroom learning activities; 2) alterations in the physical and social environment, such as changes in the seating arrangement; 3) alternative activities to which the student can shift when he or she needs a change, such as shifting to another activity or taking a break; 4) verbal scripts that can be used by adults and/or peers to help the student recompose or reengage; and, if helpful, 5) simple contingency management procedures, such as reward systems or self-monitoring/self-management activities. Items within the list can be generic supports that are to be used by anyone as needed and as appropriate (e.g., sitting next to a peer buddy) or supports that are identified in relation to specific situations or activities (e.g., in math, letting him work problems at the chalkboard instead of in his seat if he chooses to do so). In all cases, however, supports should be referenced to the specific behavior patterns.

For Brian, there were 18 short-term prevention steps and procedures, including the following:

- Give him a job to do, such as running an errand to the office (recommendation; addresses class clowning).
- Always have Brian come in slightly early to class for smooth class transitions (fixed decision; addresses resisting change, taking off, grabbing, and class clowning).
- Provide opportunities to work one-to-one with specific classmates (recommendation; addresses resisting change, taking off, and class clowning).
- Consider using a redirect as a first step when he is agitated or bored: "Do _____; then you can do _____" (fluid decision; addresses taking off).
- When he bolts from the classroom, use a preemptive strategy, in which an adult meets Brian in the hall about halfway to the place he is most likely going and offers to go with Brian to another location (fixed decision; follows taking off, but addresses dangerous situations).
- Give him an independent writing exercise to reduce anxiety in appropriate situations (recommendation; addresses resisting change, taking off).
- Arrange paraeducator support so that the paraeducator is nearby (but not right beside Brian) and is available when Brian needs help. Brian asks for adult help by producing a "come here" gesture with his hands, and this gesture is promptly honored (fluid decision; addresses taking off).

Adaptive Alternatives

Adaptive alternatives are skills that enhance the student's ability to meet personal needs, express competency in class activities, gain access to valued resources or relationships, and/or practice self-control if he or she learns them and/or begins to consistently use them. Adaptive alternatives must include, but should not be limited to, skills that directly relate to the behavioral hypotheses identified for the problem behavior patterns. The delineated skills often become part of the student's IEP.

For Brian, some of the skills that were needed to assist him in becoming more competent and to meet personal needs were as follows:

- Communicate the desire to leave one activity to engage in another by pointing to a picture of the activity that he would like to be doing.
- Communicate the need for "wait time" or "adjust time" by using a specific gesture (holding up his hand near an adult's) and/or spoken words ("Wait," "Not done yet").
- Emulate the expected activities of his typically developing peers by looking at what they are doing and selecting to either do the same activity (identical activity) or one that is similar (parallel activity). (Actual expectations are identified for each class situation, and possible choices for Brian are delineated. As Brian's competency in his classes increases with time and experience, the adaptive alternatives that are the focus of instruction also change.)

Responding to Challenging Behaviors

Responding to challenging behaviors involves creating steps and procedures for handling situations in which specific problem behaviors are in progress and/or there are safety or disruptiveness concerns. These steps and procedures may include scripted verbal routines that are employed by adults to help protect the student and others or to deescalate the behavior. They may also include authorized crisis intervention procedures. Under some conditions, they may also include consequences, but see Chapters 4 and 5 for details and considerations.

For Brian, a different pattern of adult responding was developed for each of the five behavior patterns. Here are two illustrations:

- Taking off: Give a "sit and wait" command, but then quickly ask Brian what he needs and how you can help. If Brian takes off anyway, use a preemptive strategy or go to known locations to find him if he gets away (e.g., construction site, front office, commons area). If Brian is engaged in one of his approved personal options when you find him, then honor his choice; otherwise, give him time, then start encouraging him to return to his previous activity.
- When any behavior pattern escalates and is out of control: The educator (e.g., classroom teacher, paraeducator) asks Brian in a nonthreatening way to "pull himself together now or take a break." If Brian does not do so, depending on the disruptiveness of the behavior and the educator's judgment, any one of the following can occur: 1) help him calm down by talking to him while ignoring his mumbling and grumbling, 2) escort him to the hall to soothe him and talk him through his fears or needs, 3) use noncontact block-and-protect postures, 4) remove Brian from the room by using protective removal procedures, and/or 5) remove the other students from the room. Removal is temporary, and Brian can return to the situation once he is calm.

Responsibility and Accountability

Responsibility and accountability involve creating administrative and training activities that help ensure appropriate plan implementation. Activities addressed include all of those that are associated with "implementing the plan": educational and environmental changes, professional development, crisis procedures, critical communications, problem solving, and evaluating change.

For Brian, some of the activities planned for were implementing a class schedule, crisis intervention training, and teacher-to-teacher communications.

Positive Behavioral Support at the School and Community Levels

Chapter 12

Preparing Schools for Positive Behavioral Support

"Man's actions are the
picture book of his creeds."
—Ralph Waldo Emerson

Chapter 1 examined the purposes of public education and identified its two major functions (Goodlad, 1990). First, schools are a basis for enculturation, preparing students for community life and citizenship. Second, schools are a source for academic knowledge and skills, ensuring that students have access to society's information resources. It was also pointed out that schools typically react to behavioral problems by removing the offending students from the settings in which these kinds of learning optimally take place. As noted by McLaughlin and colleagues, students who have emotional and behavioral problems "are not strangers to educational segregation" (1997, p. 16). Chapter 1 then argued that removal undermines and erodes public education's mission to appropriately educate all students.

The fact that schools have continuing, unresolved worries about educating students with behavioral problems falls squarely on their disciplinary practices. Blumstein (2000) asserted that policies for dealing with violence and similar problems in schools and other social institutions "are driven far more by ideological and emotional perspectives than by research" (p. 545). And, as Udis noted, "traditional compliance-based discipline has little effect on children who have significant problems getting along with others" (ERIC/OSEP Special Project, 1997, p. 1). This creates a dilemma for schools: It is too easy to hold students responsible for disruptions associated with conflict and to not recognize that students may be responding to conditions that schools themselves have helped create. Furlong and Morrison (2000) stressed that schools must "own their part" when searching for solutions to violence and similar problems. They also must go beyond punishment and removal (Skiba & Peterson, 2000).

The tools and techniques described previously in this book are intended to help remedy this situation because they bring together much that is known about how educators can successfully address behavioral concerns at various severity levels. Yet, the material described up to this point has largely focused on the role of individual classroom teachers, special educators, behavior specialists, and others who have direct responsibility for specific students. Many professionals have recognized and documented the futility of piecemeal approaches to the task of providing successful school experiences for all students (Brownell & Walther-Thomas, 1999; McLaughlin et al., 1997). A smattering of well-conceived and properly implemented positive behavioral support efforts by a few dedicated and thoughtful educators does not add up to a school with the capacity to support a behaviorally diverse student population in all environments. Rather, an array of positive, interconnected and mutually supportive intervention practices is required, reflecting the efforts of educators throughout a school's community. These practices must be complemented by policies that focus on the school's responsibility for educating all of its students.

This chapter, then, goes full circle, returning once again to building-level practices and the school community's responsibility to find better ways to discipline and educate its students. This chapter's main purpose is to explore ways that schools can build capacity for initiating and sustaining positive behavioral support practices. The chapter begins by considering some ways to affect school culture so as to facilitate the adoption of positive behavioral support efforts. Next, the chapter identifies and describes five schoolwide initiatives that can be conducive to support activities when adopted and implemented by a school. The final section of this chapter identifies five motifs that characterize the essential qualities of schoolwide change approaches that are designed for nurturing positive behavioral support policies and practices.

CHANGING A SCHOOL'S CULTURE AND CLIMATE TO PROMOTE POSITIVE BEHAVIORAL SUPPORT

The characteristics of a school culture that enhance acceptance of positive behavioral support include those that promote understanding and equity in instruction and discipline, as well as those that nurture growth and willingness to change in the members of the school community. Six avenues for making a school's culture more open to behavioral support are 1) schoolwide mission statement, 2) schoolwide policies and procedures for discipline, 3) collaborative professional development, 4) principles of organizational change, 5) large-scale systemic restructuring, and 6) comprehensive evaluation. These concepts are described next.

Schoolwide Mission Statement

A school's philosophy is often embodied in a mission statement or a school vision (Lewis & Sugai, 1999). A mission statement embodies schoolwide beliefs, dispositions, and values that both support and set parameters on the educational and discipline practices of teachers and other educators. Students and families should be encouraged to contribute to the development of a school's mission statement.

When a mission statement is consistent with values related to diversity in classrooms (see Chapter 3) and the tenets of positive behavioral support (see Chapter 4), then educational practices can be held to these standards (see Display 12.1). If the school's core mission is to serve all students and to view the school as a community of learners who feel connected with one another, then that school may be more forthcoming with the resources for a behavioral support plan than a school without this type of mission statement. Also, time might be more generously allocated for educa-

DISPLAY 12.1—TWO TEACHER PARADIGMS

A principal was leading a team of middle school teachers in developing a building's mission statement, which was supposed to emphasize inclusive practices. In an exercise, individual teachers described their instructional styles and the kinds of learners that they liked to have in their classes. The principal noted that teachers fell within two very different paradigms: One group of teachers viewed themselves as responsible for all children who walked through their doors; the other group of teachers viewed themselves as responsible for those children who really wanted to learn and who behaved accordingly. The following patterns characterized the responses of teachers in the "all children" paradigm and the "deserving children" paradigm:

All children paradigm	Deserving children paradigm
Provide encouragement for all children to learn, teaching at each child's level	Provide encouragement to those child ready and willing to learn, teaching at their level
Enhance community and promote self-responsibility to help children who are "on the margins"	Encourage individual self-control and self-responsibility to help those children who are "on the margins"
Help children who often interfere with others' learning; keep them in the classroom	Remove children who often interfere with others' learning

What problems do you think the team will encounter in creating a mission statement that emphasizes responsibility for and commitment to serving all students in general education classes?

What role does building leadership play in this process?

tors to attend positive behavioral support training opportunities in schools whose philosophy expresses support for all students.

Experience suggests that some schools develop a mission statement, display it in a conspicuous place, and then essentially ignore it when issues of practice are considered and decided on by individual educators. As with ensuring that inclusive schools stay aligned with their mission (Jackson, Ryndak, & Billingsley, 2000), a way to ensure that a mission statement is a "living document" is to periodically revisit it and regularly review placement, discipline, and teaching practices in relationship to it.

Schoolwide Policies and Procedures for Discipline

Chapters 6 and 7 showed that there are limits to what can be accomplished by precise rules and consequences, and it was recommended that some flexibility be incorporated into the guidelines that schools use for handling discipline concerns (i.e., heuristic decision making). In stark contrast, existing guidelines in many schools are rigid "either/or" procedures. These procedures may be codified into explicit schoolwide discipline policies that are—ostensibly for prevention—shared with students and parents and publicly posted throughout the building in abbreviated forms (e.g., no running in the halls). Regrettably, many schoolwide discipline policies focus more on delineating consequences for rule violations and less on problem prevention and long-term problem resolution.

Having voiced these concerns, let it now be said that there certainly is a place for a schoolwide plan that delineates conduct expectations and the school's responses for violations. One rationale for such a plan is that if developed with the whole school in mind, it can discourage the development of discipline procedures that differentially affect groups of students in terms of ethnic, cultural, gender, or disability criteria. For example, unless the entire student population is considered during plan development, general education students may be routinely subjected to inflexible rules involving suspension and expulsion, which may be more carefully applied with special education students; special education students may be routinely subjected to exclusionary time-out and physical restraint, which may not be applied at all with general education students.

Another argument for such a plan relates to the fact that a significant proportion of serious conflicts arise during transitions and in common areas, such as playgrounds and hallways (Astor, Meyer, & Behre, 1999; Colvin, Sugai, Good, & Lee, 1997; Kartub et al., 2000; Lewis, Sugai, & Colvin, 1998). When the school rules that are adopted in a plan apply to these areas and the school develops adult guidelines for prevention (e.g., preinstruction, active supervision), understanding (e.g., processing with the student, functional behavioral assessment), and fairness (e.g., applying consequences that match the offense, due process), the benefits are likely to include enhanced safety and more responsible student behavior. It is also possible that such standards of practice could help resolve difficulties between certain students and the school staff before such concerns escalate to the point that rule violations become behaviors that are attributed to a specific student's reputation.

It is important to stress that, if schools are to foster greater self-responsibility in students, then an effort must be made to reformulate the disciplinary plan so that the focus on negative expectations (e.g., no running or loud noise in hallways) becomes a focus on positive expectations that allows for greater latitude in understanding (e.g., be respectful to others in the hallways). The former kinds of expectations emphasize knowledge about behaviors that are appropriate or inappropriate and simple compliance to rules governing hallway conduct. The latter kinds of expectations emphasize knowledge about the rights and needs of others in the hallways and in nearby classes, as well as the use of foresight and thoughtfulness when making transitions from one place to another. When rules are violated, the former expectations call for exacting retribution, which may affect various students differently depending on their attitudes and values; the latter expectations call for honoring the community's needs through service or other consequences, which promotes continuing membership in the community and responsibility to one's peers and teachers.

Collaborative Professional Development

Senge (1990) identified characteristics of learning organizations and how individuals within these organizations attain personal mastery. Of particular relevance is Senge's emphasis on lifelong learning and the recognition that an organization develops as its people develop. Collaboration in professional development is essential for creating optimal learning communities and sustaining schoolwide change initiatives (Jenkins, Louis, Walberg, & Keefe, 1994). Just as Chapter 5 showed that positive relationships are necessary for effective teaching, so too can ongoing collegial relationships provide support for teachers in their continued learning (Walther-Thomas, Korinek, & McLaughlin, 1999). These relationships, in turn, can enhance student achievement (Moffett, 2000). Hence, good professional development is about building relationships that are conducive to realizing the school's mission to support its students' learning.

Some exemplary ways to foster relationships as part of professional development include communities of practice, study teams, peer coaching, electronic networks, and ongoing in-service opportunities. Communities of practice are groups of teachers, district personnel, and university professors who come together to plan and conduct applied research. "In these communities, learning proceeds from action, expertise is distributed, and knowledge is socially constructed" (Perry, Walton, & Calder, 1999, p. 218). In their project in which teachers developed assessments of early literacy, Perry and colleagues showed that associations between schools and higher education institutions offer opportunities for collaborative planning and reflection, merging theory and practice, and testing theory in practice.

Study groups can be especially critical for successful implementation of new schoolwide initiatives (Calhoun, 1994). Calhoun noted that study groups serve

> To provide technical support, to provide social support, to expand our conceptual understanding through discussion, and to provide a forum for regular sharing of the effects of our instruction. They support us as we engage in new learning and as we take risks and try things not in our present repertoire. (p. 30)

Powell, Berliner, and Casanova (1992) reported that "teachers gain professional knowledge and a sense of efficacy by participating in such study groups" (p. 284). These groups generally consist of four to six people, are cross-grade or cross-department, are self-formed, and meet weekly or biweekly to discuss elements of an initiative. (See Murphy, 1999, for innovative ways that schools can arrange time for these efforts.)

Peer coaching is "the collaborative work of teachers to solve problems/questions that arise during implementation" (Joyce & Showers, 1995, p. 110). The latest evolution of peer coaching practices brings the entire school faculty into the process (Showers & Joyce, 1996). Peer coaching teams are organized at the building level as a necessary first step in the implementation of a schoolwide change initiative. Teachers are typically paired on the first day of training so that they begin their collaboration during training. Teachers observe one another and give feedback, but they are not responsible for formally evaluating each other. Although both study groups and peer coaching are most often associated with curriculum changes and related issues (e.g., a new reading program, the infusion of technology), the implementation issues that are associated with positive behavioral support could certainly be addressed through these procedures.

Electronic networking is another form of ongoing professional collaboration, and it takes full advantage of the Internet. Although personal presence is missing, sites and forums on the Internet broaden one's community of discussants, mentors, and colleagues worldwide. Ruef and Higgins (1999) identified numerous web sites that offer timely and accurate information on IDEA rights and requirements, IEP team roles, functional behavioral assessment, behavior intervention plans, and other issues that are relevant to positive behavioral support. Similarly, Walther-Thomas and colleagues (1999) offered a list of web sites for school teams that are involved in professional development.

Finally, in-service opportunities can be used to impart the precepts and practices of positive behavioral support. The kinds of collaboration that are necessary for educators to meet the different students' needs can be enhanced to the extent that such in-service activities are provided to and attended by all educators in a building or district—not just special or general educators (Jackson, Ryndak, & Billingsley, 2000). In terms of the content of such in-service activities, Dunlap and colleagues (2000) described a comprehensive, long-term in-service training model for behavioral support. Their effort is designed for a multidisciplinary audience that collaborates on a case study during the training process, which promotes community building. Their model also takes into account considerations that affect the application of positive behavioral support across different service systems. For example, opportunities for ongoing practice and exchanges among the participants across agencies are a planned accompaniment of some training offerings.

Principles of Organizational Change

Research indicates that taking into account and modifying characteristics of the organization can be important steps for a successful innovation (McLaughlin et al., 1997; see also Chapter 6 of this book). Hence, systematically changing specific features of a school's organizational structure is one way that schools can make it possible to adopt and sustain a positive behavioral support initiative. Some examples of organizational changes are hiring specially trained personnel, establishing new budget line items, differentially allocating resources to maintain the initiative, and launching a new approach to overall professional development and renewal.

In a study of the impact of two systems-change variables on the success rates of positive behavioral support, Carr, Horner, and colleagues (1999) found that a broad environmental reorganization or restructuring of resources (e.g., systemic personnel changes, provision of respite services) was associated with a success rate of 65%, as compared with a rate of 50.9% when no such reorganization occurred. In addition, they found that when teachers, parents, and trainers actively worked to change their own behavioral expression as part of the intervention, the success rate was 55.2%, as compared with 41.8% when they did not do so.

Hord and colleagues (1987) are credited with two important insights about making change happen within schools. First, they asserted that change is a long-term process, not an event, and it can take as long as 5 years. Second, they contended that change primarily concerns the attitudes and actions of the individuals within the organization rather than simply the addition of new resources or curricula. These two realizations draw attention to how change facilitators should steer the change process and how they conduct their communications with others while changes are being introduced and implemented.

According to Villa and Thousand (1992), it is necessary for the people who are steering the change process to communicate positive expectations, recognize each individual's reaction to change, and accept uncertainty. Change facilitators must be straightforward and honest in their communications throughout the entire process, but especially at the beginning, when trust is being established. Moreover, everyone in the organization must be made aware of the goals, timelines, and expected outcomes. Those introducing the change should respect each individual's concerns and reaction to change, as well as how each individual will be affected by the change. Professional development is essential for supporting individuals as they adopt innovative components that are linked to the change. Facilitators need to accept uncertainty because of the unpredictable nature of events over the course of the change process. As Chapter 6 showed, schools represent complex, adaptive systems in which there are numerous interdependencies, and the outcomes of any change process are somewhat unpredictable within such systems. This implies that even simple decisions can affect many members of a school community and that such effects can become far reaching in the highly interdependent school community. This situation is analogous to tugging at one strand of a spider web and seeing changes in distant sectors of the web.

As with the task of creating and sustaining inclusive schools (Jackson, Ryndak, & Billingsley, 2000), effective leadership by individuals who are committed to positive behavioral support is essential, especially in schools that are steeped in traditional practices. This means that it is helpful if the building administrators themselves are familiar with various models for addressing behavioral concerns. It is also helpful if they know why a support model can possibly make a difference in the school's social climate and academic success of its students.

Large-Scale Systemic Restructuring

Many research-based education practices exist that are not routinely used in schools at the beginning of the 21st century (Skiba & Peterson, 2000). As Lewis and Sugai noted, "The critical step in translating empirically validated research into best practice is a systemic change in how schools approach problem behavior" (1999, p. 3).

Namkung and Ashton (2000) provided an excellent example of large-scale systemic restructuring. The Sonoma County, California, school district altered the way it serves students who are identified as being emotionally or behaviorally disturbed. The process began with a 2-day meeting of 65 interested stakeholders. The operative question that the group discussed was "If I could wipe the slate clean, what would it look like?" Three components emerged as critical in the redesign of the existing structure. They included 1) the use of wraparound plans, 2) inclusion opportunities at a student's home school, and 3) team support for classroom teachers. Of the original 65 stakeholders, 45 volunteered to be part of working groups to make the plan a reality. The final plan included elements such as family-partner links to the school, coordination with the University of Oregon's Schoolwide Positive Behavior Intervention Program, and funding for pilot programs. Preliminary outcomes of this initiative were positive on both academic and behavioral measures.

Another example of a systemic change initiative is Effective Behavior Support (EBS; Lewis, Sugai, & Colvin, 1998). As noted by Lewis and Sugai, schools that participated in EBS formalized and supported the change process by doing the following:

(a) Making the EBS effort one of their top three school improvement priorities or initiatives, (b) collecting and reporting school performance data (e.g., office discipline referrals, behavior incident reports, attendance/truancy rates) on an ongoing basis, and (c) arranging for onsite technical assistance. (1999, p. 4)

These steps illustrate that when large-scale change is being considered, it is imperative both to give it priority and to commit resources to the proposed outcomes. This ensures that the change processes have a chance of being implemented at a sufficiently broad scale to make sustainability a likely outcome.

Comprehensive Evaluation

Lewis and Sugai offered an inventory that addresses 15 features of schoolwide systems that they consider critical for successful positive behavioral support. For example, one such feature is "procedures are in place to address emergency/dangerous situations" (1999, p. 19). Their inventory permits schools to assess the current status of each feature (i.e., in place, partially in place, not in place) and the priority assigned to improving the implementation of that feature (i.e., high, medium, low). Similar checklists are also available for nonclassroom settings, classrooms, and individual student systems. Collectively, these assessments and others like them (see Display 12.2) can help school personnel rate the overall level of positive behavioral support implementation.

DISPLAY 12.2—ASSESSING SCHOOL READINESS FOR POSITIVE BEHAVIORAL SUPPORT

These selected questions, based on the work of Goplerud and Miller (n.d.), were designed to assess the readiness of intermediate educational agencies in Iowa ("Area Education Agencies") for implementing positive behavioral support practices. They have been adapted to apply to a single school.

1. Does this school's culture support the norms of risk taking, collaboration, and continuous learning that are required for learning and implementing these practices? If no, what is needed to help this occur?
2. Are there structures (e.g., work groups, committees) in place to allow collaboration to occur?
3. Will the school's culture allow time for the staff to implement these practices?
4. Do the school staff members who are implementing these practices have a good working relationship with one another?
5. Is there a history of prior successful implementation of significant change efforts, especially those that are similar to these efforts?

Can you think of other questions that would indicate a school's readiness to implement the positive behavioral support practices that are described in this book?

Examples of schoolwide and/or districtwide implementation and evaluation of positive behavioral support efforts were featured in an issue of *The Journal of Positive Behavior Interventions* (Horner & Sugai, 2000, wrote the introduction and assembled the articles). Seven articles reported ways in which school buildings or districts changed their policies and practices to foster a positive preventive approach to school discipline. Office referrals were a commonly used indicator of program success. For example, one program (Taylor-Greene & Kartub, 2000) reported that the number of office discipline referrals had declined by 68% over a 5-year period. Another program (Sadler, 2000) found that office discipline referrals declined by 35% over a 1-year period.

Although office referrals are a frequently reported measure, they are not the only data that can be used to assess improvements in both student behaviors and school capacity. Nakasato (2000) showed how school teams can learn to use data on social skills, the number and intensity of behavioral problems, and the number of students involved in behavioral incidents. He used the phrase *practical feedback loop* (p. 248) to refer to how a district-level support person gathers and reports evaluative data in a timely fashion to schools so that the data can be used by them for effective planning.

Consistent with the discussions of assessment in Chapter 8 and the assessment issues that were raised in Chapters 10 and 11, the evaluation of an initiative to broadly change behavior intervention practices at the systems level must go beyond simply assessing changes in problem behaviors. Enduring change is inadequately indicated by transitory measures of behavior change in a particular student or group of students who happen to be passing through a school at a point in time. Measures of educators' current actions to support students relative to what they once did, as well as measures of educators' confidence and competence in using behavioral support techniques (see Chapters 9, 10, and 11), may be more powerful indicators of genuine, positive change in a school's practices.

SCHOOLWIDE APPROACHES THAT ARE CONSISTENT WITH POSITIVE BEHAVIORAL SUPPORT

As indicated in Chapter 2, many innovative models for addressing learning and discipline concerns have appeared since the 1960s. The underlying assumptions, as well as the constellation and configuration of practices, often varied considerably across models; however, they were often intentionally designed to address the needs of all students rather than specific groups (e.g., students who are "at risk," are learning English as a second language, are in special education programs).

The models that were offered in Chapter 2 represented discipline approaches that could be used by individual classroom teachers and with individual students. In the 1980s and the 1990s, a number of models have emerged, some of which are versions of the models described in Chapter 2, that address disciplinary practices at the building level. Five approaches are detailed in this chapter: 1) democratic schools, 2) schoolwide behavior management systems, 3) caring schools, 4) conflict resolution schools, and 5) wraparound planning. Each approach is briefly described in terms of its definition and core values, illustrative practices, and outcomes. The major criteria for selection of a model were whether it is was a schoolwide approach that is potentially compatible with the tenets of positive behavioral support and whether it could seamlessly incorporate support practices within its overall framework.

Democratic Schools

The normative culture in democratic schools is not dictated by a small group of adults nor by an elite group of students; rather, it is consciously co-constructed by all members of the school in a dynamic process that occurs across time. Hence, students and adults alike experience ownership of the process and the outcomes. Sergiovanni stated that the key elements of democratic communities are "the standards, values, and commitments that make up a constitution for living together" (1994, p. 120). He contended that norms count more than rules in democratic communities. Schools that are configured as democratic communities offer a framework for students and adults to create their own standards for school behavior. Potentially, the democratic process can help the students meet their needs to belong, to be contributing members of a group, and to experience meaning in their lives.

Illustrative Practices   In practice, an inquiry process is often used in democratic schools to understand a challenging behavior. Thus, rather than an accusatory attitude or statement following a rule violation, a teacher in a democratic school would show respect for the student. Gathercoal stated that this is done "by asking leading questions and listening carefully" (1998, p. 207). This approach encourages students to find their own solutions to the underlying causes of their behavior and/or the social conflicts that provide the settings for problems. Educators respond to discipline problems in democratic schools by examining the disruptive event, the social contract (What are our commitments to each other, to the class, to the school?), the moral connection (How has the standard fallen?), and the natural or rational consequences to make things better. Finally, they revisit commitments (What are our commitments to each other and to this community?).

Outcomes   Outcome studies for democratic schools primarily consider dropout and suspension rates. At Kohn-Holweide, a West German school based on these tenets, only 1% of the students dropped out in 1988 as compared with the West German average of 14% (Sergiovanni, 1994). Nimmo (1998) assessed a judicious discipline model used in southern Minnesota schools and found notable positive effects. In one school, prior to the use of judicious discipline, there were as many as two or three in-school suspensions per day; "out-of-school suspensions were as high as one every other week" (p. 221). Following the implementation of judicious discipline, "a suspension was a rare event, used only with three students during the last school year" (p. 221). (See Chapter 2 in this book for more information on the judicious discipline model.)

Schoolwide Behavior Management Systems

A core value within schools that use schoolwide behavior management systems is that all students can succeed with appropriate interventions. School faculties that adopt a behavior management approach believe that support structures consisting of clear expectations and rules, instruction, and consistent consequences need to be in place to guide all students. Schoolwide behavior management systems then focus on the staff's consistent use of positive reinforcement for appropriate behaviors and consequences for violating the rules. These structures are then augmented by additional interventions for students who have more severe behavioral concerns (see Sugai, Sprague, et al., 2000).

Illustrative Practices   Most schoolwide behavior management approaches (e.g., Colvin, Kameenui, & Sugai, 1993; Rosenberg & Jackman, 1997) incorporate five common practices (ERIC/OSEP Special Project, 1997). First, there must be total staff commitment to the behavior management system that the school develops and implements. Inconsistencies in applications among staff can attenuate the effects of many practices. Second, as noted previously, a hallmark of these approaches is clearly defined and communicated expectations and rules. Third, the consequences for responding to behaviors that violate rules must be clear to all staff and students. Fourth, there is an emphasis on teaching social skills, both through natural opportunities and through direct instruction as needed. Fifth, specialized intervention plans and programs are used to address the needs of students who exhibit challenging behaviors that are not successfully addressed by in-place systems.

Outcomes   Typical measures of success within schoolwide behavior management systems are office referrals and suspensions. For example, findings from Project PREPARE, an instructional approach to managing behavior, revealed a 50% decrease in office referrals in the experimental school, as compared with a 12% increase in the control school after 1 year (Colvin et al., 1993). Taylor-Greene and colleagues (1997) showed that a schoolwide "opening day" training, coupled with a process for reinforcing appropriate behavior throughout the school year, resulted in a 42% reduction in office referrals when compared with the previous year. Rosenberg and Jackman (1997) reported on three middle schools that used Prevent, Act, and Resolve (PAR), a comprehensive behavior management model. These schools experienced reductions in office referrals and suspensions, ranging from 14% to 58%. In addition, in an interview by Brownell and Walther-Thomas (1999), Rosenberg reported that the teachers in these schools also felt less stress, greater collegiality, and more able to affect change in their classrooms.

Caring Schools: Child Development Project

The Child Development Project (Solomon, Schaps, Watson, & Battistich, 1992) is a prime example of the caring schools concept: Its underlying assumption is that schools must fulfill each child's basic psychological needs for belonging, competence, and autonomy. This classroom-based project for elementary schools emphasizes the core values of justice, tolerance, concern, and respect for others. The project stresses that these values are developed through direct, personal experience. That is, they cannot be decontextualized and taught in a class period devoted exclusively to values. Students must see school personnel intentionally reflect these values in their actions with students and with each other.

Illustrative Practices   The Child Development Project consists of five major elements: 1) a literature-based and value-oriented approach to reading instruction, 2) developmental discipline, 3) cooperative learning, 4) parent involvement, and 5) schoolwide activities (Watson, Battistich, & Solomon, 1997). Because it makes academics part of the support process, the Child Development Project's literature-based focus distinguishes it from most other schoolwide initiatives that are focused on behavioral issues. Carefully selected quality readings are used to portray certain values in literature (Lewis et al., 1996). Discussions of salient points help students ascertain the meaning and implications of the message, and educators use a variety of formats (e.g., drama, art) to elaborate on the understanding derived from the message.

Developmental discipline is directed at creating and maintaining a sense of community in the classroom and school. It encourages students to take an active role in classroom governance. For example, a sign titled "How we want our classroom to be" might be conspicuously posted in each room. Such a sign would be developed by teachers and students working together. In addition, the teachers and students collaboratively examine the impact that misbehavior has on others when problems occur, and they construct a teaching approach to problem resolution.

The Child Development Project uses cooperative learning to provide opportunities for students to practice interpersonal skills, to show respect for others, and to be concerned about one another's welfare. As noted in Chapter 3, cooperative learning strategies are particularly effective with heterogeneous groups (Stevens & Slavin, 1995). In another innovative technique that capitalizes on the value of heterogeneity, along with using reading partners from the same grade level, reading buddies across grade levels also take turns reading to one another and helping each other interpret what they have read (Viadero, 1994).

This model also has a parent involvement component. Its major purpose is to encourage warm and meaningful conversations between parents and their children. This is accomplished through family participation activities that are coordinated with the curriculum. Also, parents are represented on a "coordinating team" that plans schoolwide activities.

Finally schoolwide activities are designed to promote inclusion and the values of a caring community. Consider, for example, how activities are often designed in a typical school: There are often winners and losers (e.g., prizes at a science fair). In contrast, a caring school focuses on establishing and maintaining a sense of belonging; hence, activities are restructured to emphasize all students' strengths and gifts. For instance, each student's science fair contribution would be acknowledged for its particular and unique strengths.

Outcomes   Outcomes associated with the Child Development Project focus on a student's social and ethical development. In a multiyear, multisite research study, Battistich, Solomon, Watson, and Schaps (1997) found that the Child Development Project engendered a sense of community and that this positively affected students' social and ethical development. They also found some interesting associations, such as the following:

> Both student and teacher perceptions of community were positively associated with the frequency of class meetings, and negatively related to the use of extrinsic incentives. Students' sense of community also was strongly associated with the use of cooperative learning, and teacher's sense of community with the use of classroom activities to enhance interpersonal understanding. (p. 143)

Conflict Resolution Schools

Conflict resolution is a generic term that usually includes negotiation, mediation, and collaborative problem solving. Walker and Gresham (1997) identified schoolwide conflict resolution strategies as one of seven school-based protective factors (i.e., key characteristics of safe schools). The core premise of conflict resolution is that if schools are to be safe, orderly, and peaceful places to learn, then students must become skilled in managing conflicts constructively.

Illustrative Practices   Bodine and Crawford (1998) noted that school conflict resolution programs include

> (1) an understanding of conflict, (2) principles of conflict resolution (win-win, interest-based problem solving), (3) process steps in problem solving (for example, agreeing to negotiate and establishing ground rules for negotiation, gathering information about the conflict, explor-

ing possible solution options, selecting solution options, and reaching agreement), and (4) skills required to use each of the steps effectively (for example, active listening, reframing, understanding, and factoring into the process the impact that cultural differences have on the dispute). (p. xv)

Some of these programs also stress the use of an organized curriculum. *Teaching Students to be Peacemakers Program* (Johnson & Johnson, 1991), *Responding in Peaceful and Positive Ways (RIPP)* (Meyer & Northup, 1997), and *Resolving Conflict Creatively* (Lantieri & Patti, 1996) are three examples of school-based curricula for teaching conflict resolution skills to build positive and productive relationships among students. These programs concentrate on building a school culture that is a nonviolent learning community. For the interested reader, Bodine and Crawford (1998) offer an overview of other exemplary conflict resolution programs.

Outcomes   As of 1998, there were approximately 8,500 conflict resolution programs in public schools (Bodine & Crawford, 1998). Only some of these programs have been systematically examined. In one study, Johnson and Johnson (1996) reported on whether conflict resolution and peer mediation programs changed the strategies that students use to resolve their conflicts. They found that students' knowledge, retention, and application of negotiation strategies to resolve their conflicts consistently improved after training. Similarly, agreement (resolution) was reached in 80%–100% of the cases in which peer mediation was used. Johnson and Johnson made the important observation that this ability to manage conflicts improves relationships with others and prevents social isolation. Peer mediation schools also have been found to have a positive impact on resolving both school and home conflicts (Johnson, Johnson, Dudley, Ward, & Magnuson, 1995).

Wraparound Planning

According to Kutash and Duchnowski (1997), *wraparound planning* "is an overall approach that permits case managers to wrap services around the needs of children and families rather than requiring families to fit into existing services or programs" (p. 69). It has been widely used in gaining access to comprehensive, integrated services for children and their families (Eber & Nelson, 1997). The premise that drives wraparound planning is that all children's needs should be served in the least restrictive setting.

Illustrative Practices   Eber (1997) identified six key components of the wraparound process. These are 1) a focus on individual needs, 2) a family perspective, 3) the involvement of nontraditional participants, 4) focusing on strengths, 5) using one intervention plan across multiple life domains, and 6) team ownership of the plan. The LaGrange Area Department of Special Education Wraparound Project in Illinois (LADSE; Eber, 1996) exemplifies all of these characteristics. According to McLaughlin and colleagues, "LADSE merges individualized educational, mental health, health, social services, and juvenile justice support across multiple life domains, that is, in the student's natural family, school, and community settings" (1997, p. 18).

Representatives of public sector mental health, education, and social services; parents of children with behavioral challenges; and the children themselves are involved in intervention planning and implementation. The team reviews all aspects of a student's life: living situation, appropriate educational setting, needs for mental health services, and general health needs. Solid interagency cooperation and flexible funding practices are often necessary to provide the individualized constellation of services and supports.

Outcomes   Outcomes for wraparound planning have generally been evaluated by examining changes in placement. The Alaska Youth Initiative (Van Den Berg, 1993) is an early example of the wraparound approach. A shift was made so that youth who had previously been placed in residential, out-of-state treatment programs were served in less restrictive programs in Alaska. Eber and Nelson (1997) noted that, in Illinois, evaluation results of LADSE showed 1) children and youth making a successful transition from residential settings to their homes, while improving at school and in the community; 2) youngsters at risk for being placed outside their homes and neighborhood schools being effectively supported to prevent such moves; and 3) families reporting significant improvement in children's adaptability and high satisfaction at being included in decisions about how services are provided (p. 390).

SYNTHESIS: FIVE MOTIFS

This chapter has explored a variety of ways for schools to create a platform of practices that can be aligned with the principles of positive behavioral support. The chapter began by describing some general approaches that can be employed to effect change in a school community. These include developing and using schoolwide mission statements and discipline plans that are conducive to support values, professional development activities that involve educator collaboration, and systems change processes at the building and district levels. The chapter then examined five schoolwide models that, when implemented individually or in some combination, can provide a base for the emergence of positive behavioral support practices.

An examination of the building- and systems-level change approaches described in this chapter suggests five important motifs. These motifs, which are expressed in varying degrees within any given approach, offer clues into how building-level initiatives can contribute to positive change in schools. These motifs are 1) emphasis on community, 2) recruit and encourage student initiative and invite student participation, 3) use practices that are beneficial for all students, 4) ensure continuous and reciprocal modeling of values and practices, and 5) do not neglect academic learning.

Emphasis on community is a motif that runs through all of the approaches reviewed in this chapter. In his classic text, *Building Community in Schools*, Sergiovanni (1994) defined community as "collections of individuals who are bonded together by natural will and who are together binded to a set of shared ideas and ideals" (p. xvi). These "shared ideas and ideals" are sometimes called the school's core values, and Sergiovanni noted that "nothing is as powerful as the process that brings together the principal, staff, and parent community to reach consensus on the core values of a particular school" (p. 77). Cohesive communities can also be mobilized for unified action: Because the membership can link activities to shared values and perceptions, common purposes can emerge and be worked on by using the shared understandings as the foundation for progress. Conversely, the school that simply represents an aggregate of students and faculty who have no shared purpose nor authentic connections with each other is not a community, and such collective action for the common good is less likely to emerge. Also, as noted by Stainback and Stainback,

> [There is] growing empirical evidence that in schools where students and teachers do not establish friendships, commitments, and bonds with each other (i.e., where there is an absence of community), there are increased problems with underachievement, student

dropouts, drug abuse, exclusion of students with disabilities from the mainstream and gang activity. (1994, p. xxiv)

The change approaches that are described in this chapter share a second motif: They often *recruit and encourage student initiative and invite student participation*. This motif is consistent with a widely held belief that many of the discipline problems that plague schools could be reduced if students were allowed to participate more in decisions regarding their education and discipline. Curwin and Mendler found in their research on creating social contracts with students that "The more students are involved in the process of developing rules and consequences, the more they feel that the plan is a part of them. Ultimately, they will follow the plan if they had a say in its development" (1988, p. 52).

A third motif that is associated with a number of these change approaches is that schools should *use practices that are beneficial for all students*. Kamps and colleagues (1999) remarked that such practices are sometimes referred to as *universal interventions* because of their appeal for and applicability to all students, not just students who are described as being at risk or who have disabilities. Kamps and colleagues noted that universal interventions "promote both extended periods of appropriate social behavior with peers and high academic achievement" (p. 179). So-called "primary prevention strategies," which are intended to reduce the overall incidence of students with significant behavioral issues, are often universal interventions. This is because they are frequently designed to be applied with all students. For example, as McLaughlin and colleagues stated, "providing time during the school day to maximize the naturally occurring helping relationships between students and teachers" is a primary prevention strategy that also reflects the universal intervention concept (1997, p. 17).

The fourth shared motif is that schools need to *ensure ongoing, reciprocal modeling of values and practices* by adults with adults, adults with students, and students with students. There may be a place for discrete trial, direct instruction in the enhancement of social, academic, and behavioral skills; however, such instruction should augment embedded instruction within a variety of natural settings and never vice versa. It is the nesting of multiple observational learning and practice opportunities within the natural contexts of the general education community that provides the primary basis for both experiencing and assessing growth, whether the contexts are those of adults working with other adults to improve instruction or students working with other students to improve academic skills. Of course, what should be modeled is not just skills and values but also the gestalt of behaviors that define and constitute the notion of *community*. Nurturing and facilitating the development of these behaviors in individual learners helps ensure that each student will feel that he or she is a part of and a contributor to the school's broader membership. As Korinek, Walther-Thomas, McLaughlin, and Williams noted,

> Schools and classes where the most academic and social progress is being achieved are places where the adults assume responsibility for modeling and facilitating community among themselves and among their students at all levels. Community building requires direct instruction in prosocial behavior when needed, guided practice and feedback in natural situations, and meaningful student involvement in decision making. (1999, p. 4)

The final motif, *do not neglect academic learning*, is not as fully represented in these schoolwide approaches. Recall that this chapter opens with a reference to Chapter 1's discussion of the two primary functions of the schooling experience: enculturation and academics. Although it is conceptually useful, this dichotomy is troubling because it contributes to the view that these sets of experiences are independent of each other. From this point of view, a school can implement a schoolwide initiative that exclusively focuses on social and behavioral expectations, and this will enhance the enculturation experiences of students. As shown in Chapter 3, however, academic participation is an intricate part of the enculturation process, contributing to how students define their social affiliation choices and themselves as students. Hence, academics cannot be disregarded in efforts to reduce discipline problems precisely because the perspectives of "self" and "others" that students adopt for themselves and others are shaped by their access to and participation in the information resources that the school community values. A school fails to address the heart of the problem when it adopts an initiative that focuses on social and behavioral concerns while protecting and cherishing course and program offerings that exclude and segregate students based on presumed ability levels. Such an initiative may produce results that at first seem encouraging. Yet, the chronic, underlying malevolence that is inherent to such inequities ensures that the problems will resurface.

As a final comment, it is worth bearing in mind that schools that reflect in some profound sense the principles and values of both good teaching practices and positive behavioral support do not accomplish this feat overnight. Rather, a deliberate and concerted effort by many individuals over the course of years is required. Chapman and Hofweber (2000) reported, for example, that it can take 3–5 years for positive behavioral support to become fully operational in a school. Reaching the critical mass that is required to turn the corner from traditional to support practices requires efforts from many individuals at all levels within a school building. Whether it is the special educator's designing a solution-focused plan for a student (Chapter 10), a classroom teacher's reflecting on her practices in relation to instruction (Chapters 3 and 9), or a school faculty's agreeing to adopt a conflict resolution model for students (this chapter), each effort contributes to the shifts in practices that can make positive behavioral support a reality for a diverse range of students in upcoming generations.

Epilogue

Positive behavioral support emphasizes the merger of promising instructional practices with proactive and thoughtful disciplinary practices such that all students have the opportunity to participate in the academic curriculum and socialization experiences of their schools. The purpose of this book has been to detail the principles, processes, and outcomes of this perspective so that students and practitioners can 1) compare and contrast positive behavioral support practices with present-day classroom- and school-based instructional and discipline practices and 2) implement support practices with individuals and groups of students. It has also been stressed that effective and humane behavioral interventions are only possible when educators deliberately construct understandings of how contextual, social, affective, and experiential variables affect the responses of students and adults when there are behaviors that are in conflict with the values and expectations of their schools. This requires diligent and ongoing reflective inquiry activities in which good questions are posed to properly orient the search for useful solutions.

Throughout this book, the presentation of support concepts has been embedded within discussions of theoretical perspectives from the social and behavioral sciences. An understanding of how positive behavioral support is related to broader principles of learning, instructional design, interpersonal development, and emotional well-being allows an educator to productively address behavioral concerns that arise in situations in which there is little precedence for developing solutions.

In addition, no attempt has been made to distinguish practice issues from values issues. In fact, by example and by comparison, values such as human dignity have been woven into the discussion of practices. The bottom line is this: When answers to behavioral concerns are not straightforward or immediately forthcoming, an educator who respects, cherishes, and listens to his or her students will search for solutions that are minimally intrusive and that open rather than close doors. The lack of such a

303

grounding, however, diminishes the likelihood that an educator will arrive at solutions of a similar quality.

At this juncture, an adage comes to mind that has been informally expressed by many educators and occasionally shows up in the literature (Dwyer et al., 2000): *Do no harm*. Of course, there are times when the rights of the individual student and the common welfare of others come into conflict (see Chapter 4), and implementing a "do no harm" approach is a challenge under these circumstances. Yet, experience suggests that these kinds of compromises will not be required for the majority of students with behavioral concerns, including many who are served by special education, if educators implement positive behavioral support practices in their teaching, planning, assessment, prevention, routine support, and more intense interventions. Put differently, it is our belief that positive behavioral support provides a framework in which "do no harm" can find greater expression in educators' routine behavioral interventions.

In this epilogue, we offer some personal observations and thoughts that we hope will contribute to a roadmap for a future in which "do no harm" can find wider expression with children and youth with challenging behaviors. In this brief treatise, we propose that there is a need for a different focus in the sciences (e.g., psychology) that have traditionally defined how students with behavioral issues are perceived and how their needs are defined. We suggest that the education field has reached the point where it can clearly recognize that the medical model plays too important of a role in educational decision making and that its application can sometimes be deleterious to the well-being of those it was intended to serve.

CREATING A POSITIVE SOCIAL SCIENCE

In reflecting on their decade-long research into school reform and detracking, Oakes, Quartz, Ryan, and Lipton (2000) reiterated the imperative for creating schools that strive toward "civic virtue" and the expression of democratic ideals. They note that schools frequently struggle and are often unsuccessful in their efforts to create atmospheres that are "more deeply educative, socially just, caring, and participatory" (p. xv). These researchers offered the insight that approaching the change process from a reform perspective is often problematic in and of itself; it tends to focus people's attention on fixing unfair processes rather than on achieving positive outcomes. Oakes and colleagues offered the term *betterment* as an alternative to the concept of *reform*.

We have asserted in this book that broad changes are clearly needed in practices that are related to students with behavioral concerns. Efforts to resolve behavioral concerns through child-change interventions will likely fall on barren soil when compliance is the overarching objective, when glaring inequities in educational access exist, when certain students are viewed as being "deserving" while others are not, and when certain students consistently experience arbitrary and unfair applications of discipline codes (see Hartman & Stage, 2000; Shores, Gunter, & Jack, 1993; Smith, 2000). Given Oakes and colleagues' (2000) assessment of the results of tracking reforms, we are inclined to believe that the ideals of positive behavioral support are more likely to thrive in environments in which educators seek betterment rather than reform in their efforts to serve students with behavioral concerns. Moreover, it makes sense to view positive behavioral support as an ideal state that can never be fully reached; however, any and all schools can become better places for children and youth through the deliberate efforts of educators to use practices consistent with these principles. For this to happen, educators who serve a variety of functions—teachers, administrators, psychologists, counselors—must be able to "read" the baseline socio-cultural conditions of their school and juxtapose this information with assessment information on behavioral concerns for specific students. Then, they must generate procedures and practices that can best meet student needs while realistically acknowledging constraints that are inherent within a school's culture and structure. From this perspective, the successful practitioner is one who, given his or her position within the school community, can stretch the practices of the school just far enough to make differences in the lives of students who challenge the system but does so without adversely affecting either the students or the adults.

Most social sciences research studies that address challenging behaviors do not inquire about the foregoing processes, and these are the studies that often influence how educators define their responsibilities and construct their practices. Part of the reason for this lies in how the social sciences have defined their subject matter over the years. Seligman argued that the social sciences are marked by a "relentless focus on the negative" (1999, p. 181) and that this focus tends to misrepresent many social and psychological phenomena. Referring to what he called "remedial science," Seligman's comments suggested that the social sciences have focused largely on individual human deficits and that much of the research has centered on how these deficits can be overcome or corrected. In an interesting discussion of the future of the social sciences, Seligman called for the creation of a positive social science that would, at the individual level, take on "the delineation, measurement and promotion of human fulfillment and will" as its mission and, at the group level, view "civic virtue as its proper subject matter" (p. 182).

Consistent with Seligman (1999), we believe in the promise associated with creating a positive social science. The shift in orientation that such a science would engender could generate a base of research that is solution oriented and explores in depth how the positive qualities of both practitioners and students can be used when seeking betterment in schools and school practices. The revised paradigm shown in Chapter 3 offers one model that some social scientists may want to consider when rethinking their subject matter. Recall that the commonly used paradigm assigns causality in human performance largely to traits and properties that are within the learner. In contrast, in the revised paradigm, traits and properties within the learner are reformulated so that their causal contributions to performance are more distributed and less fixed, and social/contextual variables are given greater latitude as determinants of performance.

WIDE AWAKENESS

In our final comments, we borrow Greene's (1978) concept of *wide awakeness*. In our use of this term, we are referring to the idea that educators should continuously reflect on the impact and implications of their placement and instructional decisions, and this involves deliberately examining the theories and models that guide practices. As noted in previous chapters, the medical model has influenced how those who are concerned with problem behaviors place and instruct students. The application of the medical model often begins with diagnosis, which may then lead to assigning a label to a student that is based on behavioral traits and characteristics. The label could then be used to define student learning needs and delineate educational service requirements.

Labels can be viewed as beneficial because they can provide access to special education, and we are not questioning the potential value of this for students who need additional academic or behavioral supports. We also note that behavioral concerns can sometimes be linked to known medical conditions and that there are times when this information anticipates useful medications, dietary regimens, or precautions in treatment. As shown by Ryan (1996, 1999, 2000), this information can sometimes be helpful in designing educational supports.

What we are asking the education field to deeply question, however, is using labels such as emotional/behavioral disorders (EBD), attention-deficit/hyperactivity disorder (ADHD), or autism when a school team makes life-altering decisions about which educational experiences will or will not be provided to a particular student. Our concerns are similar to those raised by Kutchins and Kirk (1997) regarding the use of labels from the *Diagnostic and Statistical Manual of Mental Disorders, Fourth Edition* (DSM-IV; 1994) in the mental health professions. Do the educational benefits of using a label to guide specialized educational experiences outweigh the misuses and misapplications of labels given the structures and politics of schools? Has application of a diagnostic label blinded educators to individual characteristics of a learner that would have provided better guidance for educational decision making? When benefits are found for a specialized experience, is there clear evidence that the same benefits could not have been realized by using less restrictive general education procedures, perhaps with accommodations and modifications? Is the specialized experience that seems beneficial to a labeled group of children only beneficial for those children, or has something more universal been uncovered?

The precautionary principle from the physical and environmental sciences is applicable to the use of disability categories in educational decision making (Foster, Vecchia, & Repacholi, 2000). In its strongest form, the principle states that developing technologies for emerging needs or problems in a field should not be implemented whenever there are potential or proven risks for "adverse affects" (Foster et al., 2000, p. 979). For example, a new medication for treating a particular disease should not be released until it has been adequately tested for both authentic benefits and potential unintended side effects.

Educational decision-making activities that are linked to labeling should be held to this same standard. A disability classification characterizes a group of students as being distinct and different from so-called typical students. Ostensibly, this is for the purpose of enhancing students' educational experiences, but risks can be associated with such enhancements. Subfields of specialists have emerged in education to provide these enhancements. These specialists promote different educational placements, pedagogies, and definitions of needs for individuals with a given label. This can have the unintended effect of isolating and estranging these students from other students with whom association and affiliation could be reciprocally beneficial. In addition, because the students themselves have little voice in determining what is done, there is the risk that specialized techniques will have adverse affects. People who have worked in institutions for people with developmental disabilities may recall the introduction of overcorrection techniques. These techniques were broadly endorsed and applied with little consideration as to whether they were socially acceptable, whether they were really necessary, or what impact they had on the recipients' emotional well-being. R. Ryan (personal communication, January 10, 2001) noted that approximately 85% of the 4,000 people with developmental disabilities who have been served in her behavioral pharmacology clinics as of January 2001 experienced serious life traumas and/or abuse, some of it as part of their educational and/or residential programs.

Kutchins and Kirk stated that one of the problems with diagnostic categories in mental health is how they pathologize "everyday behaviors" and sweep "increasing numbers of human problems into the realm of psychiatric disorders and medical jurisdiction" (1997, p. 16). Similarly, Brennan (1995) described how patients who have serious illnesses and are elderly are at risk for being reduced to "diseased entities" and are subject to the absence of treatment, "pawning off on someone else," and "other forms of abuse" (p. 195).

These concerns should become part of the discussions among and between teachers, behavior specialists, university faculty members, administrators, and researchers. The education field's reliance on labeling continues to spawn the creation of ever more labels, and the presence of specialized services based on disability categories promotes everything from benign neglect by general educators who feel unprepared, to "technical assistance" in methodologies with little empirical backing, to the unexamined placement of students with particular labels in special programs. Brennan (1995) suggested that a "lexicon of esteem" should be developed to help professionals better treat the individuals whom they serve, especially children and youth who will be under their care and tutelage for long and formative periods of their lives.

These concerns speak to the importance of Seligman's (1999) positive social science. Given its focus on the individual, the development of such a science could encourage educators and families to exercise greater prudence when considering whether information derived from a label is really helpful. In addition, with its emphasis on valued outcomes, the science described by Seligman could emphasize educators' rethinking how educational experiences are designed and implemented. In turn, this could help education teams enhance the opportunities that are provided to all students in natural classroom communities.

As expressed throughout this book, positive behavioral support can be a force for nurturing and transforming both educational practice and the science of human behavior. In the continuing evolution of a theoretical structure and a set of values for positive behavioral support, it is important to see this work as embedded in a broader, diverse collection of works (e.g., Carr, 1997; Freiberg, 1999; Horner et al., 1990; Koegel, Koegel, & Dunlap, 1996; Kohn, 1996; Kunc, 1996; Lovett, 1996; Scotti & Meyer, 1999; Turnbull & Turnbull, 2000), each contributing in unique and important ways to the development of a rich discourse of support. As teacher educators, our hope is echoed in these words that are attributed to Archbishop Oscar Romero:

This is what we are about:
We plant seeds that one day will grow.
We water seeds already planted, knowing that they hold future promise.
We lay foundations that will need further development.

References

Achenbaum, W.A. (1998). The social compact in American history. *Generations: Journal of the American Society on Aging, 22*(4), 15–18.

Alberto, P.A., & Troutman, A.C. (1999). *Applied behavior analysis for teachers* (5th ed.). Columbus, OH: Merrill.

Albin, R.W., Lucyshyn, J.M., Horner, R.H., & Flannery, K.B. (1996). Contextual fit for behavioral support plans: A model for "goodness of fit." In L.K. Koegel, R.L. Koegel, & G. Dunlap (Eds.), *Positive behavioral support: Including people with difficult behavior in the community* (pp. 81–98). Baltimore: Paul H. Brookes Publishing Co.

Albrecht, G.L. (1992). *The disability business: Rehabilitation in America.* Thousand Oaks, CA: Sage Publications.

Alexander, P.A., Murphy, P. K., & Woods, B.S. (1996). Of squalls and fathoms: Navigating the seas of educational innovation. *Educational Researcher, 25*(3), 31–36.

Allen, L.C., Gottselig, M., & Boylan, S. (1982). A practical mechanism for using free time as a reinforcer in classrooms. *Education and Treatment of Children, 5,* 347–353.

American Psychiatric Association. (1994). *Diagnostic and statistical manual of mental disorders* (4th ed.). Washington, DC: Author.

Anderson, C.M., Bahl, A.B., & Kincaid, D.W. (1999). A person-centered approach to providing support to an adolescent with a history of parental abuse. In J.R. Scotti & L.H. Meyer (Eds.), *Behavioral intervention: Principles, models, and practices* (pp. 385–396). Baltimore: Paul H. Brookes Publishing Co.

Anderson, P.L. (2000). Using literature to teach social skills to adolescents with LD. *Intervention in School and Clinic, 35,* 271–279.

Aoki, D.S. (2000). The thing never speaks for itself: Lacan and the pedagogical politics of clarity. *Harvard Educational Review, 70,* 347–369.

Apple, M.W., & Beane, J.A. (Eds.). (1995). *Democratic schools.* Alexandria, VA: Association for Supervision and Curriculum Development.

Arlow, J.A. (1989). Psychoanalysis. In R.J. Corsini & D. Wedding (Eds.), *Current psychotherapies* (pp. 19–62). Itasca, IL: F.E. Peacock.

Armstrong, T. (1994). *Multiple intelligences in the classroom.* Alexandria, VA: Association for Supervision and Curriculum Development.

Aronson, E., Blaney, N., Stephan, C., Sikes, J., & Snapp, M. (1978). *The jigsaw classroom.* Thousand Oaks, CA: Sage Publications.

Astor, R.A., Meyer, H.A., & Behre, W.J. (1999). Unowned places and times: Maps and interviews about violence in high schools. *American Educational Research Journal, 36,* 3–42.

Au, K.H. (1997). Changing views of literacy instruction and teacher development. *Teacher Education and Special Education, 20,* 74–82.

Ayers, W. (1993). *To teach: The journey of a teacher.* New York: Teachers College Press.

Ayres, B., Hedeen, D., & Meyer, L. (1996, November). *A collaborative approach to creating positive behaviors.* Paper presented at the Annual Conference of The Association for Persons with Severe Handicaps, New Orleans, LA.

Bachman, J.E., & Fuqua, R.W. (1983). Management of inappropriate behaviors of trainable mentally impaired students using antecedent exercise. *Journal of Applied Behavior Analysis, 16,* 477–484.

Baer, D.M., Wolf, M.M., & Risley, T.R. (1968). Some current dimensions of applied behavior analysis. *Journal of Applied Behavior Analysis, 1,* 91–97.

Bahr, M.W., Whitten, E., Dieker, L., Kocarek, C.E., & Manson, D. (1999). A comparison of school-based intervention teams: Implications for educational and legal reform. *Exceptional Children, 66,* 67–84.

Baker, B. (1999). What is voice? Issues of identity and representation in the framing of review. *Review of Educational Research, 69,* 365–383.

Ball, E.W. (1997). Phonological awareness: Implications for whole language and emergent literacy programs. *Topics in Language Disorders, 17*(3), 14–26.

Bambara, L., & Knoster, T. (1998). *Designing positive behavior support plans.* Washington, DC: American Association on Mental Retardation.

Bambara, L.M., Koger, F., Katzer, T., & Davenport, T.A. (1995). Embedding choice in the context of daily routines: An experimental case study. *Journal of The Association for Persons with Severe Handicaps, 20,* 185–195.

Bandura, A. (1963). *Social learning and personality development.* Austin, TX: Holt, Rinehart & Winston.

Banks, J.A. (2000). The social construction of difference and the quest for educational equality. In R.S. Brandt (Ed.), *Education in a new era* (pp. 21–45). Alexandria, VA: Association for Supervision and Curriculum Development.

Barker, R.G. (1968). *Ecological psychology: Concepts and methods for studying the environment of human behavior.* Stanford, CA: Stanford University Press.

Barkley, R., Copeland, A., & Sivage, C. (1980). A self-control classroom for hyperactive children. *Journal of Autism and Developmental Disorders, 10,* 75–89.

Barr, R.D., & Parrett, W.H. (1995). *Hope at last for at-risk youth.* Needham Heights, MA: Allyn & Bacon.

Barth, R.S. (1990). *Improving schools from within* (2nd ed.). San Francisco: Jossey-Bass.

Bartoli, J.S. (1995). *Unequal opportunity: Learning to read in the U.S.A.* New York: Teachers College Press.

Battistich, V., Solomon, D., Watson, M., & Schaps, E. (1997). Caring school communities. *Educational Psychologist, 32,* 137–151.

Beardsley, T. (1992). Desert dynamics. *Scientific American, 267*(5), 32–36.

Beck, A. (1970). Cognitive therapy: Nature and relation to behavior therapy. *Behavior Therapy, 1,* 184–200.

Bijou, S.W. (1968). The mentally retarded child. *Psychology Today, 1,* 47–51.

Bijou, S.W., Peterson, R.F., & Ault, M.H. (1968). A method to integrate descriptive and experimental field studies at the level of data and empirical concepts. *Journal of Applied Behavior Analysis, 1,* 175–191.

Bishop, K.D., & Jubala, K.A. (1995). Positive behavior support. In M.A. Falvey (Ed.), *Inclusive and heterogeneous schooling: Assessment, curriculum, and instruction* (pp. 159–186). Baltimore: Paul H. Brookes Publishing Co.

Blair, K.C., Umbreit, J., & Bos, C.S. (1999). Using functional assessment and children's preferences to improve the behavior of young children with behavioral disorders. *Behavioral Disorders, 24,* 151–166.

Blatt, B. (1999). The controversies. In S. J. Taylor, S.D. Blatt, & D.L. Braddock (Eds.), *In search of the promised land: The collected papers of Burton Blatt* (pp. 105–119). Washington, DC: American Association on Mental Retardation.

Blatt, B., & Kaplan, F. (1996). *Christmas in purgatory.* Needham Heights, MA: Allyn & Bacon.

Blumstein, A. (2000). Violence: A new frontier for scientific research. *Science, 289,* 545.

Bodine, R.J., & Crawford, D.K. (1998). *The handbook of conflict resolution education.* San Francisco: Jossey-Bass.

Boggeman, S., Hoerr, T., & Wallach, C. (1996). *Succeeding with multiple intelligences: Teaching through the personal intelligences.* St. Louis, MO: The New City School.

Braddock, J.H., & Slavin, R.E. (1995). Why ability grouping must end: Achieving excellence and equity in American education. In H. Pool & J.A. Page (Eds.), *Beyond tracking: Finding success in inclusive schools* (pp. 7–19). Bloomington, IN: Phi Delta Kappa Educational Foundation.

Brendtro, L.K., Brokenleg, M., & van Bockern, S.V. (1990). *Reclaiming youth at risk: Our hope for the future*. Bloomington, IN: National Education Services.

Brennan, W. (1995). *Dehumanizing the vulnerable: When word games take lives*. Chicago: Loyola Press.

Briggs, D. (1996). Turning conflicts into learning experiences. *Educational Leadership, 54*(1), 60–63.

Broden, M., Hall, R.V., & Mitts, B. (1971). The effect of self-recording on the classroom behavior of two eighth-grade students. *Journal of Applied Behavior Analysis, 4*, 191–199.

Bronfenbrenner, U. (1979). *The ecology of human development: Experiments by nature and by design*. Cambridge, MA: Harvard University Press.

Browder, D.M. (1991). *Assessment of individuals with severe disabilities: An applied behavior approach to life skills assessment* (2nd ed.). Baltimore: Paul H. Brookes Publishing Co.

Brown v. Board of Education, 347 U.S. 483 (1954).

Brown, F. (1991). Creative daily scheduling: A nonintrusive approach to challenging behaviors in community residences. *Journal of The Association for Persons with Severe Handicaps, 16*, 75–84.

Brown, F. (1996). Variables to consider in the assessment of problem behaviors. *TASH Newsletter, 22*(7), 19–20.

Brown, F., Pitz, L., Rosen, F., & Velez, J. (1997, December). *From contingent electric shock to community living: One man's story*. Paper presented at the Annual Conference of The Association for Persons with Severe Handicaps, Boston.

Brown, P., & Levinson, S. (1978). Universals in language usage: Politeness phenomena. In E.N. Goody (Ed.), *Questions and politeness: Strategies in social interaction*. New York: Cambridge University Press.

Brown, W.E. (1988). Policies/practices in public school discipline. *Academic Therapy, 23*, 298–301.

Brownell, M.T., & Walther-Thomas, C. (1999). An interview with Dr. Michael Rosenberg: Preventing school discipline problems schoolwide. *Intervention in School and Clinic, 35*, 108–112.

Buck, G.H., Polloway, E.A., Kirkpatrick, M.A., Patton, J.R., & Fad, K.M. (2000). Developing behavioral intervention plans: A sequential approach. *Intervention in School and Clinic, 36*(1), 3–9.

Budoff, M. (1992). Engendering change in special education practices. In T. Hehir & T. Latus (Eds.), Special education at the century's end: Evolution in theory and practice since 1970 [Special issue]. *Harvard Educational Review*, 69–87.

Buras, K.L. (1999). Questioning core assumptions: A critical reading of and response to E.D. Hirsch's *The schools we need and why we don't have them*. *Harvard Educational Review, 69*, 67–93.

Butchart, R.E., & McEwan, B. (Eds.). (1998). *Classroom discipline in American schools: Problems and possibilities for democratic education*. Albany: State University of New York Press.

Butterworth, J., Hagner, D., Heikkinen, B., De Mello, S., & McDonough, K. (1993). *Whole life planning: A guide for organizers and facilitators*. Boston: Children's Hospital, Institute for Community Inclusion.

Cabral, A., & Salomone, P. (1990). Chance and careers: Normative versus contextual development. *Career Development Quarterly, 39*, 5–17.

Caine, R.N., & Caine, G. (1994). *Making connections: Teaching and the human brain*. Menlo Park, CA: Innovative Learning Publications.

Calculator, S.N., & Jorgensen, C.M. (1991). Integrating AAC instruction into regular education settings: Expounding on best practices. *Augmentative and Alternative Communication, 7*, 204–220.

Calhoun, E.F. (1994). *How to use action research in the self-renewing school*. Alexandria, VA: Association for Supervision and Curriculum Development.

Calne, D.B. (1999). *Within reason: Rationality and human behavior*. New York: Pantheon Books.

Cambone, J. (1995). Rethinking how we think about troubled children. *Journal of Emotional and Behavioral Problems, 3*, 12–14.

Campbell, L., Campbell, B., & Dickinson D. (1996). *Teaching and learning through multiple intelligences*. Needham Heights, MA: Allyn & Bacon.

Carr, E.G. (1977). The motivation of self-injurious behavior: A review of some hypotheses. *Psychological Bulletin, 84*, 800–816.

Carr, E.G. (1994). Emerging themes in the functional analysis of problem behavior. *Journal of Applied Behavior Analysis, 27,* 393–399.

Carr, E.G. (1997). The evolution of applied behavior analysis into positive behavioral support. *Journal of The Association for Persons with Severe Handicaps, 22,* 208–209.

Carr, E.G., Carlson, J.I., Langdon, N.A., Magito-McLaughlin, D., & Yarbrough, S.C. (1998). Two perspectives on antecedent control: Molecular and molar. In J.K. Luiselli & M.J. Cameron (Eds.), *Antecedent control: Innovative approaches to behavioral support* (pp. 3–28). Baltimore: Paul H. Brookes Publishing Co.

Carr, E.G., Horner, R., Turnbull, A.P., Marquis, J.G., McLaughlin, D.M., McAtee, M.L., Smith, C.E., Ryan, K.A., Ruef, M.B., & Doolabh, A., (1999). *Positive behavioral support for people with developmental disabilities: A research synthesis.* Washington, DC: American Association on Mental Retardation.

Carr, E.G., Langdon, N.A., & Yarbrough, S.C. (1999). Hypothesis-based intervention for severe problem behavior. In A.C. Repp & R.H. Horner (Eds.), *Functional analysis of problem behavior* (pp. 9–31). Belmont, CA: Wadsworth.

Carr, E.G., Levin, L., McConnachie, G., Carlson, J.I., Kemp, D.C., & Smith, C.E. (1994). *Communication-based intervention for problem behavior: A user's guide for producing positive change.* Baltimore: Paul H. Brookes Publishing Co.

Carr, E.G., Newsom, C.D., & Binkoff, J.A. (1980). Escape as a factor in the aggressive behavior of two retarded children. *Journal of Applied Behavior Analysis, 13,* 101–117.

Carr, E.G., Robinson, S., Taylor, J.C., & Carlson, J.I. (1990). Positive approaches to the treatment of severe behavior problems in persons with developmental disabilities: A review and analysis of reinforcement and stimulus-based procedures. *Monograph of The Association for Persons with Severe Handicaps.* Baltimore: The Association for Persons with Severe Handicaps.

Carr, E.G., Taylor, J., & Robinson, S. (1991). The effects of severe behavior problems in children on the teaching behavior of adults. *Journal of Applied Behavior Analysis, 24,* 523–535.

Carr, E.G., Turnbull, A., & Turnbull, H.R. (1997, May). *Positive behavioral support for students with challenging behavior: Research synthesis and practice/policy enhancement.* New York: American Association on Mental Retardation.

Casti, J.L. (1990). *Searching for certainty: What scientists can know about the future.* New York: William Morrow.

Chapman, D., & Hofweber, C. (2000). Effective behavior support in British Columbia. *Journal of Positive Behavior Interventions, 2,* 235–237.

Clarke, S., Dunlap, G., Foster-Johnson, L., Childs, K.E., Wilson, D., White, R., & Vera, A. (1995). Improving the conduct of students with behavioral disorders by incorporating student interests into curricular activities. *Behavioral Disorders, 20,* 221–237.

Cohen, L.G., & Spenciner, L.J. (1998). *Assessment of children and youth.* New York: Longman.

Coleman, M.C. (1992). *Behavior disorders: Theory and practice.* Needham Heights, MA: Allyn & Bacon.

Colvin, G., Ainge, D., & Nelson, R. (1997). How to defuse defiance, threats, challenges, confrontation. *Teaching Exceptional Children, 29,* 47–51.

Colvin, G., Kameenui, E.J., & Sugai, G. (1993). Reconceptualizing behavior management and school-wide discipline in general education. *Education and Treatment of Children, 16,* 361–381.

Colvin, G., Sugai, G., Good, R.H., & Lee, Y. (1997). Using active supervision and precorrection to improve transition behaviors in an elementary school. *School Psychology Quarterly, 12,* 344–363.

Coulter, D. (1996). Prevention as a form of support: Implications of the new definition. *Mental Retardation, 34,* 108–116.

Covey, S. (1989). *The 7 habits of highly effective people.* New York: Simon & Schuster.

Covington, M.V. (1996). The myth of intensification. *Educational Researcher, 25*(8), 24–27.

Crafton, L. (1994). *Challenges of holistic teaching: Answering the tough questions.* Norwood, MA: Christopher-Gordon Publishers.

Cramer, S.F. (1998). *Collaboration: A success strategy for special educators.* Needham Heights, MA: Allyn & Bacon.

Crutchfield, J.P., Farmer, J.D., Packard, N.H., & Shaw, R.S. (1986). Chaos. *Scientific American, 255*(6), 46–57.

Curwin, R.L., & Mendler, A.N. (1988). *Discipline with dignity.* Alexandria, VA: Association for Supervision and Curriculum Development.

Daniels, V.I. (1998). How to manage disruptive behavior in inclusive classrooms. *Teaching Exceptional Children, 30*(4), 26–31.

Darling-Hammond, L. (1996). The right to learn and the advancement of teaching: Research, policy, and practice for democratic education. *Educational Researcher, 25*(6), 5–17.

Demchak, M. (1993). Functional assessment of problem behaviors in applied settings. *Intervention in School and Clinic, 29*, 89–95.

Deming, W.E. (1986). *Out of the crisis.* Cambridge, MA: The MIT Press.

Derby, K.M., Fisher, W.W., & Piazza, C.C. (1996). The effects of contingent and noncontingent attention on self-injury and self-restraint. *Journal of Applied Behavior Analysis, 29*, 107–110.

Dewey, J. (1938). *Experience and education.* New York: Collier Books.

Didden, R., Duker, P.C., & Korzilius, H. (1997). Meta-analytic study on treatment effectiveness for problem behaviors with individuals who have mental retardation. *American Journal on Mental Retardation, 101*, 387–399.

Docking, J.W. (1980). *Control and discipline in schools: Perspectives and approaches.* New York: Harper & Row.

Donnellan, A.M., Mirenda, P.L., Mesaros, R.A., & Fassbender, L.L. (1984). Analyzing the communicative functions of aberrant behavior. *Journal of The Association for Persons with Severe Handicaps, 9*, 201–212.

Dörner, D. (1996). *The logic of failure: Recognizing and avoiding error in complex situations* (R. Kimber & R. Kimber, Trans.). Cambridge, MA: Perseus Books.

Dreikurs, R. (1968). *Psychology in the classroom: A manual for teachers* (2nd ed.). New York: Harper & Row.

Duchnowski, A.J. (2000). Improving family support: An agenda for the next decade. *Journal of Positive Behavior Interventions, 2*, 117–118.

Dunlap, G., & Childs, K.E. (1996). Intervention research in emotional and behavioral disorders: An analysis of studies from 1980–1993. *Behavioral Disorders, 21*, 125–136.

Dunlap, G., Hieneman, M., Knoster, T., Fox, L., Anderson, J., & Albin, R.W. (2000). Essential elements of inservice training in positive behavior support. *Journal of Positive Behavior Interventions, 2*, 22–32.

Dunlap, G., Kern, L., dePerczel, M., Clarke, S., Wilson, D., Childs, K.E., White, R., & Falk, G.D. (1993). Functional analysis of classroom variables for students with emotional and behavioral challenges. *Behavior Disorders, 18*, 275–291.

Dunlap, L.K., Dunlap, G., Koegel, L.K., & Koegel, R.L. (1991). Using self-monitoring to increase independence. *Teaching Exceptional Children, 23*(3), 17–22.

DuPaul, G.J., Ervin, R.A., Hook, C.L., & McGoey, K.E. (1998). Peer tutoring for children with attention deficit hyperactivity disorder: Effects on classroom behavior and academic performance. *Journal of Applied Behavior Analysis, 31*, 579–592.

Durand, V.M. (1990). *Severe behavior problems: A functional communication training approach.* New York: The Guilford Press.

Durrant, M. (1995). *Creative strategies for school problems: Solutions for psychologists and teachers.* New York: W.W. Norton & Company.

Dworkin, R. (2000). *Sovereign virtue: The theory and practice of equality.* Cambridge, MA: Harvard University Press.

Dwyer, K., & Osher, D. (2000). *Safeguarding our children: An action guide.* Washington, DC: U.S. Departments of Education and Justice, American Institutes for Research.

Dwyer, K.P., Osher, D., & Hoffman, C.C. (2000). Creating responsive schools: Early warning, timely response. *Exceptional Children, 66*, 347–365.

Dwyer, K., Osher, D., & Warger, C. (1998). *Early warning, timely response: A guide to safe schools.* Washingon, DC: U.S. Departments of Education and Justice.

D'Zurilla, T.J., & Goldfried, M.R. (1971). Problem solving and behavior modification. *Journal of Abnormal Psychology, 78*, 107–126.

Eber, L. (1996). Restructuring schools through the wraparound approach. The LADSE experience. *Special Services in the Schools, 11*(1/2), 135–149.

Eber, L., (1997). Improving school-based behavioral interventions through use of the wraparound process. *Reaching Today's Youth. 1*, 32–36.

Eber, L., & Nelson, C.M. (1997). School-based wraparound planning: Integrating services for students with emotional and behavioral needs. *American Journal of Orthopsychiatry, 67*, 385–395.

Edmundson, M. (1999). Psychoanalysis, American style: A review of L. J. Friedman's, *Identity's architect: A biography of Eric Erikson. New York Times Book Review, 104*(34), 11.

Education for All Handicapped Children Act of 1975, PL 94-142, 20 U.S.C. §§1400 *et seq.*

Edyburn, D.L. (Ed.). (1997). The changing roles of special educators [Special issue]. *Teaching Exceptional Children, 30*(2).

Ellis, A. (1984). *Rational-emotive therapy and cognitive behavior therapy.* New York: Springer.

Elmore, R.F. (1996). Getting to scale with good educational practice. *Harvard Educational Review, 66,* 1–26.

Englert, C.S., & Palincsar, A.S. (1991). Reconsidering instructional research in literacy from a sociocultural perspective. *Learning Disabilities Research and Practice, 6,* 225–229.

Epstein, J.L. (1995). School/family/community partnerships: Caring for the children we share. *Phi Delta Kappan, 21,* 701–712.

ERIC/OSEP Special Project. (Fall, 1997). *School-wide behavioral management systems* (Research Connections in Special Education, No. 1). Reston, VA: The ERIC Clearinghouse on Disabilities and Gifted Education.

Erikson, E. (1963). *Childhood and society* (2nd ed.). New York: W.W. Norton & Company.

Etscheidt, S. (1991). Reducing aggressive behavior and improving self-control: A cognitive-behavioral training program for behaviorally disordered adolescents. *Behavior Disorders, 16,* 107–115.

Evans, E.D., & Richardson, R.C. (1995). Corporal punishment: What teachers should know. *Teaching Exceptional Children, 27,* 33–36.

Evans, I.M., Scotti, J.R., & Hawkins, R.P. (1999). Understanding where we are going by looking at where we have been. In J.R. Scotti & L.H. Meyer (Eds.), *Behavioral intervention: Principles, models, and practices* (pp. 3–23). Baltimore: Paul H. Brookes Publishing Co.

Fahey, K.R. (2000). Classroom-based interventions for language problems. In K.R. Fahey & D.K. Reid (Eds.), *Language development, differences, and disorders: A perspective for general and special education teachers and classroom-based speech-language pathologists* (pp. 372–374). Austin, TX: PRO-ED.

Falvey, M. (1998, February). *Special and general reform: Similarities and relationships.* Paper presented at the Council for Exceptional Children Courage to Risk Annual State Conference, Colorado Springs, CO.

Farmer, T.W., Farmer, E.M., & Gut, D.M. (1999). Implications of social development research for school-based interventions for aggressive youth with EBD. *Journal of Emotional and Behavioral Disorders, 7,* 130–136.

Favell, J.E., McGimsey, J.F., & Jones, M.L. (1978). The use of physical restraint in the treatment of self-injury and as positive reinforcement. *Journal of Applied Behavior Analysis, 11,* 225–241.

Faw, G.D., Davis, P.K., & Peck, C. (1996). Increasing self-determination: Teaching people with mental retardation to evaluate residential options. *Journal of Applied Behavior Analysis, 29,* 173–188.

Feinberg, W. (1990). The moral responsibility of public schools. In J.I. Goodlad, R. Soder, & K.A. Sirotnik (Eds.), *The moral dimensions of teaching* (pp. 155–187). San Francisco: Jossey-Bass.

Field, S., LeRoy, B., & Rivera, S. (1994). Meeting functional curriculum needs in middle school general education classrooms. *Teaching Exceptional Children, 26*(2), 40–43.

Filbin, J., Rogers-Connolly, T., & Brewer, R. (1996). *Individualized learner outcomes: Infusing student needs into the regular education curriculum.* Colorado Springs, CO: PEAK Parent Center, Inc.

Fisher, R., & Ury, W. (1992). *Getting to YES: Negotiating agreement without giving in.* New York: Penguin Books.

Fogarty, R. (1999). Architects of the intellect. *Educational Leadership, 57*(3), 76–77.

Foley, G.M. (1995). Portrait of the arena evaluation: Assessment in the transdisciplinary approach. In E.D. Gibbs & D.M. Teti (Eds.), *Interdisciplinary assessment of infants: A guide for early intervention professionals* (pp. 271–286). Baltimore: Paul H. Brookes Publishing Co.

Forest, M., & Lusthaus, E. (1990). Everyone belongs with the MAPS action planning system. *Teaching Exceptional Children, 22*(2), 32–35.

Forman, S.G. (1980). A comparison of cognitive training and response cost procedures in modifying aggressive behavior of elementary school children. *Behavior Therapy, 11,* 594–600.

Foster, K.R., Vecchia, P., & Repacholi, M.H. (2000). Science and the precautionary principle. *Science, 288*, 979–981.

Freiberg, H.J. (1999). *Beyond behaviorism: Changing the classroom management paradigm.* Needham Heights, MA: Allyn & Bacon.

Freud, S. (1949). *An outline of psychoanalysis.* New York: W.W. Norton & Company.

Friedman, L.M. (1999). *The horizontal society.* New Haven, CT: Yale University Press.

Fuchs, D., Fuchs, L.S., Mathes, P.G., & Simmons, D.C. (1997). Peer-assisted learning strategies: Making classrooms more responsive to diversity. *American Educational Research Journal, 34*, 174–206.

Fullan, M. (1993). *Change forces: Probing the depths of educational reform.* London: Falmer Press.

Furlong, M., & Morrison, G. (2000). The *school* in school violence: Definition and facts. *Journal of Emotional and Behavioral Disorders, 8*, 71–82.

Gable, R.A., Arllen, N.L., & Hendrickson, J.M. (1994). Use of students with emotional/behavioral disorders as behavior change agents. *Education and Treatment of Children, 17*, 267–276.

Gable, R.A., Hendrickson, J. M., & Smith, C. (1999). Changing discipline policies and practices: Finding a place for functional behavioral assessment in schools. *Preventing School Failure, 43*, 167–170.

Gallagher, J.J. (1997, July). *Keynote address.* Presented at the OSEP/Johns Hopkins University National Symposium on Leadership Training in Special Education, Washington, DC.

Gamoran, A. (1992). Is ability grouping equitable? *Educational Leadership, 50*(2), 11–17.

Gamoran, A., Nystrand, M., Berends, M., & LePore, P.C. (1995). An organizational analysis of the effects of ability grouping. *American Educational Research Journal, 32*, 687–715.

Gardner, H. (1983). *Frames of mind: The theory of multiple intelligences.* New York: Basic Books.

Gardner, H. (1993). *Multiple intelligences: The theory in practice.* New York: Basic Books.

Gardner, H. (1995). Reflections on multiple intelligences. *Phi Delta Kappan, 77*, 200–209.

Gardner, H. (1999). *The disciplined mind: What all students should understand.* New York: Simon & Schuster.

Gardner, W.I., Cole, C.L., Davidson, D.P., & Karan, O.C. (1986). Reducing aggression in individuals with developmental disabilities: An expanded stimulus control, assessment, and intervention model. *Education and Training in Mental Retardation, 21*, 3–12.

Gathercoal, F. (1998). Judicious discipline. In R.E. Butchart & B. McEwan (Eds.), *Classroom discipline in American schools: Problems and possibilities for democratic education.* (pp. 197–216). Albany: State University of New York Press.

Gaylord, V., Abery, B., McBride, M., Pearpoint, J., & Forest, M. (Eds.). (1998). Feature issue on person-centered planning with youth and adults who have developmental disabilities. *Impact, 11*(2).

Gent, P.J., & Gurecka, L.E. (1998). Service learning: A creative strategy for inclusive classrooms. *Journal of The Association for Persons with Severe Handicaps, 23*, 261–271.

Giangreco, M.F., Cloninger, C.J., & Iverson, V.S. (1998). *Choosing outcomes and accommodations for children (COACH): A guide to educational planning for students with disabilities* (2nd ed.). Baltimore: Paul H. Brookes Publishing Co.

Giangreco, M.F., Dennis, R., Cloninger, C., Edelman, S., & Schattman, R. (1993). "I've counted Jon": Transformational experiences of teachers educating students with disabilities. *Exceptional Children, 59*, 359–372.

Giangreco, M.F., Edelman, S.W., Luiselli, T.E., & MacFarland, S.Z.C. (1997). Helping or hovering? Effects of instructional assistant proximity on students with disabilities. *Exceptional Children, 64*, 7–18.

Giannetti, C.C., & Sagarese, M.M. (1998). Turning parents from critics to allies. *Educational Leadership, 55*(8), 40–42.

Gigerenzer, G., & Todd, P.M. (1999). *Simple heuristics that make us smart.* New York: Oxford University Press.

Glasser, W. (1965). *Reality therapy: A new approach to psychiatry.* New York: Harper & Row.

Glasser, W. (1992a). The quality school. In R.A. Villa, J.S. Thousand, W. Stainback, & S. Stainback (Eds.), *Restructuring for caring and effective education: An administrative guide to creating heterogeneous schools* (pp. 61–72). Baltimore: Paul H. Brookes Publishing Co.

Glasser, W. (1992b). *The quality school: Managing students without coercion* (2nd ed.). New York: HarperCollins.

Glasser, W. (1993, February). *The quality school teacher.* Paper presented at the Strategies for Inclusive Education Conference, Denver, CO.

Goessling, D.P. (1998). Inclusion and the challenge of assimilation for teachers of students with severe disabilities. *Journal of The Association for Persons with Severe Handicaps, 23,* 238–251.

Goffman, E. (1959). *The presentation of self in everyday life.* New York: Anchor Books.

Goleman, D. (1995). *Emotional intelligence.* New York: Bantam.

Goleman, D. (1999). Both sides now: A review of Daniel Yankelovich's *The magic of dialogue: Transforming conflict into cooperation. New York Times Book Review, CIV*(41), 24.

Goodlad, J.I. (1990). The occupation of teaching in schools. In J.I. Goodlad, R. Soder, & K.A. Sirotnik (Eds.), *The moral dimensions of teaching* (pp. 3–34). San Francisco: Jossey-Bass.

Goodlad, J.I., Keating, P., & Bailey, A.Y. (Eds.). (1990). *Access to knowledge: An agenda for our schools.* New York: College Entrance Examination Board.

Goodman, K. (1993). *Phonics phacts: A common-sense look at the most controversial issue affecting today's classrooms.* Westport, CT: Heinemann.

Goplerud, D., & Miller, L. (n.d.). *The context: System development.* Unpublished manuscript.

Graden, J.L. (1989). Redefining "prereferral" intervention as intervention assistance: Collaboration between general and special education. *Exceptional Children, 56,* 227–231.

Greene, M. (1978). Wide-awakeness and the moral life. In M. Greene (Ed.), *Landscapes of learning* (pp. 42–52). New York: Teachers College Press.

Greenwood, C.R., Carta, J.J., Kamps, D., & Arreaga-Mayer, C. (1990). Ecobehavioral analysis of classroom instruction. In S. Schroeder (Ed.). *Ecobehavioral analysis and developmental disabilities: The twenty-first century* (pp. 33–63). New York: Springer-Verlag.

Greenwood, C.R., Delquadri, J., & Carta, J.J. (1988). *Classwide peer tutoring.* Seattle: Educational Achievement Systems.

Greenwood, C.R., Delquardri, J.C., & Hall, R.V. (1989). Longitudinal effects of classwide peer tutoring. *Journal of Educational Psychology, 81,* 371–383.

Hagner, D., Helm, D.T., & Butterworth, J. (1996). "This is your meeting": A qualitative study of person-centered planning. *Mental Retardation, 34,* 159–170.

Hahn, H. (1993). The political implications of disability. *Journal of Disability Policy Studies, 4*(2), 41–52.

Hall, A., Neuharth-Pritchett, S., & Belfiore, P.J. (1997). Reduction of aggressive behaviors with changes in activity: Linking descriptive and experimental analysis. *Education and Training in Mental Retardation and Developmental Disabilities, 32*(4), 331–339.

Hall, R.V., Panyan, M., Rabon, D., & Broden. M. (1968). Instructing beginning teachers in reinforcement procedures which improve classroom control. *Journal of Applied Behavior Analysis, 1,* 315–322.

Hanson, F.A. (1993). *Testing, testing: Social consequences of the examined life.* Berkeley: University of California Press.

Harré, R., & Gillett, G. (1994). *The discursive mind.* Thousand Oaks, CA: Sage Publications.

Hartman, R., & Stage, S.A. (2000). The relationship between social information processing and in-school suspensions for students with behavioral disorders. *Behavioral Disorders, 25,* 183–195.

Hartup, W.W. (1985). Relationships and their significance in cognitive development. In R.A. Hinde, J. Stevenson-Hinde, & A.N. Oerret-Clermont (Eds.), *Social relationships and cognitive development* (pp. 66–82). New York: Oxford University Press.

Helff, C.M., & Glidden, L.M. (1998). More positive or less negative? Trends in research on adjustment of families rearing children with developmental disabilities. *Mental Retardation, 36,* 457–464.

Helwick, G., & Jackson, L.B. (1999, April). *Teaming for prevention.* Paper presented at the Behavior Summit, Longmont, CO.

Helwick, G., & Jackson, L.B. (2000, February). *Collaboration for difficult learning and behavior problems.* Paper presented at the Council for Exceptional Children Courage to Risk Annual State Conference, Colorado Springs, CO.

Henderson, J.G. (1992). *Reflective teaching: Becoming an inquiring educator.* New York: Macmillan.

Hendrickson, J.M., Gable, R.A., Conroy, M.A., Fox, J., & Smith, C. (1999). Behavioral problems in schools: Ways to encourage functional behavior assessment (FBA) of discipline-evoking behavior of students with emotional and/or behavioral disorders. *Education and Treatment of Children, 22*(3) 280–290.

Henley, M. (1997). Points, level systems, and teaching responsibility. *Reaching Today's Youth, 6,* 24–29.

Hileman, L.R. (1985). Exploring drama with emotionally disturbed adolescents. *Pointer, 30*(1), 12–15.

Hobbs, N. (1966). Helping disturbed children: Psychological and ecological strategies. *American Psychologist, 21,* 1105–1115.

Hodapp, R.M., & Dykens, E.M. (1994). Mental retardation's two cultures of behavioral research. *American Journal on Mental Retardation, 98,* 675–687.

Hoerr, T.R. (1992). How our school applied multiple intelligences theory. *Educational Leadership,* 67–68.

Holdsworth, R. (1988). Student participation projects in Australia: An anecdotal history. In R. Slee (Ed.), *Discipline and schools: A curriculum perspective.* Melbourne: Macmillan.

Hoover, R.L., & Kindsvatter, R. (1997). *Democratic discipline: Foundation and practice.* Columbus, OH: Merrill Education.

Hord, S.M., Rutherford, W.L., Huling-Austin, L., & Hall, G.E. (1987). *Taking charge of change.* Alexandria, VA: Association for Supervision and Curriculum Development.

Horner, R.H. (1994). Functional behavioral assessment: Contributions and future directions. *Journal of Applied Behavior Analysis, 27,* 401–404.

Horner, R.H., Anderson, J.L., Sailor, W., Dunlap, G., Carr, E., Koegel, R.L., & Koegel, L.K. (1995, August). *Positive behavioral support.* Presentation at a workshop sponsored by the Rehabilitation Research and Training Center, Denver, CO.

Horner, R.H., & Carr, E.G. (1997). Behavioral support for students with severe disabilities: Functional assessment and comprehensive intervention. *Journal of Special Education, 31,* 84–104.

Horner, R.H., Day, H.M., & Day, J.R. (1997). Using neutralizing routines to reduce problem behaviors. *Journal of Applied Behavior Analysis, 30,* 601–614.

Horner, R.H., Dunlap, G., Koegel, R.L., Carr, E.G., Sailor, W., Anderson, J., Albin, R.W., & O'Neill, R.E. (1990). Toward a technology of "nonaversive" behavioral support. *Journal of The Association for Persons with Severe Handicaps, 15,* 125–132.

Horner, R.H., & Sugai, G. (2000). School-wide behavior support: An emerging initiative. *Journal of Positive Behavior Interventions, 2*(4), 231–232.

Hoyt, M.F. (Ed.). (1994). *Constructive therapies.* New York: The Guilford Press.

Huberman, M. (1999). The mind is its own place: The influence of sustained interactivity with practitioners on educational researchers. *Harvard Educational Review, 69,* 289–319.

Hughes, C., Guth, C., Hall, S., Presley, J., Dye, M., & Byers, C. (1999). "They are my best friends": Peer buddies promote inclusion in high school. *Teaching Exceptional Children, 31*(5), 32–37.

Individuals with Disabilities Education Act Amendments of 1997, PL 105-17, 20 U.S.C. §§ 1400 *et seq.*

Iwata, B.A., & Bailey, J.S. (1974). Reward versus cost token systems: An analysis of the effects on students and teachers. *Journal of Applied Behavior Analysis, 7,* 567–576.

Iwata, B.A., Dorsey, M.F., Slifer, K.J., Bauman, K.E., & Richman, G.S. (1982). Toward a functional analysis of self-injury. *Analysis and Intervention in Developmental Disabilities, 2,* 3–20.

Jackson, L.B. (1992, December). *Ecological assessment: Exemplary applications.* Paper presented at the International Symposium on Assessment of Exceptional Children, Taiwan, Republic of China.

Jackson, L.B. (1996). *A manual for assessing and analyzing communication capabilities and communication needs.* Greeley: University of Northern Colorado, Division of Special Education.

Jackson, L.B. (1998, April). *Making the shift from managing to supporting students with "problem" behaviors.* Keynote address at the Conference for Teachers and Families, Wilmington, Delaware.

Jackson, L.B., Barnes, J., Padilla, M., McClure, B., & Anson, T. (1998, December). *Constructing support plans for students who have escalating behavior patterns.* Seattle: Annual Conference of The Association for Persons with Severe Handicaps.

Jackson, L.B., Dobson, D., Wimberley, V., & Shepler, S. (1993, February). *Communication, empowerment, and challenging behavior*. Paper presented at the Strategies for Inclusive Education Conference, Denver, CO.

Jackson. L.B., & Leon, M.Z. (1995, February). *Developing behavior support plans for students in inclusive education settings*. Paper presented at the Strategies for Inclusive Education Conference, Denver, CO.

Jackson, L.B., & Leon, M.Z. (1996a, February). *Advances and new developments in behavior support*. Paper presented at the Strategies for Inclusive Education Conference, Denver, CO.

Jackson, L.B., & Leon, M.Z. (1996b, November). *Growing good behavior*. Paper presented at the Southeastern Colorado BOCES 12th Annual Educational Conference, Lamar, CO.

Jackson, L.B., & Leon, M.Z. (1997a, February). *Developing behavior support plans I: Essential elements for effective support*. Paper presented at the Colorado Inclusion Conference: Strategies for Success for All Students, Denver.

Jackson, L.B., & Leon, M.Z. (1997b, February). *Developing behavior support plans II: Solution-focused plans*. Paper presented at the Colorado Inclusion Conference: Strategies for Success for All Students, Denver.

Jackson, L.B., & Leon, M.Z. (1998a). *Developing a behavior support plan: A manual for teachers and behavioral specialists* (2nd ed.). Colorado Springs, CO: PEAK Parent Center, Inc.

Jackson, L.B., & Leon, M.Z. (1998b, February). *The nuts and bolts of building effective behavior support plans*. Paper presented at the Conference on Inclusive Education, Denver, CO.

Jackson, L.B., Ryndak, D., & Billingsley, F. (2000). Useful practices in inclusive education: A preliminary view of what experts in moderate to severe disabilities are saying. *Journal of The Association for Persons with Severe Handicaps, 25*, 129–141.

Jackson, L.B., Ryndak, D., Keefe, E., & Kozleski, E. (2000, April). *Defining roles for the special education teacher in the 21st century*. Paper presented at the Annual Convention of the Council for Exceptional Children, Vancouver, Canada.

Jackson, L.B., Ryndak, D., Keefe, L., McCaleb, K., Moore, M., Holthaus, C., & Moore, V. (2000, November). *Emerging roles of special education teachers: The imperative for change in teacher education*. Paper presented at the Annual Conference of the Teacher Education Division of the Council for Exceptional Children, Las Vegas, NV.

Jackson, L.B., Shepler, S., & Dobson, D. (1991, November). *Effectively managing challenging behaviors in regular education classrooms: Configuring old techniques for new settings*. Paper presented at The Association for Persons with Severe Handicaps Conference, Washington, DC.

Jalongo, M.R. (1992, April). Teachers' stories: Our ways of knowing. *Educational Leadership*, 68–73.

Janney, R.E., & Meyer, L.H. (1990). A consultation model to support integrated educational services for students with severe disabilities and challenging behaviors. *Journal of The Association for Persons with Severe Handicaps, 15*, 186–199.

Janney, R.E., & Snell, M.E. (1996). How teachers use peer interactions to include students with moderate and severe disabilities in elementary general education classrooms. *Journal of The Association for Persons with Severe Handicaps, 21*, 72–80.

Jenkins, J.M., Louis, K.S., Walberg. H.J., & Keefe, J.W. (1994) *World class schools: An evolving concept*. Reston, VA: National Association of Secondary School Principals.

John-Steiner, V., & Mahn, H. (1996). Sociocultural approaches to learning and development: A Vygotskian framework. *Educational Psychologist, 31*, 191–206.

Johnson, D.W., & Johnson, R.T. (1991). *Teaching students to be peacemakers*. Edina, MN: Interaction Book Co.

Johnson, D.W., & Johnson, R.T. (1996). Conflict resolution and peer mediation programs in elementary and secondary schools: A review of the research. *Review of Educational Research, 66*, 459–506.

Johnson, D.W., Johnson, R., Dudley, B., Ward, M., & Magnuson, D. (1995). The impact of peer mediation training on the management of school and home conflicts. *American Educational Research Journal, 32*, 829–844.

Johnson, D.W., Johnson, R.T., Holubec, E.J., & Roy, P. (1984). *Circles of learning: Cooperation in the classroom*. Alexandria, VA: Association for Supervision and Curriculum Development.

Jones, E. (1959). *Sigmund Freud: Collected papers: Vol. 1*. New York: Basic Books.

Jones, E.E., & Nisbett, R.E. (1979). The actor and the observer: Divergent perceptions of the causes of behavior. In W.A. Gamson & A. Modigliani (Eds.), *Conceptions of social life* (pp. 82–94). Lanham, MD: University Press of America.

Jones, V.F., & Jones, L.S. (1998). *Comprehensive classroom management: Creating communities of support and solving problems* (5th ed.). Needham Heights, MA: Allyn & Bacon.

Joyce, B., & Showers, B. (1995). *Student achievement through staff development: Fundamentals of school renewal* (2nd ed.). New York: Longman.

Kamps, D., Kravits, T., Stolze, J., & Swaggart, B. (1999). Prevention strategies for at-risk students and students with EBD in urban elementary schools. *Journal of Emotional and Behavioral Disorders, 7*, 178–188.

Karoly, P. (1984). Self-management problems in children. In E.J. Mash & L.G. Terdal (Eds.), *Behavioral assessment of childhood disorders* (pp. 79–126). New York: The Guilford Press.

Karp, S. (1997). Educating for a civil society: The core issue is inequality. *Educational Leadership, 54*(5), 40–43.

Kartub, D.T., Taylor-Greene, S., March, R.E., & Horner, R.H. (2000). Reducing hallway noise: A systems approach. *Journal of Positive Behavior Interventions, 2*, 179–182.

Katsiyannis, A., & Maag, J.W. (1998). Disciplining students with disabilities: Issues and considerations for implementing IDEA '97. *Behavioral Disorders, 23*, 276–289.

Kauffman, S.A. (1991). Antichaos and adaptation. *Scientific American, 265*(2), 78–84.

Kavale, K.A., Mathur, S.R., Forness, S.R., Quinn, M.M., & Rutherford, R.B. (2000). Right reason in the integration of group and single-subject research in behavioral disorders. *Behavioral Disorders, 25*, 142–157.

Kazdin, A.E., & Bootzin, R.R. (1972). The token economy: An evaluative review. *Journal of Applied Behavior Analysis, 5*, 343–372.

Kelly, B. (1994). Student disruptions in the cooperative classroom: Experiences in a New Brunswick, Canada, school district. In J.S. Thousand, R.A. Villa, & A.I. Nevin (Eds.). *Creativity and collaborative learning: A practical guide to empowering students and teachers* (pp. 103–114). Baltimore: Paul H. Brookes Publishing Co.

Kennedy, C.H. (1994). Manipulating antecedent conditions to alter the stimulus control of problem behavior. *Journal of Applied Behavior Analysis, 27*, 161–170.

Kennedy, C.H., & Itkonen, T. (1993). Effects of setting events on the problem behavior of students with severe disabilities. *Journal of Applied Behavior Analysis, 26*, 321–327.

Kennedy, C.H., & Meyer, K.A. (1996). Sleep deprivation, allergy symptoms, and negatively reinforced problem behavior. *Journal of Applied Behavior Analysis, 29*, 133–135.

Kennedy, M.M. (1997). The connection between research and practice. *Educational Researcher, 26*(7), 4–12.

Kern, L., Childs, K.E., Dunlap, G., Clarke, S., & Falk, G.D. (1994). Using assessment-based curricular intervention to improve the classroom behavior of a student with emotional and behavioral challenges. *Journal of Applied Behavior Analysis, 27*, 7–19.

Kern, L., Wacker, D.P., Mace, F.C., Falk, G.D., Dunlap, G., & Kromrey, J.D. (1995). Improving the peer interactions of students with emotional and behavioral disorders through self-evaluation procedures: A component analysis and group application. *Journal of Applied Behavior Analysis, 28*, 47–59.

Kincaid, D. (1996). Person-centered planning. In L.K. Koegel, R.L. Koegel, & G. Dunlap (Eds.), *Positive behavioral support: Including people with difficult behavior in the community* (pp. 439–465). Baltimore: Paul H. Brookes Publishing Co.

Klingner, J.K., & Vaughn, S. (1999). Students' perceptions of instruction in inclusion classrooms: Implications for students with learning disabilities. *Exceptional Children, 66*, 23–37.

Kluger, R. (1976). *Simple justice.* New York: Alfred A. Knopf.

Knight, T. (1988). Student discipline as a curriculum concern. In R. Slee (Ed.), *Discipline and schools: A curriculum perspective.* New York: Macmillan.

Knoster, T. (1998). Creating effective support plans. *The Positive Behavior Support Newsletter, 3*(1), 1–3.

Knowlton, E. (1998). Considerations in the design of personalized curricular supports for students with developmental disabilities. *Education and Training in Mental Retardation and Developmental Disabilities, 33*, 95–107.

Koegel, L.K., Koegel, R.L., & Dunlap, G. (Eds.). (1996). *Positive behavioral support: Including people with difficult behavior in the community.* Baltimore: Paul H. Brookes Publishing Co.

Koegel, L.K., Koegel, R.L., Kellegrew, D., & Mullen, K. (1996). Parent education for prevention and reduction of severe problem behaviors. In L.K. Koegel, R.L. Koegel, & G. Dunlap (Eds.), *Positive behavioral support: Including people with difficult behavior in the community* (pp. 3–30). Baltimore: Paul H. Brookes Publishing Co.

Koegel, L.K., Stiebel, D., & Koegel, R.L. (1998). Reducing aggression in children with autism toward infant or toddler siblings. *Journal of The Association for Persons with Severe Handicaps, 23,* 111–118.

Kohn, A. (1993). *Punished by rewards: The trouble with gold stars, incentive plans, A's, praise, and other bribes.* Boston: Houghton Mifflin.

Kohn, A. (1996). *Beyond discipline: From compliance to community.* Alexandria, VA: Association for Supervision and Curriculum Development.

Kohn, A. (1997, February). *On bribing students to learn: Second thoughts about A's, praise, stickers, and contests.* Paper presented at the Colorado Inclusion Conference: Strategies for Success for All Students, Denver.

Kohn, A. (1998). Only for *my* kid: How privileged parents undermine school reform. *Phi Delta Kappan, 79*(8), 569–576.

Korinek, L., Walther-Thomas, C. McLaughlin, V.L., & Williams, B.T. (1999). Creating classroom communities and networks for student support. *Intervention in School and Clinic, 35,* 3–8.

Kozleski, E., & Jackson, L.B. (1993). Taylor's story: Full inclusion in her neighborhood elementary school. *Exceptionality, 4,* 153–175.

Kozulin, A. (1996). The concept of activity in Soviet psychology. In H. Daniels (Ed.), *An introduction to Vygotsky* (pp. 99–122). New York: Routledge.

Krippner, S. (1994). Humanistic psychology and chaos theory: The third revolution and the third force. *Journal of Humanistic Psychology, 34*(3), 48–61.

Krystal, S. (1999). The nurturing potential of service learning. *Educational Leadership, 56*(4), 58–61.

Kunc, N. (1992). The need to belong: Rediscovering Maslow's hierarchy of needs. In R.A. Villa, J.S. Thousand, W. Stainback, & S. Stainback (Eds.), *Restructuring for caring and effective education: An administrative guide to creating heterogeneous schools* (pp. 25–39). Baltimore: Paul H. Brookes Publishing Co.

Kunc, N. (1996, March). *Rocking the boat without sinking the ship! Managing conflict in inclusive schools.* Paper presented at the Creating Inclusive School Communities Conference, Grand Junction, CO.

Kunc, N., & Van der Klift, E. (1995a). *A credo for support* [Video]. Nanaimo, Canada: Axis Consultation & Training Ltd.

Kunc, N., & Van der Klift, E. (1995b, March). *Learning to stand still: Supporting individuals with puzzling behavior.* Paper presented at the Council for Exceptional Children Courage to Risk Annual State Conference, Colorado Springs, CO.

Kutash, K., & Duchnowski, A.J. (1997). Create comprehensive and collaborative systems. *Journal of Emotional and Behavioral Disorders, 5,* 66–75.

Kutchins, H., & Kirk, S.A. (1997). *Making us crazy: DSM—The psychiatric bible and the creation of mental disorders.* New York: The Free Press.

Lakin, K.C., & Bruininks, R.H. (1985). Social integration of developmentally disabled persons. In K.C. Lakin & R.H. Bruininks (Eds.), *Strategies for achieving community integration of developmentally disabled citizens* (pp. 3–25). Baltimore: Paul H. Brookes Publishing Co.

Lalli, J.S., Casey, S., & Kates, K. (1995). Reducing escape behavior and increasing task completion with functional communication training, extinction, and response chaining. *Journal of Applied Behavior Analysis, 28,* 261–268.

Lantieri, L., & Patti, J. (1996). The road to peace in our schools. *Educational Leadership, 54*(1), 28–31.

Larsen, L.A. (1976). Deinstitutionalization. In M.A. Thomas (Ed.), *HEY, don't forget about me!* (pp. 124–145). Arlington, VA: The Council for Exceptional Children.

Lenkowsky, R.S. (1987). Bibliotherapy: A review of analysis of the literature. *The Journal of Special Education, 21,* 123–132.

Lennox, D.B., & Miltenberger, R.G. (1989). Conducting a functional assessment of problem behavior in applied settings. *Journal of The Association for Persons with Severe Handicaps, 14,* 304–311.

Leon, M.Z., & Jackson, L.B. (1995, October). *Building behavior support plans.* Paper presented at a statewide workshop sponsored by the Colorado Department of Education, Breckenridge, CO.

Leon, M.Z., & Jackson, L.B. (1996, January). *Developing behavior support plans for students in integrated educational settings.* Paper presented at School Restructuring and Inclusion: Equity and Excellence for All Conference, Nashua, NH.

Leone, P.E., Mayer, M.J., Malmbren, K., & Meisel, S.M. (2000). School violence and disruption: Rhetoric, reality, and reasonable balance. *Focus on Exceptional Children, 33*(1), 1–20.

Lepper, M.R., & Greene, D. (Eds.). (1978). *The hidden costs of reward: New perspectives on the psychology of human motivation.* Mahwah, NJ: Lawrence Erlbaum Associates.

Leyden, G., Newton, C., & Wilson, D. (1998). Circles of Friends in planning with students. *Impact, 11*, 14–15.

Lewis, C.C., Schaps, E., & Watson, M.S. (1996). The caring classroom's academic edge. *Educational Leadership, 54*(1), 16–21.

Lewis, T.J., & Daniels, C. (2000). Rethinking school discipline through effective behavioral support. *Reaching Today's Youth, 4*(2), 43–47.

Lewis, T.J., & Sugai, G. (1999). Effective behavior support: A systems approach to proactive schoolwide management. *Focus on Exceptional Children, 31*(6), 1–24.

Lewis, T.J., Sugai, G., & Colvin, G. (1998). Reducing problem behavior through a school-wide system of effective behavioral support: Investigation of a school-wide social skills training program and contextual interventions. *School Psychology Review, 27*, 446–459.

Lipsky, D.K., & Gartner, A. (1997). *Inclusion and school reform: Transforming America's classrooms.* Baltimore: Paul H. Brookes Publishing Co.

Lloyd, J.W., & Heubusch, J.D. (1996). Issues of social validation in research on serving individuals with emotional or behavioral disorders. *Behavioral Disorders, 22*, 8–14.

Lohrmann-O'Rourke, S., & Zirkel, P.A. (1998). The case law on aversive interventions for students with disabilities. *Exceptional Children, 65*, 101–123.

Lohrmann-O'Rourke, S.L., Knoster, T., & Llewellyn, G. (1999). Screening for understanding: An initial line of inquiry for school-based settings. *Journal of Positive Behavior Interventions, 1*, 35–42.

Long, N.J., & Morse, W.C. (1996). *Conflict in the classroom: The education of at-risk and troubled students* (5th ed.). Belmont, CA: Wadsworth.

Lovett, H. (1996). *Learning to listen: Positive approaches and people with difficult behavior.* Baltimore: Paul H. Brookes Publishing Co.

Lucas, S.R. (1999). *Tracking inequality: Stratification and mobility in American high schools.* New York: Teachers College Press.

Luiselli, J.K. (2000). Case demonstration of a fading procedure to promote school attendance of a child with Asperger's syndrome. *Journal of Positive Behavior Interventions, 2*, 47–52.

Luiselli, J.K., & Cameron, M.J. (Eds.). (1998). *Antecedent control: Innovative approaches to behavioral support.* Baltimore: Paul H. Brookes Publishing Co.

Maag, J.W. (1999). Why they say no: Foundational precises and techniques for managing resistance. *Focus on Exceptional Children, 32*, 1–16.

Maag, J.W., Rutherford, R.B., & DiGangi, S.A. (1992). Effects of self-monitoring and contingent reinforcement on on-task behavior and academic productivity of learning-disabled students: A social validation study. *Psychology in the Schools, 29*, 157–172.

Macht, L. (1990). *Managing classroom behavior: An ecological approach to academic and social learning.* New York: Longman.

Mackintosh, N.J. (1998). *IQ and human intelligence.* New York: Oxford University Press.

Malette, P., Mirenda, P., Kandborg, T., Jones, P., Bunz, T., & Rogow, S. (1992). Application of a life style development process for persons with severe intellectual disabilities: A case study report. *Journal of The Association for Persons with Severe Handicaps, 17*, 179–191.

Mamlin, N. (1999). Despite best intentions: When inclusion fails. *Journal of Special Education, 33*, 36–49.

Martin, G., & Pear, J. (1999). *Behavior modification: What it is and how to do it* (6th ed.). Upper Saddle River, NJ: Prentice Hall.

Maslow, A. (1970). *Motivation and personality* (2nd ed.). New York: Harper & Row.

Massing, A. (1993). Effects of lingering Nazi world views in family life. In B. Heimannsberg & C.J. Schmidt (Eds.), *The collective silence: German identity and the legacy of shame* (pp. 95–108). San Francisco: Jossey-Bass.

Mathur, S.R., Kavale, K.A., Quinn, M.M., Forness, S.R., & Rutherford, R.B. (1998). Social skills interventions with students with emotional and behavioral problems: A quantitative synthesis of single-subject research. *Behavioral Disorders, 23*, 193–201.

Matusov, E. (1996). Intersubjectivity without agreement, *Mind, Culture, and Activity, 3*, 25–45.

May, R., & Yalom, I. (1989). Existential psychotherapy. In R.J. Corsini & D. Wedding (Eds.), *Current psychotherapies* (pp. 363–402). Itasca, IL: F.E. Peacock.

Mayer, G.R. (1995). Preventing antisocial behavior in the school. *Journal of Applied Behavior Analysis, 28*, 467–478.

Mayer, M.J., & Leone, P.E. (1999). A structural analysis of school violence and disruption: Implications for creating safer schools. *Education and Treatment of Children, 22*, 333–358.

Mazaleski, J.L., Iwata, B.A., Vollmer, T.R., Zarcone, J.R., & Smith, R.G. (1993). Analysis of the reinforcement and extinction components in DRO contingencies with self-injury. *Journal of Applied Behavior Analysis, 26*, 143–156.

McEwan, B., Gathercoal, P., & Nimmo, V. (1999). Application of judicious discipline. In H.J. Freiberg (Ed.), *Beyond behaviorism: Changing the classroom management paradigm* (pp. 98–118). Needham Heights, MA: Allyn & Bacon.

McIntyre, T. (1996). Guidelines for providing appropriate services to culturally diverse students with emotional and/or behavioral disorders. *Behavioral Disorders, 21*, 137–144.

McLaughlin, M.J., Leone, P.E., Meisel, S., & Henderson, K. (1997). Strengthen school and community capacity. *Journal of Emotional and Behavioral Disorders, 5*(1), 15–23.

McLeskey, J., Henry, D., & Hodges, D. (1998). *Inclusion: Where is it happening? Teaching Exceptional Children, 31*(1), 4–10.

Meadows, N.B. (1999). A university–public school collaborative project for including students with learning and behavior problems in general education classrooms. In J.R. Scotti & L.H. Meyer (Eds.), *Behavioral intervention: Principles, models, and practices* (pp. 175–193). Baltimore: Paul H. Brookes Publishing Co.

Mehan, H., Hertweck, A., & Meihls, J.L. (1986). *Handicapping the handicapped: Decision making in students' educational careers.* Stanford, CA: Stanford University Press.

Meichenbaum, D.H. (1977). *Cognitive-behavior modification: An integrative approach.* New York: Plenum.

Meichenbaum, D.H., & Goodman, J. (1971). Training impulsive children to talk to themselves: A means of developing self-control. *Journal of Abnormal Psychology, 77*, 115–126.

Metcalf, L. (1995). *Counseling toward solutions: A practical solution-focused program for working with students, teachers, and parents.* Englewood Cliffs, NJ: The Center for Applied Research in Education.

Meyer, A.L., & Northup, W.B. (1997). What is violence prevention, anyway? *Educational Leadership, 54*(8), 31–33.

Meyer, L.H., & Evans, I.M. (1989). *Nonaversive intervention for behavior problems: A manual for home and community.* Baltimore: Paul H. Brookes Publishing Co.

Meyer, L.H., & Evans, I.M. (1993). Science and practice in behavioral intervention: Meaningful outcomes, research validity, and usable knowledge. *Journal of The Association for Persons with Severe Handicaps, 18*, 224–234.

Meyer, L.H., & Park, H. (1999). Contemporary, most promising practices for people with disabilities. In J.R. Scotti & L.H. Meyer (Eds.), *Behavioral intervention: Principles, models, and practices* (pp. 25–45). Baltimore: Paul H. Brookes Publishing Co.

Miller, D.W. (1999). The black hole of educational research. *The Chronicle of Higher Education, 45*(48), A17–A18.

Miller, L., Epp, J., & McGinnis, E. (1985). Setting analysis. In F. Wood, C.R. Smith, & J. Grimes (Eds.), *The Iowa Assessment Model in Behavioral Disorders: A training manual* (pp. 61–149). Des Moines, IA: State Department of Public Instruction.

Mills v. Board of Education of the District of Columbia, 348 F. Suppl. 866 (D.D.C., 1972).

Milofsky, C. (1992). Why special education isn't special. In T. Hehir & T. Latus (Eds.), Special education at the century's end: Evolution in theory and practice since 1970 [Special issue]. *Harvard Educational Review*, 47–67.

Moberg, C.L., & Cohn, Z.A. (1991). René Jules Dubos. *Scientific American, 264*(5), 66–74.

Moes, D.R., & Frea, W.D. (2000). Using family context to inform intervention planning for the treatment of a child with autism. *Journal of Positive Behavior Interventions, 2*, 40–46.

Moffett, C.A. (2000). Sustaining change: The answers are blowing in the wind. *Educational Leadership, 57*(7), 35–38.

Morgan, H. (1996). An analysis of Gardner's theory of multiple intelligence. *Roeper Review, 18,* 263–269.

Morningstar, M.E., Kleinhammer-Tramill, P.J., & Lattin, D.L. (1999). Using successful models of student-centered transition planning and services for adolescents with disabilities. *Focus on Exceptional Children, 31,* 1–19.

Morris, W. (Ed.). (1969). *The American heritage dictionary of the English language.* New York: American Heritage Publishing Co.

Mount, B., & Zwernik, K. (1988). *It's never too early, it's never too late: An overview of personal futures planning.* St. Paul, MN: Governor's Planning Council on Developmental Disabilities.

Munk, D.D., & Repp, A.C. (1994). The relationship between instructional variables and problem behavior: A review. *Exceptional Children, 60,* 390–401.

Murphy, C.U. (1999). Use time for faculty study. *Journal of Staff Development, 20,* 20–25.

Nakasato, J. (2000). Data-based decision making in Hawaii's behavior support effort. *Journal of Positive Behavior Interventions, 2,* 247–250.

Namkung, J., & Ashton, D. (2000, April). *Serving students who are emotionally disturbed more effectively: How one system changed.* Paper presented at the Council for Exceptional Children Convention, Vancouver, Canada.

Neef, N.A., Shafer, M.S., Egel, A.L., Cataldo, M.F., & Parrish, J.M. (1983). The class specific effects of compliance training with "do" and "don't" requests: Analogue analysis and classroom application. *Journal of Applied Behavior Analysis, 16,* 81–99.

Nelson, J.R., Martella, R., & Galand, B. (1998). The effects of teaching school expectations and establishing a consistent consequence on formal office disciplinary actions. *Journal of Emotional and Behavioral Disorders, 6,* 153–161.

Nichols, P. (2000). The role of cognition and affect in a functional behavioral analysis. *Exceptional Children, 66,* 393–402.

Nimmo, V.L. (1998). But will it work? The practice of judicious discipline in southern Minnesota schools. In R.E. Butchart & B. McEwan (Eds.), *Classroom discipline in American schools* (pp. 217–236). Albany: State University of New York Press.

Noddings, N. (1992). *The challenge to care in schools: An alternative approach to education.* New York: Teachers College Press.

Oakes, J. (1985). *Keeping track: How schools structure inequality.* New Haven, CT: Yale University Press.

Oakes, J., & Lipton, M. (1990). Tracking and ability grouping: A structural barrier to access and achievement. In J.I. Goodlad, P. Keating, & A.Y. Bailey (Eds.), *Access to knowledge: An agenda for our schools* (pp. 187–204). New York: College Entrance Examination Board.

Oakes, J., Quartz, K.H., Ryan, S., & Lipton, M. (2000). *Becoming good American schools: The struggle for civic virtue in education reform.* San Francisco: Jossey-Bass.

Oakes, J., Selvin, M., Karoly, L., & Guiton, G. (1992). *Educational matchmaking: Academic and vocational tracking in comprehensive high schools.* Santa Monica, CA: RAND.

O'Brien, G.V. (1999). Protecting the social body: Use of the organism metaphor in fighting the "menace of the feebleminded." *Mental Retardation, 37,* 188–200.

O'Brien, J. (1987). A guide to life-style planning: Using *The Activities Catalog* to integrate services and natural support systems. In B. Wilcox & G.T. Bellamy (Eds.), *A comprehensive guide to The Activities Catalog: An alternative curriculum for youth and adults with severe disabilities* (pp. 175–189). Baltimore: Paul H. Brookes Publishing Co.

Odom, S.L., Peterson, C., McConnell, S.R., & Ostrosky, M. (1990). Ecobehavioral analysis of early education/specialized classroom settings and peer social interaction. *Education and Treatment of Children, 13,* 316–330.

O'Hanlon, B. (1994). The third wave. *The Family Therapy Networker, 18*(6), 18–29.

O'Leary, S.G., & Dubey, D.R. (1979). Applications of self-control procedures by children: A review. *Journal of Applied Behavior Analysis, 12,* 449–465.

Oliva, C., & Brown, F. (1994, December). *Continuous analysis of the communicative intent of problem behaviors: Using supporters' judgement.* Paper presented at the Annual Conference of The Association for Persons with Severe Handicaps, Atlanta, GA.

Ollendick, T.H., & Hersen, M. (1984). An overview of child behavioral assessment. In A.P. Goldstein & L. Krasner (Eds.), *Child behavioral assessment principles and procedures.* (pp. 3–19). New York: Pergamon Press.

Olson, G.B. (2000). Designing a new material world. *Science, 288,* 993–998.

Olson, R.L., & Roberts, M.W. (1987). Alternative treatments for sibling aggression. *Behavior Therapy, 18,* 243–250.

O'Neill, R.E., Horner, R.H., Albin, R.W., Sprague, J.R., Storey, K., & Newton, J.S. (1997). *Functional assessment and program development for problem behavior: A practical handbook* (2nd ed.). Pacific Grove, CA: Brooks/Cole Thomson Learning.

O'Neill, R.E., Horner, R.H., Albin, R.W., Storey, K., & Sprague, J.R. (1990). *Functional analysis of problem behavior.* Sycamore, IL: Sycamore Publishing Company.

O'Reilly, M.F. (1995). Functional analysis and treatment of escape-maintained aggression correlated with sleep deprivation. *Journal of Applied Behavior Analysis, 28,* 225–226.

O'Reilly, M.F. (1997). Functional analysis of episodic self-injury correlated with recurrent otitis media. *Journal of Applied Behavior Analysis, 30,* 165–167.

Orelove, F.P., & Sobsey, D. (1991). *Educating children with multiple disabilities: A transdisciplinary approach* (2nd ed.). Baltimore: Paul H. Brookes Publishing Co.

Oseroff, A., Oseroff, C.E., Westling, D., & Gessner, L.J. (1999). Teachers' beliefs about maltreatment of students with emotional/behavioral disorders. *Behavioral Disorders, 24,* 197–209.

Overton, S.S. (1997). The forgotten intervention: How to design environments that foster friendship. *Reaching Today's Youth, 2,* 6–10.

Palincsar, A.S., & Brown, A.L. (1986). Interactive teaching to promote independent learning from text. *Reading Teacher, 39,* 771–777.

Parsons, M.B., Reid, D.H., Reynolds, J., & Bumgarner, M. (1990). Effects of chosen versus assigned jobs on the work performance of persons with severe handicaps. *Journal of Applied Behavior Analysis, 23,* 253–258.

Patterson, G.R., Jones, R., Whittier, J., & Wright, M.A. (1965). A behavior modification technique for the hyperactive child. *Behavior Research and Therapy, 2,* 217–226.

Pearpoint, J., Forest, M., & O'Brien, J. (1996). MAPs, Circles of Friends, and PATH: Powerful tools to help build caring communities. In S. Stainback & W. Stainback (Eds.), *Inclusion: A guide for educators* (pp. 67–86). Baltimore: Paul H. Brookes Publishing Co.

Pearpoint, J., O'Brien, J., & Forest, M. (1993). *PATH: A workbook for planning positive possible futures.* Toronto: Inclusion Press.

Pennsylvania Association for Retarded Citizens v. Commonwealth of Pennsylvania, 334 F. Suppl. 1257 (E.D.Pa 1971).

Perry, N.E., Walton, C., & Calder, K. (1999). Teachers developing assessments of early literacy: A community of practice project. *Teacher Education and Special Education, 22,* 218–233.

Perske, R. (1988). *Circles of Friends.* Nashville: Abingdon Press.

Powell, J.H., Berliner, D.C., & Casanova, U. (1992). Empowerment through collegial study groups. *Contemporary Education, 63*(4), 281–284.

Prater, M.A., Hogan, S., & Miller, S.R. (1992). Using self-monitoring to improve on-task behavior and academic skills of an adolescent with mild handicaps across special and regular education settings. *Education and Treatment of Children, 15,* 43–55.

Putnam, J.W. (Ed.). (1998). *Cooperative learning and strategies for inclusion: Celebrating diversity in the classroom* (2nd ed.). Baltimore: Paul H. Brookes Publishing Co.

Quinn, M.M., Kavale, K.A., Mathur, S.R., Rutherford, R.B., & Forness, S.R. (1999). A meta-analysis of social skill intervention for students with emotional or behavioral disorders. *Journal of Emotional and Behavioral Disorders, 7,* 54–64.

Rapport, M.D., Murphy, H.A., & Bailey, J.S. (1982). Ritalin vs. response cost in the control of hyperactive children: A within-subject comparison. *Journal of Applied Behavior Analysis, 15,* 205–216.

Ratner, C. (n.d.). *Historical and contemporary significance of Vygotsky's sociohistorical psychology* [Online]. Available: http://www.humboldt1.com/~cr2/sociohis.htm.

Redl, F. (1966). *When we deal with children.* New York: The Free Press.

Reichle, J., & Johnston, S.S. (1993). Replacing challenging behavior: The role of communication intervention. *Topics in Language Disorders, 13*(3), 61–76.

Reid, D.K. (1996). Learning disorders: Theoretical and research perspectives. In D.K. Reid, W.P. Hresko, & H.L. Swanson (Eds.), *Cognitive approaches to learning disabilities* (pp. 213–247). Austin, TX: PRO-ED.

Repp, A.C. (1999). Naturalistic functional assessment with regular and special education students in classroom settings. In A.C. Repp & R.H. Horner (Eds.), *Functional analysis of problem behavior: From effective assessment to effective support* (pp. 238–258). Belmont, CA: Wadsworth.

Repp, A.C., & Horner, R.H. (Eds.). (1999). *Functional analysis of problem behavior: From effective assessment to effective support.* Belmont, CA: Wadsworth.

Repp, A.C., & Singh, N.N. (1990). *Perspectives on the use of nonaversive and aversive interventions for persons with developmental disabilities.* Sycamore, IL: Sycamore Publishing Company.

Reynolds, L.K., & Kelley, M.L. (1997). The efficacy of a response cost-based treatment package for managing aggressive behavior in preschoolers. *Behavior Modification, 21*(2), 216–230.

Rhode, G., Jensen, W.R., & Reavis, H.K. (1995) *The tough kid book: Practical classroom management strategies* (5th ed.). Longmont, CO: Sopris West.

Rhodes, W.C. (1967). The disturbing child: A problem of ecological management. *Exceptional Children, 36,* 306–314.

Rich, J.M. (1982). *Discipline and authority in school and family.* Lanham, MD: Lexington Books.

Richardson, J.G. (1994). Common, delinquent, and special: On the formalization of common schooling in the American states. *American Educational Research Journal, 31,* 695–723.

Riordan, R.J., & Wilson, L.S. (1989). Bibliotherapy: Does it work? *Journal of Counseling and Development, 67,* 506–508.

Risley, T. (1996). Get a life! Positive behavioral intervention for challenging behavior through life arrangement and life coaching. In L.K. Koegel, R.L. Koegel, & G. Dunlap (Eds.), *Positive behavioral support: Including people with difficult behavior in the community* (pp. 425–437). Baltimore: Paul H. Brookes Publishing Co.

Roberts, G., Becker, H., & Seay, P. (1997). A process for measuring adoption of innovation within the support paradigm. *Journal of The Association for Persons with Severe Handicaps, 22,* 109–119.

Rock, E.E., Rosenberg, M.S., & Carran, D.T. (1995). Variables affecting the reintegration rate of students with serious emotional disturbance. *Exceptional Children, 61,* 254–268.

Rockland, L.H. (1989). *Supportive therapy: A psychodynamic approach.* New York: Basic Books.

Rodis, P., Garrrod, A., & Boscardin, M.L. (2000). *Learning disabilities and life stories.* Needham Heights, MA: Allyn & Bacon.

Rogers, E.M. (1995). *Diffusion of innovations* (4th ed.). New York: The Free Press.

Rogers, S., Ludington, J., & Graham, S. (1999). *Motivation and learning.* Evergreen, CO: Peak Learning Systems, Inc.

Rogers, S., & Renard, L. (1999). Relationship-driven teaching. *Educational Leadership, 57*(1), 34–37.

Rolider, A., & Axelrod, S. (2000). *How to teach self-control through trigger analysis.* Austin, TX: PRO-ED.

Romero, O. *Prophets of a future not our own* [On-line]. Available: http://rrnet.com/~sedaqah/oarpry.htm.

Rooney, K.J., & Hallahan, D.P. (1985). Future directions for cognitive behavior modification research: The quest for cognitive change. *Remedial and Special Education, 6,* 46–51.

Rosenbaum, M.S., & Drabman, R.S. (1979). Self-control training in the classroom: A review and critique. *Journal of Applied Behavior Analysis, 12,* 467–485.

Rosenberg, M.S., & Jackman, L.A. (1997). Addressing student and staff behavior: The PAR model. *The Fourth R, 79,* 1–12.

Rosenberg, M.S., Wilson, R., Maheady, L., & Sindelar, P.T. (1997). *Educating students with behavior disorders.* Needham Heights, MA: Allyn & Bacon.

Ross, G., & Schuster, P. (1996, October). *A solution-focused approach to behavioral problems.* Paper presented at the International Adolescent Conference: Programming for the Needs of Adolescents with Behavioral Disorders, Snowmass, CO.

Rotter, J.B. (1982). Social learning theory. In J.B. Rotter (Ed.), *The development and application of social learning theory: Selected papers* (pp. 301–323). New York: Praeger.

Ruef, M.B., & Higgins, C. (1999). Look it up on the web: Practical behavioral support information. *Teaching Exceptional Children, 31,* 332–334.

Ruef, M.B., Turnbull, A.P., Turnbull, H.R., & Poston, D. (1999). Perspectives of five stakeholder groups: Challenging behavior of individuals with mental retardation and/or autism. *Journal of Positive Behavior Interventions, 1,* 43–58.

Ruelle, D. (1994). Where can one hope to profitably apply the ideas of chaos? *Physics Today, 47*(7), 24–30.

Ryan, R. (1996). *Handbook of mental health care for persons with developmental disabilities.* Denver, CO: Community Circle Publications.

Ryan, R. (1999, April). *Behavior pharmacology: The effects of medication and brain chemistry on behavior.* Paper presented at the Summit on Behavior, Longmont, CO.

Ryan, R. (2000, April). *Post-traumatic stress disorder.* Paper prsented at the Summit on Behavior, Longmont, CO.

Ryndak, D., Jackson, L.B., & Billingsley, F. (1999–2000). Defining school inclusion for students with moderate or severe disabilities: What do experts say? *Exceptionality, 8*(2), 101–116.

Sadler, C. (2000). Effective behavior support implementation at the district level: Tigard-Tualatin school district. *Journal of Positive Behavior Interventions, 2,* 241–243.

Sapon-Shevin, M. (1996). Full inclusion as disclosing tablet: Revealing the flaws in our present system. *Theory into Practice, 35*(1), 35–45.

Sapon-Shevin, M. (1999). *Because we change the world: A practical guide to building cooperative, inclusive classroom communities.* Needham Heights, MA: Allyn & Bacon.

Sapon-Shevin, M., Ayers, B.J., & Duncan, J. (1994). Cooperative learning and inclusion. In J.S. Thousand, R.A. Villa, & A. Nevin (Eds.). *Creativity and collaborative learning: A practical guide to empowering students and teachers* (pp. 45–58). Baltimore: Paul H. Brookes Publishing Co.

Schenko, L. (1994). *Structuring a learner-centered school.* Palatine, IL: IRI/Skylight Publishing.

Scheuermann, B., Webber, J., Partin, M., & Knies, W.C. (1994). Levels systems and the law: Are they compatible? *Behavioral Disorders, 19,* 205–220.

Schmuck, R.A., & Schmuck, P.A. (1988). *Group processes in the classroom* (5th ed.). Dubuque, IA: Wm. C. Brown Publishers.

Schreibman, L., Whalen, C., & Stahmer, A.C. (2000). The use of video priming to reduce disruptive transition behavior in children with autism. *Journal of Positive Behavior Interventions, 2,* 3–11.

Schulman, J.L., Suran, B.G., Stevens, T.M., & Kupst, M.J. (1979). Instructions, feedback, and reinforcement in reducing activity levels in the classroom. *Journal of Applied Behavior Analysis, 12,* 441–447.

Scott, T.M., & Nelson, C.M. (1998). Confusion and failure in facilitating generalized social responding in the school setting: Sometimes 2 + 2 = 5. *Behavioral Disorders, 23,* 264–275.

Scott, T.M., & Nelson, C.M. (1999a). Functional behavioral assessment: Implications for training and staff development. *Behavioral Disorders, 24,* 249–252.

Scott, T.M., & Nelson, C.M. (1999b). Using functional behavioral assessment to develop effective intervention plans. *Journal of Positive Behavior Interventions, 1,* 242–251.

Scotti, J.R., Evans, I.M., Meyer, L.H., & Walker, P. (1991). A meta-analysis of intervention research with problem behavior: Treatment validity and standards of practice. *American Journal on Mental Retardation, 96,* 233–256.

Scotti, J.R., & Meyer, L.H. (Eds.). (1999). *Behavioral intervention: Principles, models, and practices.* Baltimore: Paul H. Brookes Publishing Co.

Seligman, M.E.P. (1999). Positive social science. *Journal of Positive Behavior Interventions, 1,* 181–182.

Senge, P. (1990). *The fifth discipline: The art and practice of the learning organization.* New York: Doubleday Broadway Publishing Group.

Sergiovanni, T.J. (1994). *Building community in schools.* San Francisco: Jossey-Bass.

Serow, R.C. (1983). *Schooling for diversity: An analysis of policy and practice.* New York: Teachers College Press.

Shapiro, E.S. (1996). *Academic skills problems* (2nd ed.). New York: The Guilford Press.

Sharan, Y., & Sharan, S. (1992). *Expanding cooperative learning through group investigation.* New York: Teachers College Press.

Shores, R.E., Gunter, P.L., & Jack, S.L. (1993). Classroom management strategies: Are they setting events for coercion? *Behavioral Disorders, 18,* 92–102.

Showers, B., & Joyce, B. (1996). The evolution of peer coaching. *Educational Leadership*, *53*(6), 12–16.

Sidman, M. (1989). *Coercion and its fallout*. Boston: Authors Cooperative.

Silberman, M. (1996). *Active learning: 101 strategies to teach any subject*. Needham Heights, MA: Allyn & Bacon.

Singer, G.H.S. (2000). Ecological validity. *Journal of Positive Behavior Interventions*, *2*, 122–124.

Singer, J. (1974). *Imagery and daydream methods in psychotherapy*. San Diego: Academic Press.

Singh, N.N., Winton, A.S.W., & Ball, P. (1984). Effects of physical restraint on the behavior of hyperactive mentally retarded persons. *American Journal of Mental Deficiency*, *89*, 16–22.

Skiba, R.J., & Peterson, R.L. (2000). School discipline at a crossroads: From zero tolerance to early response. *Exceptional Children*, *66*, 335–347.

Skinner, B.F. (1953). *Science and human behavior*. New York: Appleton-Century-Crofts.

Skinner, B.F. (1968). *The technology of teaching*. New York: Appleton-Century-Crofts.

Skovron, D. (1999, October). *Conflict management: Skills for life*. Paper presented at the Summit on Behavior, Longmont, CO.

Skrtic, T.M. (1995). Special education and student disabilities as organizational pathologies: Toward a metatheory of school organization and change. In T.M. Skrtic (Ed.), *Disability and democracy: Reconstructing (special) education for postmodernity* (pp. 190–232). New York: Teachers College Press.

Slavin, R.E. (1997). Including inclusion in school reform: Success for All and Roots and Wings. In D.K. Lipsky & A. Gartner (Eds.), *Inclusion and school reform: Transforming America's class-rooms* (pp. 375–387). Baltimore: Paul H. Brookes Publishing Co.

Smith, C.R. (2000). Behavioral and discipline provisions of IDEA '97: Implicit competencies yet to be attained. *Exceptional Children*, *66*, 403–415.

Smith, J.D. (1999). Thoughts on the changing meaning of disability: New eugenics or new wholeness? *Remedial and Special Education*, *20*, 131–133.

Snell, M.E., & Brown, F. (2000). Meaningful assessment. In M.E. Snell & F. Brown (Eds.), *Instruction of students with severe disabilities* (5th ed., pp. 67–114). Upper Saddle River, NJ: Prentice Hall.

Snell, M.E., & Janney, R.E. (2000). Teachers' problem-solving about children with moderate and severe disabilities in elementary classrooms. *Exceptional Children*, *66*, 472–490.

Solnick, J.V., Rincover, A., & Peterson, C.R. (1977). Some determinates of the reinforcing and punishing effects of time-out. *Journal of Applied Behavior Analysis*, *10*, 415–424.

Solomon, D., Schaps, E., Watson, M., & Battistich, V. (1992). Creating caring school and class-room communities for all students. In R.A. Villa, J.S. Thousand, W. Stainback, & S. Stainback (Eds.), *Restructuring for caring and effective education: An administrative guide to cre-ating heterogeneous schools* (pp. 41–60). Baltimore: Paul H. Brookes Publishing Co.

Soo Hoo, S. (1990). School renewal: Taking responsibility for providing an education of value. In J.I. Goodlad & P. Keating (Eds.), *Access to knowledge: An agenda for our nation's schools* (pp. 205–236). New York: College Entrance Examination Board.

Sprague, J., & Walker, H. (2000). Early identification and intervention for youth with antiso-cial and violent behavior. *Exceptional Children*, *66*, 367–379.

Sprick, R., Sprick, M., & Garrison, M. (1993). *Interventions: Collaborative planning for students at risk*. Longmont, CO: Sopris West.

Stainback, W., & Stainback, S. (1996). Collaboration, support networking, and community building. In S. Stainback & W. Stainback (Eds.), *Inclusion: A guide for educators* (pp. 193–199). Baltimore: Paul H. Brookes Publishing Co.

Stainback, W., Stainback, S., Raschke, D., & Anderson, R.J. (1981). Three methods for encour-aging interactions between severely retarded and nonhandicapped students. *Education and Training in Mental Retardation*, *16*, 188–192.

Stainback, W.C., & Stainback, S.B. (1994). Introduction. In J.S. Thousand, R.A. Villa, & A.I. Nevin (Eds.), *Creativity and collaborative learning: A practical guide to empowering students and teachers* (pp. xxiii–xxvi). Baltimore: Paul H. Brookes Publishing Co.

Stanford, G. (1977). *Developing effective classroom groups: A practical guide for teachers*. New York: Hart Publishing.

Stanger, C. (1996). Behavioral assessment: An overview. In M. Breen & C.R. Fiedler (Eds.), *Behavioral approach to assessment of youth with emotional/behavioral disorders* (pp. 3–22). Austin, TX: PRO-ED.

Stevens, R.J., & Slavin, R.E. (1995). The cooperative elementary school: Effects on student's achievement, attitudes, and social relations. *American Educational Research Journal, 32*(2), 321–351.

Stokes, T.F., & Baer, D.M. (1977). An implicit technology of generalization. *Journal of Applied Behavior Analysis, 10,* 349–367.

Strachey, J. (Ed.). (1961). *The standard edition of the complete psychological works of Sigmund Freud: Vol. XIX (1923–1925).* London: The Hogarth Press and the Institute of Psycho-Analysis.

Sugai, G., & Colvin, G. (1997). Debriefing: A transition step for promoting acceptable behavior. *Education and Treatment of Children, 20,* 209–221.

Sugai, G., Horner, R.H., Dunlap, G., Hieneman, M., Lewis, T.J., Nelson, C.M., Scott, T., Liaupsin, C., Sailor, W., Turnbull, A.P., Turnbull, H.R., Wickham, D., Wilcox, B., & Ruef, M. (2000). Applying positive behavior support and functional behavioral assessment in schools. *Journal of Positive Behavior Interventions, 2,* 131–143.

Sugai, G., Horner, R.H., & Sprague, J.R. (1999). Functional-assessment-based-behavior support planning: Research to practice to research. *Behavioral Disorders, 24,* 253–257.

Sugai, G., Lewis-Palmer, T., & Hagan, S. (1998). Using functional assessment to develop behavior support plans. *Preventing School Failure, 43,* 6–12.

Sugai, G., & Maheady, L. (1988). Cultural diversity and individual assessment for behavior disorders. *Teaching Exceptional Children, 20*(1), 28–31.

Sugai, G., Sprague, J.R., Horner, R.H., & Walker, H.M. (2000). Preventing school violence: The use of official discipline referrals to assess and monitor school-wide discipline interventions. *Journal of Emotional and Behavioral Disorders, 8,* 94–101.

Sullivan, M.A., & O'Leary, S.G. (1990). Maintenance following reward and cost token programs. *Behavior Therapy, 21,* 139–149.

Sulzer-Azaroff, B., & Mayer, G.R. (1991). *Behavior analysis for lasting change.* Fort Worth, TX: Harcourt College Publishers.

Taylor, C.C., & Bailey, J.S. (1996). Reducing corporal punishment with elementary school students using behavioral diagnostic procedures. In L.K. Koegel, R.L. Koegel, & G. Dunlap (Eds.), *Positive behavioral support: Including people with difficult behavior in the community* (pp. 207–225). Baltimore: Paul H. Brookes Publishing Co.

Taylor, S.J. (1988). Caught in the continuum: A critical analysis of the principle of the least restrictive environment. *Journal of The Association for Persons with Severe Handicaps, 13,* 41–53.

Taylor, S.J., & Bogdan, R. (1984). *Introduction to qualitative research methods: The search for meaning* (2nd ed.). New York: John Wiley & Sons.

Taylor-Greene, S., Brown, D., Nelson, L., Longton, J., Gassman, T., Cohen, J., Swartz, J., Horner, R., Sugai, G., & Hall, S. (1997). School-wide behavioral support: Starting the year off right. *Journal of Behavioral Education, 7,* 99–112.

Taylor-Greene. S., & Kartub, D.T. (2000). Durable implementation of school-wide behavior support: The high five program. *Journal of Positive Behavior Interventions, 2,* 233–234.

Thomas, S.B., & Rapport, M.J.K. (1998). Least restrictive environment: Understanding the direction of the courts. *Journal of Special Education, 32,* 66–78.

Tilly, W.D. (1999). *The what and why of problem solving.* Presentation to the Iowa Administrative Law Judges and Mediators, Des Moines, IA.

Tilly, W.D., Knoster, T.P., Kovaleski, J., Bambara, L., Dunlap, G., & Kincaid, D. (1998). *Functional behavioral assessment: Policy development in light of emerging research and practice.* Alexandria, VA: National Association of State Directors of Special Education.

Todd, P.M. (1999). Reason now and then: A review of D.B. Caine's *Within reason: Rationality and human behavior. Science, 286,* 1861–1862.

Tomasello, M., Kruger, A.C., & Ratner, H.H. (1993). Cultural learning. *Behavioral and Brain Sciences, 16,* 495–552.

Tomlinson, C.A. (1995a). *Differentiating instruction for mixed-ability classrooms* [Inquiry kit]. Alexandria, VA: Association for Supervision and Curriculum Development,

Tomlinson, C.A. (1999). *The differentiated classroom: Responding to the needs of all learners.* Alexandria, VA: Association for Supervision and Curriculum Development.

Tomlinson, S. (1995b). The radical structuralist view of special education and disability: Unpopular perspectives on their origins and development. In T.M. Skrtic (Ed.), *Disability and democracy: Reconstructing (special) education for postmodernity* (pp. 122–134). New York: Teachers College Press.

Touchette, P.E., MacDonald, R.F., & Langer, S.N. (1985). A scatter plot for identifying stimulus control of problem behavior. *Journal of Applied Behavior Analysis, 18*, 343–351.

Townsend, B. (2000). The disproportionate discipline of African American learners: Reducing school suspensions and expulsions. *Exceptional Children, 66*, 381–392.

Turnbull, A., & Turnbull, H.R. (1999). Comprehensive lifestyle support for adults with challenging behavior: From rhetoric to reality. *Education and Training in Mental Retardation and Developmental Disabilities, 34*, 373–394.

Turnbull, A., & Turnbull, H.R. (2000). Achieving "rich" lifestyles. *Journal of Positive Behavior Interventions, 2*, 190–192.

Turnbull, H.R., Wilcox, B.L., Stowe, M., Raper, C., & Hedges, L.P. (2000). Public policy foundations for positive behavioral interventions, strategies, and supports. *Journal of Positive Behavior Interventions, 2*, 218–230.

Tustin, R.D. (1995). The effects of advance notice of activity transitions on stereotypic behavior. *Journal of Applied Behavior Analysis, 28*, 91–92.

Tyack, D., & Tobin, W. (1994). The "grammar" of schooling: Why has it been so hard to change? *American Educational Research Journal, 31*, 453–479.

Uditsky, B. (1993). Natural pathways to friendships. In A.N. Amado (Eds.), *Friendships and community connections between people with and without developmental disabilities* (pp. 85–95). Baltimore: Paul H. Brookes Publishing Co.

Van Den Berg, J.E. (1993). Integration of individualized mental health services into the system of care for children and adolescents. *Administration and Policy in Mental Health, 20*, 247–257.

Van der Klift, E., & Kunc, N. (1994). Beyond benevolence: Friendship and the politics of help. In J.S. Thousand, R.A. Villa, & A.I. Nevin (Eds.), *Creativity and collaborative learning: A practical guide to empowering students and teachers* (pp. 391–401). Baltimore: Paul H. Brookes Publishing Co.

Van der Klift, E., & Kunc, N. (1995, February). *Hell-bent on helping: Friendship, benevolence, and the politics of help.* Denver, CO: Strategies for Inclusive Education.

Vandercook, T., York, J., & Forest, M. (1989). The McGill action planning system (MAPS): A strategy for building vision. *Journal of The Association for Persons with Severe Handicaps, 14*, 205–215.

Vaughn, B.J., & Horner, R.H. (1997). Identifying instructional tasks that occasion problem behaviors and assessing the effects of student versus teacher choice among these tasks. *Journal of Applied Behavior Analysis, 30*, 299–312.

Viadero, D. (1994). Learning to care. *Education Week, XIV*(8), 31–33.

Villa, R.A., & Thousand, J.S. (1992). Restructuring public school systems: Strategies for organizational change and progress. In R.A. Villa, J.S. Thousand, W. Stainback, & S. Stainback (Eds.), *Restructuring for caring and effective education: An administrative guide to creating heterogeneous schools* (pp. 109–137). Baltimore: Paul H. Brookes Publishing Co.

Villa, R.A., & Thousand, J.S. (1994). One divided by two or more: Redefining the role of a cooperative education team. In J.S. Thousand, R.A. Villa, & A.I. Nevin (Eds.), *Creativity and collaborative learning: A practical guide to empowering students and teachers* (pp. 79–101). Baltimore: Paul H. Brookes Publishing Co.

Vittimberga, G.L., Scotti, J.R., & Weigle, K.L. (1999). Standards of practice and critical elements in an educative approach to behavioral intervention. In J.R. Scotti & L.H. Meyer (Eds.), *Behavioral intervention: Principles, models, and practices* (pp. 47–69). Baltimore: Paul H. Brookes Publishing Co.

Vollmer, T.R., Iwata, B.A., Zarcone, J.R., Smith, R.G., & Mazaleski, J.L. (1993). The role of attention in the treatment of attention-maintained self-injurious behavior: Noncontingent reinforcement and differential reinforcement of other behavior. *Journal of Applied Behavior Analysis, 26*, 9–22.

Vygotsky, L.S. (1962). *Thought and language.* Cambridge, MA: The MIT Press.

Vygotsky, L.S. (1978). *Mind and society: The development of higher psychological processes.* Cambridge, MA: Harvard University Press.

Wacker, D.P., Cooper, L.J., Peck, S.M., Derby, M., & Berg, W.K. (1999). Community-based functional assessment. In A.C. Repp & R.H. Horner (Eds.), *Functional analysis of problem behavior* (pp. 31–56). Belmont, CA: Wadsworth.

Wacker, D.P., Harding, J., Cooper, L.J., Derby, K.M., Peck, S., Asmus, J., Berg, W.K., & Brown, K.A. (1996). The effects of meal schedule and quantity on problem behavior. *Journal of Applied Behavior Analysis, 29,* 79–87.

Waldron, N.L., McLaskey, J., & Pacchiano, D. (1999). Giving teachers a voice: Teachers' perspectives regarding elementary inclusive school programs. *Teacher Education and Special Education, 22,* 141–153.

Walker, H.M., Colvin, G., & Ramsey, E. (1995). *Antisocial behavior in school: Strategies and best practices.* Pacific Grove, CA: Brooks/Cole Thomson Learning.

Walker, H.M., & Gresham, F.M. (1997). Making schools safer and violence free. *Intervention in School and Clinic, 32,* 199–204.

Walker, H.M., Horner, R.H., Sugai, G., Bullis, M., Sprague, J.R., Bricker, D., & Kaufman, M.J. (1996). Integrated approaches to preventing antisocial behavior patterns among school-aged children and youth. *Journal of Emotional and Behavioral Disorders, 4*(4), 194–209.

Walther-Thomas, C., Korinek, L., & McLaughlin, V.L. (1999). Collaboration to support student's success. *Focus on Exceptional Children, 32*(3), 1–18.

Watson, M., Battistich, V., & Solomon, D. (1997). Enhancing students' social and ethical development in schools: An intervention program and its effects. *International Journal of Educational Research, 27,* 571–586.

Wayson, W., & Pinnell, G. (1982). Creating a living curriculum for teaching self-discipline. In D. Duke (Ed.), *Helping teachers manage classrooms.* Alexandria, VA: Association for Supervision and Curriculum Development.

Webb, N.M., Nemer, K.M., Chizhik, A.W., & Sugrue, B. (1998). Equity issues in collaborative group assessment: Group composition and performance. *American Educational Research Journal, 35,* 607–651.

Webb-Johnson, G.C. (1999). Cultural contexts: Confronting the overrepresentation of African American learners in special education. In J.R. Scotti & L.H. Meyer (Eds.), *Behavioral intervention: Principles, models, and practices* (pp. 449–464). Baltimore: Paul H. Brookes Publishing Co.

Weeks, M., & Gaylord-Ross, R. (1981). Task difficulty and aberrant behavior in severely handicapped students. *Journal of Applied Behavior Analysis, 14,* 449–463.

Wehby, J.H., Symons, F.J., & Canale, J.A. (1998). Teaching practices in classrooms for students with emotional and behavioral disorders: Discrepancies between recommendations and observations. *Behavioral Disorders, 24,* 51–56.

Wehmeyer, M., & Schwartz, M. (1997). Self-determination and positive adult outcomes: A follow-up study of youth with mental retardation or learning abilities. *Exceptional Children, 63,* 245–255.

Wehmeyer, M.L. (1992). Self-determination and the education of students with mental retardation. *Education and Training in Mental Retardation, 97,* 302–313.

Weigle, K.L. (1997). Positive behavioral support as a model for promoting educational inclusion. *Journal of The Association for Persons with Severe Handicaps, 22,* 36–48.

Wells, G. (1999). *Dialogic inquiry: Toward a sociocultural practice and theory of education.* New York: Cambridge University Press.

Whiston, S.C., & Sexton, T.L. (1998). A review of school counseling outcome research: Implications for practice. *Journal of Counseling and Development, 76,* 412–426.

Wiggins, G., & McTighe, J. (1998). *Understanding by design.* Alexandria, VA: Association for Supervision and Curriculum Development.

Wilson, C.C., Robertson, S.J., Herlong, L.H., & Haynes, S.N. (1979). Vicarious effects of time-out in the modification of aggression in the classroom. *Behavior Modification, 3,* 97–111.

Winett, R.A., & Winkler, R.C. (1972). Current behavior modification in the classroom: Be still, be quiet, be docile. *Journal of Applied Behavior Analysis, 5,* 499–504.

Wolf, M.M. (1978). Social validity: The case for subjective measurement or how applied behavior analysis is finding its heart. *Journal of Applied Behavior Analysis, 11,* 203–214.

Wolf, M.M., Risley, T.R., & Mees, H. (1964). Application of operant conditioning procedures to the behavior problems of an autistic child. *Behavior Research and Therapy, 5,* 103–112.

Wolfgang, C.H. (1995). *Solving discipline problems: Methods and models for today's teachers* (3rd ed.). Needham Heights, MA: Allyn & Bacon.

Wolfgang, C.H., & Glickman, C.D. (1986). *Solving discipline problems: Strategies for classroom teachers* (2nd ed.). Needham Heights, MA: Allyn & Bacon.

Wood, M.M., & Long, N.J. (1991). *Life space intervention*. Austin, TX: PRO-ED.

Woodward, J.R., & Elliott, M. (1992, May/June). What a difference a word makes! *The Disability Rage*, 14–15.

Xie, H., Cairns, R.B., & Cairns, B.D. (1999). Social networks and configurations in inner-city schools: Aggression, popularity, and implications for students with EBD. *Journal of Emotional and Behavioral Disorders, 7*, 147–155.

Yankelovich, D. (1999). *The magic of dialogue: Transforming conflict into cooperation*. New York: Simon & Schuster.

Yell, M.L., & Rozalski, M.E. (2000). Searching for safe schools: Legal issues in the prevention of school violence. *Journal of Emotional and Behavioral Disorders, 8*, 187–196.

Ysseldyke, J., & Christenson, S. (1994). *The Instructional Environment System–II: A system to identify a student's instructional needs*. Longmont, CO: Sopris West.

Suggested Readings

CHAPTER 1

Goodlad, J.I., Keating, P., & Bailey, A.Y. (Eds.). (1990). *Access to knowledge: An agenda for our schools.* New York: College Entrance Examination Board.

Mehan, H., Hertweck, A., & Meihls, J.L. (1986). *Handicapping the handicapped: Decision making in students' educational careers.* Stanford, CA: Stanford University Press.

Shapiro, H.S., & Purpel, D.E. (Eds.). (1998). *Critical social issues in American education.* Mahwah, NJ: Lawrence Erlbaum Associates.

Shapiro, J.P. (1993). *No pity: People with disabilities forging a new civil rights movement.* New York: Times Books.

Skrtic, T.M. (Ed.). (1995). *Disability and democracy: Reconstructing (special) education for post-modernity.* New York: Teachers College Press.

CHAPTER 2

Butchart, R.E., & McEwan, B. (Eds.). (1998). *Classroom discipline in American schools: Problems and possibilities for democratic education.* Albany: State University of New York Press.

Coleman, M.C. (1992). *Behavior disorders: Theory and practice.* Needham Heights, MA: Allyn & Bacon.

Frieberg, H.J. (1999). *Beyond behaviorism: Changing the classroom management paradigm.* Needham Heights, MA: Allyn & Bacon.

Glasser, W. (1992). *The quality school: Managing students without coercion* (2nd ed.). New York: HarperCollins.

Jones, V.F., & Jones, L.S. (1998). *Comprehensive classroom management: Creating communities of support and solving problems* (5th ed.). Needham Heights, MA: Allyn & Bacon.

Kounin, J. (1970). *Discipline and group management in classrooms.* New York: Holt, Rinehart & Winston.

Scotti, J.R., & Meyer, L.H. (1999). *Behavioral intervention: Principles, models, and practices.* Baltimore: Paul H. Brookes Publishing Co.

Singh, N.N. (Ed.). (1997). *Prevention and treatment of severe behavior problems: Models and methods in developmental disabilities.* Pacific Grove, CA: Brooks/Cole Thomson Learning.

Wolfgang, C.H. (1995). *Solving discipline problems: Methods and models for today's teachers* (3rd ed.). Needham Heights, MA: Allyn & Bacon.

CHAPTER 3

Bandura, A. (1963). *Social learning and personality development.* New York: Holt, Rinehart & Winston.

Dewey, J. (1938). *Experience and education.* New York: Collier Books.

Kunc, N. (1992). The need to belong: Rediscovering Maslow's hierarchy of needs. In R.A. Villa, J.S. Thousand, W. Stainback, & S. Stainback (Eds.), *Restructuring for caring and effective education: An administrative guide to creating heterogeneous schools.* (pp. 25–39). Baltimore: Paul H. Brookes Publishing Co.

Oakes, J. (1985). *Keeping track: How schools structure inequality.* New Haven, CT: Yale University Press.

Sapon-Shevin, M. (1999). *Because we can change the world: A practical guide to building cooperative, inclusive classroom communities.* Needham Heights, MA: Allyn & Bacon.

Schmuck, R.A., & Schmuck, P.A. (1988). *Group processes in the classroom* (5th ed.). Dubuque, IA: Wm. C. Brown Publishers.

Stanford, G. (1977). *Developing effective classroom groups: A practical guide for teachers.* New York: Hart Publishing.

Vygotsky, L.S. (1978). *Mind and society: The development of higher psychological processes.* Cambridge, MA: Harvard University Press.

CHAPTER 4

Charney, R.S. (1991). *Teaching children to care: Management in the responsive classroom.* Greensfield, MA: Northeast Foundation for Children.

Dwyer, K., & Osher, D. (2000). *Safeguarding our children: An action guide.* Washington, DC: U.S. Departments of Education and Justice, American Institutes for Research.

Dwyer, K., Osher, D., & Warger, C. (1998). *Early warning, timely response: A guide to safe schools.* Washington, DC: U.S. Departments of Education and Justice.

Leone, P.E., Mayer, M.J., Malmbren, K., & Meisel, S.M. (2000). School violence and disruption: Rhetoric, reality, and reasonable balance. *Focus on Exceptional Children, 33*(1), 1–20.

Lovett, H. (1996). *Learning to listen: Positive approaches and people with difficult behavior.* Baltimore: Paul H. Brookes Publishing Co.

Scotti, J.R., & Meyer, L.H. (Eds.). (1999). *Behavioral intervention: Principles, models, and practices.* Baltimore: Paul H. Brookes Publishing Co.

Yell, M.L., & Rozalski, M.E. (2000). Searching for safe schools: Legal issues in the prevention of school violence. *Journal of Emotional and Behavioral Disorders, 8,* 187–196.

CHAPTER 5

Amado, A.N. (1993). *Friendships and community connections between people with and without developmental disabilities.* Baltimore: Paul H. Brookes Publishing Co.

Brown, F. (1991). Creative daily scheduling: A nonintrusive approach to challenging behaviors in community residences. *Journal of The Association for Persons with Severe Handicaps, 16,* 75–84.

Butterworth, J.H., Hagner, D., Heikkinen, B., Faris, S., De Mello, S., & McDonough, K. (1999). *More like a dance: Whole life planning for people with disabilities.* Boston: University of Massachusetts, Children's Hospital.

Carr, E.G., Horner, R.H., Turnbull, A.P., Marquis, J.G., McLaughlin, D.M., McAtee, M.L., Smith, C.E., Ryan, K.A., Ruef, M.B., & Doolabh, A. (1999). *Positive behavioral support for people with developmental disabilities: A research synthesis.* Washington, DC: American Association on Mental Retardation.

Jackson, L., & Leon, M. (1998). *Developing a behavior support plan: A manual for teachers and behavioral specialists* (2nd ed.). Colorado Springs, CO: PEAK Parent Center, Inc.

Morningstar, M.E., Kleinhammer-Tramill, P.J., & Lattin, D.L. (1999). Using successful models of student-centered transition planning and services for adolescents with disabilities. *Focus on Exceptional Children, 31,* 1–19.

Rogers, S., Ludington, J., & Graham, S. (1999). *Motivation and learning.* Evergreen, CO: Peak Learning Systems, Inc.

Walker, H.M., Colvin, G., & Ramsey, E. (1995). *Antisocial behavior in school: Strategies and best practices.* Pacific Grove, CA: Brooks/Cole Thomson Learning.

CHAPTER 6

Cramer, S.F. (1998). *Collaboration: A success strategy for special educators.* Needham Heights, MA: Allyn & Bacon.

Fisher, R., & Ury, W. (1992). *Getting to YES: Negotiating agreement without giving in.* New York: Penguin Books.

Fullan, M. (1993). *Change forces: Probing the depths of educational reform.* London: Falmer Press.

Hargreaves, A. (Ed.). (1997). *Rethinking educational change with heart and mind.* Alexandria, VA: Association for Supervision and Curriculum Development.

Hord, S.M., Rutherford, W.L., Huling-Austin, L., & Hall, G.E. (1987). *Taking charge of change.* Alexandria, VA: Association for Supervision and Curriculum Development.

Rogers, E.M. (1995). *Diffusion of innovations* (4th ed.). New York: The Free Press.

Senge, P., Kleiner, A., Roberts, C., Ross, R., Roth, G., & Smith, B. (1999). *The dance of change: The challenges of sustaining momentum in learning organizations.* New York: Doubleday.

Wiggins, G., & McTighe, J. (1998). *Understanding by design.* Alexandria, VA: Association for Supervision and Curriculum Development.

Yankelovich, D. (1999). *The magic of dialogue: Transforming conflict into cooperation.* New York: Simon & Schuster.

CHAPTER 7

Dörner, D. (1996). *The logic of failure: Recognizing and avoiding error in complex situations* (R. Kimber & R. Kimber, Trans.). Cambridge, MA: Perseus Books.

Hord, S.M., Rutherford, W.L., Huling-Austin, L., & Hall, G.E. (1987). *Taking charge of change.* Alexandria, VA: Association for Supervision and Curriculum Development.

Repp, A.C., & Horner, R.H. (Eds.). (1999). *Functional analysis of problem behavior: From effective assessment to effective support.* Belmont, CA: Wadsworth.

Scotti, J.R., & Meyer, L.H. (Eds.). (1999). *Behavioral intervention: Principles, models, and practices.* Baltimore: Paul H. Brookes Publishing Co.

CHAPTER 8

Artesani, A.J., & Mallar, L. (1998). Positive behavior supports in general education settings: Combining person-centered planning and functional analysis. *Intervention in School and Clinic, 34,* 33–38.

Carr, E.G., Levin, L., McConnachie, G., Carlson, J.I., Kemp, D.C., & Smith, C.E. (1994). *Communication-based intervention for problem behavior: A user's guide for producing positive change.* Baltimore: Paul H. Brookes Publishing Co.

Horner, R.H., & Carr, E.G. (1997). Behavioral support for students with severe disabilities: Functional assessment and comprehensive intervention. *Journal of Special Education, 31,* 84–104.

Jackson, L.B., & Leon, M.Z. (1998). *Developing a behavior support plan: A manual for teachers and behavior specialists* (2nd ed.). Colorado Springs: PEAK Parent Center, Inc.

Repp, A.C., & Horner, R.H. (1999). (Eds.). *Functional analysis of problem behavior: From effective assessment to effective support.* Belmont, CA: Wadsworth.

Snell, M.E., & Brown, F. (2000). Meaningful assessment. In M.E. Snell & F. Brown (Eds.). *Instruction of students with severe disabilities* (5th ed., pp. 67–114). Upper Saddle River, NJ: Prentice Hall.

Stanger, C. (1996). Behavioral assessment: An overview. In M. Breen & C.R. Fiedler (Eds.), *Behavioral approach to assessment of youth with emotional/behavioral disorders* (pp. 3–22). Austin, TX: PRO-ED.

Sugai, G., Lewis-Palmer, T., & Hagan, S. (1998). Using functional assessments to develop behavior support plans. *Preventing School Failure, 43,* 6–12.

CHAPTER 9

Bambara, L., & Knoster, T. (1998). *Designing positive support plans.* Washington, DC: American Association on Mental Retardation.

Jones, V.F., & Jones, L.S. (1998). *Comprehensive classroom management: Creating communities of support and solving problems* (5th ed.). Needham Heights, MA: Allyn & Bacon.

Keel, M.C., Dangel, H.L., & Owens, S.H. (1999). Selecting instructional interventions for students with mild disabilities in inclusive classrooms. *Focus on Exceptional Children, 31,* 1–16.

Maag, J.W. (1999). Why they say no: Foundational precises and techniques for managing resistance. *Focus on Exceptional Children, 32,* 1–16.

Putnam, J.W. (Ed.). (1998). *Cooperative learning and strategies for inclusion: Celebrating diversity in the classroom* (2nd ed.). Baltimore: Paul H. Brookes Publishing Co.

Reid, R. (1999). Attention deficit hyperactivity disorder: Effective methods for the classroom. *Focus on Exceptional Children, 32,* 1–20.

Schmuck, R.A., & Schmuck, P.A. (1988). *Group processes in the classroom* (5th ed.). Dubuque, IA: Wm. C. Brown Publishers.

CHAPER 10

Durrant, M. (1995). *Creative strategies for school problems: Solutions for psychologists and teachers.* New York: W.W. Norton & Company.

Hoyt, M.F. (Ed.). (1994). *Constructive therapies.* New York: The Guilford Press.

Lohrmann-O'Rourke, S.L., Knoster, T., & Llewellyn, G. (1999). Screening for understanding: An initial line of inquiry for school-based settings. *Journal of Positive Behavior Interventions, 1,* 35–42.

Metcalf, L. (1995). *Counseling toward solutions: A practical solution-focused program for working with students, teachers, and parents.* Englewood Cliffs, NJ: The Center for Applied Research in Education.

CHAPTER 11

Buswell, B.E., Schaffner, C.B., Jackson, L.B., & Schiappacasse, J. (1999). Behavior: Strategies, supports, and structures. In B.E. Buswell, C.B. Schaffner, & A.B. Seyler (Eds.), *Opening doors: Connecting students to curriculum, classmates, and learning* (pp. 41–47). Colorado Springs, CO: PEAK Parent Center, Inc.

Jackson, L.B., & Leon, M.Z. (1998). *Developing a behavior support plan: A manual for teachers and behavioral specialists* (2nd ed.). Colorado Springs, CO: PEAK Parent Center, Inc.

Koegel, L.K., Koegel, R.L., & Dunlap, G. (Eds.). (1996). *Positive behavioral support: Including people with difficult behavior in the community.* Baltimore: Paul H. Brookes Publishing Co.

Meyer, L.H., & Evans, I.M. (1989). *Nonaversive intervention for behavior problems: A manual for home and community.* Baltimore: Paul H. Brookes Publishing Co.

Scotti, J.R., & Meyer, L.H. (Eds.). (1999). *Behavioral intervention: Principles, models, and practices.* Baltimore: Paul H. Brookes Publishing Co.

CHAPTER 12

Bodine, R.J., & Crawford, D.K. (1998). *The handbook of conflict resolution education.* San Francisco: Jossey-Bass.

Burke, K. (1992). *What to do with the kid who . . .: Developing cooperation, self-discipline, and responsibility in the classroom.* Arlington Heights, IL: Skylight Training and Publishing.

Fullan, M.G. (1991). *The new meaning of educational change* (2nd ed.). New York: Teachers College Press.

Joyce, B., & Showers, B. (1995). *Student achievement through staff development: Fundamentals of school renewal* (2nd ed.). New York: Longman.

Lewis, T.J., & Sugai, G. (1999). Effective behavior support: A systems approach to proactive schoolwide management. *Focus on Exceptional Children, 31,* 1–24.

Noddings, N. (1992). *The challenge to care in schools: An alternative approach to education.* New York: Teachers College Press.

Appendix
Intervention Planning Forms

Competing Pathways Analysis Form
Scatter Plot Data Collection Form
Typical Person Inventory
Expectations and Supports
A Checklist for Self-Assessment of Enhanced Practices
Solution-Focused Behavior Intervention Planning Form
Solutions Organizer
Plan Summary
Implementation Checklist

Competing Pathways Analysis Form

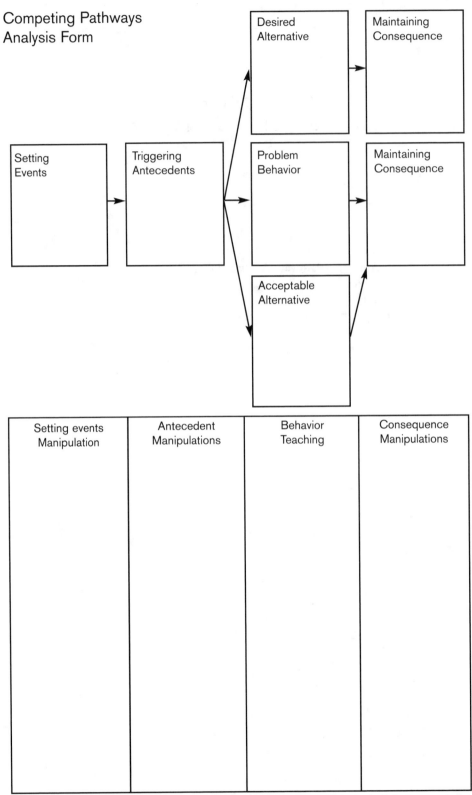

| | | Desired Alternative | Maintaining Consequence |

| Setting Events | Triggering Antecedents | Problem Behavior | Maintaining Consequence |

| | | Acceptable Alternative | |

Setting events Manipulation	Antecedent Manipulations	Behavior Teaching	Consequence Manipulations

From Sugai, G., Lewis-Palmer, T., & Hagan, S. (1998). Using functional assessments to develop behavior support plans. *Preventing School Failure, 43*(1), 11. Adapted with permission of the Helen Dwight Reid Educational Foundation. Published by Heldref Publications, 1319 Eighteenth Street, NW, Washington, DC 20036-1802. Copyright © 1998.

Positive Behavioral Support in the Classroom: Principles and Practices by Lewis Jackson and Marion Veeneman Panyan

Scatter Plot Data Collection Form

Name of student: _____   Name of observer: _____   Dates: _____

	8:00 to 8:15	8:15 to 8:30	8:30 to 8:45	8:45 to 9:00	9:00 to 9:15	9:15 to 9:30	9:30 to 9:45	9:45 to 10:00	10:00 to 10:15	10:15 to 10:30	10:30 to 10:45	10:45 to 11:00	11:00 to 11:15	11:15 to 11:30	11:30 to 11:45	11:45 to 12:00	12:00 to 12:15	12:15 to 12:30	12:30 to 12:45	12:45 to 1:00	1:00 to 1:15	1:15 to 1:30	1:30 to 1:45	1:45 to 2:00	2:00 to 2:15	2:15 to 2:30	2:30 to 2:45	2:45 to 3:00
MON	1 2 3	1 2 3	1 2 3	1 2 3	1 2 3	1 2 3	1 2 3	1 2 3	1 2 3	1 2 3	1 2 3	1 2 3	1 2 3	1 2 3	1 2 3	1 2 3	1 2 3	1 2 3	1 2 3	1 2 3	1 2 3	1 2 3	1 2 3	1 2 3	1 2 3	1 2 3	1 2 3	1 2 3
TUE	1 2 3	1 2 3	1 2 3	1 2 3	1 2 3	1 2 3	1 2 3	1 2 3	1 2 3	1 2 3	1 2 3	1 2 3	1 2 3	1 2 3	1 2 3	1 2 3	1 2 3	1 2 3	1 2 3	1 2 3	1 2 3	1 2 3	1 2 3	1 2 3	1 2 3	1 2 3	1 2 3	1 2 3
WED	1 2 3	1 2 3	1 2 3	1 2 3	1 2 3	1 2 3	1 2 3	1 2 3	1 2 3	1 2 3	1 2 3	1 2 3	1 2 3	1 2 3	1 2 3	1 2 3	1 2 3	1 2 3	1 2 3	1 2 3	1 2 3	1 2 3	1 2 3	1 2 3	1 2 3	1 2 3	1 2 3	1 2 3
THU	1 2 3	1 2 3	1 2 3	1 2 3	1 2 3	1 2 3	1 2 3	1 2 3	1 2 3	1 2 3	1 2 3	1 2 3	1 2 3	1 2 3	1 2 3	1 2 3	1 2 3	1 2 3	1 2 3	1 2 3	1 2 3	1 2 3	1 2 3	1 2 3	1 2 3	1 2 3	1 2 3	1 2 3
FRI	1 2 3	1 2 3	1 2 3	1 2 3	1 2 3	1 2 3	1 2 3	1 2 3	1 2 3	1 2 3	1 2 3	1 2 3	1 2 3	1 2 3	1 2 3	1 2 3	1 2 3	1 2 3	1 2 3	1 2 3	1 2 3	1 2 3	1 2 3	1 2 3	1 2 3	1 2 3	1 2 3	1 2 3

KEY
1 = _____
2 = _____
3 = _____

Comments: _____

Positive Behavioral Support in the Classroom: Principles and Practices by Lewis Jackson and Marion Veeneman Panyan
© 2002 Paul H. Brookes Publishing Co.

Typical Person Inventory

Name of student: _____

Classroom environment: _____

Activity: _____

Date: _____

Support person	Classroom routine	Pre	Post	Discrepancy analysis	Adaptations	Related objectives

Positive Behavioral Support in the Classroom: Principles and Practices by Lewis Jackson and Marion Veeneman Panyan
© 2002 Paul H. Brookes Publishing Co.

Expectations and Supports

Name of student: _____ Class or activity: _____

Student activities	Desired behavior	Acceptable behavior	Natural supports	Added supports

Positive Behavioral Support in the Classroom: Principles and Practices by Lewis Jackson and Marion Veeneman Panyan
© 2002 Paul H. Brookes Publishing Co.

A Checklist for Self-Assessment of Enhanced Practices

Type of support	Needs more information	Needs practice and reflection	Uses technique and can share with others
Affective supports Neutralizing routines			
Social interpretation or reframing			
Relationship transfer			
Positive unconditional regard			
Use of literature			
Positive communication between school and home			
Schedule and activity supports Choice making			
Predictable routines and signals			
Rest and break options			
Anticipation cues			
Accommodation and modification			
Creative scheduling			
Peer supports Peer buddy			
Cooperative learning			
Classwide peer tutoring			
Base group			
Extracurricular activities			
Peer mediators			
Teacher style supports Rapport building			
Debriefing			
Behavioral momentum			
Embedding instructions			
Self-monitoring			
Stepping back			

Positive Behavioral Support in the Classroom: Principles and Practices by Lewis Jackson and Marion Veeneman Panyan
© 2002 Paul H. Brookes Publishing Co.

Solution-Focused Behavior Intervention Planning Form

for

_____

(Name of student)

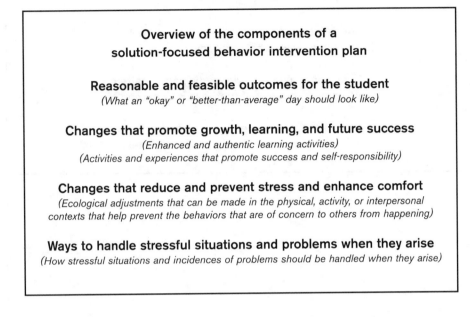

**Overview of the components of a
solution-focused behavior intervention plan**

Reasonable and feasible outcomes for the student
(What an "okay" or "better-than-average" day should look like)

Changes that promote growth, learning, and future success
(Enhanced and authentic learning activities)
(Activities and experiences that promote success and self-responsibility)

Changes that reduce and prevent stress and enhance comfort
*(Ecological adjustments that can be made in the physical, activity, or interpersonal
contexts that help prevent the behaviors that are of concern to others from happening)*

Ways to handle stressful situations and problems when they arise
(How stressful situations and incidences of problems should be handled when they arise)

Facilitator:_____   Date of plan:_____

Plan development participants:

_____

_____

_____

_____

_____

_____

_____

Positive Behavioral Support in the Classroom: Principles and Practices by Lewis Jackson and Marion Veeneman Panyan
© 2002 Paul H. Brookes Publishing Co.

Component 1
Reasonable and feasible outcomes for the student

Focus Questions

• What does a good day look like now?
Is this a reasonable outcome for the near future?

• What learning and activity participation patterns
would be happening if progress is occurring?

• What minimum changes are necessary for us to
feel that the plan is working in several weeks?

Time = 10 minutes

Component 2
Changes that promote growth, learning, and future success

Focus Questions

• If the student is isolated from the mainstream, are there some ways
we can reduce that isolation that could be successful for the student?

• Can we create new roles or responsibilities for
the student to encourage greater autonomy?

• Are there some ways we can help the student
more effectively communicate basic needs?

• Are there some ways we can help the student
more effectively participate in classroom activities?

• Do some of the activities or strategies that we are using
with this student devalue or degrade him or her?

• What responses can we encourage that honor the student's
attention, affiliation, or power needs?

• In what activities is the student successful now?
Can access to these be increased?

• How else can we further enrich what the student
is doing throughout the school day?

Time = 20 minutes

Positive Behavioral Support in the Classroom: Principles and Practices by Lewis Jackson and Marion Veeneman Panyan
© 2002 Paul H. Brookes Publishing Co.

Component 3
Changes that reduce and prevent stress and enhance comfort

Focus Questions

• Are there things that reliably upset the student? Do we know why?

• Are there things that we now do that reduce or alleviate
stress, fear, or uncertainty?

• Are there other activity, material, or outcome adaptations that may reduce stress
by clarifying expectations or ensuring success? Are there peers who could help?

• Does the student need more breaks or opportunities
to rest or more access to food or drink?

• Are there reliable refocus or redirect signals?

• Are there coping strategies that the student can use
to help control stressful situations?

• Are there safety or predictability signals that we can use when
the student is agitated?

• Are there before- or after-school precipitating
circumstances that can be simply resolved?

• How can we promote greater comfort in relationships between
the student and his or her peers?

• Are there reasonable schedule adaptations that can help with transitions?

Time = 20 minutes

Positive Behavioral Support in the Classroom: Principles and Practices by Lewis Jackson and Marion Veeneman Panyan
© 2002 Paul H. Brookes Publishing Co.

Component 4
Ways to handle stressful situations and problems when they arise

Focus Questions

• What behavior patterns are of particular concern to the school community?

• In what settings do we have these concerns?

• At what times of day and in what specific activities do we have these concerns?

• What can we do when the situation is out of control?
Who can we recruit to help us?

• If temporarily removed,
what will the student be expected to do?

• How can we promote understanding and acceptance from the other students?

Time = 10 minutes

Solutions Organizer

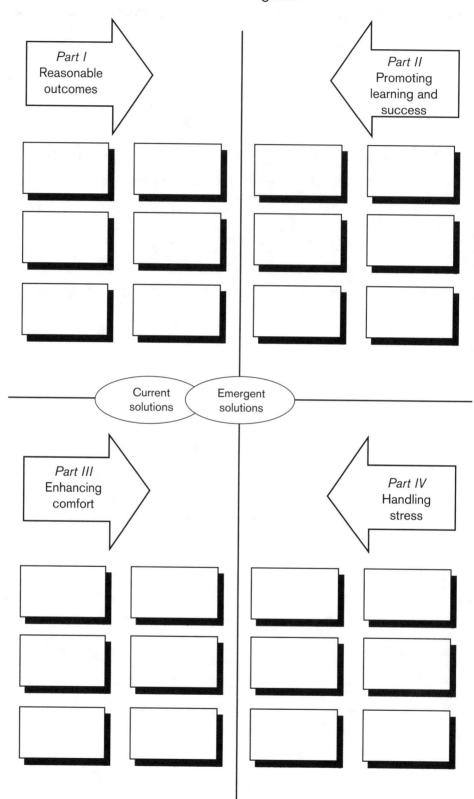

Plan Summary

Name of student:_____   Date of plan:_____

Relevant setting(s):_____

Reasonable and feasible outcomes for the student

Changes that promote growth, learning, and future success

Changes that reduce and prevent stress and enhance comfort

Ways to handle stressful situations and problems when they arise

Implementation Checklist

Behavior plan goal	Rating 0 = no progress 1 = some progress 2 = excellent progress	Comments

Positive Behavioral Support in the Classroom: Principles and Practices by Lewis Jackson and Marion Veeneman Panyan
© 2002 Paul H. Brookes Publishing Co.

Behavior plan item	Implementation Rating 0 = not at all 1 = occasionally 2 = consistently	Contribution Rating 0 = not at all 1 = helpful 2 = very helpful	Comments

Positive Behavioral Support in the Classroom: Principles and Practices by Lewis Jackson and Marion Veeneman Panyan
© 2002 Paul H. Brookes Publishing Co.

Index

Page numbers followed by *f* indicate figures; those followed by *t* indicate tables.